This book is published in memory of Norman Hall,
1892-1967, late of the Lancashire Fusiliers,
pictured above as a captain in 1916,
and of his comrades in arms in the Great War,
especially those who did not survive,

and remembering the dedication referenced by Norman himself in Volume 2 of his diary:

"In proud memory of long days and nights in the trenches; of patrols, wiring parties, and carrying parties; of the duty done by all ranks in many places; of days passed under shell fire, Machine Gun fire, and Gas attacks; of raids by night and attacks by night; of a stubborn defence, and a glorious advance, and the final overthrow of the enemy.

Of days, months, and years devoted to our King's and Empire's service.

In proud and solemn memory of our fallen, of those who suffered wounds and mutilation in a just and righteous cause.

In sincere hope of a glorious and lasting peace; of difficulties to be met and dangers overcome by cool heads and stout hearts, and of generations to come who shall prove themselves worthy of the great deeds of their fathers."

(Lieutenant Colonel E.G. Hoare)

CONTENTS   Page

PREFACE

Norman Hall was born on 28th February 1892 in Bury, the son of George Hall, a wool merchant, and Sarah Elizabeth Anne Hall. He had two older brothers, John Russell (Jack, born 1884) and George (born 1886), an older sister, Mary Marjorie (born 1888), and a younger sister, Kathleen Margaret (born 1897, also known as "Bill"). At the outbreak of the First World War in 1914 his parents, his brother George, and his younger sister Kathleen, were living at Ravensdale, 217 Walmersley Road, Bury. By then Jack had married Nora, and Mary had married Jack Ashworth. Both couples still lived nearby.

Norman attended Bury Grammar School, and then Owens College in Manchester, one of the original colleges of Manchester University, where he studied Chemistry and joined the OTC (Officers' Training Corps). On graduating in about 1913 he went to work in the Chemical Engineering Laboratory of Lever Brothers in Port Sunlight, and had been working there for about a year when he enlisted, shortly after war broke out.

This diary tells the story of what happened to him during the First World War, which he was fortunate enough to survive.

After the War he went back to Lever Brothers in Port Sunlight for a short time, until in November 1919 he went to work for the then newly formed British Dyestuffs Corporation at Blackley in Manchester, which also had a plant at Dalton in Huddersfield, and in 1926 was one of four companies which merged to form ICI (Imperial Chemical Industries).

In 1923 he married Norah Hall, no relation, but also from Bury. They had three children, John Kenneth (almost certainly named after the Kenneth Waterhouse who features in the diary), Christine Elizabeth, and David Malcolm, who all went on to have their own children, giving Norman and Norah a total of eight grandchildren.

During the 1920s Norman moved to Huddersfield, and continued to work for the British Dyestuffs Corporation/ICI for a total of 35 years, holding many posts in plant management, until his retirement in 1954, when he and Norah went to live at Craigwen, Llandegfan, Anglesey. Norah died in 1962, and Norman then moved to be near Christine in Cambridge, where he died on 21st December 1967.

The original diary is handwritten, and occupies five volumes (pictured on page 15), which are stored for safe-keeping in the archives of the Imperial War Museum, London, and can be accessed there by appointment. Eventually the Imperial War Museum will have access to a complete typed transcript of all five volumes of the original diary, and it is intended that research staff at the Fusilier Museum in Bury (www.fusiliermuseum.com) will also have such access.

The first three volumes of the original diary deal mainly with Norman's time with the 2/5th Lancashire Fusiliers up to 13th September 1916, while the last two volumes deal with the period from then on, for most of which Norman was with the 1/5th Lancashire Fusiliers. This edited version of the diary focuses on the first three volumes, with the contents of the last two being summarised in the *Afterword*.

In Chapter 1, under the heading *"First Impressions, First Decisions, First Actions"*, covering the period from 1st August 1914 to 19th November 1914, Norman writes, on page 19, *"now – in 1919 …"*, thus making it clear that he commenced writing the diary in 1919, soon after the end of the War. In the same section he writes *"When the Peace is really signed …"* thus indicating that he was writing this section before the Treaty of Versailles was signed on 28th June 1919. He also writes, in the section covering 8th November 1914 to 13th December 1914, *"now (in 1919) …"* (page 28).

The question of how long he took to write the diary, and when he completed it, is more difficult. The very last page of manuscript, signed by Norman, is dated 30th March 1928, but by then he had included accounts of the Victory March on 19th July 1919, and the unveiling of the Memorial to the 55th Division at Givenchy on 15th May 1921, as well as other passages that appear to be addenda to the main text, such as the actions of the 1/5th Lancashire Fusiliers from the date when Norman left them on 29th July 1918 to Armistice Day, and the arrival of the Lancashire Fusiliers' Cadre back in Bury on 11th April 1919, so the main text must have been completed earlier, perhaps much earlier.

Turning to the sources that Norman used for the diary, as well has his own personal recollection of events (which will no doubt have been quite vivid, at least when he began writing the diary) he also had reference to the following aides-memoire:

1. He had access to a fairly significant collection of letters written by him to people at home – there are 167 referenced in the text of the first three volumes of the diary. There are markedly fewer in the last two volumes, nor are the letters referred to in the last two volumes numbered sequentially, unlike in the first three volumes. None of the letters survive.
2. He had pocket diaries, the entries in which were presumably contemporaneous, containing brief details of day to day activities and the weather on each day. Three surviving pocket diaries, spanning the period covered by the last two volumes of the diary, are also in the archives of the Imperial War Museum. No pocket diaries survive for the earlier period, but pocket diaries must surely have been available to Norman at the time of writing the first three volumes. He writes in the entry for 19th October 1914, *"I did not keep a daily diary at this time"*, the implication being that that was the exception rather than the rule.
3. In the entry for 12th August 1915 he refers to starting to keep a stick with the names of places in code, but exactly how the code worked is not clear; no stick is extant. He is, however, remarkably meticulous and detailed when reporting routes of train travel or marches, complete with timings, though on one occasion, 20th March 1917, describing a journey from London to Bury, he is unusually brief, and includes the comment *"lost records"*.
4. He may have had reference to other people's diaries; for example, when Dr Thompson, the MO, leaves the 2/5th Lancashire Fusiliers on 8th March 1916, he specifically quotes from Thompson's own diary for a description of their parting. Also, the description of refugees fleeing from the Front in the entry for 23rd March 1918 is remarkably vivid and personal, even though Norman himself was not there at the time (though this could have been based on an oral account from one of his comrades rather than a diary).

5. He will have had access to official Regimental and Divisional records, particularly for details of engagements where he was not present, and records of numbers of killed and wounded; in the diary entry for 14th September 1916, describing the Battle of Ginchy after he had been wounded, he mentions specifically having had reference to the *Lancashire Fusiliers' Annual*.

6. He sometimes refers to published books that he has read, for example, Ian Hay's *The First Hundred Thousand*, referred to in the description of life on the front line in October 1915, and *My War Memories 1914-1918* by Erich Ludendorff,[1] referred to in the entry for 10th July 1918 in connection with the failed German Spring Offensive of March 1918. It is worth mentioning here that he quite often puts a few words, or even whole sentences, in inverted commas, without identifying the source, so that it is not clear whether the quotation is from literature, a historical account, the press, a common saying of the day, a letter, or someone else's diary etc.

The illustrations in this book are almost all from the original diary. They include hand-drawn sketches of trench layouts, systems of attack and defence, gas masks etc., and documents pasted into the original diary by Norman, such as maps, letters, postcards, newspaper cuttings, official documents relating to Norman's Army Service, original Operation Orders, and photographs; many of the latter will have been taken by Norman himself, as he refers to numbered VPK (Vest Pocket Kodak) photographs, but a separate numbered collection of photographs is not thought to be extant.

This edition of the diary is, up to September 1916, barely abridged, and almost entirely in Norman's own words, while from September 1916 onwards the original account is summarised in an *Afterword*. Any editing up to September 1916 has had the following objectives:

(i) To achieve a fairly uniform narrative style, using, for the most part, complete, grammatically correct, sentences;

(ii) To use, for the most part, correct and consistent punctuation, while preserving immediacy by the prolific use of dashes for moments of high drama etc.;

(iii) To use conventional modern spelling fot place names, and to correct obvious errors in, e.g., spelling, the inadvertent use of the wrong word, the omission of a word, and, occasionally (but only if clear), dates;

(iv) To achieve consistency in the way in which, e.g., dates, distances and ranks are written (ranks are written in full);

(v) To achieve consistency in the use of capital letters, while preserving the use of capitals where they appear to be used for effect, e.g. to add emphasis;

(vi) To minimise the use of acronyms (which might involve excessive reference to a glossary), instead writing the words in full;

(vii) To achieve consistency in the use of headings and sub-headings;

(viii) To avoid overmuch repetition; so, for example, if there are two descriptions of essentially the same procedure or location, combining the key elements together in only one place in the diary;

---

[1] Erich Friedrich Wilhelm Ludendorff was a powerful German general who promoted the unsuccessful German Spring Offensive.

(ix)   In some places to run together a number of dated entries, so as to give a summary of what Norman was doing and/or thinking over a period of time, rather than a precise day by day account, for example for some periods when he was on leave or when no individually significant events were happening at the front;

(x)   To omit some details that are unlikely to interest most readers today, and do not contribute to the overall picture, for example, shortening some of the lists of places visited on marches or train journeys, and omitting the list that Norman gives detailing all the units in the 51st Division, retaining details of only the units in his own Brigade; also, leaving out some chance meetings with people whose characters are not developed elsewhere, and also not including details of every football match etc. referred to in the diary, while preserving enough such details to give a good impression and understanding of the part that such social interaction and sporting activities played in the life of a person in Norman's position;

(xi)   To omit some details of merely incidental news of family and friends at home which have no particular bearing upon Norman's experience of the War;

(xii)   To omit some passages which distract from the narrative and are not personal to Norman, for example, some of the extensive quotations from Shakespeare's *Henry V*;

(xiii)   Very occasionally to substitute a different word where the word that Norman used has either become archaic or acquired different connotations today from those it had at the time the diary was being written; only three words have been replaced, as follows:

(a) "native", which Norman uses in the sense of "from a non-Western ethnic background"; as he is referring to Indians at the time, I have simply used the word "Indian";

(b) "ripping" and "topping", which in Norman's time would have been in common usage amongst the middle classes as adjectives describing something good or enjoyable, but now tend to be used only to mimic or pillory a certain type of upper class "toff"; I have substituted "great", " very fine", "excellent", or "splendid", depending on the context.

Arabic numerals in superscript in the text of the diary refer to footnotes at the bottom of the page on which such numbers appear; Roman numerals in superscript in the text of the diary refer to endnotes at the end of the diary, listing Norman's narrow escapes from injury or death. The list is completed by insertion of a table below the endnotes containing brief details of narrow escapes mentioned in Volumes 4 and 5 of the original diary, which are not included in this edited version (unless touched on in the *Afterword*).

The intention behind publishing this version of the diary is twofold:

(i) To provide Norman's grandchildren and great-grandchildren with a tangible and accessible memento of their grandfather/great-grandfather; and

(ii) To raise funds for charity, primarily a charity or charities for the welfare of servicemen and/or ex-servicemen, to be nominated by the family, and also to benefit organisations honouring the memory of the Lancashire Fusiliers, for example by allowing Bury's Fusilier Museum to purchase copies at cost.

My reading of the diary suggests that both the types of cause mentioned in (ii) above would have been dear to Norman's own heart.

Thanks are due: first, to my grandfather, for leaving such a complete and beautifully written record of his experiences; secondly to my aunt and fellow grandchildren for supporting me in the project of typing, editing and publishing the diary, in particular John Sharpe who took some of the photographs that appear in this volume (reproducing my grandfather's photographs), Geoffrey Sharpe who visited the Imperial War Museum to review the private papers of Major General J.C. Latter, and Sue and Nick Tanton who have put me up on my many visits to access the original work in the Imperial War Museum; thanks are due also to Penny Ward who helped with the Bedford section, and to Andrew Riddoch, one of the authors of *When the Whistle Blows: the Story of the Footballers' Battalion in the Great War*, for his helpful suggestions as to how I might bring the publication of the diary to the attention of prospective readers. I gratefully acknowledge reference to Major General J.C. Latter's *History of the Lancashire Fusiliers 1914-1918,* and to a number of websites containing information about the First World War, including The Great War Forum www.greatwarforum.org , The Long, Long Trail www.longlongtrail.co.uk , the Commonwealth War Graves Commission's website www.cwgc.org , the Imperial War Museum's website www.iwm.org.uk , the Comprehensive Guide to the Victoria and George Cross www.vconline.org.uk, and www.firstworldwar.com , to name but a few. I am indebted also to the estate of Barbara Bruce Littlejohn, the daughter of Captain Bruce Bairnsfather, for permission to include four of Captain Bairnsfather's cartoons on pages 111, 134 and 182, and his poem *My Dug Out* (© 2020 The Estate of Barbara Bruce Littlejohn. All Rights Reserved). Finally, I owe a huge debt of gratitude to Priscilla Balkwill, who proofread the entire work for me (any errors now present have been introduced post-proofreading), and to David Ramshaw of P3Publications who has helped me to publish it, both providing their services free of charge in view of the book's charitable objectives; and last, but not least, to my husband, Graham, who took some of the recent photographs reproduced in this book, and over many, many months has endured being a virtual computer screen widower while I have brought the project to fruition.

Patricia Rothwell, granddaughter of Norman Hall, August 2020

Ravensdale, 217 Walmersley Road, Bury in 2019; the house was Norman Hall's family home in 1914

George Hall senior ("Father")

Sarah Elizabeth Anne Hall ("Mother")

George junior as a 2ⁿᵈ Lieutenant in 1914

Mary, who married Jack Ashworth (see below)

Norman, photographed c. 1913

Kathleen, otherwise known as Kit or "Bill"

See the footnote on page 280 for George and his family

Kathleen "put her hair up" in May 1915, began nursing classes in June 1915, and was given a Lancashire Fusiliers' brooch for her 18th birthday in September 1915; she was with Norman on Armistice Day in Blackpool

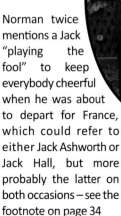

Norman twice mentions a Jack "playing the fool" to keep everybody cheerful when he was about to depart for France, which could refer to either Jack Ashworth or Jack Hall, but more probably the latter on both occasions – see the footnote on page 34

Mary and Jack Ashworth on their wedding day

John Russell (Jack) with (left) Herbert P. Cain (for the latter, see the footnotes on pages 32 and 34)

The Hall Family

8

Above:
Bury Grammar School Lower Sixth, c. 1907;
Norman is in the middle of the front row

Left:
Norman on graduating with a chemistry degree
from Owens College (later part of Manchester
University), c. 1913

Education

Glossary of Acronyms

AF	Army Form
BEF	British Expeditionary Force
CB	Companion of the Most Honourable Order of the Bath
CCS	Casualty Clearing Station
CDS	Chief of Divisional Staff
CMG	Companion of the Most Distinguished Order of St Michael and St George
CO	Commanding Officer
DCM	Distinguished Conduct Medal
DHQ	Divisional Headquarters
DSO	Distinguished Service Order
FGCM	Field General Court Martial
FRCS	Fellow of the Royal College of Surgeons
GHQ	General Headquarters
GOC	General Officer Commanding (or in Command)
HE	High Explosives
HMHS	His Majesty's Hospital Ship
HMS	His Majesty's Ship
HQ	Headquarters
KCB	Knight of the Most Honourable Order of the Bath
MC	Military Cross
MD	Medical Doctor
MM	Military Medal
MO	Doctor of Medicine
MVO	Member of the Royal Victorian Order
NCO	Non-commissioned Officer
OC	Officer Commanding (or in Command)
OTC	Officers' Training Corps
POW	Prisoner of War
PUO	Pyrexia of Unknown Origin
RAMC	Royal Army Medical Corps
RE	Royal Engineers
RMS	Royal Mail Ship
RNVR	Royal Naval Volunteer Reserve
SAA	Small Arms Ammunition
SS	Steam Ship
VC	Victoria Cross
VD	Volunteer Officers' Decoration
WD	War Department
YMCA	Young Men's Christian Association

My Experiences in the
Great War
1914 – 1919

2

Norman Hall
5th Lancashire Fusiliers

---

2 This, the badge of the Lancashire Fusiliers, is drawn in the diary at the beginning of Volume 3.

Introduction
The Origin of the War

Before reviewing my own personal experiences in the Great European War of 1914 to 1920, it seems to be of considerable interest to consider for a brief moment the points of interest which led up to this World Wide War. Some people call it a Calamity; whether this be so or no can only be proved by history, by the effects of the War on the life of Nations – great or small – in future generations. Those of us who have had the honour and privilege of helping our Empire, our Allies – and the World – in an attempt to stamp out for ever "Military Domination" will probably never see the real fruits of our labours and sacrifices. If we have helped, and our children, and children's children, are guaranteed "a Freedom from the sufferings and hardships which the world has endured since August 4th 1914" then I say the glorious sacrifices of life, of comfort, of pleasure, and the desolation of France, Belgium, the Balkans, and Russia, will not have been in vain.

The immediate result of an enterprise cannot always be reckoned on a financial basis.

The origin of most modern Wars is at once complicated and simple. They start as a rule in some incident, not in itself of more than local importance. Their driving power is always that multitude of national susceptibilities and ambition which lie only half concealed beneath the routine of peace. When the people of England read in their newspapers on June 29th 1914 of the murder of the hereditary Archduke of Austria and his wife at Sarajevo, no one imagined that this brutal and apparently remote event was to be the spark to kindle the fire and plunge Europe into War. The ordinary individual in the nation had very little interest in the Balkan States. Amongst themselves they had been constantly at variance. We had no "direct British interests" in Serbia. So that, when Austria made the murder a ground of accusation against the Serbian people, we Britishers considered it yet another inexplicable Balkan affair. Universal sympathy was extended towards the Austrian Royal Family. The attitude of Austria towards Serbia, meanwhile, became alarmingly threatening. Serbia seemed defiant and impertinent, and the European reader was inclined to take the side of Austria. Past history and difference soon had its sway.

On further examination one found it to be a story of racial struggle, in which naturally the lesser and oppressed race calls for sympathy – the Serbs and Slavs. Many Serbian Slavs had in previous times been forcibly incorporated along with their territory into the Austrian Empire. These Serbs had long wished to unite with the Slavian Serbia in forming a new and greater Serbia. Militant Societies had their influence in Austria on this question, which had been a source of worry to Austria. Several times during the present century the two countries had nearly gone to War, and, if Italy had supported Austria in 1913, Serbia would have been finished. The "Sarajevo Outrage" was seized as an opportunity to renew the attempt and finish her at last.

Austria maintained that the crime was committed under the knowledge and encouragement of the Serbian Government.

Many reasons rather contradict this point:

1. Serbia had <u>not</u> recovered from the Balkan War;
2. The Serbian Government therefore wished to avoid giving Austria further cause for interference;
3. Actually Serbia had very little ammunition, arms, supplies;
4. She had practically concluded an economic and military Union with Montenegro, the benefits of which required time to mature.

In 1909 Count Forgách – the Austro-Hungarian Minister of Belgrade – was charged with forging documents to prove that Austrian Slavs and Serbian Slavs were forming a conspiracy. The same method was adopted by him in 1914, even though he had been condemned by Austrian Courts as a forger in 1909. The feeling in Vienna and Budapest in June and early July 1914 was decidedly in favour of War. Serbia meanwhile awaited Austrian demands. Diplomatic Circles believed that Austria's terms would cause no difficulty, but that the affair would blow over.

It was known that Austria had drawn up a note – but the only Ambassador at Vienna who knew the details was Von Tschirschky, the German Ambassador, a noted Russo-phobe and an Anti-Serbian; he openly stated that nothing but War could settle the dispute.

Further indications in support of this view were:

1. Troops called up for training were kept with the Colours;
2. Gold was gradually withdrawn from the market;
3. The Chiefs of the German and Austrian General Staff had several interviews.

Russia as a protector of the Slavs, and France as Russia's Ally were keenly interested.

The contents and date of the presentation of Austria's note were kept secret. The note was actually presented on July 23rd 1914. The Ambassadors of the Entente were surprised and dumbfounded. The contents were extortionate, and a 48 hours' time limit was made for reply. It was indeed an ultimatum. It was intended to take Serbia and Europe by surprise. Austria must have expected a refusal – indeed hoped for it – for she desired War.

Just as in 1909 Austria surprised Europe by annexing Bosnia and Herzegovina, so now she hoped to localise this quarrel, and she believed that Russia was not in a position to interfere. Serbia appealed to Russia. A plea was made for an extension of the time by the Entente Powers, especially Russia. Documents were submitted to the Powers by Austria but no time was given for the study of them. This was neither reasonable nor courteous. Serbia presented her reply in 47¾ hours, accepting 9 out of 10 of the most humiliating terms ever proposed by one Modern State to another. Austria broke off relations and immediately proceeded to mobilise on the Serbian Frontier.

1. From July 25th to August 1st 1914 the Serbian question was the work of every Foreign Office and Embassy in Europe;
2. On August 1st the interest moved to Belgium and the French Frontier.

These two periods in the origin of the War interest us most.

The main aim of the Entente was:

1. To arrest Austrian preparations;
2. To bring Austria and Russia to confer, Russia having refused to stand aside and see Serbia crushed.

"Austria's determination of Serbia would be as intolerable to Russia as the dependence of the Netherlands on Germany would be to Great Britain".[3]

Sir Edward Grey proposed that Germany, Britain, France, and Italy should mediate at Vienna and Petrograd, which proposal was agreed to by all four. The "Horror of War" hanging over Europe became more feverish and dreadful.

There seems to be no record on official documents of what passed between Vienna and Berlin between Austria's note being presented and the outbreak of War. Germany promised to mediate at Vienna. Without her help mediation was futile – but she only promised.

"It has been perhaps the Secret of Germany's Predominance and of the strain which Europe has lived for the past decade, that Germany has always shown her power, but has never taken it into her confidence".[4]

Germany professed to have given Austria a free hand in her action towards Serbia, and to be disinclined to interfere. This was unlike Germany! She denied having previous knowledge of Austria's note, which is practically contradicted by the evidence of the French and British Ministers abroad.

Sir Maurice de Bunsen stated that he knew that the German Ambassador at Vienna knew the text of the note prior to the dispatch to Serbia, and telegraphed it to the German Emperor. Germany professed

---

[3] Norman does not say where this quotation comes from.
[4] Norman does not say where this quotation comes from.

to desire the Peace of Europe, but she made little or no effort to secure it. Berlin had the key to the situation, but wouldn't unlock the door to Peace.

Did Germany then desire War? One cannot say. But the time may have seemed favourable to her.

Russia was re-organising her Army – which would be completed in 1917. Britain, it was expected, would remain neutral. She didn't seem fitted for War with her Army, and Ireland in uproar. France's President and the President of her Council were in Russia on July 23rd 1914 and could not reach France until July 28th.

Consider for a moment the relations of France and Germany. Germany's ambition was to catch France at a disadvantage and complete her efforts of 1870. The favourite topic of conversation in Germany, after the humiliation in the Morocco Crisis of 1911, was War with France and then with England. Germany's dream was to conquer the World.

Limitless possibilities were opening out for German manufacture, German trade, and expansion. They believed that the future belonged to them, and undoubtedly in 1914 Germany was a great Nation. Germany considered France with her 40 million inhabitants a Second Rate Power.

France on the other hand was determined to make good her rights and refused to be intimidated any longer. This annoyed Germany. In 1912 to 1913 Germany increased her Army to give her preponderance in the field; to which France replied with her Three Years' Service Bill for the Active Army.

Germany had a Great Revival of the War of Liberation (1813) and Centenary Celebrations to rouse patriotic and military sentiment. Commemorations of the First French Campaign and first entry of the Prussians into Paris were held.

Left: The five volumes of the original diary, now in the Imperial War Museum

Introduction

The German People were educated to the fact that "Our Armaments are an answer to the Armaments and Policy of France", "An offensive war on our part is a necessity in order to combat the provocation of our adversaries" and "Under the heavy weight of powerful allurements, considerable sacrifice, and strained political relations, an outbreak of war would be a relief, because after it would come decades of peace and prosperity as after 1870". Finally "No efforts on any Nation's part will turn us from our aim to protect and extend *Deutschtum*[5] all over the World". Such was Germany's creed in 1913.

On July 28th Austria declared War on Serbia. Russia thereupon warned the Powers that she was preparing to mobilise in the South. This is really the first step towards the outbreak of hostilities in the European War.

A state of feverish diplomacy is now accompanied by the element of mobilisation. For a moment it seemed as if the efforts of Britain and France might be successful; even as late as July 31st the German Emperor and the Czar exchanged telegrams.

On July 31st Germany presented an ultimatum to Russia, demanding that Russia should begin demobilising not only against Germany, but also against Austria, within 12 hours. Practically all the powers were mobilising by this time.

Such a demand had but one result. By the evening of August 1st 1914 Germany and Russia were at War. When Germany saw that her mobilisation on the Western Front had sufficiently advanced, she declared War on France on August 3rd.

Germany contended that Russia concealed her general mobilisation, and still holds Russia responsible for the first declaration of War. The truth appears to be that the Czar ordered partial mobilisation of his Army on July 29th, but refused a general mobilisation. Further preparations for general mobilisation were made by his Staff secretly in answer to Germany's secret mobilisation.

Germany had undoubtedly taken steps for mobilisation as early as July 25th. On July 27th, her requisitions were completed and her covering troops were in position. Railways were warned prior to this date, and on the 29th individual Reservists had been called up. By this date Germany was beyond negotiation. She was the last nation in Europe capable of negotiation on the brink of War. Her institutions, her national character, her perfection of military organisation prevented it. A state of uncertainty was intolerable to her nerves. Her military machine was too vast. Mobilisation to her was not a military preparation, it was an offensive action. Her Armies did not merely concentrate, they marched.

What would England do? This worried Germany. We were expected to remain neutral. Some Nations believed that if we had definitely taken our stand by France and Russia at the very beginning there would not have been War. Our attitude was that "If Germany was not involved, and even France", we should not intervene – but that no definite pledge could be given either way. Precautions were taken.

The Fleet, concentrated at Portland, received orders on July 27th not to disperse for manoeuvre leave. On July 29th Germany first made a bid for British neutrality.

---

[5] Germanness.

The Chancellor of Germany asked if we would stand by if French territory were respected – no mention being made of French Colonies – nor did he guarantee Belgian neutrality. France had given her word to respect Belgian neutrality.

On August 1st we were pressed by Germany to name conditions of neutrality, and by France to declare ourselves on her side. We still remained free.

On August 2nd we assured France that if the German Fleet came into the Channel or through the North Sea to undertake hostile operations against French shipping or her coast, the British Fleet would take action.

On August 2nd early German troops had invaded Luxembourg – later on this date they were reported to be across the French Frontier at Cirey and near Longwy.

On August 3rd (War having been declared on France) the German advanced guard was at Gemmerich in Belgium. But Berlin was almost silent. In London, Paris, and Brussels vain attempts were still being made to avoid War. In Germany the control of events had passed from the Foreign Office to the General Staff.

The violation of Belgian neutrality finally decided Great Britain to take part in the War. It had been a common thought for years that Germany intended to attack France through Eastern Belgium. Since 1906 Germany had constructed an elaborate network of railways from the Rhine to the Belgian Frontier, through a barren, thinly populated area – deliberately constructed for sudden attack on Belgium. Great Britain and France had, in view of this action, discussed plans of protection with Belgium. Germany found these plans in Brussels and tried to make them her cover for the violation of Belgian neutrality. Germany asked with threats on August 2nd for a free passage through Belgium. It was refused, but the Frontier was crossed. But Germany said "Necessity knows no law". Belgium exercised patience and fortitude, but on August 4th appealed to Britain and France for protection. On August 4th Britain presented her ultimatum to Germany – demanding Germany to refrain from further Belgian violation.

For Britain it was a matter of life and death for her honour to keep her solemn compact with Belgium – "To defend her neutrality if attacked".

At 4.00pm on August 4th War was declared on Germany. We were late in the field, but our Navy was early.

Mobilisation of our Standing Army – Reserves, Navy and Territorials – began. The scheme of concentration was carried out wonderfully.

On August 9th the first elements of the Expeditionary Force embarked. Nine days later the greater part had been landed in France and was moving by way of Amiens to assist the French. What they did, and their successors have done to translate diplomacy into action in the War of liberty is now known and will be the glory of our history.

CHAPTER 1
First Impressions, First Decisions, First Actions, Liverpool and Bury
1st August 1914 to 7th November 1914

01.08.14

and

02.08.14

It is not my intention to write a history of the War, but merely to give a resume of my own personal experiences, to be a reminder in the days to come of the small part I took in "The Great War".

Perhaps my experiences are more or less typical of the average individual. This diary may give some idea of the part played by one amongst many million of our Great Empire Army. On August 1st [6], which incidentally is a great day in my Regiment, the Lancashire Fusiliers, – Minden Day – I was employed by Lever Bros at Port Sunlight, in the Chemical Engineering Laboratory. Personally I was engaged on the determination of glycerin values (which compound by the way proved to be of tremendous value to this Country during the War, as an intermediate product in the manufacture of explosives).

I was living with Harold Downham in digs at Mr Parrot's, 1 Queens Road, Rock Ferry. Both of us went over to Bury on August 1st 1914 for the week-end and naturally that week-end was one of intense excitement and anxiety. Everyone was talking about the possibilities of war and the probabilities, but rather in the light of "How could war be avoided?"

03.08.14

We returned to Rock Ferry on Monday evening – a Bank Holiday. Newsboys had the time of their lives selling their special editions which contained little or no news. Little did the boys care. They got just whatever they asked for the papers.

04.08.14

In the evening everyone walked about, worried, and eager for the latest news. Late that evening Germany's reply was expected. Our hopes of Peace were shattered. WAR WAS DECLARED ON GERMANY.

05.08.14

I went to work as usual. Even so quickly the Government Factory at Walton Abbey were pressing us for glycerin.

On this date Mobilisation Orders were received to the Army and Navy Reservists, and the Territorials. Army and Navy Reservists were ordered to report to their respective Depots, Territorials to their own Units at their own Drill Halls. The Mobilisation Orders were posted up at Public Buildings, Town Halls, Police Stations, Post Offices, Places of Worship.

Naturally to many of us who were not in the Army or Territorials at the outbreak of hostilities came many questions to our minds.

How is this going to affect the Country?

How is it going to affect me personally?

What part shall I have to take in it (if any)?

---

[6] The Battle of Minden, or The Battle of the Roses (so called because the victorious side are said to have plucked flowers from the hedgerows as they advanced), took place on 1st August 1759, when British and Prussian Allies fought against French and Saxon soldiers at Minden in North West Germany, and won, although outnumbered four to five. The XXth Foot, from whom the Fusiliers traced their origins, took part in the battle, and commemorated it, inter alia, by the wearing of "Minden Roses".

Remember that <u>at this time</u> everyone not actually in the Army, Navy, or Terriers[7] was a free man.

Thoughts travelled quickly – quicker than action, either national or personal. I personally wondered whether a General Mobilisation order would be issued.

The general feeling prevailing throughout the Nation was that such a titanic struggle – already involving Britain, France, Russia, Belgium and Serbia on the one hand, and, on the other, Germany and Austro-Hungary – couldn't possibly last long.

The Economic Question seemed to govern the situation. How long could the Nations stand the Financial Strain? The Food Question also seemed to be Vitally important.

People in the British Isles imagined that our food supply would run out in the course of a few days. England became temporarily panic stricken. Food prices increased enormously. Some people almost filled their houses with stores as if in preparation for a siege, and then what? Unnecessary shortage and exorbitant prices for a time.

In a few days the Country regained its reason, and resumed a calmer realisation of the Seriousness of things – but <u>NOT</u> in real earnest. They appreciated that now was the time to be British. But not for many months, years, almost two years, in 1916, did the Country really appreciate the fact that the War was really a matter of life and death, not alone of the individuals, but a question of the very existence of the Country and the Great British Empire.

While we at home were talking and wondering, "our Contemptible Little Army"[8] was fast mobilising, and being dipatched to France to support the French and the Belgians on the Western Front.

Now it was quite obvious that our Reserves would be insufficient to maintain the Army in the field for many months without thousands of additional Recruits.

The Great Cry throughout the Country was for <u>Recruits</u>. The British Bull Dog Spirit, his love of Adventure, his love of his Country, and the Excitement of the Day brought many thousands to the Colours, especially old soldiers. The saying "Once a soldier, always a soldier" proved true enough. Gradually Territorial Battalions were brought up to Mobilisation and War Basis strength, not only in men, but in transport, and equipment. Horses and Vehicles of all description were commandeered – many of course had been subsidised for years by the Government.

The Territorials – which had hitherto been rather despised – proved their value without doubt, and now – in 1919 – we all know and appreciate this fact beyond all praise.

Although for many years prior to the War the Country had refused to listen to the appeals of such fine Patriarchs as Lord Roberts, who advocated a system of National Service, yet, when the crisis came, we wished we had taken their advice. Fortunately for our Empire we had some level-headed, far-seeing men living – Lord Roberts, Lord Kitchener, Lord Derby, for example. When the Peace is really signed[9] and we English – British – realise

---

[7] Territorials.

[8] On 19th August 1914 Kaiser William II issued an order that General French's "Contemptible Little Army" be defeated forthwith.

[9] This happened on 28th June 1919.

"Der Tag"[10], we shall appreciate what these men did for Greater England.

Within a week of the Outbreak of War these men appealed to the Country to supply Recruits – not only as Reserves for the Armies then embodied, but to form an additional force.

At first Lord Kitchener appealed for the "First Hundred Thousand" – these he got easily.

Further appeals were made – men simply flocked to the Colours, and we know how many real volunteers came forward, before it was deemed necessary to introduce the "Attestation Scheme"[11] – still voluntary – and then followed later by the "Conscript Scheme", or Compulsory Service Act, in varying degrees.[12]

Surely the Britisher responded to the call right nobly as if in answer to this appeal.

O Noble English
Awake remembrance of the valiant dead,
And with your puissant arm renew their feats.[13]

Germany despised our original expeditionary Force of 1914 calling them "The Contemptible Little Army" – those heroes of the Battle of Mons and the Marne. The World knows what they did.

We were laughed at because of our keenness on sport of all kinds; and English character may be easy going, light hearted, rather believing in the old saying:

"Never trouble trouble till trouble troubles you";

but when the British latent determination was roused undoubtedly the very best of England's – Britain's – manhood, and later womanhood, responded to the Country's Call.

So far I've talked of what other people did. What did I do?

Was I one of the occupants of *"the nest of bones"*.[14] Thank God No! My pride, my will, and the small amount of Englishman I am, governed my decision.

I never had any pugilistic tendencies. Only once in my school days do I remember having a real fight – and that with a fellow who gave me a thrashing. He unfortunately is no more, for, having served his Country before the War and through the War until February 1919, he unfortunately died in Egypt.

So I cannot say that it was a lust for fighting, and it wasn't any love of adventure, that made me join – for I was always a greater lover of my own home and my own folk – and it wasn't for honour and glory. Often have I been asked the question – "Whatever made you enlist when you did, when did you feel that first spark of enthusiasm which made you give up a useful occupation, necessary to the Country and to the Army, and join the Army?" The question is difficult to answer.

---

[10] Literally "The Day". This was a toast by German Imperial Naval Commanders when they were going to engage in battle with the British Royal Navy, and after the War was applied by the British to the day on which the German Fleet surrendered to the Allies, 21st November 1918.

[11] This scheme was introduced by Lord Derby in the autumn of 1915; under it men could enlist voluntarily by attesting that they were willing to go to war, but could defer actually going to war until they were called up at a later date.

[12] In this sentence Norman is referring to The Military Service Act, passed in January 1916, which introduced a "Conscript Scheme", and also to subsequent Military Service Acts which extended the scope of conscription.

[13] Here are set out extensive extracts from Shakespeare's *Henry V*, beginning with a quotation from *Act 1 Scene 2*; in the earlier part of the diary, Norman has included a number of quotations from this play, and he was clearly impressed by what he saw as strong analogies between the way in which Henry V's troops dealt with the situation faced by the English in Shakespeare's play, and the way in which the British dealt with the situation faced by them in the First World War.

[14] Another quotation from *Henry V*; Norman refers to the *"nest of bones"* as reminding him of *"the Irish trouble – the Shirkers – the Conscientious Objectors, the cowards"*.

06.08.14   My first real feelings of "Get away and do something" came as early as Thursday August 6th 1914.

After a hard day's work I thought I would go over to Liverpool from Rock Ferry and see what was doing. So I took the ferry across for a ride.

On approach, the Prince's Landing Stage (a place familiar to me by frequent visits, and to me always full of interest) presented a very busy and unusual appearance.

Several moveable cranes were drawn up alongside the landing stage, boardings had been created on the stage, and lying in the Mersey were a number of strange large boats, also there were two berthed alongside the stage – quite unusual.

When I got off the ferry and walked along the stage, I found it barricaded, and an armed sentry on duty. Walking up to Prince's Parade I saw one mass of line upon line of motor lorries – all shapes and sizes – collected from all over the Country. Each had been hurriedly marked with the Government sign, a broad arrow and the initials of the War Department "[↑WD]", so familiar in later days. Officers were rushing about looking worried and carrying bundles of paper. Loading was merrily going on – whistles blowing, motor cycle dispatch riders rushing about. On examination I found all the lorries bore the chalk marks "6th Transport Column BEF" (British Expeditionary Force).

It was this sight that made me first realise that England really was at war. I felt interested – more than that – keen – full of excitement. I felt I ought to do something.

It wasn't any idea of fighting for Neutral States or Violation of Scraps of Paper or the Rights of Weaker Nations that made my mind up. England – the British Empire – was at war. She had done a great deal for me – here was a chance to give something back. – I must have a real share in the War.

I had been willing enough to play at soldiers in the School and University – I was keen in those times. I had learnt a little of military matters, and had some great times at the Country's expense. Couldn't my little knowledge be made some use of somewhere?

How was I to start – how could I take an active part?

That night I went back to my digs and turned the question over in my mind.

08.08.14   On Saturday August 8th I went home to Bury. Bury was busy, the Territorials were all living in Town awaiting orders. Some were living at the Drill Hall[15], some at the Athenaeum, some at the Co-operative Hall, and some at home. Orders were received to establish a Brigade Camp at Turton for the Lancashire Fusiliers Brigade (later the 125th Infantry Brigade), which happened on August 10th.

10.08.14   We had been going to go to Cromer, Norfolk, for a holiday, but had to cancel that because
to   of traffic difficulties etc. So Father, Mother, Kathleen and I went over to Cleveleys Hydro
23.08.14   for a week. We had a very enjoyable time playing golf, tennis, bathing and walks, the universal topic being the War and following the newspapers for movements of the armies in France.

I was on holiday until Sunday August 23rd. During the last few days of my holidays I tried to get a recommendation for a commission through the University OTC, but I was rejected on

---

[15] The Drill Hall was built in 1868 on the site of Bury Castle, and still stands in the centre of Bury (see the photograph on page 34). The Athenaeum was part of a neo-classical development on Market Street designed by Sidney Smirke in 1850, comprising the Derby Hotel, Derby Hall (the old Town Hall) and the Athenaeum; only Derby Hall survives, the rest having been demolished in the 1960s. The whereabouts of the Co-operative Hall is not known.

chest measurement at the RAMC Headquarters in Manchester. Then I made enquiries at the Drill Hall in Bury to try and get away with the 1/5th Lancashire Fusiliers – but with no avail.

24.08.14   When I got back to the Works everyone was talking of enlisting. But nothing definite was done until the movement came forward to recruit for "Pals" Battalions in Liverpool. It took some little time for the authority to form these units to come through and we were very busy at the Works on glycerin production at this time, and I really couldn't get away.

29.08.14   I went over to Bury for the week and found that everyone I knew seemed to be joining – Tom Cornall, Alec Smith, Roger Smith, and Sydney Ramsbottom. One group – Tom, Alec, Walter Wearing, Jimmy Hopkinson, and Charles Peacock – joined the Cavalry, were posted to the 11th Hussars, and went to Scarborough.
Many of the fellows I knew joined the Manchester "Pals" (Infantry).
On my return to Port Sunlight on Monday August 31st we all determined to enlist in something. We considered things over. Harold Downham and I talked it over very seriously in our digs at night.

02.09.14   At breakfast we agreed that we would decide definitely that night. However Harold telephoned me to the Works from Liverpool and said he was off to Bolton to try to join the Engineers. He went to Bolton, couldn't get in the REs, so went on to Bury and joined the Lancashire Fusiliers, being sent to Turton at once and posted to the 7th Battalion. Harold went to Egypt with them, also Gallipoli, France. However, I shall have more to say about Harold later.[16]
With Harold joining I was stranded.

03.09.14   I decided I really must do something. I went down to the Works and told them my intentions. Several fellows from the Chemical Engineering Laboratory had joined the previous day.
However I went straight over to Liverpool to Exchange Station to telephone to Jack to ask him to see Major Gow at the Drill Hall and see if there was a 12th hour chance of going away with the 1/5th. I anxiously awaited Jack's reply. After lunch I rang up Jack again, but no luck. During the morning I had decided that if no news came from Bury I should join the "Pals" in Liverpool.
So at about 3.30pm on Thursday September 3rd I went to St George's Hall Recruiting Centre. At first I got into the wrong place, where they were recruiting for the Line Battalions – they seemed a rough crowd and I must admit I was a bit doubtful. On finding the mistake out, I went to the correct room. There I found a line of fellows waiting with similar intentions to my own. We were given several forms to fill in. Then we were told to strip for medical inspection. Being the first time I had been medically inspected in public, I felt

---

[6] Harold Downham was a fellow Bury Grammar School pupil two years older than Norman. Norman met him from time to time during the War, and he features in diary entries for 23rd August 1917, 9th September 1917, and 9th October 1917, all during the period when Norman was with the 1/5th Lancashire Fusiliers on the Belgian front; on the third of these meetings Harold is described as "*sitting on the road side coming down from the Line, on his way … home to go to a Cadet School to get a commission*". Norman probably also intended to tell of his death, as Harold, by then a 2nd Lieutenant, was wounded near Trescault, and died shortly afterwards on 29th September 1918, aged 28. The son of John and Fanny Downham of 194 Walmersley Road, Bury, and married (only two months before his death) to Fanny, he is buried at Grévillers British Cemetery, reference XV.A.8.

somewhat embarrassed; however, it had to be done – so now for it.

A Sergeant took me in hand first. He took my chest measurement. "Eh lad th'yll have to do better than that. Take a deep breath. Eh, go on, deeper" – eventually by not holding the tape too tight across the back I <u>only just</u> reached the required standard. This measurement was duly recorded on one of the Army Forms. Then I had to be weighed. The Sergeant seemed very struck with my slimness – of course I never was really fat! On the scales I jumped, and turned it at 7 stone 11 pounds,[17] to the amusement of the Sergeant who said, "Eh, mon, you'll never make a soldier with that weight. Are you a jockey? Anyway, we'll soon make a man of you in the Army." Then I had my eyes tested, my lungs, and several other odd tricks. The final decision was alright – "Are you keen?" – to which I replied "Yes – what do you think I came here for if I wasn't?" We then dressed – and returned to be sworn in.

I was given a form describing my general appearance etc. and out I went – a Soldier – feeling as proud as punch and inches taller.

That evening I went home to Rock Ferry. I went down to see Mr Howson at his digs and told him I had enlisted and shouldn't be in at the Works the following morning. We had been instructed to proceed home and await further instructions.

04.09.14 I collected all my belongings at Queen's Road, packed up and went home, arriving in Bury in time for dinner.

I was then in the 3rd City Battalion, King's Liverpool Regiment, as a Private.

Friday evening I went down to see Major Gow at the Drill Hall to ask him to recommend me for a commission in the King's Liverpool Regiment. We had a chat and he asked me whether I would like to put my name down for the Lancashire Fusiliers. There was some talk of forming a Reserve Battalion to the 5th Lancashire Fusiliers (Territorial Force) but the authority had not been given. He suggested I should be able to get a transfer from the King's Liverpool Regiment. I decided to consider the question and arranged to call and see him in a day or two.

A few days later the authority was given to recruit for a Reserve Battalion, and my name was put on the list of prospective officers along with H. Barnes, J.B. Packman, Norman Kemp, Malcolm Young and Manse Evans. Then George (my brother) and Bob Ashworth applied, also Geoffrey Hutchinson.

07.09.14 I went down to the Drill Hall and reported to Major Gow.

We got about 60 Recruits that day. These men were formed into a Recruits Squad and were instructed by Corporal Crawford – later Regimental Sergeant Major – and Corporal Collier. The officers were also to be drilled with this Squad and in addition we instructed ourselves in Elementary Drill and Musketry in the Officers' Quarters. Sergeant Major Ash also came over and gave us short lectures on Guard Duties, Saluting etc.

08.09.14 I went down to Knowsley Street Station[18] in the afternoon to watch the entraining of the East Lancashire Brigade. This Brigade had been in Camp at Chesham Fields since August 10th. They entrained from the Cattle Siding. They were going to Egypt.

---

[17] 49.4 kilograms.

[18] The station was closed on 5th October 1970, and subsequently demolished, but the line running through it was re-opened in 2003 by the East Lancashire Railway, a heritage railway.

Little did anybody think that these troops would ever see any fighting. The average person scarcely imagined fighting probable in Egypt, but how time proved this surmise entirely wrong. For, after being stationed in various parts of Egypt – Alexandria, Cairo, Suez, and East of the Canal – these same men were in the thick of the fighting on Gallipoli, and later at Kantara and the fighting preliminary to the Gaza Offensive, and General Allenby's wonderful fighting in Palestine in 1918. In February 1917 the 42nd Division came over to France. I shall describe more fully their work in France as I was later (in June 1917) posted to the 1/5th Lancashire Fusiliers.[19]

09.09.14 to 11.09.14	We paraded daily at the Drill Hall. Recruits came in steadily and by the end of the week we had about 200 to 250 men. Colonel John Hall had accepted the position of Commanding Officer of the 5th Reserve Battalion Lancashire Fusiliers and proceeded to Turton to take over the command of the Residue of the 1/5th Lancashire Fusiliers – men who for various reasons were unable to volunteer to proceed abroad with the Battalion. At that time (1914) there was no obligation on a Territorial Officer or Soldier to serve outside the United Kingdom, and officers or men had to volunteer to serve overseas if they were needed overseas on mobilisation. The officers left behind with the 1/5th Lancashire Fusiliers at Turton were Captain Stonestreet, 2nd Lieutenant Laughlin, and 2nd Lieutenant Frizelle.
12.09.14	On Saturday September 12th Colonel Hall came over to Bury to interview the few of us who had applied for consideration for commissions. I went down to the Drill Hall, Bury, at 9.00am. This was the morning that Kenneth Waterhouse and Hartley Goldsmith first reported, and applied for commissions in the 5th Reserve Lancashire Fusiliers. We formed an Officers Squad and had a short instruction under Corporal Crawford in the Drill Hall. I received orders from Liverpool to report at the Riding School, Dingle, at 2.30pm, so I went over there in the afternoon. Several hundred fellows were collected there. We formed up under the sheds. Then we paraded in the yard according to the Rolls called. I was in Nº 6 Platoon "B" Company. Later in the afternoon we received our pay and billeting allowance for the 10 days' service – in all 20 shillings. We were then told to parade at Sefton Park at 10.00am on Monday September 14th, and we were dismissed at about 8.00pm. The training at Sefton Park consisted in Physical Drill, Squad Drill, Platoon and Company Drill. Later each company went to Musketry in turn, as there were only a limited number of DP rifles[20]. We used to have two Route Marches a week – Wednesdays and Saturdays. Each week-end I used to go home, but had to catch the 6.29am train on Monday morning to Liverpool. I was picked out as Corporal of my section, Nº 7 Section, "B" Company. We never got any uniforms while I was in Liverpool – but we were measured for them. During this period of training I was anxiously waiting to be gazetted to the 5th Reserve Lancashire Fusiliers. This Battalion was rapidly increasing – Recruits coming up daily. During my absence from Bury the following officers joined the Battalion: Captain J.D. Barnsdale, Duckworth, Bloy, Kirkman, and Thompson (junior).

---

[19] See the *Afterword* page 274 ff.
[20] Drill purpose rifles, i.e. rifles which had been disabled.

Colonel John Hall made several attempts to get me transferred from the Liverpool Regiment but nothing could be done until I was actually gazetted.

14.10.14   I went on the 8.30am boat as usual from New Ferry. I bought the *Times* as usual and to my astonishment found I was gazetted 2nd Lieutenant in the Lancashire Fusiliers [see page 320]. I was very excited. I went to Sefton Park as usual, and saw my Company CO before Parade, and showed him the *Times*. He took me before the Colonel very soon, and I was dismissed to go to the Orderly Room to make arrangements for my transfer. My papers were made out, and I was paid up to date and clear of the 3rd City Battalion King's Liverpool Regiment by 12 noon – after just six weeks' service. I went over to Port Sunlight, packed my things and left Liverpool at 8.00pm, arriving at Bury at about 10.30pm. When I arrived home, my brother George came in shortly afterwards in uniform. The Battalion had been to the theatre, kindly invited by Mr Wrigley.

16.10.14   I reported to the Drill Hall. The Battalion had grown considerably in my absence, and was formed into 8 companies – about 600 strong. I took over N° 3 Company with Duckworth as my sub. We went down to the Golf Links and did Squad Drill. In the afternoon George and I went down to Manchester. I ordered my uniform from Milton and Jones, also my camp kit at Finnigans.

19.10.14   The greater part of the 5th Reserve (Home Service) Battalion Lancashire Fusiliers moved from Mossborough to Southport. Thus the following officers proceeded to Southport to join their men, namely Waterhouse, Hutchinson, Barnsdale, Bloy, Kirkman, Laughlin, Frizelle, Major Milnes, Major Kay, and Kemp.

Major P.G. Gow was in command at the Depot at Bury, and Captain G. Stonestreet returned from Mossborough to be Depot Adjutant, Sergeant Major Ash being Regimental Sergeant Major. Duckworth and I were sent to join Goldsmith who was with a detachment at Heywood. Thus at Bury we had Major Gow, Captain Stonestreet, George, Packman, Evans, Young, and at Heywood, Goldsmith and Duckworth and myself.

Training proceeded briskly and with good heart.

We were all keen and <u>so were the men</u>.

The training was carried out in the Drill Hall, Bury Ground, and down at Redvales. We used to do Battalion, Company, Platoon, and Squad Drill, Musketry. I used to take the Squads in Musketry. We used to have Route Marches round Holcombe, Tottington, Ramsbottom, Pilsworth, Bolton Road and Radcliffe. Goldsmith lived at the Drill Hall and we used to take turns in staying down with him each night.

Colonel Hall wired for me to proceed to Southport on October 20th, but, as my uniform and kit had not arrived, I was unable to go.

At this time the separate dates are not very clear, as unfortunately I did <u>not</u> keep a daily diary at this time.

About 26.10.14   I was ordered to take over the Radcliffe Detachment to save the men coming from Radcliffe each day. 2nd Lieutenant J.B. Packman went with me. We were busy with recruiting and in a few days had increased our numbers from about 20 to over 100. We had difficulty in finding a drill ground. We did fairly useful work down there during our short stay.

06.11.14   We received a warning order that we might move to Southport any day.

07.11.14   At about noon we received orders to parade the Radcliffe Section and march to Bury immediately after dining.

This done we arrived at Bury Drill Hall at about 3.15pm. Colonel Hall had come over from Southport. The Battalion was formed up and they were selecting men out to be NCOs.

Men with previous experience and ex-soldiers were first selected. I mention this because I distinctly remember two men falling out on the left flank of N° 3 Company. These two men were ex-Sergeant Ashworth who was later Company Sergeant Major of "Y" Company and ex-Corporal Joe Howard late of the 4th King's Own Royal Lancasters, and later of "Z" Company – my own Company. We shall hear more of his doings. But I mention it as being the first time he came to my notice.

The men were warned about the move to Southport which was to be on the next day. After making a speech to the Battalion Colonel Hall dismissed the Parade.

This concludes the first period of my service with the 5th Reserve Battalion Lancashire Fusiliers, the preliminary recruiting period in Bury.

**Norman as a 2nd lieutenant
in 1914**

**Norman's travel pass to secure rail transport from
Liverpool to Seaforth following his recruitment in
September 1914**

CHAPTER 2
Southport and Bury
8th November 1914 to 18th April 1915

08.11.14   George and I had a great rush to get our kit packed ready to move to Southport on
to   November 8th 1914.

13.12.14   Waddicar (my servant) and Dick Bradburn (George's servant) – who had been coming up home daily since October 15th cleaning our uniform etc. – packed our kit and took it down to the Drill Hall. It was a pouring wet morning and cold. The Battalion paraded at the Drill Hall at 9.00am under Colonel Hall.

At this time, of course, the men were in mufti. The Battalion was divided into Right and Left Half Battalion. The Right Half Battalion was to go on the first train, and the Left Half Battalion on the second train. Colonel Hall took the Right Half Battalion. And I took the Left Half Battalion.

Before the Battalion moved off from the Drill Hall the Mayor – Councillor Hacking – addressed us and wished us all good luck.

Colonel Wike, Honorary Colonel of the 5th Lancashire Fusiliers, also spoke. The Mayor presented the men with cigarettes before leaving.

The Borough Brass Band headed the Column, but did not play much as it was so wet. Large numbers of people turned out to see the Battalion march off by Market Street and Knowsley Street to Knowsley Street Station. I was in the rear of the Column.

Mother watched us march out from the Athenaeum.

The first train got away, and was quickly followed by the second train.

It was fine when we arrived at Chapel Street Station, Southport, at about 11.30am. Captain Cummins met us at the station, and we marched out headed by the Band.

Just outside the station we passed Mr and Mrs Bentley in a landau.[21]

We marched to the billeting area where we were met by Major Kay, Major H.N. Milnes, Captain Barnsdale, Hutchinson, Bloy, Kirkman, and 2nd Lieutenant Kemp.

The Battalion HQ, Orderly Room Stores, Boot Shop and Guard Room were at 3, Victoria Street and the men's billets were at Bath Street, Victoria Street and Neville Street. It took almost one and a half hours to get the men fixed up in billets. George and I joined at a bedroom.

Battalion HQ Mess was at Victoria Hotel. I remember feeling very nervous the first night at Mess, but it was great. We usually had our own little crowd at the top end of the table,

---

[21] A landau was a luxury city horse drawn carriage. Frank Mercer Bentley and Horace M. Bentley were friends of Norman and his brother, George. Frank was born in 1881 and attended Bury Grammar School briefly from 1892 to 1894, when the family moved away. The father, Arthur Frank Bentley, a businessman and proprietor of the Bury Times, died in 1895, and the 1911 census shows the mother, Mary Ellen Bentley, living back in Bury at 125 Walmersley Road with her five children, Frank and Horace being the eldest and youngest siblings. Perhaps *Mr and Mrs Bentley* were relatives (grandparents?). Frank was gazetted to the 3/5th Lancashire Fusiliers in August 1915, and in January 1917 he was with them at Colchester (as was George), while Horace was in "B" Company of the 1/5th Lancashire Fusiliers when Norman joined them in France in June 1917, and is mentioned several times in that part of the diary. Frank won the MC in the 3rd Battle of Ypres in October 1917, suffering a wound to his leg which necessitated a period of recovery in Britain. On 13th October 1918, soon after returning to France to join the 1/5th Lancashire Fusiliers, he was killed by a shell at Briastre on the River Selle. He is buried at St Souplet British Cemetery, reference II.A.1.

Captain Waterhouse, Goldsmith, Barnsdale, George, and myself.

During the afternoon Colonel Hall told me that I was to take over command of "B" Company – all "A" Company and "B" Company were Home Service men left behind by the 1/5th Lancashire Fusiliers when they went to Egypt.

Writing this diary now (in 1919) I cannot give daily details of our work at Southport; I can only summarise the General Routine.

Daily Routine:

7.00am	Rouse Parade
7.45am	Breakfast
8.20am	Commanding Officer's orders
9.00am	Battalion Parade opposite Pier, Birkdale Golf Links or Sands
2.00pm	Company Parades – Sands or Birkdale Park
4.20pm	Tea
7.30pm	Dinner

On Rouse Parade we used to turn out in any old dress. Footer knickers etc. Manse Evans was always prominent with very short socks. We used to do Physical Drill or have a run along the promenade (if too cold for the promenade we used to go into Lord Street). It was a great stunt turning out in semi-darkness – climbing up a lamp post to light the gas to call the Roll. It was always some job turning the fellows out of billets these cold mornings.

On the morning parade we used to march out with the Band to the Golf Links and do Squad Drill, Physical Training, Extended Order Drill, always marching back with the Band, and marching on to the Parade Ground to the Regimental March.

Colonel Hall used to get very annoyed with the admiring ladies who would crowd on to the Parade Ground.

One day he got very annoyed and cursed the crowd, and then was so upset he made the officers repeat their salute before dismissing.

Gradually we got the old red uniforms over from Bury – half the men being in khaki and half in red – with a few still in mufti.

We had very few rifles, about 100.

Captain Hutchinson[22] trained a class of NCOs in Musketry.

In the afternoons we used to do Company Drill on the Sands or give our men a lecture.

My Colour Sergeant was Colour Sergeant Ferguson – a very good administrative Sergeant but a poor disciplinarian on parade. However, he was exceedingly useful in getting out the Pay, Pay and Mess Book, and Billeting Certificates. All these details worried me no end – as it was all entirely new work to me. 2nd Lieutenant N.D. Thompson (Jellicoe) was my subaltern. There was a considerable amount of detail in organising Companies and it took a great deal of spare time. In fact with Company orders, inspecting billets etc., kit inspections, pay, and billeting payments on Fridays – we worked pretty hard and hadn't a great deal of time free. My NCOs were pretty hopeless – several old Sergeants left behind by the 1/5th Lancashire Fusiliers, and no wonder!

---

[22] This, and the Captain Hutchinson mentioned at the top of page 33, are probably not the Geoffrey Hutchinson mentioned in the diary entry for 4th September 1914, as the latter started out as a 2nd lieutenant, though he was a captain by the time the Battalion departed for France on 3rd May 1915.

Lance Corporal Howarth, who was my Company Orderly Clerk, was very useful and did excellent work. He was Orderly Room Sergeant later in France, and won the DCM on July 31st 1917 at Ypres.[23]

Bathing Parades were held for each company once a week at the Baths near the Pier. The men seemed frightened of water and we had great difficulty in getting them to bathe. Many a man had his bath in his clothes because he was pushed in.

Very often we used to have tea at Thom's Café in Lord Street. Bloy always used to excel in the cake line – eating about a dozen daily. We used to play billiards in the evenings.

Major Milnes, Waterhouse, Goldsmith, George, and Barnsdale often gathered at the "Deep End" in Lawdie's little abode.

Sundays we went to Christ Church for service at 9.15am. Then there was always a party for golf at Birkdale.

We always had a long Route March on Saturday morning to Ormskirk, Birkdale, Ainsdale, etc. Major Kay was Mess President.

Dinners were always rather humorous, especially when the CO told tales; then the little stout waitress, who was always called "Mother", was always asked to find a job of work elsewhere – shame!

The following officers were with the 5th Reserve Lancashire Fusiliers – later known as the 2/5th Lancashire Fusiliers.[24]

Colonel John Hall

Major J. Kay

Major H.N. Milnes

Captain Cummins, Adjutant

Major J.W. Cook, Medical Officer

Lieutenant J. Bowd, Quartermaster

"A" Company: 2nd Lieutenant R.S. Ashworth, 2nd Lieutenant R.W. Kirkman, 2nd Lieutenant G. Hall

"B" Company: 2nd Lieutenant N. Hall, 2nd Lieutenant R.N. Thompson

"C" Company: Captain J.D. Barnsdale, 2nd Lieutenant L. Bloy, 2nd Lieutenant W. Duckworth

"D" Company: 2nd Lieutenant H. Frizelle, 2nd Lieutenant J.B. Packman, 2nd Lieutenant Isherwood

"E" Company: 2nd Lieutenant G.C. Hutchinson, 2nd Lieutenant Evans, 2nd Lieutenant Young

"F" Company: 2nd Lieutenant Laughlin, 2nd Lieutenant H. Barnes

"G" Company: 2nd Lieutenant Goldsmith

"H" Company: 2nd Lieutenant K. Waterhouse, 2nd Lieutenant N. Kemp

During the early days at Southport the men were vaccinated. This upset training rather badly as many of the men were very seedy.

---

[23] Sergeant F. Howarth was still with the 2/5th Lancashire Fusiliers when he won his DCM in the 3rd Battle of Ypres on 31st July 1917. The 2/5th Lancashire Fusiliers were in an action at Spree Farm under Lieutenant Colonel Best-Dunkley, who was mortally wounded in the action. After Best-Dunkley fell, it was not known whether any officers were left alive, so Sergeant Howarth took command of the Battalion for a time. Norman was by then with the 1/5th Lancashire Fusiliers at Gommecourt, so not involved in the action, but Thomas Hope Floyd, like Norman a Bury Grammar School pupil, gives a detailed account of it in his book, *At Ypres with Best-Dunkley*.

[24] Norman gives details of what happened to most of these men when they got to France; we know virtually nothing about any of them at this stage, but gradually get to learn more about those who turned out to be Norman's closest comrades. See also the footnote to the diary entry for 3rd May 1915, when Norman's unit first landed in France.

A postcard which Norman sent from Southport to his sister Kathleen on 7th December 1914, showing the Victoria Hotel, with his and George's room marked

14.12.14
to
20.12.14
About 10 of us were struck down with food poisoning and were in bed for about a week. George and I were both in the same room. George just kept groaning and saying "Oh God, I am ill – I'm going to die." That didn't make me feel any better. Doctor got two nurses to look after us. One nurse, Nurse Piggott, was quite a cheery soul. She really did very well for us, in spite of us grumbling at everything she did, and didn't do just as we liked. Mother came over to see George and me on December 16th, but apparently we were both very rude to her, and not very interesting.

Mother saw Kenneth Waterhouse for the first and only time on the day she came over.

24.12.14
I got a week's leave and went home with George, or, rather, I followed on a later train. I had a very good time over Xmas, with all of us at home. I returned to Southport on December 28th with George and Duckworth.

31.12.14
It was New Year's Eve, and most of the officers went to the Palladium to a show, while George and I went up to spend the evening with the Hopkinsons.

We had a very enjoyable evening, quite a party, and came back about 1.15am on January 1st 1915. George was the Orderly Officer, but he had forgotten, and put his dinner jacket on, so I turned out the guard for him on our return.

I found Major Milnes, Waterhouse, Goldsmith, Bloy, Laughlin, and Hill in the "Deep End" with Lawdie, and stayed until 2.30am. Then I retired to the ante-room, where there were heated arguments involving Cummins and Jimmy Bowd – both tight! I finally went to bed at 3.00am – tired.

We did trips along landings with luggage trucks – quite mad! There had been a fire alarm while we were away.

So ended 1914!

01.01.15
Everyone got up feeling very tired.

The Battalion Band played outside the Hotel. They were requested to stop by Major Kay.

The Battalion paraded at 9.00am – marched down the promenade towards Birkdale and returned via Lord Street. It was a cold wet morning. Parade was dismissed for kit inspections.

I spent the remainder of the day getting out my Pay and Mess Book for December.

I was very worried. I heard later about this month's account from the War Office Accountant Board in January 1917 when I went to Ripon.[25]

03.01.15   We had Church Parade. In the afternoon the Band played outside the Hotel. About this time the khaki clothing and web equipment[26] came along.

06.01.15   I heard that I was gazetted Lieutenant from December 28th 1914.[27]

10.01.15   I was detailed to proceed to Bury to train men who were then at the Depot – about 500 men. These men formed the nucleus of the 3/5th Battalion Lancashire Fusiliers. Ashworth and Thompson were also detailed to proceed to Bury. Ashworth and Thompson were both Home Service at this time. I was NOT. I never could understand why I was sent. I handed over my Company to George.

11.01.15   I left Southport with Bob Ashworth about 2.00pm. I reported at the Drill Hall in Bury.
to   Captain Stonestreet was then in Command.
04.04.15   A few days later Major Kay came back to Bury and took over as OC of the Depot. Thank God! At about this time the Battalion at Southport was re-organised into four company formation. A few days later George and Barnes came back to Bury.
Barnes – with Laughlin and Frizelle – received orders to proceed to Egypt to join the 1/5th Lancashire Fusiliers.
The Daily Routine was as follows:

9.30am   Parade in Drill Hall, Physical Drill on Golf Links
11.00am to 12.30pm Squad, Platoon and Company Drill – sometimes at Chamber Hall
2.00pm to 4.30pm   Afternoon Parade, varied
Route Marches three times a week – Holcombe, Whitefield, Heywood, Birtle
A certain amount of Musketry was also taken. This was my job.

The officers used to sleep at the Drill Hall in turn. We generally had breakfast at the Derby. George and I lived at home while we were at Bury, and we really had some very good times. I got on very well with Major Kay.
One week-end the Band came over from Southport. Major Kay gave them a hot-pot supper in the Squad Room on the Monday evening. George and I went down for an hour. Sergeant Major Ash was chairman.
In the evening we often used to fire on the Miniature Range.
There was an old Sergeant, Sergeant Glover, at the Drill Hall in charge of the details, about six men too old to go abroad. Old Glover was very amusing at times. He thought he had taught us all we knew.

---

[25] Norman does not mention this when writing about his time in Ripon later in the diary, let alone expand upon it.

[26] This was equipment made of a strong woven cloth pioneered by the Mills Equipment Company in the USA. Typically it comprised a belt, ammunition pouches, haversack and large pack. The British Army was the first European Army to replace leather belts and pouches with those made of this material.

[27] In fact the promotion of Norman to temporary Lieutenant featured in the supplement to the *London Gazette* on 7th January 1915, to take effect from 23rd December 1914; see the extract reproduced on page 320.

Some time after this Gladys[28] was at the Drill Hall on Red Cross work.

My name happened to be mentioned at which old Glover pricked up his ears. Gladys said, "Why do you know Captain Hall?" – to which old Glover immediately replied, "Know him, why I reared him."

About the beginning of April rumours got about that the 2/5th Battalion were going to move. They had been training very hard and had got well through with their Musketry at Altcar using the Japanese Service Rifle. The rumours were that they were going to Malvern. Naturally we at Bury wondered what would happen to us; especially as George and I, being keen to do as much as possible and going anywhere, wanted to go with the 2/5th Battalion. Also they had got quite a number of new officers since we were at Southport and we didn't want to be cut out by these fellows.

Then another rumour came along and that was that they were going abroad. We could hardly credit this as they had only been in training since September 1914.

05.04.15   The Battalion at Bury was inspected by Brigadier General Garston from Southport. Arrangements had been made for the inspection to be on the Golf Links. We marched down to the Links in a snow storm. When we had got thoroughly wet, orders came down that we were to proceed to the Drill Hall. We marched back and were then inspected. Colonel Hall came over with the Brigadier.

Rapid arrangements were made for the men to be inoculated immediately. George and I were both done. It didn't affect me, but George was a bit groggy for a day or two.

We were then called on to find drafts for the 2/5th at Southport – especially to replace a considerable number of Home Service men, several of whom were also sent to other battalions of the 2nd and 1st East Lancashire Division.

Most of our best men – especially the NCOs whom we had carefully selected – were picked out.

11.04.15   This was a <u>very</u> busy week for us in Bury. The 2/5th Battalion were due to leave Southport
to   on Sunday April 18th and go to Bedford to join the 51st Highland Division. Although they
18.04.15   were <u>NOT</u> known by that number at that time.

Altogether we equipped about 150 men for the 2/5th out of the 3/5th at Bury.

We also sent about 100 men to the 2/7th Manchesters from Bury.

On April 15th George took a draft over to the 2/5th at Southport. He saw Colonel Hall and tried to get us transferred back to them so that we could go with the 2/5th. No avail! Curses on old John. We were both very fed up at being left behind as so many new officers were going with them.

On April 16th I took a draft over to the 2/7th Manchesters. Then I went to see the officers at the Victoria. Everyone was just up to the eyes in work in preparation for the move on Sunday.

On April 17th George was detailed to take another draft over to Southport this Saturday

---

[28] Gladys was probably one of Norman's cousins, as in the original diary entry for 6th January 1915 he refers to having tea with Gladys and Auntie Polly at the Palladium in Bury. She was probably married to Herbert Cain, as Herbert Cain joined them for the tea, and later, on 6th June 1917, Norman visited "Herbert, Gladys and Auntie" at West Bank, Bury. There is a photograph of Herbert Cain on page 8.

afternoon. I took the remainder of the men for a Route March round Holcombe and arrived back at 12.45pm. I found on my return that the arrangements regarding the conducting of the draft had been altered.

Major Kay had decided that I should go to a Musketry Course at Altcar[29] for a month. He suggested that I should take the draft to Southport to see Captain Hutchinson about the course, as he had just come back. I got lunch at the Derby and left with the draft at 2.38pm. I handed over the men to the Adjutant at the Orderly Room, then went across to the Victoria for tea. All very worried. I saw Colonel Hall and told him how fed up George and I were at being left behind, especially as we were amongst the first half dozen officers to join the 2/5th Lancashire Fusiliers when it was formed. Nothing could be done. I'm afraid I was really rude to the CO. I said goodbye to all my pals, who wanted me to stay dinner but I couldn't face it.

I arrived back in Bury at 10.30pm. Feeling very annoyed, I went to the Drill Hall to drown my sorrows.

On arrival there Sergeant Glover met me.

"I think as there's a bother on Sir – Aye! Th'Major's come, and yer George, and an old chap with a grey beard (Father). They're up yon in t' Mess all a looking at papers and things."

"Very interesting," I thought to myself.

Sure enough, Sam was right – There in the ante-room were Father, Major Kay, George, and Arthur Webb, all busy looking at telegrams, time tables etc. – and looking <u>very</u> worried. It all seemed so strange – yet so warlike. The news affected me – Colonel Hall had telephoned Major Kay – and also wired me:

"Instruct Lieutenant N. Hall to proceed to Bedford early tomorrow, Sunday, to join Battalion, Urgent."

I could scarcely believe my own eyes, for only a few hours before I had said "Goodbye" to them all at Southport.

It seemed like a dream!

Major Kay talked to me privately, rather wanting me to stay with him I think.

However, here was an order. I made my mind up quickly. Go I must! The very chance I had hoped for for months.

I left word for Waddicar – my servant – to be sent for to his home the next morning, Sunday, at 6.00am, collect my things on his way up to the Drill Hall and be at Ravensdale (my home) at 7.30am.

Then Father, George, and I went home and broke the news. Everyone took it very calmly. Perhaps glad to get rid of me!

That night was rather a restless night. I was very excited and full of wonder.

Where were we going to?

Why had Colonel Hall changed his mind so quickly about me?

I did get some sleep – but very little, and I was up early on Sunday morning April 18th 1915.

---

[29] Norman never actually went on this course, and, in fact, never seems to have attended any significant courses at all throughout the War; see the footnote on page 304 of the *Afterword*.

The Drill Hall in Bury in 2019

18.04.15   I got up quite early, collected most of my kit together, and after breakfast went to settle things up at the Drill Hall – cash etc.

I got my travelling warrant. Waddicar came up to Ravensdale as ordered, then went home to tell his wife the news. I ordered him to be at the Bolton Street Station[30] at 3.15pm.

George ran me down to West Bank[31] in his side-car before dinner.

Jack and Mary, and Jack and Nora, came for dinner.

Then came the parting. It was by no means easy to leave home this particular day.

Going abroad – not knowing where I was going or when – also how long it would be before I came home again. It might be never – I was really going to the War!

In fact it was very hard to appear cheerful and unconcerned. Jack absolutely saved the ship by playing the fool. I shall never forget him. It just made all the difference.[32]

At last the cab arrived and I left home at about 2.45pm. Waddicar was at the station with his wife and mother. Herbert met Father and George at the station. The train left at 3.20pm.

So I started on my travels – wondering when (if ever) I should see Bury again. Very many times had I travelled on that same line to Manchester, but never under quite the same circumstances.

On arrival at Victoria I took a taxi across to Central Station, and got my kit fixed up and on the train. Then I had a short walk up Oxford Street for some cigarettes. I came back to the station and met George, who had ridden over on his motorbike. The London train left at 5.15pm to the minute – naturally, when I wanted a few minutes more. At last I really seemed to be off on a job of work.

---

[30] The station was closed for conventional rail services in 1980, but reopened in 1987 by the East Lancashire Railway, a heritage railway.
[31] West Bank, Bury was the home of Auntie Polly and cousin Gladys, and probably also Herbert Cain – see footnote 28 on page 32; Herbert Cain is probably the Herbert referred to later on this page.
[32] This probably refers to Norman's brother, John Russell Hall, rather than Jack Ashworth, as Norman again mentions a Jack *"playing the fool"* to cheer everyone up when he is about to depart for the front on 31st December 1918, when Jack Ashworth was not present.

It was a glorious evening. The first few miles I spent in silent thought. I couldn't read – so I ordered some tea and then wrote one or two letters.

The country looked glorious – so nice and peaceful. The train was very full, but quite comfortable. Derbyshire looked just gorgeous and I felt, as I never felt quite before, that England was a wonderful country. At Derby we had dinner and this helped matters considerably.

Oakley House, Bedford, in about 1900

We ran into Bedford at about 9.00pm. The station was very busy. With some difficulty I managed to get a "growler"[33] and went round to the Mess which was at Oakley House, Bromham Road. It was really a school, and one which turned out to be of interest; for St Barbe[34] – of whom I shall have something to say later – was there at one time. I met Colonel Hall at the Mess, who sent me to my billet at Mrs Eaton Turner's, 58 Adelaide Square where I found Young and Norman Kemp.

58 Adelaide Square, Bedford in 2019

The Turners were extremely kind to Kemp, Young, and myself. We were <u>very</u> happy at "58".

Most of the officers were billeted away from the Mess – in pairs. The men were billeted in empty houses. I got Waddicar fixed up for the night.

Meanwhile, the Battalion had travelled down from Southport that day, and were getting settled into billets when I arrived.

They had paraded on the Pier approach at Southport at 8.30am, with quite a crowd assembled to see them march away. The Mayor of Southport made a farewell speech, and the Massed Bands of the Brigade played the Battalion to the station. Colonel John Hall made one of his famous speeches – and typical:

"The Battalion will move. Men, I can say no more. Home Service men, stand fast. What the devil is that man moving in the rear of N° 4 Company for, and that man in N° 2 Company standing with his nose in one parish and his heels in another?"

Then the Battalion marched off down Neville Street. The old sailor at the shop at the bottom greeted them as he had done many times before: "Good Boys, your Country's proud of you. There are VCs amongst you." – which proved all too true later.

19.04.15   I reported at the Orderly Room in Bromham Road and found that I had been sent for to take over duties of Signalling Officer to the Battalion. It seemed that on Saturday evening April 17th the Colonel suddenly found that he wanted a Signalling Officer. Someone suggested I knew signalling – so he wired for me; and Ainscow, whose kit was actually on the train, was ordered to remain behind and proceed to Bury. Jolly bad luck on him.[35]

---

[33] A horse drawn four-wheeled cab, called a *"growler"* because of the noise its wheels made on cobbled streets.

[34] St Barbe was a fellow officer of Norman's in the 1/5th Lancashire Fusiliers from June 1917. There is more about him in the *Afterword* – see the footnote to the passage covering the period June/July 1917 on page 275.

[35] Ainscow eventually joined the 2/5th Lancashire Fusiliers in France in November 1915 – see the diary entry for 15th November 1915.

It was rather humorous as I had forgotten what little signalling I ever knew/had learnt on the Wireless Section in the Manchester University OTC.

No one seemed to know what my duties were – so I had to worry the job out for myself. I found out what equipment was required and took immediate steps to indent on Ordnance to complete signalling stores to War Establishment. Many were the visits I paid to the Ordnance at Ampthill Road to draw stores and worry the Deputy Assistant Director Ordnance Services.

I must describe my first meeting with Colonel Hall at Bedford. His first remark was:

"Do you know why you've come?"

"Yes, Sir, I was wired for and ordered to proceed to Bedford urgent."

"Well my boy – we wanted a Signalling Officer so I wired for you. I don't know anything about it. We may be off any day – You've got to run the show yourself. Here's a book of equipment. Now get to work." So I did.

The impression on seeing Bedford was one of real work – something definite, and serious. The Division we were posted to was the 1/1st Highland Division. We were part of the 3rd Brigade, a West Lancashire Brigade comprised of:

1/4th King's Own Royal Lancasters

1/4th Loyal North Lancashires

1/8th Liverpool Regiment (Irish)

The town was literally a mass of troops, Artillery, Ammunition Columns, Transport Columns, Signalling Sections, Royal Engineers etc.

General rumour seemed to say we should have a short stay in Bedford. Where we were going or when was very indefinite. A Secret! This gave me all the less time to get my Signal Section organised.

I paraded the Section to see my men.

They were a really excellent crowd who proved my judgment right:

Sergeant Hindle	Private Harrison
Sergeant Collins	Private Bowden
Private Nuttall J.R.	Private Ogden
Private Taylor	Private Armitage
Private Pearson	Private Bland
Private Green	Private Turner J.
Private Atherton	Private Turner R.
Private Walker	Private Wilkinson K.
Private Street	

I gave them some Flag Drill. During the afternoon I interviewed the Brigade Signalling Officer who gave me some very useful information, and advised me to train my fellows in buzzer work. I immediately bought some buzzer units in Bedford, also I made some small lamps – electric – and my fellows soon got very keen and worked hard – all hours of the day and night. But so much for this day's work.

At lunch I met all the officers for the first time. I had a good chat with my old friends and felt very happy to be with them all again.

In the afternoon the Battalion went to the Corn Exchange for a lecture by General Moran on Tips for the Front, Care of Arms on Service etc. He had just returned from La Bassée (a place I shall describe later[36]).

I found out my fellows were supposed to be trained in Morse, Semaphore, Lamps, Telephones, Cable Laying, Heliograph.

I imagined my fellows would be miles behind other units. However, under Sergeant Hindle (who had spent 8 years with the 8th Irish Hussars) and Sergeant Collins (who had spent 12 years with the Manchester Regiment), who were both capable instructors, they made rapid progress.

20.04.15   There were further rumours of an early move. Kits were to be reduced to 35lbs[37] weight, which meant we could take very little; I was especially keen on having plenty of socks.

We had a lecture from Major J.W. Cook on the First Field Dressing – interrupted by Colonel Hall wanting all officers immediately at the Orderly Room. This became a "Daily Wind Up", and we got used to it.

21.04.15   I decided it would be advisable to train some Reserve Signallers. So I got one per section – 64 in all. They knew nothing. I took my parade out daily to a field on the Railway Side – opposite the County Cricket Ground, on the left entering Bedford from the North. As soon as I got this squad interested and making good progress it was decided they were unnecessary. However I earmarked several of the men, for future reference.

We all got our hair close clipped, officers and men – we looked like a lot of convicts.

We adopted the web equipment[38] and discarded Sam Browne Belts. I got my revolver holster, ammunition pouch, and glasses' case painted khaki.

Our Battalion stores came in rapidly, General Service Limbers,[39] Field Cookers, Mess Cart, Maltese Cart,[40] Horses, Mules etc.

I got flags, electric signalling lamps, telephones, wire, telescopes etc.

23.04.15   All my kit was packed. Waddicar had it weighed at the Pork Butchers – 35lbs, just with a pair of boot laces transferred to my pocket. I put my great coat, pair of boots, socks, shaving things, and towel, in my pack. Some pack – some weight too!

Some of the units were ready to move at a moment's notice – officially!

It was almost certain France was our objective.

Although the Battalion had new clothes and kit before leaving Southport, all this was changed for precisely similar stuff within a week – simply because we had come into another Command; Army Red Tape – imagine the expense and unnecessary labour entailed by such methods.

---

[36] Referred to in the *Afterword*, covering the period from November 1917 to February 1918 (page 290 ff.).
[37] 35 pounds, which is about 16 kilograms.
[38] See the footnote to the diary entry for 3rd January 1915.
[39] A limber was a horse drawn cart which was well-suited to travelling over rough ground, often used (coupled to a gun carriage) for carrying ammunition, or alternatively for "General Service", carrying rations, tools, and other equipment used in the trenches.
[40] A small two-wheeled cart, unsprung, drawn by a single animal, horse, pony, donkey or mule, capable of carrying one or two passengers.

25.04.15   We still had many preparations to complete. We had no rifles.

At about 11.00pm we received orders to be ready to move in four hours. What a hurry and bustle!

We simply drew rifles for 1000 men in about an hour. We were busy in pouring rain until 2.00am, then the order "Stand By" in billets came. But to be ready to move at an hour's notice. There was a rumour of an intended invasion on East Coast, and as a matter of fact trains were always ready to move the Division quickly anywhere.

But we didn't go – except to bed! And Monday came, and we seemed just as likely to be in Bedford for months. No one knew definitely even yet where we should go.

26.04.15   I was busy with my Signallers. Having just 17 men I got to know them very well. One couldn't help studying their individual characters, so I got to understand them very well, and love them. Care had to be taken in selecting them, as Signallers' work is very responsible and often secret. So the men must be reliable. They were.

I impressed on them at home the possibility of not being able to write very often, also that I should not be able to say where I was or what I was doing.

I bought the wrist watch which served me throughout the war until Armistice Day, November 11th 1918 – when I had it stolen at Blackpool.[41]

The Hanging Gate c. 1925

28.04.15   On April 28th I borrowed a bicycle, had a ride
to   round on my way back from the Range, and
30.04.15   called for tea at the Hanging Gate.[42] The following day I spent the day completing drawing of stores and drew nine bicycles for Signallers. On April 30th I drew two Machine Guns – prehistoric things – very slow. Almost Battle of Waterloo type!

01.05.15   In the early morning orders were received that the Transport would move at 11.00pm from the station. They loaded during the morning, taking our valises.

General Service Wagons, Tool Carts, Machine Gun Limbers,[43] Field Kitchen, Maltese Cart,[44] Machine Gunners, nine Cyclist Signallers, and Water Carts all paraded at 9.00pm under Major Milnes, Lieutenant Abbotts, and Lieutenant Hill (Machine Gun Officer).

Mules were kicking – wheels creaking – then shouting – and the CO raging and swearing. However, off they went. It seemed like a funeral march – at night with very few lights about. In the morning we had our photograph taken.[45]

---

[41] Actually it seems that it was stolen on 16th November 1918 – see the account in the *Afterword* on page 305.
[42] This beerhouse, at 1861 Old Harrowden Road, Bedford, was first licensed in 1843, later becoming a Public House. In 1915 the licensee was William Mann. Latterly it was known simply as "The Gate". It became a private residence c. 2011.
[43] See footnote 39 on page 37. General Service Wagons were larger than General Service Limbers, with four wheels rather than two, less suited to rough ground.
[44] See footnote 40 on page 37.
[45] See page 42.

Lieutenant R.N. Thompson, RAMC, who turned out to be a great fellow, joined us as Doctor, also Captain Gillenders as Padre – also a very good sort.

02.05.15   News of the first Gas attack at Ypres on April 26th reached us – there was a hurried attempt to make Gas Respirators of cotton wool mouth and nose pads.

03.05.15   The Division as it moved out from Bedford was the 1st Highland Division, later the 51st Highland Division, made up of a number of Brigades, including the 3rd Infantry Brigade, an East Lancashire Brigade, later the 154th Brigade, comprising:

> 1/4th King's Own Royal Lancasters
> 1/8th King's Liverpool Regiment (Irish)
> 1/4th Loyal North Lancashires
> 2/5th Lancashire Fusiliers

The Division was in the Indian Corps. We were therefore a rather potpourri Battalion, an East Lancashire Battalion in a West Lancashire Brigade, in a Scottish Division, in an Indian Army Corps.

The 3rd Infantry Brigade Staff were:

> Brigadier General Hibbert
> Major Bruce, Brigade Major
> Captain Jackson, Staff Captain

This particular morning, May 3rd, I got up early. The Battalion paraded in full marching order for Route March, including blanket rolled round pack. We went through Bromford with Major Barnsdale in command. It was very hot. The Route March was a rotten idea, as we were leaving England that afternoon – just like the Army to make men fed up before they start. We arrived back at 12.30pm.

At 3.00pm the Battalion paraded in full marching order ready to move. Quite a crowd gathered in Bedford to see us away.

The men were carrying two days' rations, 4lb tins of bully beef,[46] bread, butter, cheese, jam. There was no Band to play us away. All our bandsmen were allotted to companies as stretcher bearers.

The following officers proceeded with the Battalion:[47]

Headquarters:	Lieutenant Colonel John Hall, CO
	Major H.N. Milnes
	Captain J.J.P. Cummins, Adjutant
	Lieutenant J. Bowd, Quartermaster
	Lieutenant Abbotts, Transport Officer
	Lieutenant Hill, Machine Gun Officer
	Lieutenant N. Hall, Signals Officer
	Lieutenant R.N. Thompson, MO
	Captain Gillenders, Chaplain

---

[46] 1lb, or one pound, is approximately half a kilogram; bully beef, or bully, is a type of tinned meat similar to corned beef.
[47] Norman has recorded what happened to most of these officers while they were serving in France; a table on page 321 shows the date of the diary entry when each man is mentioned for the last time in the diary, and the editor has added a footnote to that final entry summarising what is known about the individual in question.

"A" Company	Captain G.H. Goldsmith
	Captain Ramsden
	2nd Lieutenant G. Gray
	2nd Lieutenant H. Waterhouse
	2nd Lieutenant H.H. Noton
"B" Company	Major J.D. Barnsdale
	Captain L.H. Bloy
	2nd Lieutenant W. Duckworth
	Lieutenant A.V. Barwood
	2nd Lieutenant J. Hartington
"C" Company	Captain G.C. Hutchinson
	Lieutenant R.W. Kirkman
	2nd Lieutenant B.H. Rothband
	2nd Lieutenant M.H. Young
	2nd Lieutenant M.P. Evans
	2nd Lieutenant J.B. Packman
"D" Company	Captain K. Waterhouse
	Captain J.W. Hedley
	Captain E.C. Simon
	2nd Lieutenant J.C. Latter
	2nd Lieutenant N. Kemp
	2nd Lieutenant J.F. Harker

At last we were really going away – but even now we didn't know where definitely, though pretty certainly France.

The first train, carrying HQ, "A" Company, and "B" Company, left at 5.00pm.

The second train, carrying "C" Company and "D" Company, left at 5.30pm.

I travelled in a carriage with Captain Ramsden and Jimmy Bowd.

As the train started we were very cheery and "full of beans" – moving with a light heart rather than feelings of sadness. Yet there was the inward doubt as to whether we should come back again. Many we knew wouldn't – but we did not know who the unfortunate ones would be – what a blessing. So we went off – knowing that this was the spirit:

Each man would do his best,
I doubt not that; since we are all well persuaded
We carried not a heart with us from hence
That grows not in a fair consent with ours
Nor leave not one behind that doth not wish
Success and conquest to attend on us.[48]

The journey from Bedford was amusing. Jimmy Bowd was very funny. He and Captain Cummins had met some old friend in Bedford in the morning. They had both imbibed freely rather than wisely. Jimmy was consequently very talkative. We didn't even know the port of embarkation but Bowd insisted we were off to France. Some kind friend had given Jimmy a periscope, and he insisted on telling Ramsden and me the story.

---

[48] *Henry V Act II Scene 2.*

"You see this periscope, Gentlemen, well I had this periscope given to me in Bedford this morning by an old friend of mine. Captain Cummins got one too. It's a very good periscope, and I'm very fond of it." This tale was repeated a score of times before we reached Dover. Unfortunately the periscope had a sad accident later.[49]

It was a glorious evening – eventually we reached London, and, passing over the river, we got a glimpse of St Paul's.

Finally we arrived at Dover. It was dark and cold, with a strong wind blowing. Ramsden and I went on board first with the Naval Embarkation Officer. The ship was the SS *Victoria*.[50]

SS *Victoria*

The first trainload soon came on board, followed about 15 minutes later by the second train. All were issued with life belts, and settled down. I took off my kit and went on deck with Kemp. We had quite a nice time going out of Dover, escorted by two destroyers. So we had actually started. One's mind travelled back – the shores and lights of England gradually faded away. Perhaps for ever! Who knew!

When we got clear, Kemp and I went down for some food, which we enjoyed. Harker was soon quite ill, also several others. After dinner Kemp and I went on deck again. It was very cold and began to rain heavily. We were on deck when we landed in Boulogne. We could see the light at Pointe de la Crèche several miles before we actually went into harbour. Also the sky was swept with searchlights.

A war base such as Boulogne was developed into a very busy port. Very similar to an ordinary seaport town, Boulogne itself is quite a nice place, but this visit I did not see much of it. Several Hospital Ships were berthed alongside the Quay when we arrived. They could be easily distinguished by the broad green line and big red cross – all the hull otherwise being painted white. The red cross and green band were lighted up distinctly with coloured electric lights. These ships were chiefly waiting for wounded from the 2nd Battle of Ypres.

We disembarked after some waiting. It was fairly dark, except for large flare lights along the Quay. We marched over railway lines along the docks. I was with Joe Hedley, who remarked, "Wouldn't it save a lot of trouble if we were going back on one of those ships?" It might! We marched over the bridges and on to the town.

It was still raining <u>hard</u>, and we were fully loaded. We went through the town over slippery cobbled pavements, then up a <u>very</u> steep hill to St Martin's Camp. I lost a pair of gloves. The camp was a tent camp situated on the high ground East of Boulogne, overlooking the harbour and the Channel. It was an awful night; wet through, we got the men settled down in tents – after issuing hot tea to them. Then we turned in ourselves and had some tea. I slept with Young, Kemp, and Harker. It was very cold. We turned in at about 2.00am.

---

[49] Norman presumably intended to tell the story of what happened to the periscope later, but it does not get further mention.

[50] SS *Victoria* was a paddle steamer built in 1907; during the First World War she was in service with the South Eastern and Chatham Railway Company.

30 of the 31 officers who departed for France with the 2/5th Lancashire Fusiliers on 3rd May 1915; Norman is in the back row, second from the left; note that the officers at either end of the back row have been rather expertly "photo-shopped", early twentieth century style, as on the left the brick wall can be seen where the officer's body should be, while on the right the hedge and wall is missing behind the officer's neck and shoulders; presumably these two were not available for some reason at the time the group photograph was taken.

CHAPTER 4
Boulogne, Norrent-Fontes, Cornet Malo, Caionne-sur-la-Lys, Merris, La Gorgue, Wallon-Cappel
4th May 1915 to 19th May 1915

04.05.15   It was a glorious spring morning. I got up early, even though I had only turned in at 2.00am. Everyone put the kit out to dry. We saw the men's breakfast issued. Then we officers went to a farm nearby for breakfast. K. Waterhouse and Noton saved the day by knowing French rather well. One table was set inside the farm, and one outside. I am not sure which was the preferable place to avoid a horrible smell – the interior smelt as bad as the manure heap outside. However the omelettes were very good eaten quickly.

Colonel Hall was very funny, trying to talk French to the old Madame.

Breakfast over, we inspected rifles and issued "Iron Rations" – these were issued like gold (one tin of bully beef, ¾lb biscuits, a tin containing tea and sugar), only to be used in an emergency and only by permission of an officer. Iron Rations were always a source of annoyance, and responsible for many days' Field Punishment.

We paraded at 2.00pm in full marching order and left St Martin's Camp. We had no valises at this time as they were with the Transport, which had crossed to Havre.

It was very hot marching to the station where we were to entrain, Pont de Briques, a pretty little village about 4 miles from Boulogne. We waited for the train coming from Havre with our Transport on board. It arrived about 5.00pm. The men travelled in cattle trucks marked:

HOMMES 20   **CHEVAUX 8** [51]

They had straw to lie on. The officers were more fortunate as we got a corridor passenger coach. Major Milnes, Hill, and Abbotts were on board with our mess kits and Fortnum and Mason's parcel, so we were fortunate. We travelled six in a compartment.

We steamed out towards Boulogne slowly not knowing where we were going – except North. The men were in great spirits – full of beans and ready for anything. Considering their short training – six months – they were a credit to themselves and to their officers. But of course they needed more training, and we were promised this before we left England, but the chance of getting it seemed very remote, as the Army around Ypres and Armentières were being very hard pressed. The Boche had broken through the French and the 1st Canadian Division had been pushed in hurriedly to fill the gap. The Northumbrian Division – the 50th – had been rushed up North only a few days ago.

To continue the journey – we went up North, skirting the coast to Wimereux, then to Marquise and on to Calais. It was then about 8.30pm and getting dark. We had had very little rest since Sunday and were feeling tired. I couldn't go to sleep. I was too excited and interested, my mind full of conjecture. At Calais we stayed about half an hour in the Troop Siding. I went down to see my Signallers, and found them very cheery and making themselves comfortable. I got them some hot water to make tea.

From Calais we went via Audruicq, Watten and Serques to St Omer. GHQ was then at St Omer, and the GOC in Chief was General French.

---

[51] This must be a slip of the pen on Norman's part, as the trucks were in fact marked: HOMMES 40 CHEVAUX 8.

While in the station we saw a Hospital Train coming from Ypres – going South. The men had only been in action one day, and went off home wounded – only out from England five days. What of our chances! Should we be the same?

Well if we were, it couldn't be helped – it was our job. We were actually going to have a biff at the Boche at last!

Fellows are always keen on their first battle – they are ignorant of it all and enthusiastic – this enthusiasm soon wears off.

Practically every man had the spirit expressed so aptly by Shakespeare, *Henry V Act III Scene 1:*

Once more unto the breach, dear friends, once more,
Or close the wall up with our English dead ...

From St Omer we went to Wallon-Cappel, Ebblinghem, Hazebrouck, Steenbecque, Thiennes, Aire, Molinghem and then Berquette (on the Béthune line), where we detrained at about 11.30pm.

The detraining of the Transport took some time. We got the men out and formed up by Companies, and then we lay down. Many of the men were tired out after travelling for six and a half hours in cramped trucks.

At 1.00am we marched off from Berquette to Norrent-Fontes, only 6 miles – but what a march. It was very foggy and the fog made it cold – but we soon got too hot. The march discipline was not good and it was with great difficulty we kept the men in Column. Several men were hanging on to limbers.[52] I was with Joe Hedley and Jimmy Bowd.

I must have travelled 10 miles – running up and down collecting men. Not an easy job with a full pack and blanket as well. Still I kept going by sheer determination.

05.05.15   We finally arrived at Norrent-Fontes at about 3.30am. Colonel Hall and Captain Simon went ahead for billeting purposes. It was still dark. Billeting the men took some time. I found the Signallers their billet, but could not find mine. So I took off my equipment and actually lay down on the hedge bottom. I was soon disturbed by Colonel John asking me who I was and why the devil I didn't go to my billet, which I found quite near. It was in a Chateau – good rooms and well furnished; evidently the occupants had left rather hurriedly – pots etc. left on the tables.

Eventually I found a crowd of our officers in the billiard room. So I settled down on the floor – <u>stone</u> – very hard. But with my great coat and air pillow – and feeling very tired – I was soon asleep. Joe Hedley was on the billiard table – a strong one luckily! Dr Thompson, the MO, wakened up in great spirits and did balancing tricks. At about 10.00am, after breakfast, I went to see my men. They were having breakfast and were all very fit and comfortable in the attic. I arranged my cyclist orderly duties. Then I tried to get on the telephone to Brigade from the Civil Post Office. Of course it was impossible and absurd – as I realised later. Then I rode over to Brigade who were billeted at Ham-en-Artois, a lovely picturesque village, at the Chateau – quite a quaint old place. I met Major Bruce and Brigadier General Hibbert for the first time. They were both very nice. I fixed up about the telephone being put over to the Battalion HQ. We could <u>just</u> hear the guns in the distance with a North East wind – from Ypres. I came back through St Hilaire – 3 miles. It was a glorious morning.

----

[52] See footnote 39 on page 37.

I went to buy potatoes with Long Waterhouse on my return. The country round this part was flat and well wooded – singularly devoid of hedges as we see them in England, the farms being divided by dikes. The country people were decidedly primitive in their living and habits – hard working and sturdy, and the number of old people working in the fields was very marked. A rather characteristic point about many of the houses is the doors – they are made in two halves split horizontally like a stable door in England.

Horses are generally used for haulage, although I saw several quaint ideas:

A small cart drawn by a huge dog;

A farm cart with a cow yoked to the shaft.

Also the water supply is mainly from wells. The people carry their water in buckets – steadying their loads by yokes.

The chief means of living is by agriculture. Every available square yard is tilled. What a contrast to England.

The farms are grouped together in the village round the church – usually well wooded. You seldom, if ever, see isolated farms, as in England. The people often have considerable distances to walk to their own particular fields. Most of the farms churn butter, and in many cases the churn is worked mechanically by a driving shaft running to the outside of the building where there is a large cage wheel – like a water wheel. A dog is put into the double wheel and he works as a on a tread-mill – this drives the churn. It struck me as rather cruel! So much for a brief description of the civilian population.

06.05.15   I had a very good night's rest. During the night there was heavy motor traffic on the road, an endless stream of wagons and cars. The Column continued to pass till late in the afternoon. They were French troops being rushed up to fill in the gap in the French Line after the first Cloud Gas attack at Ypres. These troops had come from another part of the Front and had been travelling for hours. They were simply white with dust.

After lunch there were rumours of a move. I sat in the garden, in an orchard, and slept, taking the chance while I had it. I saw my first aeroplane on Active Service. It was quite an event to see an aeroplane even these days – there were not a great number used. We packed up our kit.

The Battalion paraded at 7.30pm. We synchronised watches and marched off at 8.00pm. It started to rain. There was no moon, and it was very dark.

The Colonel told us (before starting) that, when we completed our march that night, we should be 5 miles from Hill 60 of fame.[53]

We marched through St Hilaire to the railway crossing at Lillers on the Béthune to Hazebrouck line. Colonel John had words with the Divisional Staff Captain, who accused him of being two minutes late. The CO swore he was that many minutes early.

We were marching independently by Battalions in our Brigade, and we had a terrific time trying to keep touch with the Brigade who were in front. I got very tired running ahead – still with full kit – trying to keep in touch; eventually Long Waterhouse borrowed Walker's bicycle and rode ahead. He had a misfortune with the bike, breaking it, and we had to leave it behind, not knowing whether we should ever see it again.

---

[53] The scene of a battle between 17th April and 7th May 1915.

Eventually I put out a chain of Signallers as connecting, having made touch with the rear of the Brigade Transport.

We marched through Busnes and Robecque, along the canal bank to Rue de Vaches, St Floris, Caionne-sur-la-Lys, and Cornet Malo (of interest in the Boche Offensive of March 1918, because the Boche broke through to this place and the Front Line was established here). It was simply raining in sheets.

We had done about 16 miles and arrived at about 1.45am, very tired. Simon had ridden ahead billeting, and weren't we pleased to see him standing in the road with a lamp waiting for us. Of course, the Signallers were billeted right through the village quite a mile and a half further than "W" Company (or "A" Company as they were then). Green, one of my men, was very ill with fatigue on the march, but I gave him some of my brandy which bucked him up, and he stuck to it the whole way, although the last mile he was almost carried in. The men's feet were very sore – most of them having new boots.

We were billeted at a nice little farm. The men were in the barn, and they soon settled in. Then I turned into my billet, and found Madame and her two daughters waiting for me. They had kept some food hot, and some very good coffee, which I enjoyed. Then they gave me a very nice room, with a very nice bed and clean sheets. I undressed, as I was _very_ wet.

07.05.15 I got up at about 8.00am. Waddicar made my breakfast. The Company billets were very scattered. Colonel Hall was very keen to have telephones at Company HQ and Battalion HQ. I had never laid out telephones before, and was not sure how to lay so long a circuit with five call offices. However we had a shot at it, and by 1 o'clock all Companies, Transport and Battalion HQ were in communication. I organised three Signallers at each station to work in reliefs and arranged for the men to draw their rations with the Companies they were attached to.

The wires were broken several times by the cows. The difficulty was getting the wires high enough, as we had no poles, and the road had to be crossed several times. However, we overcame the difficulties one by one. Even though we had very poor wire, communication was good.

08.05.15 Brigadier General C. Hibbert (Snappy) and Major Bruce inspected the Battalion. They were rather fed up with things.

In the afternoon I cycled into Merville, about 8 miles away. It was very full of troops and very busy.

Packman went home.[54]

09.05.15 We were now acting as a Reserve Division – a flying Column for any part of the Front from Ypres to Armentières, at that time in reality in Reserve for the Battle of Fromelles.

We could easily hear the guns, and each night we used to see the flare rockets from the Line. The Line here seemed to circle all round us, with us being in the centre of a circle of about 15 miles' radius.

I saw my first Observation Balloon – Sausage, as we called them.

---

[54] The Battalion War Diary entry for 10th May 1915 (not 8th May 1915) is *"J.B. Packman to England – sick"*.

An Observation or Kite Balloon, nicknamed "Sausage" for obvious reasons; this photograph was taken over a year later in the Somme area, and appears in the diary beside the entry for 18th August 1916.

I joined "D" Company Mess – by invitation of Captain Waterhouse and Joe Hedley. I was very happy to be with "D" Company Mess, comprising Captain Waterhouse, Captain Hedley, Captain Simon, 2nd Lieutenant Kemp, 2nd Lieutenant Latter, 2nd Lieutenant Harker, and myself – "We are seven".

Kemp, Latter, Harker and I slept in a dirty old room, very grubby. The night was rather cold. There was a peculiar old woman at the farm who made very good omelettes.

We got very good food – augmented by shopping expeditions into Merville.

This is a typical menu:

Breakfast: Bacon – Eggs – Marmalade – Toast
Lunch: Bully Beef – Salad – Fruit – Coffee
Tea: Usual
Dinner: Tomato Soup, Roast Beef, Potatoes, Swedes, Prunes, Custard, Coffee

We were always hungry.

About this time we heard about the sinking of the *Lusitania*[55] but couldn't believe it.

10.05.15 and 11.05.15	Most of the men went for a swim in the Canal at Caionne-sur-la-Lys. It was cold but very enjoyable. Company Swimming Races were organised. Lance Corporal Hutton of "D" Company won the first prize. "C" Company played "D" Company at football.

Kemp pinched a horse from the Transport Lines to ride into Merville. Abbotts, our Transport Officer, was very fed up.

The Battalion was warned to "Stand By" ready to move. "D" Company closed in and stacked kits etc. in a field opposite Company HQ

Many Indian wounded were coming through all day from Fromelles. One Indian was very proud of a Boche's head he was carrying – probably living in hopes of taking it home as a souvenir.

The weather was very wet.

---

[55] A passenger liner sunk on 7th May 1915 by a German Submarine; this caused particular outrage as it disregarded rules of conduct previously respected by both sides, to the effect that civilians would not be deliberately targeted.

12.05.15   I went to Merville with Ken and Joe to buy mess stores.

13.05.15   We were still "Standing By". It rained all day.

14.05.15   Orders were received at 5.00am by telephone to be ready to move at 8.00am. I got up, took in the telephone wires, collected the instruments, and packed them on a limber. It was still raining heavily. We marched off at 8.30am, from Caionne-sur-la-Lys through Merville, striking North East to Neuf-Berquin, La Couronne, Vieux-Berquin, and Merris to near Outtersteene, arriving at about 1.00pm; a 12 miles' march over Belgian-type roads – stone setts with a big crown on the road, edged by thick mud badly churned up by Motor Transport. We bivouacked "D" Company and the Signallers near Battalion HQ, then got Field Cookers going and made dinners for the men. By about 7.00pm our billets, which had been occupied by King Edward's Horse when we arrived, were clear, and we took over. They were good billets in a large farm. I laid out telephone wires to Company billets, which were again very scattered, and we had a lot of high road crossing wires to fix. I finished at about 10.30pm.

15.05.15   The weather was glorious. The country was very nice, though flat. We were now about 17 miles North West of Lille, 8 miles from Armentières, and 15 miles South West of Ypres. It was a great hop growing district. The hops were beginning to grow properly. Almost every farm had its hop garden – conspicuous by the huge frames, some 90 feet high. The ground was also very well cultivated. There were still few hedges, but the flowers in the gardens were glorious, helped by hot sunshine.

Long Waterhouse and I went into Bailleul on bikes. Bailleul is a fairly large country town with a few good shops. We bought some mess stores, also bulbs for torches etc.

Many wild and unfounded rumours reached Bury regarding our movements – all fairy tales; up to now we had done nothing – we were just a flying Column in Reserve for any old scrap.

In Bailleul I saw my first sight of wounded coming down from the Lines. They came from Ypres and Armentières, convoy after convoy of ambulances. There had been a big Show at Fromelles, in an attempt to take Aubers Ridge, without success.

We went through Méteren, where the 2nd Battalions of the Lancashire Fusiliers and 8th Warwickshires fought heavily in 1914, and came across the graves of Lieutenant Colonel Loring[56] and Major Christie.[57] The CO was quite pleased with my communication efforts. I really found out that Ken Waterhouse and Joe Hedley were <u>fine</u> fellows. They were just like two brothers to me, although I wasn't really one of "D" Company. I began to feel I was one of them.

---

[56] Lieutenant Colonel Walter Latham Loring of the 2nd Battalion Royal Warwickshire Regiment, mentioned in dispatches, son of the Reverend E.H. Loring, died aged 46 on 23rd October 1914; he is commemorated at the Ypres (Menin Gate) Memorial, West-Vlaanderen, Belgium, Panel 8. This is a little unexpected in view of the fact that Norman records having seen his grave at Méteren. Either what Norman saw was merely a memorial, or his grave was later lost or destroyed.

[57] Major William Charles Christie of the 1st Battalion Royal Warwickshire Regiment, elder son of the late John Robert and Margaret Christie of Llandaff, Glamorgan, and husband of Florence Violet Christie of Newton Abbot, died aged 41 on 13th October 1914; he was a member of the Order of the Medjidie, and had twice been mentioned in dispatches, during the Sudan Campaign of 1898, and during the South African Campaign of 1899 to 1902; he is buried at the Méteren Military Cemetery, reference I.N.332.

16.05.15   In the evening the Battalion paraded for a Route March at 5.30pm. I was left behind with the Signallers. The Battalion didn't leave word where they were going, which proved very awkward, as urgent Operation Orders came while they were out, ordering us to be ready to move at an hour's notice.

I immediately ordered my cyclists to turn out on various roads to find the Battalion, giving copies of the orders to each cyclist. Then I collected the men who were in billets – very few. I got them rolling blankets, and stacking them, ready for loading. I went round to warn Jimmy Bowd, the Quartermaster, and the Transport Officer, to get ready loaded up. Consequently <u>when</u> (!) the Battalion returned at about 8.15pm, the stores etc. were all ready to move. However, the orders were cancelled for that night.

The Adjutant made a remark on their return – "Blast their eyes" – which Harker imitated perfectly – much to the amusement of people many times after.

It was lucky the move was postponed as the men were very nearly done up – they had been unnecessarily messed about for a few days.

17.05.15   We were "Standing By" all day, having received orders to be ready to move in half an hour. Things were very pressing somewhere. We expected to be in a Show <u>very</u> soon. During the day orders came through to move at 8.30pm.

The CO usually told me of moves and times, so I could reconnoitre the route to the Starting Point. This night he said nothing to me.

We paraded at 8.15pm, the Signallers leading, followed by "D" Company.

We marched off at 8.30pm, and were due at the railway crossing South West of Merris at 9.10pm. The Adjutant took the wrong turning at the beginning; I told him he was wrong, but he replied, "Mind your own business."

Then the CO asked me if I knew the way – how could I? – I hadn't seen the place before, and he refused me permission to fall out to look at my map. However I knew the way to the main road where the RAMC were, and sent cyclists ahead to reconnoitre the route, and also went myself. When we got to the RAMC Camp I told Colonel Hall I wasn't acquainted with the route, and again asked permission to look at my map, and was again refused with anything but courtesy. So I simply washed my hands of further responsibility regarding the route. The CO took the wrong turning and got the wind up – halted the Column and about turned them, and rode up and down furiously – swearing at me and telling the whole Battalion, "That Bloody Fool Hall is responsible for this." And again, "You're a B ——— idiot – Sir, as I should but say." The result was we were late at the Starting Point and had to increase our march rate to catch up.

It started to rain heavily, and rained all night. The roads were awful – long, straight, cobbled roads lined with trees – which never seemed to end. We went through Merris, Vieux-Berquin, and La Couronne, where we caught up the Brigade and halted for two hours. I was with Ken and Joe, and feeling very fed up at messing things up, although the CO was really to blame. We lay down in the road in spite of the wet and cold, and my brandy flask was much appreciated. We went on to La Gorgue, arriving at about 3.30am, very tired and sore – a march of 16 miles. I got the men fixed up and then found my billet. I slept in a loft on straw with Barnsdale, Bloy, Ken Waterhouse, Hedley, Simon, Hill, Bowd, Kemp, Harker, and Long Waterhouse.

We were all very tired, and soon went to sleep in spite of being wet through.

18.05.15   I got up at 7.00am and saw rations issued, then got some eggs and coffee at an estaminet. Orders were issued to be ready to move at 9.00am.

We found out our Battalion was to move back instead of into the Line as we expected. Orders had suddenly come through that the 2/5th Lancashire Fusiliers had to proceed to GHQ to complete their training, as was the idea when we left England, but, owing to the Boche pressure, we had been taken forward with the Division.

At 10.00am we moved off from La Gorgue. Everyone was very fed up, to say nothing of being very tired. However we started. Colonel John ordered me to march in the rear of the Column with the Signallers and consider myself in disgrace for the previous evening. So I marched along with Major Milnes, Dr Thompson and Jimmy Bowd.

We marched via La Gorgue on to the main road to Cassel. Colonel John took the wrong turning soon after we started. Major Milnes rode forward to tell him – the CO was very annoyed. He halted, about turned, and ordered me to wait and join rear of Column again. Well, we marched up the same road we had travelled over only a few hours before – Neuf-Berquin, La Couronne, Vieux-Berquin, where we had a half hour halt, and ate biscuits and bully. Then we went through Strazeele, Pradelles and Borre to Hazebrouck, passing the Forest of Nieppe (a forest some 6 miles wide, famous in the fighting in March 1918 when the Germans captured Merville and partly held this forest), and finally to Wallon-Cappel, arriving at this small village at 6.00pm.

Harker arrived looking like an Italian Organ Grinder – with a huge waterproof cape thrown over his kit, and carrying about three rifles. Many men fell out on this march – they were dog tired and footsore, having done 24 miles this day, and about 40 miles in 22 hours, with very little food.

We had tea at the 2nd Life Guards' HQ. Colonel John apologised to me for his treatment the previous evening.

The men had fairly good billets. I was billeted in a school, and had an impromptu hot bath, and changed my socks – some treat! Then I had a good dinner, and felt very fit and cheery, but turned in early. We slept on the school forms. I got a letter from home, even though we had been continuously moving about – rather wonderful the Mail. We heard about the casualties in the Dardanelles.[58]

---

[58] This may be a reference, in particular, to the engagement on 25th April 1915 known as the Lancashire Landing, at the start of the Gallipoli Campaign, when members of the 1/5th Lancashire Fusiliers famously won "six VCs before breakfast".

CHAPTER 5
Arques
20th May 1915 to 8th July 1915

20.05.15[59]   It was a glorious morning. I gave my Signallers a rest.

I went to see Gillenders, the Padre, at his billet – a very nice cottage. We were now many miles away from the Line again, which was rather disappointing.

We got ready to move at 2.00pm. It was a very hot day. We marched through Ebblinghem to Arques, arriving at about 5.30pm after an 8 mile march. We were inspected en route by General Stopford, GOC of GHQ troops, and Major Needham, GHQ Staff. The march discipline was anything but good, but the men were very tired and footsore after long marching with irregular food and sleep.

So we arrived at Arques after many miles of useless wandering.

Bennison[60] excelled himself by getting drunk.

Perhaps a few remarks about Arques would not be out of place here. We had come down here for strenuous training, and we got it. But we also had a very enjoyable time.

Arques is a small country town of about 2000 inhabitants. There are three chief streets, and a large market place with quite a nice modern Hotel de Ville. It is about 2½ miles from St Omer. The railway from St Omer (from Calais to Béthune) passes through Arques. There is also the Canal – Neuf Fosse – which connects with Aire, Béthune and lLa Bassée. Arques is just at the head of the valley in which St Omer is situated. This raises quite an interesting point in reference to the Canal. There is a very fine lift on the Canal for raising barges from the lower to the upper level. This lift is a fine feat of engineering, the power being hydraulic, with the effect of one barge coming down raising the barge coming up.

There are a few shops in Arques, but most people shop in St Omer, quite a nice sized town with some good shops, fine buildings, nice parks and a very fine church. We often used to go over there to do our shopping.

The chief occupations in Arques are glass working, corn milling, brickworks, sugar beet factories, sewing, and lace making. The surrounding district is well cultivated – very productive in molinary cereals.

The country all round Arques is exceedingly nice, hilly and well wooded, with villages – often very pretty – hidden amongst trees.

The Battalion was very fortunate in getting good billets, rather scattered but comfortable. "D" Company were especially fortunate, as they got fitted up in billets with a big garden where the men could thoroughly lazy about under the trees. There were a lot of flowers and fruit in this garden. Some of the accommodation was in greenhouses.

My Signallers got a very nice billet with a married girl called Martha. They had two good barns, and Martha cleared one of the rooms in the house to make a nice large room for the men to use as a common room, which they appreciated. Martha's husband was a French soldier, so she seemed to have a fellow sympathy for my men, and was extremely

---

[59] In the original this diary entry has both 19th and 20th May beside it. The Battalion War Diary shows that the latter is correct, and that Norman's dates for the last week have been a day adrift as a result of his having omitted a day at Caionne-sur-la-Lys.
[60] Bennison is only mentioned once more, with rather more affection, namely when he left the Army on 29th February 1916 (see the diary entry for that date).

good to them. I lived with "D" Company. "D" Company HQ Mess was in a nice house belonging to the Mayor of Arques. The Mess Room was a jolly nice room, quite nicely furnished, and we had a nice piano – Latter turned out to be quite a musician.[61] I had very happy times in "D" Company Mess. Almost every evening we had someone down to dinner, or else we were out calling on other companies. I also had some jolly good times with Joe and Ken Waterhouse, and went in to have dinner in St Omer once or twice with them.

The Mayor and Mayoress were very kind to us all, and we gave them a set of carvers as a parting gift when we moved on.

The Mayor and Mayoress of Arques with Norman, Captain K. Waterhouse, Captain J.W. Hedley, Captain E.C. Simon, 2nd Lieutenant N. Kemp and 2nd Lieutenant J.C. Latter.

23.05.15   Ken Waterhouse and Joe Hedley slept in the Mayor and Mayoress's house. The rest of us slept out at houses quite near. I lived with Monsieur Louis Saintoyen.

There was a mother, father, and a girl, Marie Antoinette, about 16. Monsieur Saintoyen was manager of a glass works in Arques. They really were exceedingly kind to me. My room was very comfortable and I always had fresh flowers daily.

24.05.15   It was a glorious day. I spent the afternoon writing in the garden.
to
30.05.15   Newspapers were easy to get at Arques. Sometimes we got the English papers the same day of issue at about 8.00pm.

---

[61] Latter's nickname was "Ludwig", possibly after Ludwig van Beethoven in recognition of his musical talent.

We were out training each day.

Each day was a similar programme so a typical day will suffice to show how we spent our time:

7.00 – 7.30am	Physical Drill
8.00am	Breakfast
8.30am	CO's orders
9.00am	Parade
Hours of work:	10.30am – 12.30pm
	1 hour for dinner
	2.00pm – 4.00pm

We were actually working from 7.00am till 5.15pm at night.

Each company used to train on its own, doing Close Order Drill, Field Exercises, Bayonet Fighting, Attack Formation, and Musketry.

My Signallers worked directly under my control. I divided the time up, doing Flag Work, Morse and Semaphore, Cable Laying, Buzzer Work, Discs etc.

I also gave them lectures on Map Reading, Communication, Telephone, Road Reconnaissance, Reports on Villages, Country, etc. We found this most interesting and enjoyable work. At one time and another we reconnoitred the following villages near St Omer:

Blendecques, Wizernes, Hallines, Esquerdes, Noir Cornet, Helfauc, Bilques, Inghem, Ecques, Quiestède, Wittes, Racquinghem, Wardrecques, Campagne, Thérouanne, Aire, Wisques, Longuenesse, Forêt de Clairmarais.

We also did Night Marches, Route Marches, Night Attacks and Bivouacs.

One afternoon, when out cycling with my Signallers, we saw the 1st Indian Cavalry returning from Ypres Salient for a rest. It was a very fine sight as they came down an avenue on a hillside in Quiestède. There were many stragglers – poor fellows – feet almost red raw. They looked absolutely war worn – with that vacant blood shot eye so characteristic of long marching, fatigue, weariness and reaction.

Often some of the remarks made by the Company were extremely amusing.

One fellow was heard to remark during the day, "I wish I were in a lunatic asylum. At any rate you have someone to look after you there."

Another man lost his Gas helmet and called to his pal "Eh, Bill, 'as ti sin my perspirator?"

While at Arques I used to censor my men's letters, and I found it a very great help in studying their various true characters. It is impossible to deal with men fairly and tactfully unless you understand their peculiarities.

On Friday May 28th I went through the glass works with Monsieur Saintoyen. It was very interesting, and I actually blew a bottle myself. I saw them making Benedictine wine bottles, also small glasses for Price's night lights.

Several of the men used to go over these works and often got crests etc. put into glass for paper weights etc.

The weather was glorious, and it was our usual daily pastime to bathe in the Neuf Fosse canal. We used to swim to an old barge, and had great sports – making rafts, diving boards etc. Hutty was always in great form on the unofficial bathing parades. Once he rode down a board on one of my bicycles into the Canal. On May 26th, after bathing with Harker, Kemp and Young, we had a glorious 2 mile walk to St Omer along the canal bank, which was lined with tall poplar trees all the way.

Also on May 26th Waddicar had rather a bad attack of colic – so called – really the beginning of his appendicitis trouble.

We were quite a long way from the firing line, but we used to see a great deal of motor traffic etc. going to and fro from the Line from the Ypres direction.

31.05.15 to 05.06.15	I formed a Reserve Signal Section for training men to replace casualties. I got some good men, Coupe, Jack, Longton, Packer, and K. Wilkinson. It was quite a busy time, but they were all keen and hard working. I went round the glass works again with Dr Thompson and Captain Gillenders. Things began to change in the Battalion with the first moves towards Colonel John Hall and Captain Cummins, the Adjutant, leaving us. I received a letter from Kit (Kathleen) telling me she had put her hair up.[62]
06.06.15 to 12.06.15	During this week there was a fishing competition in the lake between Gray, Hartley Goldsmith, Long Waterhouse, Noton and Ramsden, "A" Company officers. Dead heat – no catch! One day I saw a whole Column of London Motor Omnibuses painted grey, the first I had seen out in France – very useful. I also saw Mr Asquith in a motor car going up North towards Cassel, going to see his pals the Boche I suppose! Another day I saw General French and the Prince of Wales in St Omer.
13.06.15 to 20.06.15	During the week we had changes on the HQ staff. Lieutenant Colonel John Hall[63] relinquished the command of the Battalion, being succeeded by Major H.J. Shirley CMG, MD, FRCS, of the Artists' Rifles. His pre-war name was Herbert Johan Scharlieb – son of Dr Mary Scharlieb.[64]

---

[62] See the photograph on page 8.

[63] Lieutenant Colonel John Hall VD and Captain Cummins, Commanding Officer and Adjutant respectively, were thus the first officers to leave the 2/5th Lancashire Fusiliers of those who were with the Battalion when they landed in France on 3rd May 1915; Lieutenant Colonel John Hall was Commanding Officer when Norman joined the Battalion in September 1914, and Captain Cummins was Adjutant from at least 8th November 1914 in Southport. Lieutenant Colonel Hall comes across as a well-meaning, but rather irascible man. Norman generally writes of him with affection, but was happy to regale his comrades with anecdotes of his doings (see the diary entry for 8th October 1915). Examples of passages which give an insight into Lieutenant Colonel Hal's style of command are the account of him on the Parade Ground in the diary entry for 8th November to 13th December 1914, the speech to the troops on leaving Southport on 18th April 1915, the instructions to Norman to take over as Signalling Officer in the diary entry for 19th April 1915, the difference of opinion with the Divisional Staff Captain on 6th May 1915 as to whether he was two minutes late or two minutes early, and the episode when the Battalion got lost at La Gorgue as described in the diary entry for 17th May 1915, when he blamed Norman for what Norman says was his own error, but then apologised the following day. In the photograph on page 42 he is the white-haired man in the middle of the front row. In *The History of the Lancashire Fusiliers 1914-1918* Major General J.C. Latter, describing the early training of the 2/5th Lancashire Fusiliers under Lieutenant Colonel Hall's leadership as using selected NCOs to train the whole Battalion rather than each section being trained by its own NCOs, says that this was not conventional at the time and probably led to the Battalion being selected for overseas service ahead of other Territorial Battalions, and then adds: *John Hall was never conventional. He became famous in Southport for his sayings. He was indefatigable and he paid great attention to detail.*
Captain Cummins is also mentioned in the La Gorgue episode as having made an error in navigation but being unwilling to listen to an alternative suggestion, and in the diary entry for 16th May 1915 his expression *"Blast their eyes"*, used to express his annoyance with the temporary absence of the Battalion, is taken up and mimicked to good effect by Freddy Harker. He is also mentioned as having been in an argument with Jimmy Bowd, the Quartermaster, on 31st December 1914, when they were both *"tight"*, and as travelling with Jimmy Bowd on the train on 3rd May 1915 on their way to France, at which point they had both *"imbibed freely rather than wisely"*.

[64] A well known gynaecologist at the Royal Free Hospital; her son changed his name by deed poll in 1914.

We also got a new Adjutant. Captain Cummins proceeded to Base Depot at Calais and was succeeded by Captain Jeffreys, a Regular, who was Adjutant to the 1/6th Durham Light Infantry, having also commanded the Battalion up at Ypres. I soon began to get to know Colonel Shirley and Captain Jeffreys, and found them to be very fine fellows.

Captain Jeffreys was a pukker[65] soldier, a strict disciplinarian and a thorough gentleman, with a very sympathetic and kind manner. He was a great favourite and the new combination really did a great deal in improving the efficiency of the Battalion, with all due respect to the hard, unceasing efforts of Colonel John, to whom is undoubtedly due endless praise for his work in raising the 2/5th Lancashire Fusiliers and training them in the early days. In my opinion the only reason for his losing his command was that he was too old to command a Battalion in the present war. A vigorous active man of younger years was required to stand the strain of this war. This proved the case time and time again.

Before Colonel Hall went away we had a farewell evening up at the HQ Mess. All the officers were there. It was rather a sad parting, because I feel all of us appreciated all the work the Colonel had done and we were really sorry to lose him. But it was without doubt a sound move. The Colonel also made a farewell speech to the Battalion. He was <u>very</u> upset and almost broke down.

We heard later that Colonel Hall took over command of the 3/5th Lancashire Fusiliers.[66]

On Wednesday June 16th I was Orderly Officer, so I had a busy morning going round billets, cook houses, Quartermaster stores, Transport Lines etc. I heard that Captain Oldfield of the 8th Manchesters had been killed.[67]

On Thursday June 17th there were tremendous thunderstorms – we were out at Blendecque and were caught in the storm. I never heard such thunder or saw such lightning – and the Rain! – just as if the Heavens had burst. On the way home I thought some of my men were struck by lightning – they were positively thrown from the road, and several fell. However nobody was hurt. I felt the heat myself.[i]

On Sunday June 20th Captain Gillenders left us to go to our old Division at Festubert. A Padre who used to be at Bolton Abbey came to us, a narrow and conceited man with high ideas – not a bit suitable for Lancashire men.

We went to a service at St Omer, joining with one Battalion of the London Rifle Brigade, who were very greatly reduced in numbers through very heavy fighting. The sermon was rotten but the service very enjoyable.

About this time we re-lettered the Companies:

> "A" Company became "W" Company
>
> "B" Company became "X" Company
>
> "C" Company became "Y" Company
>
> "D" Company became "Z" Company

The chief reason was the similarity between B, C, and D when speaking over the telephone.

On June 21st we left Arques at 8.30am to visit the GHQ Machine Gun School in the old

---

[65] Pukker (more normally spelt pukka or pucca) is slang for "proper", derived from the Hindustani for "cooked" or "ripe".
[66] This information about what happened to Colonel Hall is given later in the original diary, in the entry for 9th to 10th August 1915.
[67] Captain Edmund George William Oldfield, son of the late Reverend Edmund Oldfield, Vicar of Reddish, later Vicar of Spratton, and Mrs Emma Oldfield, who had served in the South African War and had been mentioned in dispatches, died aged 33 on 5th June 1915, and is commemorated at the Helles Memorial in Turkey (Gallipoli), on Panel 159 to 171.

21.06.15 to 30.06.15	Convent at Wisques, a fine hall in beautiful grounds. We travelled on motor buses, many of which had been used in the retreat from Antwerp. We had a good look round, and saw Hill and Harker, who were both doing a course at Wisques. The Army was just beginning to appreciate the value of the Machine Gun as a supplementary infantry weapon.

During this period I got my first parcel of Japanese cakes, which we christened "Arques Cakes". One day I walked into St Omer with Joe Hedley, and we had "tea at a café"

.Another day we had a long Route March – Arques, Renescure, Ebblinghem, Wardrecques, Belle Croix, down main road to Arques – 17 miles, and very hot, but the men were in much better form. My chief complaint was blistered feet.

"How can one have a blister and keep going on a Route March with another 6 miles to do?" – one of the soldier's problems.

I heard that Kathleen had started her nursing classes.

Sunday was a very peaceful day. We could hardly imagine we were really only a few miles from the firing line. In the evening I went out taking compass bearings with Joe Hedley and the Skipper – Ken Waterhouse was always known as "The Skipper" from this date, and Joe Hedley as "Hell Fire Joe". Why the latter I don't know, because he was anything but what is implied by that name.

I managed to buy a football for my Signallers in St Omer. They were very pleased. We played Kemp's Platoon – and lost.

I first started to ride, and quite enjoyed it. I didn't realise at this time that a horse would be my downfall later – on July 29th 1918.[68]

There was another fishing competition between Gray and Long Waterhouse. Gray won, with 14 to his line in three hours.

01.07.15	We had a lecture on bomb throwing at Blendecques. We all threw live bombs for the first time – the old jam tin type with a 5 second fuse, often known as "Tickler's Artillery".[69]

I heard that Thewlis (Lord Mayor of Manchester's son) was killed.[70] We were in the OTC together, and he went to Warwick Barracks with us in 1913; we also worked in the same laboratory at Owens.[71]

Our training period at Arques was completed. We received orders that we were to move up to the Line again any day, probably to join our old Division, who had had a severe time in the fighting at Festubert, especially our old Brigade, who had lost heavily, and it had been necessary to bring the 1/6th Scottish Rifles into the Brigade.

04.07.15	I had a walk after Church Parade with the Skipper and Uncle Joe.

The Padre received orders to leave us when we moved. Thank God!

---

[68] See the *Afterword*, page 304.
[69] Thomas Tickler was elected as MP for Great Grimsby in May 1914. He had a jam company, T.G. Tickler Ltd, which won a contract to supply jam to the forces at the front. The empty jam tins were used to make makeshift grenades, hence the name, "Tickler's Artillery".
[70] Harold Darling Thewlis, "C" Company 1/7th Manchester Regiment, son of James Herbert and Isabella Thewlis of Victoria Park, Manchester, died aged 24 on 4th June 1915, and is commemorated on the Helles Memorial in Turkey (Gallipoli), Panel 159 to 171.
[71] Owens was one of the colleges which became Manchester University, where Norman studied chemistry, graduating about a year before the War began.

05.07.15   We had a Route March from 9.00am to 2.00pm, quite an easy day, followed by a glorious swim in the "Cut".

Captain Simon left "Z" Company and went to "Y".

Harker rode down from Wisques on a horse belonging to an Indian Cavalry Officer. He came down in great style with an Indian Groom – just like Freddy's cheek. He once borrowed a horse in St Omer to ride up to Wisques on and then found it belonged to the CO of the 1st Life Guards. Some cheek!

08.07.15   The Battalion paraded at 9.30am. The Transport with valises, stores etc. had gone on by road the previous day. We formed up in the Square at Arques. There were about 40 motor buses waiting for us.

We started off in Column of Route of Buses at 10.00am. Quite a number of people came to see us away and gave us a good send off. I was on a bus at the front of the Column with Uncle Joe, the Skipper, Freddy Harker, Kemp, and Latter. The two immediately behind us had on board Goldsmith, Ramsden,[72] Hill, Gray, Long Waterhouse, and Noton. This bus soon dropped a heavy barrage on our line of advance – not with shells, just potatoes (!), some old ones found in a box on the bus. We went through country which had become quite familiar to us along the main St Omer to Aire road, through Campagne, Wardrecques, Racquinghem and Wittes to Aire. It was very hot and very dusty. It must have been the limit in the rear of the Column.

We could see distinctly the pyramidical piles of colliery waste at collieries near Béthune about 20 miles away. These piles became familiar to me at a later date in 1917.[73]

From Aire we went to Isbergues, just through the outskirts of Berquette (where we detrained on May 4th 1915), then on to Guarbecque, where we halted the Column and had some food. Colonel Shirley took a photograph of the Column.[74] After about half an hour halt we went on to St Venant crossing the Aire to La Bassée Canal. We went along the bank of the Canal de la Lys, through St Floris, past our old billets of May 9th at Cornet Malo to Merville, through Merville and on to La Gorgue, a place we had anything but pleasant memories of (for it was from here we had retraced our steps to St Omer on May 18th), then on to Estaires. Here we debussed after a trip of about 30 miles. It was about 3.00pm when we arrived. The whole of the Battalion was billeted in a weaving mill and bleach works combined. Many of the machines had Walker Radcliffe, England on them. The men were very soon quite at home carrying cops and baskets working the looms. Several of us slept in some offices over the engine house. It was not very clean and had a very hard floor. Still we were very happy, and all very "full of beans".

Many of the officers went into Estaires for dinner. Joe, the Skipper and I had food at a little estaminet – eggs, omelette, salad etc. It was very good, and we were very hungry. We retired to bed early.

---

[72] Captain E.R. Ramsden was with "A" Company of the 2/5th Lancashire Fusiliers when they first landed in France on 3rd May 1915, and there have been a couple of references to him in the diary since then, but he is not mentioned again. The Battalion War Diary entry for 16th July 1915 reads "*Captain Ramsden to Hospital sick (15/07/15)*", followed on 22nd July by "*Captain E.R. Ramsden to England sick*".

[73] In the text of the diary Norman says that the later period when the "piles" became familiar to him was October 1917, but in fact the first diary entry in 1917 when he mentions Béthune is 28th November 1917 when he arrived in the La Bassée Sector with the 1/5th Lancashire Fusiliers; he stayed there until 8th February 1918.

[74] This photograph does not appear to be in the diary.

Lieutenant Colonel H.J. Shirley

CHAPTER 6
Estaires and Laventie
9th July 1915 to 27th July 1915

09.07.15   We were quite near the firing line now, only about 2½ miles away, and could hear the guns occasionally, but nothing very exciting.

We had now come back to our old Division, the 1/1ˢᵗ Highland Division, in the same Brigade.

It was now imperative, owing to my signalling duties, to take up residence with HQ and mess with them. I was very reluctant at leaving old "Z" Company and my pals there, but it couldn't be helped. HQ was now very different from the old crowd. We were quite a small party, Lieutenant Colonel Shirley, Major Milnes, Captain Jeffreys, Lieutenant Hill, Dr Thompson and myself. Of course I took Waddicar along with me to HQ.

We received orders to move to Support in front of Laventie, and marched off at 2.00pm. As we were only taking a Support Line over we took the Transport up with us.

We moved along the La Bassée road with platoons at 200 yards distance, as we were now in the danger zone for shelling. We cut along towards Sailly-sur-la-Lys, and then South East to Laventie. At Laventie we really got our first sight of a village badly damaged by shell fire. It struck me very very much, and I realised, as I never had done before, what shell fire could do. The houses and church were very badly damaged, and there were cautionary notices about "*loitering*" and "*troops only allowed to move in small parties past this point*" and so forth.

We got through quite peacefully – no shelling at all.

We found our billets fairly easily, picking up guides from the 1/6ᵗʰ Argyll and Sutherland Highlanders at Laventie Church. The men were billeted in houses and occupied defence works in their vicinity for Alarm Posts. We were about a mile from the Front Line. Companies were occupying Posts along the Rue de Bacquerol, and the Battalion HQ was at Dead End Lane Farm, Picantin.

We very soon got the men fixed up. I took over Signals, and found I had communication by telephone to Brigade HQ, who were on the Rue de la Lys, and also with Reserve Battalion HQ and Front Line HQ.

I had no communication with the Companies. I went round to see the location of the Companies with the Colonel, and then laid out wires to each Company HQ. I completed this by 10.00pm, and then turned in for some dinner – I was quite ready.

The farm was quite good, but dirty. Major Milnes, Captain Jeffreys and I slept in the same room – not a palace. The CO had the next room.

10.07.15   We suffered the first casualty to the Battalion – a man hit in the knee by a spent bullet. He was lying in a field outside the trenches – quite a cushy Blighty.[75]

I got my signal office cleaned out, and then – as usual – received orders to move again, only about 2 miles back towards Laventie, about 2 miles from Sailly-sur-la-Lys. I went to

---

[75] Blighty is slang for "Britain" or "home", and is derived from Hindustani "bilayati", meaning "foreign land". In the context of a wound, it means a wound bad enough to secure a passage home.

the Reserve Battalion HQ of the 1/4th Loyal North Lancashires at Red House, and met Major Harry Nickson[76] for the first time.

Life was anything but monotonous, always busy and full of change and fresh interests.

Well, we moved back at 3.00pm, about 3 miles. The men were bivouacked in an orchard, and we had a very good billet for HQ. Hill and I slept on our valises on the floor as usual – this time a stone one, <u>very</u> hard and rather cold. Dr Thompson joined HQ Mess. The rest of the officers slept at a farm near.

11.07.15   It was quite a slack day. We had Church Parade in a field near Laventie. It was a glorious day, and the flies were very troublesome – there were thousands of them.

The Colonel suddenly took it into his head always to address me as "This Boy". We got on quite well together and I quite liked living at HQ. Major Milnes was great.

Spy fever was prevalent! Two small kids were arrested under suspicion and sent to the Assistant Provost Marshal in Estaires for cross examination. I was called out during the night to the next farm to listen to suspicious tapping noises rather like a wireless apparatus. I didn't discover anything.

One officer per Company, and Lieutenant Hill, Machine Gun Officer, went up to the trenches as we were taking over on Monday. They left at about 6.00pm. Hill did a very odd thing. He packed his valise and said, "Now look here old bean – if anything happens to me my kit is all ready to send home." He must have felt uneasy somehow, for he was hit through the head next morning on his way down the Communication Trench.

12.07.15   In the morning I was busy organising my Signallers. I rode up to Front Line HQ to get particulars of the Communications, Plan of Lines, etc, and number of stations required, then came back, put one or two things on one side to take up with me, and packed my valise to go to Transport Lines.

13.07.15   Hill was wounded at about 11.15am coming down from the Line, badly hit through the head. It was very bad luck so soon. He was the first officer casualty in the 2/5th Lancashire Fusiliers. Colonel Shirley[77] got a car and went to the Casualty Clearing Station to see if there was anything he could do. But he was too late, as Hill had been sent right away to Merville[78]. I went off with my Signallers and Joe Hedley at about 6.15pm and got to Battalion HQ at about 7.30pm. I fixed up telephones there and went on up the Line with Joe.

It was a very peculiar feeling going up to the trenches proper for the first time. I had mixed

---

[76] Norman spells the surname "Nixon", but the correct spelling is "Nickson".

[77] Lieutenant Colonel Shirley had been a medical doctor in his own right before the War – see the footnote to the diary entry for 21st June 1916.

[78] Lieutenant Hill was the Machine Gun Officer with the 2/5th Lancashire Fusiliers when they first landed in France on 3rd May 1915. He was first mentioned in the diary in the entry for 31st December 1914, when Norman found him and various other officers at the "Deep End" or "Lawdie's" in Southport. He is mentioned as having been on a Machine Gun course with Harker at Wisques in the diary entry for 21st June 1915 to 30th June 1915. He was the first officer with the 2/5th Lancashire Fusiliers to be wounded. The Battalion War Diary gives this account of his injury: "*Lieutenant C.W.B. Hill shot through head in No 17 Communication Trench on return from visit to trenches for instructional purpose. Believed serious*". Subsequently it records that he was invalided to England on 31st July 1915. This is the last mention of him in the diary, and it is not clear what happened to him afterwards.

feelings of excitement, full of novelty, and at the same time – I must admit – a sense of fear. All went well. It was very quiet – a few stray bullets, but no shelling on our Front. We went up past the Picantin Post, a white cottage, and along a small railway to the Rue Tilloloy. We got into the Communication Trench on the Rue Tilloloy. It was now getting dark – fortunately, as the Communication Trench was only knee deep in most places; however, it deepened as we got nearer to the Line.

We followed "Z" Company up. It was quite a typical relief, a case of "Step short in front"… …"All closed up in the rear"…"Mind the wire"…"Hole here" – and so forth, quite the usual passwords on going up Communication Trenches. Each Platoon had its guides sent down by the 1/8th Liverpool Regiment, whom we were relieving in the Front Line.

The trenches at this sector were not trenches proper. The ground being very flat and marshy, you could not dig down more than a couple of feet without striking water; consequently, the defences had to be built up with sand bags and revetments, made into breastworks. There were thousands of sand bags. The Front Line was fairly well protected, but along the back of the trench the parados was not continuous. Also the Line was very irregular and crescent shaped, which made it possible for the Boche to be behind our Line in certain places. This was dangerous as he could snipe any movement by day.

At first when we got into the Front Line we seemed lost – at least, I did.

As I had previously ordered three Signallers to go up with each Company, I came up to go round each Company Station and see that everything was in order. Joe and I went to see the Skipper at Company HQ, a very small dug out, only a weather-proof shelter really – not even splinter-proof. It had two beds. We found the OC of "D" Company 1/8th Liverpool Irish, Joe Chamberlain, a great fellow, whom we got to know very well later.

A misfortune happened here. Joe Chamberlain was showing us a flare pistol and, not realising it was loaded, pressed the trigger and hit one of his subalterns with the burning flare light – the fellow lost three fingers – and the dug out was filled with fumes. This misfortune fixed up, Joe Hedley, Joe Chamberlain and I walked round the Line.

My first experience of "No Man's Land" came along very soon. The three of us went out through one of our saps to look at our barbed wire. I don't mind admitting I wasn't too keen on going out this first time – but Pride wouldn't let me say no – I didn't want to appear soft. So I pulled myself together and out we went for about 200 yards along our wire. This was quite a nightly trip later on.

I didn't find it as terrible as I expected, but I wasn't sorry to get back.

Then I went round to my Signals, and found all stations working quite well, except one, where we had to lay a new line out to a detached point on a salient. I got this fixed up and then had a chat with Goldsmith. By this time it was about 2.30am. I decided to remain up the Line until "Stand Down". I wanted to see what happened. I met Captain Jeffreys who was very annoyed with me for not letting them know at HQ where I was. They imagined that I had followed Hill's example. I think – "Not me – by intent!" So Jeffreys and I walked round, and I learnt quite a lot.

14.07.15 It came light. The men all "Stood to", which means that each man occupied his Battle Position in the Front Line bays. Each man must know his fighting position in case of alarm, and must be able to get to it quickly.

We went up to Red Lamp Corner. At this point we were only 80 yards from the Boche, and this morning we were greeted by "Good Morning Lancashire Fusiliers" from the Boche. How they knew that we had come up was just one of those many unanswerable questions.

Going back across an open bit of trench Jeffreys and I were shot at – the bullet just missed me – I felt the wind of it and stumbled with surprise. The Adjutant quite thought I was hit. But no![ii]

We went along and had some coffee with the Skipper, calling to see Hutty and Barnsdale on our way, then we made tracks for home, HQ. We were sniped at again near the trench railway, which we found on further acquaintance was a favourite line of some old Boches. We got back at about 5.00am – a glorious summer morning – birds singing etc.

I couldn't find my trench bundle, but found a valise. It turned out that when HQ's packs came up my valise was missing, so Jeffreys had sent down to the Transport especially for it – just like him. He was always doing these little kind acts for me. So we went to bed about 5.15am and slept until 10.00am, then had a good breakfast.

We had a look round the HQ Farm. We were lucky. It was quite a typical French farm, with a manure heap in the middle of the farm and the buildings built round it. There was a rather peculiar thing here, a tree growing from the inside of one of the rooms, through the roof, spreading blossom all over. There was also a swallow's nest in our Mess Room. So we called the place "Swallow Tree Farm".

Captain Jeffreys got a wire to say his brother had been killed in France with the Duke of Cornwall's Light Infantry.[79]

Battalion Headquarters, Laventie, Swallow Tree Farm

---

[79] Captain Darrell Richard Jeffreys of the 1st Battalion Devonshire Regiment (not the Duke of Cornwall's Light Infantry Regiment as stated by Norman), son of Florence Hall Jeffreys and the late John Jeffreys of Canterton Manor, Hampshire, died on 11th July 1915, aged 33, as a result of a British shell falling short. He is buried at Chester Farm Cemetery, West-Vlaanderen, Belgium, reference III.F.15. The full name of the Captain Jeffreys who was Adjutant to the 2/5th Lancashire Fusiliers was John William Jeffreys, born in 1876, and he rose to be Lieutenant Colonel commanding the 1/6th Durham Light Infantry.

In the afternoon I went out with Nuttall and Manock[80] sorting wires along the Rue Tilloloy and Front Line. We collected quite a lot of obsolete telephone wire, which had been left behind by the 7th Division; it was good stuff, and came in very useful.

In the evening I went round the Line with Colonel Shirley. There was sniping reported from behind our Line. Hill had been wounded and another fellow killed at the same spot. We lay out in the grass outside the trench for a full hour trying to find out by ear where the shot came from. One or two were fired but we couldn't locate the rifle. We suspected a farm nearby, and searched it without result.

Soon after the CO and I left the spot that we had been watching a second man was killed near the gap in the hedge.[iii]

Very often we were fired on from behind our Front Line on this sector, so it was necessary to patrol the roads behind the Line.

Rations came up on mules in the evening.

16.07.15   I got up early and went to the Line. I spent the morning repairing wires with Sergeant Collins. I had another escape on coming into the trench. Unfortunately the bullet hit Private Gates of "Y" Company, Simon's servant – who was just in front of me. Undoubtedly the bullet was meant for me, as Gates wasn't visible until he came out from behind the parados, just as I was coming in.[iv] I'm glad to say that he recovered after several months, and came to my Company in the 1/5th Lancashire Fusiliers in February 1918 at Houchin.

I had lunch with Joe and the Skipper at "Z" Company HQ. We went to "W" Company at Red Lamp Corner, and saw mining operations. We went down one shaft – it was very wet. We got shelled on our return along the Rue Tilloloy. We got to HQ for tea.

17.07.15   It was a quiet day. In the evening I helped to bury a dead horse at HQ, which was smelling very badly. I went out wire hunting, and lost one of the gold studs which Uncle George had given me for a 21st birthday present.

18.07.15   It was another quiet day. I was up the Line all day. The Boche shelled a bit in the afternoon, and caught "Z" Company party working in the immediate Support Line. Latter was busy making "chevaux de frise"[81] of barbed wire at "Grange", "Z" Company's work house.

I returned to HQ. While at dinner I got an urgent telephone message from Goldsmith, reporting heavy shelling from the Boche – they were having a very rough time. I tried to get retaliation. We had very few guns covering us, only one Battery of a 15 pounder and two 4.7 inch Naval Guns – and very little ammunition. After a great deal of persuasion they fired six rounds, but it did no good – only irritated the Boche still more, so that they put down quite a barrage, and really messed our Line about, blowing many breaches in the

---

[80] Norman spells this "Maynock".

[81] A mediaeval defensive anti-cavalry measure consisting of a portable frame (sometimes just a simple log) covered with many projecting long iron or wooden spikes or spears. During the First World War, armies used chevaux de frise made of barbed wire temporarily to plug gaps in the wire in front of the trenches.

breastworks. Hartley Goldsmith was in an awful funk. I also spoke to Waterhouse. His Company, "Z" Company, was not being troubled much. In fact the Skipper, with his usual coolness on such occasions, wanted to know if he should send down for rations as usual. Jeffreys very much admired Waterhouse's coolness.

It was the first time the 2/5th Lancashire Fusiliers had been really under fire. Several of the men got the wind up, but taken all round they behaved splendidly.

We had several fellows killed, several wounded, and a few shell shocks. Lieutenant R.W. Kirkman[82] and Company Sergeant Major Marshall returned to England. Marshall was very badly crushed from being buried. One Machine Gun Post was blown in and Quinlan[83] was killed. He was buried just behind the trenches.

Jeffreys wouldn't let me go up to the Line. So, while he and the Colonel went up, I organised Ammunition Supply Parties in the event of attack. Jeffreys was quite bucked with this. Eventually I took a wire repairing party up with Sergeant Hindle, Nuttall and Taylor, as our wires were broken down and we had no communication. One of my Signal Stations at "X" Company HQ was blown in, but luckily there were no casualties. We had a rotten time that night mending wires under shell fire, but were too busy to worry. We got all straight again by daylight.

19.07.15   I was out repairing wires again all day. I had quite an interesting time coming home with Nuttall. We suspected an old man of spying and telephoning to the Boche. He was cutting corn in front of one of our Battery positions. After stalking him for some time, joined by Harker, we arrested him. Jeffreys was very amused, and called me a fool for doing it, but later admitted that he had suspected the same man only a few days previously. It was a much quieter day, and the Boche behaved himself, but the men were a bit jumpy.
It rained heavily, and was very wet and muddy.

20.07.15   There was the usual work up the Line. I came down with Jeffreys and gathered flowers – roses etc. Jeffreys was really a fine soldier and jolly good fellow.
Sergeant Bampton[84] was killed by a sniper.

22.07.15   We received orders of relief next day and were busy making preparations.

23.07.15   I went round all the wires. We were relieved at about 8.30pm by the 2nd Argyll and Sutherland Highlanders, 28th Division.
This particular evening was glorious – a fine moonlit night, quite sharp.

---

[82] Lieutenant R.W. Kirkman was with "C" Company of the 2/5th Lancashire Fusiliers when they first landed in France on 3rd May 1915, having joined the Lancashire Fusiliers as an officer in or about September 1914 (see the diary entry for 12th September 1914). Norman gives the impression that Kirkman returned to England immediately after this engagement, while the Battalion War Diary has an entry for 21st July 1915, which reads "Captain R.W. Kirkman to Hospital sick", and he is reported to have been subsequently invalided to England on 11th August 1915. He is mentioned only once more, when Norman met him in Colchester in January 1917, while he (Norman) was on Home Service at Ripon.
[83] Private Richards Quinlan, Service no 2582, is recorded in the Commonwealth War Graves Commission's records as having died on 19th July 1915; he is commemorated on the Le Touret Memorial, Pas de Calais, Panel 12.
[84] Lance Sergeant Tom Bampton, Service no 1589, son of George William and Elizabeth Bampton of Heywood, is recorded in the Commonwealth War Graves Commission's records as having died on 23rd July 1915, aged 18; he is buried at Rue-du-Bacquerot (13th London) Graveyard, Laventie, reference F.17.

We moved off independently. I marched with the Signallers from Picantin Post to Laventie along Rue de la Lys, closely followed by "Z" Company. My men were very chirpy – singing all the way. We went through Estaires – I left a stick near a house in the Square and came back for it next day. The cooks' wagons were at Estaires, and we waited there for the rest of the Battalion and had tea.

We were billeted at a very nice Chateau with a glorious garden. I waited until all the Battalion came in, and reported in at about 3.30am. I sent Bland to report to the Brigade, then went to bed. It <u>was</u> bed this time – a <u>real</u> one. Major Milnes was quite settled in bed when the Adjutant and I turned in. I had my clothes off for the first time in 10 days.

24.07.15   I got up at about 10.00am. It was a glorious morning, and I had a walk round the billets after a jolly good bath. I cleaned up the telephones and straightened up my stores.

In the afternoon I went to Estaires with Hartley Goldsmith, Waterhouse, and Harker for hot baths. We found them full up, so had tea at the Hotel.

We saw a fine view of the Boche shelling one of our planes.

We were not likely to be in the Line for a few days.

25.07.15   We had Church Parade – Captain Gillenders rejoined our Battalion.[85]

Later I went into Estaires and got a hot bath, then had a jolly good lunch at the same Hotel, and in the afternoon I lazed about in the garden.

26.07.15   News of a move was received. It was rumoured that we should move down South to the Somme District. The French were holding the Line there and we were to relieve them.

27.07.15   I went down to Estaires Station to arrange entraining for our Battalion the following day. We were busy preparing for the move.

"X" Company:

From left to right:
Lieutenant A.V. Barwood,
Lieutenant W. Duckworth,
2nd Lieutenant J.E. Hartington,
Major J.D. Barnsdale.

This photograph was almost certainly one of those taken in September 1915 at Senlis in the Somme area by Lieutenant Colonel Shirley – see page 97.

---

[85] Captain Gillenders, described by Norman as *"a very good sort"*, was chaplain to the 2/5th Lancashire Fusiliers when they first landed in France on 3rd May 1915. He left for a short time on 20th June 1915, but rejoined on 25th July 1915, as mentioned in this diary entry. However, this is the last mention of him, and it is not clear when he again left, but as Captain Davenport joined the Battalion as a new Padre on 4th January 1916 it may have been then, or shortly before.

CHAPTER 7
Corbie, Bouzincourt, Albert, Aveluy, Martinsart and Senlis
28th July 1915 to 28th August 1915

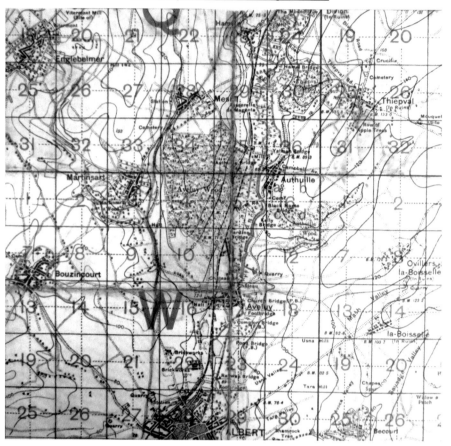

28.07.15   We got up at 4.15am. We left our fine billet at the Chateau and entrained at Estaires at 6.45am – quite cold so early.

We passed through Merville again, and the Forest of Nieppe, then to Hazebrouck, and through Arques, our old training centre, then on to St Omer, Watten, Audruicq and on to Calais, where we stayed half an hour. We got a glimpse of the English Channel once again, which made me wish I was going on leave. No such luck yet a bit!

Travelling down the main line from Calais towards Paris we passed through Wimereux, where the railway passes along the edge of the cliffs, and there were very large Base Hospitals.

We passed through Boulogne, and soon after we left Boulogne the crowd started to play bridge. I preferred to look at the scenery. It was all new and full of interest.

The country is very like England although not quite as green, even in these parts not directly affected by war's ravages. It began to appeal to me, perhaps by force of circumstances because I had to live in it. Jeffreys was also very keen on Nature's beauties – nothing appealed to him so much as a fine view or a gorgeous sunset.

It seemed quite strange to see the Paris to Boulogne Boat Train – quite civilised with corridor coaches and dining cars.

We went along the coast line through Camiers – also a big Base Hospital Centre – and on to Étaples, which was one of the biggest Infantry Base Depots in France. Here nearly all reinforcements for the Line first reported, and were then sent off to their various units. I shall describe Étaples more fully later as I had the misfortune to spend a few days there once or twice during the War.[86]

The next place of any size we came to was Noyelle, then Abbeville. From there we followed the River Somme along the Somme Valley through Pont-Remy, Longpré, Hangest, Picquigny and St Sauveur to Amiens, and then to Corbie. We got the men billeted and then turned in ourselves.

29.07.15   In the morning I did practically nothing at all, except look round the town. It is a pretty place with lots of trees and beautiful gardens. There are five rivers running into the Somme at Corbie. The town is in a valley with hills all round, and consequently it is very hot. We fixed up to mess at the Café de la Gare.

In the afternoon I got orders to reconnoitre several villages towards the Line. So I started off on my bike with two Signallers, Green and Bland. The country was quite different from up North, hilly and open. The roads were very busy with French troops, and all the villages had French troops billeted in them. We were practically the first British troops down in this

district, so that we seemed to cause quite an interest. We rode up to Heilly, Méricourt, Buire, Dernancourt, Laviéville, and Millencourt to Bouzincourt. Here were many French troops, chiefly Gunners. At Bouzincourt I called at a French Artillery Brigade HQ and the officers were very sociable and gave me some very nice wine. Then we went down to Albert. Albert is also down in a valley, the valley where the River Ancre (later famous) flows. It looked quite nice in the distance, with the well known church of Albert with the falling Virgin on the spire.

When we got into the town itself we found it had been <u>very</u> badly damaged by shell fire – especially round the railway station and Square. In 1914 the Germans occupied

Albert Cathedral in 1916

Albert and even spent 19 days in Amiens. We had a quick look round Albert. It really was a very impressive sight to see a one time flourishing town almost levelled to the ground in places. The railway was literally torn up. It made you realise that the tales about poor little Belgium and the sacking of Louvain and places up North were really true, and what war meant to the would-be peaceful citizen.

The restored spire in 2018

[86] June 1917, and March and July 1918.

Surely the Germans – the Kaiser and his staff – were determined to lay every part of France they could – to waste.[87] [88]

We retraced our steps to Corbie, via Méaulte and Dernancourt. Here we saw a French Observation Balloon being hauled down. It was worked by a huge motor on a motor carriage. We saw it come right down and the observers get out of the basket.

Then we pushed on home and arrived back ready for dinner.

30.07.15 In the morning I had another look round Corbie. I went into the church and up the spire, and got a good view of the country. It was quite similar to Salisbury Plain, with hilly slopes, and here and there the strata protruding through the close springy turf. This part was also very well cultivated, with a great many fruit-orchards.

At about 1.00pm we paraded in full kit, and we and the Transport moved out of Corbie towards Albert, over the ground I had reconnoitred the previous day, by Route Nationale Nº 10 to Méricourt. At Méricourt we were inspected by General Monro, the Corps Commander. It was a glorious day – but, oh, how hot! We went through the usual ceremonial for inspections and were quite glad when it was over. It was rather tedious to have these things on Active Service and only a few miles from the Line, but undoubtedly they serve a good purpose.

The inspection over the men settled down to tea, and we soon followed. We just lay out on the grass near a little brook, quite a picnic under the trees – a glorious spot. We had a jolly good tea <u>and</u> we were ready; tongue, salad, eggs, cake and fruit.

Then we had a jolly good wash in the stream, and at 7.15pm we were again ready to move

---

[87] There follows a further lengthy quotation from *Henry V, Act III Scene 3*.

[88] Later diary entries for 2nd January and 4th September 1916 refer to Albert, and there are some photographs of the damage accompanying the latter entry. On 23rd August 1917 Norman again returned to Albert with the 1/5th Lancashire Fusiliers. His diary entry for that day reads: *"Albert was more damaged than when I was here back in 1916. But the Cathedral still stood and the hanging Virgin was still hanging. Before the War Albert had been a prosperous industrial town of 7000 inhabitants. Lying at the foot of a hill on both sides of the River Ancre, originally known as Ancre, it was given its name when it became the property of Charles d'Albert, Duke of Luynes in 1619. Early in the War in 1914 fierce fighting took place in its immediate neighbourhood, but the Germans were repulsed with heavy losses at La Boiselle and in front of Fricourt. September 29th 1914 saw the town heavily shelled and, the shelling continued until it was annihilated, the Iron Works, Sugar Factories, Brick Kilns, Mechanical Workshops being the main targets. No public buildings were spared – not until 1916 was Albert again out of range of German Guns. In March 1918 it was again in German hands, and remained in German hands until 22nd August when the final British Offensive cleared the Boche out for the last time. The Church of Notre Dame de Brebières was famous for its Virgin Statue, and known to nearly all British troops. The brick belfry was 200 feet high, and was surmounted by a copper dome on which stood a gilt statue of the Virgin 26 feet high, holding the infant Jesus in her arms. Early in the War a shell struck the top of the dome and burst against the socle of the statue. The base gave way but did not entirely collapse, the statue overturning and remaining suspended in mid-air. For several years it remained there and there was a saying that "The War will end when the Virgin Statue of Albert falls". The Spring Bombardment of 1918 completed the ruin of the Church. The belfry collapsed carrying with it the Virgin. Actually I was told by Watson – a 2nd Lieutenant of the 2nd Howitzer Battery – that their Battery actually knocked the Virgin down in a competition with another Battery, this shoot costing some thousands of rounds."* Norman met 2nd Lieutenant Watson, an alumnus of Uppingham School, at No 74 General Hospital in June 1918 (see the *Afterword*, page 303). Watson was with 2nd Siege Battery, Royal Garrison Artillery, 85th Brigade. This Brigade's War Diary for 16th April 1918 reads: *"The Statue of the Virgin on Albert Cathedral was brought down at 3.30pm this afternoon."* The Diary does not say that the Brigade shot at the Virgin, but they could surely see it. The 89th Brigade's Diary records the fall of the cathedral tower at 3.36pm while its 57th Siege Battery were firing at it.

off, through Treux and Ribemont to Buire, then past a very large Sugar Factory up a <u>very</u> steep hill and out across country on the Route Nationale N° 29, the main Amiens – Cambrai – Péronne road, a beautiful road, one long avenue, up hill and down dale – indeed a fine road, and so typical of the fine French National roads, very wide and bordered on each side with grass and the trees sown along it many years ago. The fine roads were part of Napoleon's wonderful defence scheme. The road marking's are done exceedingly well, and sign posts are a great feature. England might copy the scheme with advantage. We passed to the south of Bresle and Laviéville, and came into Millencourt, where we began to drop down into Albert, crossing over the Amiens – Albert – Arras line. It was now about 10.15pm.

We marched through Albert to the North end and billeted the men in houses. They were all fairly tired. Marching in full kit on a hot summer night in July on the Somme is <u>not</u> easy work. By 11.00pm we had given the men tea and settled them down. They were very impressed – even in the dark – by the damage done by shell fire.

Before I turned in I had to report our arrival in billets to the French General who was at Senlis, about 6 miles away. I had to report by telephone. Joe Hedley came with me to find the French Army Signals, who were billeted in a house on the Albert to Bapaume road. No sentries were posted, so we walked in, upstairs, found no one on duty – they were all comfortably settled in bed. This Signal Office corresponded to our Divisional HQ Signals – imagine the trouble if our Signallers acted similarly. With difficulty we wakened one of the "Poilus",[89] and explained what we wanted. He assured us it was useless at that time of night – there wouldn't be anyone up at Corps HQ. However, as they were expecting our message, we persuaded the man to ring up. After waiting quite half an hour, we got an answer, in a very sleepy way, and spoke to a French Staff Officer. All correct, we retraced our steps to our billet, for I had arranged to sleep with Joe at a very nice billet he had got, with a real bed. We found the billet with difficulty and were jolly glad to turn in.

We slept well until 9.00am, and then had breakfast at HQ Mess – a glorious morning. We had a look round Albert, and received orders to move up the Line that night. I was to move before the rest of the Battalion with my Signallers, and we were to get up to the Line before dark. One officer per company also had to go up in advance to have a look over the Line prior to taking over.

It is a point of interest to mention that we Territorials – unlike Kitchener's Army Pets[90] – had to go into the Line direct, without instruction, and learn the routine of trench warfare by experience and mistakes, and, knowing little about war, we still had to hold the Line and carry on in as near the same routine as regular trained troops had done before us. The fact remains that we did it by sheer perseverance and hard work by officers and men alike. The men supported us loyally, though at first the conditions were not so good as later on; later we got used to running the Battalion as well as possible for the men's comfort, no matter where we were, whether in trenches or in billets.

When the bulk of Kitchener's Army Divisions came out, they had every facility given them for tours of instruction by platoons and companies in the Line, with seasoned troops, like we became in a few months. It was a fine scheme for them and undoubtedly helped these

---

[89] French private soldiers.

[90] Men who responded to Lord Kitchener's call for volunteers from August 1914, who were formed into an entirely new army, with the intention that they would be fully trained by mid-1916, though they were in fact first used earlier, at the battle of Loos in September 1915. See also the diary entry for 5th August 1914.

Divisions very considerably.

This brings us to an interesting place of the War. Until this time the total length of Line held by British troops on the Western Front was 27 miles from just North of Ypres to the South of the La Bassée Canal to Vermelles.

When we took over a long stretch of Front from Hébuterne to Vaux to just East of Bray and along the North bank of the Somme, the British Line was extended from 27 miles to just over 60 miles in length, chiefly due to the completion of training of Kitchener's Divisions who came out to the Bases, relieving trained troops who were in Reserve, resting after hard fighting. The troops were then available to take over new Lines.

31.07.15

205 — ALBERT (environs) - Un escalier rustique construit par nos poilus dans un bois

I moved off from Albert about 2.30pm with the Signallers. We went along the Albert to Arras road to Aveluy, a small village of only a few hundred inhabitants, fairly well in repair, but with a few houses badly damaged.[91]

We went right down to the French Brigade HQ at the Chateau, a glorious place with a very fine garden. The River Ancre ran at the bottom of the garden. There were also some very fine stables. The Chateau belonged to a man in Paris who made electrical lights. He was also very keen on race-horses, and a one time Derby winner was bred in these stables. But that is a point of interest rather off our object.

At the Chateau I got a guide, a second class French "Poilu".[92] He was a man of 40 to 45, tall, well built, with a black beard and moustache. He spoke English quite well. After a few minutes' chat with Captain Jackson, our Brigade Major, I set off with my guide. It was about 3 miles' walk up to the Front Line, but rather less to Battalion HQ. I found my guide a most interesting man. He had been Vice-Consul for the French Government in Beirut before the War, and military attaché to the Serbian Army during the Balkan War of 1911, so he was an intellectual man. He gave me a good description of the Line we were to take over, also the habits of the

---

[91] This is in contrast to later in 1916, by which time Aveluy had been severely damaged; photographs accompany the diary entry for 4th September 1916, when Norman again visited Aveluy.

[92] A French private soldier.

Boche, and the general topographical features of the district.

It was quite a nice walk up to the Line from Brigade HQ. We crossed over the River Ancre, then on to Crucifix Corner, where there was an iron crucifix in good repair. We turned North here, leaving the by-road which went across to La Boiselle, there to meet the main Albert to Bapaume road – incidentally a road which became very famous at a later date in 1916.[93]

We followed the Arras road towards Authuille for half a mile, then cut off East along a field track. We were not under observation at this place because of high ground between us and the Boche Line; also the Boche on Serre Ridge could not get direct observation on to the main road because of the woods giving cover from view.

The geographical features may be compared with Bury, with Albert to Aveluy being Limefield, and the Front Line being along Birtle Edge, and with Serre Ridge, a few miles North, corresponding to Whittle Pike, thus commanding the view down to Bury (or Albert). Leaving the main road we very soon entered a very thick wood – Aveluy Wood – the scene of very heavy fighting in September 1914 when the French unsuccessfully attempted to stop the German Army from gaining Albert and Amiens. I was told that there were fully a thousand Boche buried in this wood. We passed up the wood along a wood-land ride. This wood is really Authuille Wood, or part of it. As we went along the wood it was gorgeous, very quiet and peaceful, hardly a sign of war until we came to some French Field Kitchens and the Support dug outs. Outside these dug outs under the trees were rustic seats and tables, with little pagodas near the dug outs – more like a tea gardens.

Then we came to Communication Trenches, which we crossed over by small bridges, and on to small paths until we came to a sunken road. Built into the banks of this road were more large underground tunnels, for the Support Company. Passing on another 200 yards we came to a second sunken road which we turned up, for Battalion HQ was at the top of this road.

What a surprise! The place looked just like a tea garden again, with two fine wooden huts made of logs built on the banks of the wood. Steps led up to a terrace in front of the huts and the French had laid out flower beds railed round with rustic railings. The whole effect was very beautiful – and all this, our new home, right in the middle of a huge wood.

It was now about 5.30pm, so quite light. Having reported to the Major commanding the Battalion we were to relieve (for a Major commands a Battalion in the French Army, and a Colonel corresponds to our Brigadier and commands one of their Regiments or three Battalions) I proposed to leave my HQ Signallers to take over Battalion HQ Lines and go round the Line to settle my Company Signallers and see the lie of the land.

It was some distance to each Company HQ, and, being new ground, it seemed further. However I got a move on and went to the Left Company, Left Centre, and got to the Right Centre at about 7.45pm. It was getting dusk, especially in the wood. The birds sounded glorious. They were just singing their evening hymn so to speak. The beauty of the whole surroundings was disturbed only by the hideous chalk trenches – which very greatly disfigured the place. At the Left Centre Company I ran across Major Barnsdale. He was with his French Company Commander. After the usual introductions they very kindly asked me to stay to

---

[93] In July 1916, the Battle of Albert.

dinner. Trust me I accepted! But I just wanted to see the Right Company Signallers fixed up, so I trotted off over there – not very far – and then came back for dinner. We had a very good dinner and most interesting conversation with the two French officers.

It had now got to 9.00pm, and was quite dark. We expected the Battalion up very soon, so I decided to get down to HQ.

After receiving directions from the French officer I started off. Imagine being stranded in a thick wood at night and told to go to a place half a mile away. I started off down the Communication Trench, took the wrong turn very soon, and got lost. Then the Boche started to fire a few shells, which echoed right through the wood; also a couple of Machine Guns. There was I, all alone and lost, and not quite sure where the Boche was. I didn't feel quite comfortable – not by any means! I decided to retrace my steps to Barnsdale's HQ – if I could find the place! Luckily I did. I got fresh directions and started off again. This time I was more successful and found HQ – easily – but I never went down a Communication Trench so quickly – I was hot and cold all over – in other words – frightened! It was now 10.15pm. There was no sign of the Battalion. However at about 11.15pm the first party arrived, Sergeant Beetson with the mess stores, a good sign. The Colonel wouldn't be long <u>now</u>!

Very soon the Companies came along. "Z" Company with the Skipper went up "Maisoncelle Communication Trench". All the trenches were called after French officers. Major Milnes was then OC of the Battalion, Colonel Shirley being on leave. He arrived with Captain Jeffreys. I waited up until 2.30am to collect in the Company handing over certificates. The relief took an abnormally long time – due to it being an inter-allies' change over. I reported to Captain Jeffreys who then turned in. I then eventually got through to our Brigade HQ at Aveluy by telephone, and to the French Divisional HQ at Senlis, also by telephone. At 3.45am I turned in too – to sleep in the Mess. I had been too busy to find a dug out. I went to sleep on a chair at first. Then I settled down on the floor with just my burberry,[94] however I went to sleep. When I wakened up at 9.00am of course it was quite light. I felt very comfortable for I had several blankets and another coat over me.

I found out that Captain Jeffreys had wakened up during the night, spotted the set up, and covered me with his clothes. It was just typical of his kindness and thought. He really was far too kind to me and I certainly appreciated it.

01.08.15	Unfortunately, as we were in the Line, we couldn't celebrate our Regimental Battle Honour – and unfortunately the roses did not turn up, although they had been ordered.
Minden	
Day[95]	The first thing I did was to ensure that communication was alright. Then I had breakfast and then looked round for a dug out. Eventually I found Dr Thompson had a spare bed in his dug out at the Aid Post – "Post de Secours" – quite near HQ. This was also a fine piece of work, the dug out being built into the bank of the sunken road leading up to "Maisoncelle Communication Trench". They were all made of huge trees, very well done.

The Aid Post was like a small infirmary with about 20 bunks, a waiting room, and a consulting room – all compact.

---

[94] A waterproof trench coat, made of gabardine, a material which had been invented by William Burberry in 1879; he submitted a design for the coat to the British Army in 1901, and it was adopted as optional wear for officers,
[95] See the footnote to the diary entry for 1st August 1914.

Dr Thompson and I had a very nice little dug out, with two beds, two tables, chairs, a window, and a wooden floor. We put some Kirchner[96] pictures on the walls, and I put my photographs up and really made the place look very cosy. We had a nice flower garden outside.

There was about 8 feet of earth on our roof with huge tree trunks – but it was only about 4.5 inch shell-proof – however, good enough! And chance our luck with anything heavier. About 10 o'clock I took Sergeant Hindle, Nuttall, and Taylor round the lines. We traced every wire on our sector and made a plan of the lines. We visited all Signal Stations and arrived back at 4.00pm, quite hungry and tired, for it was a very hot day.

The HQ Signal Office was quite a complicated place. When we got rid of the French Signallers – who were an awful nuisance – we relaid our wires into the office and made a new switch board; also, we made switch boards for each Company HQ, and relaid several new lines, taking up the old ones which were short-circuiting. In "Z" Company Line there were about 20 old wires which we cleared away entirely.

The telephone system was roughly:

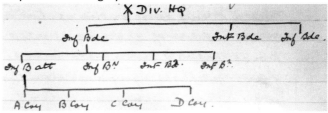

Our particular lines were:

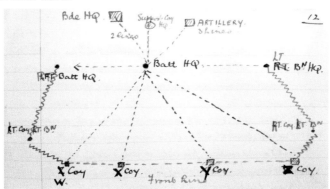

In addition to telephone communication, we also established Visual Stations with Division (7 miles), and Brigade (3 miles), Flank Battalions with Flag and Lamp by day, and with Lamp only by night.

---

[96] Kirchner is a German or Austrian name. At least three artists named Kirchner were working at the material time:

(i) Ernst Ludwig Kirchner (1880-1938), a German expressionist painter, who volunteered for army service in the First World War, but suffered a breakdown (he ultimately committed suicide by gun shot some 23 years later). In 1915 he painted *Self-portrait as a Soldier*. Earlier work included wood cuts, female nudes and Berlin Street Scenes.

(ii) Eugen Kirchner (1865-1938), a German who was one of the founders of the Munich Secession, whose caricature-type drawings appeared in magazines and prints;

(iii) Raphael Kirchner (1876-1917), an Austrian illustrator who moved to Paris in 1900 and the United States in 1914. According to an entry on the website www.firstworldwar.com *"his erotic 'pin up' sketches proved popular during the First World War not only among his compatriots but also among British and French servicemen"*. He is therefore by far the most likely candidate of the three Kirchners. See the next page for examples of his work.

Certain Signallers were detailed off as linesmen. Their job was to inspect the lines daily – twice a day or more – and to effect minor repairs.

All Infantry lines were laid on the North and West side of trenches, while all Artillery lines were laid on the South and East side. We found it quite a good idea to lay our wires about a foot from the trench floor, set into grooves in the trench side. Where it was necessary to cross the trench we buried the wire 2 feet deep.

All our wires were labelled and numbered on little wooden labels with the number painted on. This facilitated tracing and repairs. We also set in test boxes at intervals so that we could test the line easily and localise the faults. Constant work and attention was necessary, especially when the Boche strafed our Line – because we needed communication more than ever then.

Taken all round the telephones were very satisfactory. As the War grew older improvements were introduced.

Typical posters featuring the work of Raphael Kirchner: Riquette et son chien and Le Coup de la Jarretelle

02.08.15 to 06.08.15 The weather broke down very badly. We got a lot of rain, and, as we were on limestone with a clay sub-soil, it got frightfully muddy – quite up to one's knees in thick wet slimy "mood" in places. Still, we carried on as usual, mostly keeping very fit and in good spirits. Even sleeping in wet clothes became quite a matter of course.

At one point several of us were a bit groggy with food poisoning. I had a day in bed in my dug out. Sergeant Collins left us with appendicitis. I was very sorry to lose him; he was a good Signaller, but rather a fool of a man – always tight.

One day we went out on a reconnaissance. We met old General Hibbert fishing for trout in the Ancre. He was a funny old boy. If he couldn't get a bite, he used to get his servant and drag the river, which was quite narrow. He also used to go wild duck shooting on the marshes near Mesnil and Beaumont-Hamel.

The rifle fire and Machine Gun fire was quiet generally – just a little sniping by day. The Boche seemed to choose meal times for his little Hates, usually with pip-squeaks (77mm shells) – shrapnel – bursting overhead. They did whistle through the wood. We usually did a Derby[97] into cover when he started.

---

[97] i.e. ran like a horse competing in the Derby.

We divided the German shells into three classes:

a. Heavy Crumps, in these days up to 6 inches.

b. Shrapnel – 77mm – bursting forward, throwing about 150 to 200 small bullets.

c. High Explosive – 77mm.

One night we wanted Artillery Support, and, as French "Soixante Quinze" – 75mm – were covering us, it took some time to get them to fire; but when they started we couldn't stop the beggars for about an hour – they just delighted to show we English what they could do.

As these seven days in the Line were comparatively quiet, I got a very good idea of the Line. I will describe it briefly, and have drawn a sketch plan below, and see the detail on page 79.

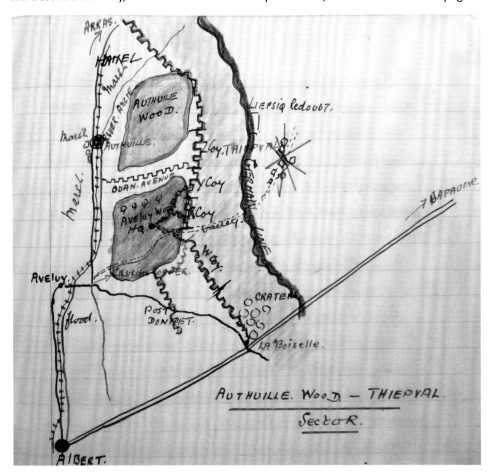

"W" Company, the Right Company, were in fairly deep trenches, all chalk. They had a break in their Line on the left and no Front Line communication with "X" Company.

"W" Company had a very pretty HQ. A wooden front to the dug out was built into the roadside, with quite a nice garden in front, just on the edge of the wood. A French officer took a photo of several of us outside. It was on a road – a by-road in this case, a cart track really.[98]

"X" Company, the Right Centre Company, held the front of the wood, rather a bad place and very wet, on sloping ground.

---

[98] This photograph does not appear to be in the original diary.

"Y" Company, the Left Centre Company, had a good Line, very deep, 19 to 15 feet deep in places, with steps up to the fire step, and fairly good dug outs.

"Z" Company, the Left Company, had a good Line, rather wet, with a good Company HQ. There were four saps in their Line, and at one point the Boche were only 50 yards away. The approach up Maisoncelle Communication Trench past my dug out was very pretty. There was an excellent Observation Post off Maisoncelle. You could see all the Boche Front Line, Pozières Church, La Boiselle, and Mouquet Farm (a famous spot and scene of a great battle in 1916).

07.08.15	We were relieved in the trenches by the 1/4th Loyal North Lancashires. We left the trenches at about 10.15pm, through the wood – raining in torrents – ankle deep in mud; I thought of Bill[99] dancing in the ballrooms at Cleveleys Hydro – some comparison. Even in the dark, when I called out to a party coming up, "Keep to the Right", a reply came to my voice "Well, I'm damned, is that Hall?" It was Lindsay of the 1/4th Loyal North Lancashires – an old Manchester University OTC fellow. Fancy meeting in a wood in France.
	We marched about 5 miles to Martinsart, where we arrived at about 12.30am. My men had a good village billet. After some food at HQ Mess I turned in. My billet was in a funny little house, very dirty, but we settled down for the night, very tired after seven days in the Line.
08.08.15 to 13.08.15	We were now the Battalion in Reserve.
	On August 8th I got up at 8.30am, had a bath, and got some clean clothes. We spent part of the morning fumigating HQ Mess with burning sulphur to try to get rid of the flies and mosquitos – hundreds of them. I also fixed up a telephone office.
	Hartley Goldsmith asked me whether I ever got any rest in the Line because I always seemed to be turning up at all hours of the day and night to see if anyone wanted any odd job of work doing.
	Martinsart is a small village with one street, a village green, and a church. It is practically surrounded by woods. The nearest villages are Aveluy, Englebelmer, Mesnil, and Bouzincourt, where our Transport Lines were.
	One point of interest was the threshing machines, worked by a horse. He walked up a rolling staircase idea, but never got to the top, and this endless band drove the machine. "Sandy Mac" – Skipper's three-quarter time comic circus pony – hated these machines. "Z" Company had a good billet on the left hand side of the Mesnil Road, the last farm in the village. We thoroughly cleaned up our billet, and Waddicar scrubbed our bedroom floor. We could also see through the window when he had spring cleaned. We had plenty of rats for company at night – dear little things!
	During our week in Reserve we moved from Martinsart to Senlis, about 5 miles. Senlis was a bigger place than Martinsart – cleaner and much nicer. The Divisional HQ of the 51st Division was here.
	We arrived at Senlis late at night. Waddicar, in trying to get to the Mess Cart, which was in the HQ Mess farm yard near the manure pond, slipped in up to his waist, only saving himself by holding on to the cart wheel – imagine the mess he was in.
	The week in Reserve was very enjoyable. We had a good rest and got some sleep – making

---

[99] Norman's sister, Kathleen

up a little lost time. In the mornings we did a little quiet training. We made a special point of getting the men bathed, giving them a change of clothing, generally cleaning up, polishing buttons etc., and steady drill to smarten them up after trench life.

I was feeling quite fit again.

One day I went down to Major Boon's 4.5 inch Low Battery in position near a wood on the right of the Mesnil Road, East side. He asked me to go down to advise him about his telephones, and very kindly showed me his guns – their mechanism, and also the action of shell fuses etc. – very interesting.

They had brought a 4.7 inch Naval Gun up to shoot at a Boche Observation Balloon about 6 miles away. I stayed for lunch to watch the show. No luck, we didn't hit the old Sausage, but got several air bursts quite near to it – and evidently made the German observer uncomfortable as they hauled the Balloon down.

A Division of Kitchener's Army[100] arrived; we were surprised – we thought Kitchener's Army had decided to remain neutral – they were so long in coming out to France! We were embodied at the same time, but had been out nearly four months now.

I started to make my stick with the names of places on in code.[101]

Some of our fellows wrote most wonderful accounts of our fighting and hardships – and some imagined they had won VCs before they had heard a shot fired. Why, we had had a good time so far – almost a holiday.

Skipper Waterhouse went on leave. Lucky beggar! – seven days only.

We received photos of Teddy Horsfall in the Dardanelles.[102]

14.08.15 During Saturday morning we prepared to move up to the Line. We moved out of Senlis at about 2.30pm on to the Hédauville to Albert road. It was a very clear afternoon and, as Boche Observation Balloons were up, and could observe the road that we had to pass along, we were compelled to halt for a couple of hours. Eventually we started at 4.30pm and got a hurried brew of tea on the road for the men. I rode one of Colonel Shirley's horses. We moved via Bouzincourt (where our Transport Lines were to stay) to Albert, then on through Aveluy village, the Battalion moving up by platoons at 200 yards' distance. It was a perfect evening, and the country, though disfigured by trenches, looked glorious. We arrived up in the Line at about 8.30pm. There was a slight "German Hate" to greet us, and several fellows were wounded, Sergeant Stewart was quite badly shot through the kidneys, and Thompson and I thought he wouldn't live. We were up with him all night. I'm glad to say that he recovered completely.

---

[100] See footnote 90 on page 69.

[101] It is not clear how this code worked or what it recorded; no stick is extant.

[102] Norman met up with Teddy Horsfall quite frequently from June 1917 onwards, while he was serving with the 1/5th Lancashire Fusiliers, for example at Ytres on 24th June 1917, at Albert on 22nd August 1917, at Toronto Camp near the Ypres Salient on 16th September 1917, at Coxyde on 20th October 1917, and at Coigneux on 2nd May 1918. On the last mentioned occasion Norman was on the verge of going down with trench fever, and says of Teddy *"he was always like a tonic"*. At the end of the diary, in Volume 5, is pasted a Christmas card sent in 1916 *by "Captain Edward Horsfall MC of the 1/8th Manchester Regiment, 42nd East Lancashire Division"*, from the Egyptian Front.

14.08.15 to 19.08.15	This tour in the Line seemed full of interesting incidents and adventures. The saying is that "it never rains but it pours". It is difficult for me to be precise about exact dates of all the incidents on this tour, but where I can allocate specific dates I will. Captain Joe Hedley was in command of "Z" Company while the Skipper was on leave. I went up several nights to the Front Line to spend the night with Joe. I appreciated being able to ramble all over our Battalion Sector. It must have been very monotonous being confined to a Company Sector of Line. Joe and I had some interesting prowls round the Line. One night the Boche got a Machine Gun trained on Oban Avenue where "Z" Company HQ was, firing right down the trench. Joe started to go out a few yards in front of me, and rather humorously turned back, saying, "Give me my umbrella, old thing, it sounds as if it was raining." In reality it was bullets whizzing overhead – luckily Fritz was firing high or else, well! Who knows?[v]

Another night, going past a place where our fellows were working outside the trench on the parapet face, suddenly the same Machine Gun opened out – a man bounded over the parapet, and fell headlong into the trench crying out, "Somebody's hit mi' wi' a b —— brick." It was Private Scully. Then he fainted; so we carried him to Company HQ, examined him, and found he had got a beautiful clean bullet wound through his arm. He soon cheered up with some brandy, food and a smoke, and we packed him off to the Aid Post. Latter, Kemp, Harker and I had some rather good sport ratting. The Line was very bad for rats – swarms of big fat devils. We used to mount guard on a rat hole in Latter's dug out and fire our revolvers at the beasts. Latter was quite a crack shot. The back of his chair in the dug out had several holes through – where he had missed his target.

The wood near HQ got rather unpleasant periodically during the day time – just short quick strafes, chiefly whizz-bangs[103] – old Fritz taking pot shots in the hopes of catching some one. Had several near squeaks but "a miss is as good as a mile". Anyway I picked up one or two quite nice shell fuses.[vi]

On August 16th the Germans started rather a heavy "Hate" in the afternoon for about an hour, however we retaliated by getting our guns on to Pozières and set one or two houses on fire.

During that particular afternoon (August 16th) Hutty and Captain Simon were engaging a Boche Sniper. Rather foolishly they were lying on the top of a dug out firing. Simon was spotting for Hutty and when he got up on to his knees the Boche hit Simon through the abdomen – a very nasty wound. He was brought down to the Aid Post. Colonel Shirley[104] and Thompson did all they could for him and he was sent down to the Casualty Clearing Station at Millencourt – where unfortunately he died and was buried.[105]

---

[103] Army slang for a type of high velocity shell, usually the 77mm type.

[104] Lieutenant Colonel Shirley had been a medical doctor in his own right before the War – see the footnote to the diary entry for 21st June 1916.

[105] Captain Eric Conrad Simon, son of Henry and Emily Simon, born at Didsbury, Manchester, married to Winifred R. Simon (nee Levy) of Hampstead, died aged 27 on 17th August 1915, and is buried at Millencourt Communal Cemetery, reference F.63, where his gravestone is engraved with the Star of David, in recognition of the fact that he was a Jew. The account in the Battalion War Diary reads: *"Captain Simon had been making an observation of enemies' lines and when returning was shot through the stomach."* Captain Simon was with "D" Company (later called "Z" Company) of the 2/5th Lancashire Fusiliers when they first landed in France on 3rd May 1915. Norman got to know him well when Norman joined "D" Company's Mess from 9th May 1915 until they finished their training at Arques on 8th July 1915, and he has featured frequently in the diary up to his death. He moved to "Y" Company on 5th July 1915, and was the

During this week up the Line we actually had some of "Kitchener's Army" up for instruction. We got the 11th Middlesex Regiment of the 18th Division. Many of these men came from Bury and actually wanted to join the 2/5th Lancashire Fusiliers early in September 1914 before we got authority to form the Battalion. They were very disgusted at coming into the Line for instruction with Territorials, especially a 2nd Line Battalion like ours; they were quite jealous of us having been out so long. Tommy Lucas was with them.[106]

This reminds me of a short story in connection with this instruction. Our guides went down one night to conduct the 11th Middlesex Platoon up to the Line. When they found they were coming to Territorials they were disgusted and made several pertinent remarks to our guide. He waited his opportunity, and when his party got up the Communication Trench which was about 8 feet deep, and as safe as possible, the guide turned to the party and said, "Get down here lads – it's very dangerous and under observation." So the whole Middlesex Platoon got down on their hands and knees in full kit – packs, Gas helmets, rifles, bayonets, rations etc.

After about 50 yards had been covered in this way on all fours, the guide said to the officer, "It's alright now, Sir, quite safe now." So the men got up very hot and excited. Our guide turned to them saying, "That will teach you to laugh at Territorials, why, this trench is as safe as a bloomin' house."

On August 19th the Skipper returned from leave.

The Boche Line in front of Aveluy Wood was over a crest opposite "Z" Company, thus:

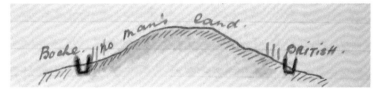

The Line at this point ran as under:

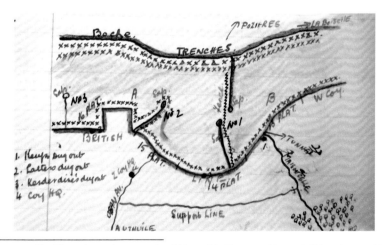

first of the original officers to die. There is a photograph of him with Norman, Kenneth Waterhouse, Hedley, Latter, Kemp, and the Mayor and Mayoress of Arques, taken between 20th May 1915 and 8th July 1915 on page 52.

[106] See footnote 90 on page 69 for "Kitchener's Army". Thomas Turner Lucas, a Bury Grammar School pupil, son of Robert Millett Lucas (who had died in 1904) and Hannah Gee Lucas of the Queen's Hotel, Bury, enlisted in September 1914 as a private with the 12th Battalion (not the 11th) of the Middlesex Regiment, won the DCM at Chérisy in May 1917, then was promoted to Company Sergeant Major. He transferred to the 2/2nd London (Royal Fusiliers) Regiment in April 1918, and died near Amiens on 1st May 1918. He is buried at Crouy British Cemetery, reference I.D.10.

It was not difficult to see, as the Skipper pointed out, that it was imperative that <u>we</u> should occupy the high ground in No Man's Land. If the Boche sapped forward from his Line unknown to us he could gain a vantage point from which he could observe all our movements to his front and indeed to the North and South, for so ran the Line here.

The Skipper drew up a scheme by which this neutral ground was constantly under observation, patrolled, and indeed occupied – thereby in reality becoming ours and no longer No Man's Land. The scheme also included the digging of a trench from Point A on the above diagram, including N° 2 Sap, across to Point B including No 1 Sap, Point B being in "Y" Company's Line.

The Skipper and Joe Hedley, indeed all of us interested in the scheme, were very keen and felt confident of its success.

The points in its favour were

1. Occupation of the high ground in No Man's Land
2. Prevention of the Boche encroaching on No Man's Land
3. Giving <u>us</u> better observation of the Boche
4. Bringing us nearer to the Boche for minor offensive action, raids, patrols etc.
5. Shortening our Line by abolishing the re-entrant AB in our Line
6. Giving us a better field of fire
7. Abandonment of the N° 1 and N° 2 Saps which were long saps (about 200 yards out from our own Line in the case of No 1 Sap)
8. Further, the hedge running across No Man's Land as shown had our N° 1 Sap on the North side and the Boche sap running down the South side. These saps' heads were about 40 yards apart, almost within bombing distance. The holding of N° 1 Sap required six men by night and three by day, and was a constant strain on the men.

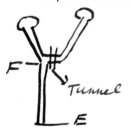

Latter's Platoon held this sap, which had a forked head, as shown in the diagram on the left.

We had previously pushed this sap out 50 yards from the East, the original position. This entailed a lot of work, for the sap from E to F was underground, so as to reduce the chances of the Boche spoiling our new work. Many hours did we dig at this. I used to go up to "Z" Company from HQ to help in the work.

This scheme had been in being from about August 1ˢᵗ. The Skipper had put it forward to the CO, then to Brigade who awaited consent from the Division. They replied that it was under consideration, and – but for the War being over – it would doubtless still be under consideration by some keen energetic "staff loving" Staff Officer.

"Z" Company men were very keen on doing this job. They also saw some chance of getting a real live Boche – just what they wanted!

Constant patrol in No Man's Land was a tremendous strain on officers and men. The men who undertook this work were all volunteers for the job – Corporal Hoyle, Corporal MᶜKay, Lance Corporal Burgon,[107] Lance Corporal Hampson, Private Ronksley, Watts, Wilcox, Greenwood, and Corporal Lord.

---

[107] The only other mention in the diary of Lance Corporal Burgon of "Z" Company is when when he was being presented with the Military Medal at Ripon in April 1918 while Norman was on Home Service there (see the *Afterword* page 273).

Latter and Kemp did most of the work from the commanding point of view. I went out several times with Kemp and Latter on patrol while with the 2/5th Lancashire Fusiliers.

I remember going up to "Z" Company one night. Kemp was due to go out to relieve the day patrol under Latter, but he wasn't fit, so in a weak moment I said I would do his turn for him until Kenderdine came on duty and would come out and relieve me [this night must have been some time after August 23rd 1915, as Kenderdine did not arrive at the Front until then, as desbribed in the diary entry for that date].

I hadn't been out on patrol properly before but I felt very keen to have a go out this night. So with Company Sergeant Major Howard, Lance Corporal Hampson, and two privates, we started out. We found Latter with his fellows anxiously waiting to be relieved as they were very tired and hungry. The relief passed off without incident.

When we had been out for about half an hour I began to feel more at home, for up to then I had felt decidedly uncomfortable, but daren't show that I was frightened. However I spotted a form moving in the grass, then a second, a third, directly in front. The right and left observers also reported movement on their respective flanks – in other words we had encountered a Boche Patrol at least twice our strength, probably more.

I must admit I felt decidedly doubtful what action to take. By this time the Boche were within 15 yards of us and creeping round our flanks; whether they saw us or not I cannot say. Company Sergeant Major Howard was full of beans and bucked me up tremendously.

"We shall get the 'ole bloomin' lot, Sir – or else they'll get us – but there bain't be much fear ow that. Just take it easy, Sir."

We certainly had an advantage. We were waiting for them, looking uphill, which gave us a slight sky line against which their forms and every movement were clearly visible.

The flank observers were withdrawn slightly and our rear guard connecting file kept a keen eye on his job, lest the old Boche drew our attention in front while his pals crept round in rear and cut off our line of retreat back to the Line – thus giving us a free passage to Germany, personally conducted by the old Huns.

Waiting several seconds while the Boche crept nearer and nearer through the long beet-grass – which, being dry, cracked and sounded like guns – my heart seemed to be beating so hard that I felt sure the Boche would hear it. I was intensely excited – strung up to the very highest nerve pitch. For me it was the first time really face to face with a Boche, and a chance of either taking one or more, or killing them.

Seconds seemed like hours. Then our chance – the old Hun within 10 yards. "Hands up you devils!" They made no attempt to come up – taken by surprise they fired their rifles any old way – luckily for us. We, being more prepared, took a more or less (!) deliberate aim. I got my man – at least I heard him curse and saw him roll over.[108] Then there was a few moments of intense excitement and rifle fire.

The Boche got up and ran, dragging his wounded pal with him.

Unfortunately we were prevented from following him by a cross fire from the Boche trench, which was decidedly unpleasant and very low. We were compelled to lie low for some time, then we patrolled the ground to see if we could find any Boche lying about,

---

[108] This is the first of two occasions when Norman describes firing at an individual and either wounding or killing him; see also the diary entry for 4th and 5th August 1916.

but no luck. The bird had flown!

I stayed out for about three hours and was then relieved by Kenders!

It was a <u>great evening</u> – but I will admit when I got back to the trench it felt as safe as a house in a rain storm. I was quite ready for a snack and incidentally a wee tot of brandy. So ended my first patrol – we had no casualties but certainly did several Boche in nicely.

I have described this at some length because it is typical of the class of work which had to be done on the days of Peace Warfare – just carrying on watching and waiting, day after day, night after night, fine weather and wet.

At about this time Captain Jeffreys, the Adjutant, was recalled to his unit, the 1/6th Durham Light Infantry, to command them. We were all very sorry to lose him, but realised what a splendid CO he would be, and wished him good luck in his command. Captain L.H. Bloy took over duties as Adjutant, and, considering his short experience, it was surprising how soon he fell into his new work and did it well. Meanwhile, Colonel Shirley had returned from leave. On his return he brought a sentry dog back with him – one of Major Richardson's. He was a fine big Airedale terrier and we christened him "John Minden".[109] He always wore a Lancashire Fusiliers' badge on his collar with a little plate "*John Minden – 2/5 Lancs Fus – Lt Col H.J. Shirley*".

On the reverse of the original photograph is written "John Minden, Our Regimental Pet"

---

[109] Named after Minden Day – see the footnote to the diary entry for 1st August 1914.

He was no use as a sentry dog; the first time he was taken out on patrol by "X" Company, Barnsdale's Company, John barked – nearly got shot – and lost favour as a protector. But in spite of this he was a great pet and favourite. He had a marvellous sense of loyalty, and would find his way anywhere around the Line. He knew all the short cuts home – especially when he was tired and hungry.

When he first came out – just like the foolish human being – he took a great delight in listening to see shells skimming overhead. In fact he used to run along with his head and ears pricked up and follow them – but one day a Boche 77mm shell burst quite near to him. He got sprinkled with bits of shrapnel. He was not hurt, but he was frightened and ran into the dug out with his tail between his legs. Ever after that experience he learnt what dug outs were made for and, on the first indication of shell fire, you would see "John Minden" discreetly making for cover – so like ourselves.

He was very fond of my bed and often – both in and out of the Line – he used to sleep at the bottom of my bed and, if I wasn't in bed, he used to take up residence on the top.

20.08.15 I fixed up a telephone in my own dug out – from which place I had communication to the Companies in the Line, Flank Battalions, Brigade HQ and the Artillery – quite convenient. I made several switch boards out of wood bases with French cartridges for plugs, so that we had a cut-out system all over our sector – quite an improvement.

22.08.15 It was a glorious day. I went up to see the Skipper and Joe, and had lunch with them. "Z" Company had a very good Company HQ [marked on the plan on page 79], a huge big dug out with a wooden floor, two beds at one end of the dug out, a large dining room table, several chairs, cupboards, shelves, and a stove (the French type, for coal). Opening out of one end of the dug out was a door which led out to some steps and on to a very nice verandah looking away from the Line across the River Ancre valley to Martinsart, Englebelmer, Mesnil, Authuille and Beaumont-Hamel – a glorious view.

There was a table and chairs on the verandah where we used to have afternoon tea.

This particular afternoon nearly ended disastrously for us all. We had all been sitting out on the verandah, talking and smoking and enjoying life, when the Boche put one or two shells over rather near – too near to be pleasant.

The Skipper, being a sensible fellow, advised a temporary retirement to the dug out. Rather against our wishes we went. We just got inside when the Boche <u>very rudely</u> put a shell right on to the verandah where we had all been sitting a few minutes before. What a mess – all our chairs, tables, pots, split! But what a lucky escape for us all.[vii] But it was our beautiful verandah that worried us most and occupied our minds, not the escape from practically certain death, for some of us anyway. We examined the debris and held a council of war as to what should be done with the sight. Skipper had a great scheme. As it was coming winter, a verandah was not a necessity – nor a luxury – so he proposed to dig the place down about 20 feet and make a Mess Room, cut a passage through to the servants' dug out and kitchen, and so make a suite of rooms.

This was an excellent plan – which was eventually put into action and completed. It was a big job but when finished it was great.

The Mess Room was all wooden floor and walls, with a window. A table and more chairs were purloined from Authuille village. Then we covered the walls with green canvas and got some pictures and made quite a cosy home, large enough to seat twelve at the table. However more of this later [in the diary entry for 11th September 1915].

Later the Hun had a rare old Hate at us, shells, Machine Guns, rifle fire – flares – all gone mad. Quite a fine sight, and luckily he did no damage.

I heard that George had been promoted to Lieutenant – quite time too.

23.08.15   Four new officers joined the Battalion:[110]

Lieutenant Kenderdine	Lancashire Fusiliers
2nd Lieutenant S.L. Moffatt	Lancashire Fusiliers
2nd Lieutenant C.H. Moffatt	Lancashire Fusiliers
Lieutenant Humble	Notts and Derby

They arrived at Battalion HQ at about 8.45pm, had some dinner, and then went up to their Companies. Kenderdine and Moffatt C.H. went to "Z" Company, Moffatt S.L. went to "X" Company, and Humble went to "W" Company. I took Kenderdine and Moffatt up to "Z" Company at about 10.00pm.

For some nights previous to this Fritz seemed to have taken either an intense dislike or affection to the Communication Trench running up past my dug out – the Aid Post – and up Maisoncelle to "Z" Company Front Line. He used to sweep round in bursts every few minutes. When we started off I warned Kenderdine and Moffatt about this Machine Gun and told them to be ready to lie down quickly.

They thought I was pulling their leg, it being their first time in the Line. But very soon after we left HQ, Fritz started his little game, and it was only by pushing Kenderdine down that he missed being hit. We lay down for almost 10 minutes. One bullet made rather a mess of the heel of my boot – nothing worse.[viii] Then we made our way up to "Z" Company. I got back at about 2.00am.

25.08.15   On this particular day I received orders from the Brigade Signalling Officer, Lieutenant Peak RE,[111] that I was to establish visual signalling by electric lamp from a point near HQ in the Line to a point near Divisional HQ at Senlis – as the crow flies a distance of about 7 miles – and also with Brigade HQ Station which was situated at the point where the Decauville Railway[112] crosses the Aveluy – Bouzincourt – Martinsart – Albert road, the point being

---

[110] The Battalion War Diary agrees that four officers joined the Battalion that day, but names them as Humble, Kenderdine, Lieutenant S. Cooper and 2nd Lieutenant E.H. Fryer; the Moffatt brothers' Medal Cards suggest that they in fact joined on 11th November 1915, but the Battalion War Diary for November to December 1915 is missing. Norman does not mention them again before 11th November 1915, apart from Cecil once on page 99.

[111] Norman says of Peak (sometimes spelt "Peake"): "*He was an exceedingly nice fellow. He was about my own age and we really got on very well together. He was an old Cheltonian, and a pre-war Cadet at Woolwich Military Academy, or "The Shop", as it is better known in the Army.*"

[112] Decauville was a manufacturing company which was founded by Paul Decauville (1846-1922), specialising in the manufacture of light narrow-gauge railway track produced in ready-made sections. These light railway tracks clearly had their uses, but were not always problem-free. For example in his diary entry for 29th June 1917 Norman writes: "*From Ypres to Neuville on the edge of Havrincourt Wood there ran up a Decauville Railway track – this being a narrow gauge track with small trucks and engine. I was detailed as Rail Transport Officer for the move ... I travelled on the fourth train with "B" Company, with Horace Bentley. One of the couplings broke on our 'diner', and Horace had to run after the first portion to get them to come back for us. It was a fine track; you had to hold hard or else slip off – they were open trucks, and we sat on the sides or floor or any old place.*" On 2nd September 1917, when a light railway was used to bring troops from Ypres to Goldfish Chateau, Norman says it was "*a scheme which was voted by the officers and men as rather more trouble than it was worth for the short time.*"

marked on the maps as Halt, it being a place where the narrow gauge train from Albert used to stop in Peace time [see page 66 and the sketch of Aveluy on page 89].

I chose my position on the Western edge of Aveluy Wood, a few minutes' walk from Battalion HQ. It was near a Support Post governing Authuille village, which Post at this time was held by a detachment of Bengal Lancers belonging to the 1st Indian Cavalry Division, who were holding the sector on our left.

Knowing this Post to be held by Indian troops I thought it advisable to warn their Regimental HQ in Authuille of my intention to establish a Signal Station near their Detached Post. I thought it might save trouble.

So on the evening of August 25th about 10.00pm I took two of my Signallers – Nuttall and Taylor – to this place, with a lamp. We set up our lamp, and got an alignment on the Brigade Station, and established communication. Whilst busy signalling we were challenged in some foreign lingo from our right. Turning round I saw two huge burly black figures in turbans – below which I could distinguish a black face and a black moustache and beard – the blackness only relieved by two rows of white teeth. I also heard movement in the thick undergrowth in the wood behind and saw a figure stealthily creeping behind us, but passing us and posting himself on our left – being the direction from which we had come. This fellow had a nice shining bayonet which scarcely looked hospitable in the bright moonlight – for it was a perfect night. Then the challenge came again.

To argue, or to continue our work, was futile. To ignore the challenge was merely asking for trouble. So I answered, "Friend – Lancashire Fusiliers."

By this time I had a bayonet pointed at my chest, and only a few inches away. When I moved, so moved the bayonet. It was useless to try to explain what I was doing there. No one could speak or understand English. So I decided to give myself up and told Nuttall and Taylor to remain with the lamp until I returned. I motioned to the village and asked to be taken to a British officer. So I was marched off under escort of two Black Bengal Lancers. On the way down across the fields to Authuille village, I decided to have a cigarette, but the mere fact of my getting out my case seemed to rouse the suspicions of my escort, and evidently I wasn't popular.

However, we reached the village without incident and I was taken to the Adjutant whom I had seen in the afternoon. I explained my object in signalling, and then related how his men had arrested me. He and the other officer in the Mess were very amused. However, after a quiet chat, smoke, and drink, the Adjutant explained to the escort that I was quite harmless – not a Boche – and we were to be allowed to continue our signalling without interruption. So I retraced my steps to the wood, along the Aveluy to Authuille road.

It really was a gorgeous moonlit night – not a sound – no shells – no rifle fire – just a few birds could be heard bidding one another good night – but, apart from these sounds of Nature's life, everything was quiet. The War might have been miles away, instead of us being scarcely half a mile from the Front Line. Yet how quickly – without warning – could the whole scene have been changed into one of noise and death; and this uncertainty – the constant strain – never knowing from one minute to another what might happen – really made fellows appreciate life in a way they had never done before, or, as Captain Jeffreys used to say in his characteristic manner, "You know, it makes you think."

As I went down the road I passed a group of Indian soldiers making their evening prayers. There was a special enclosure just outside the village on the roadside set apart for religious ceremonies for the Indians.

Then my escort – but no longer escort (for I was a free man) – grinning all over his face and showing his white teeth said "Compris Hindustan?", but I didn't compris Hindustan, so that what might have developed into an interesting conversation never materialised.

So I arrived back to the Alarm Signal Station, very much relieved to find Nuttall and Taylor quite safe. It was a rather unpleasant experience all round, but it might have been worse, for the Indian troops are fine soldiers; they shoot first and apologise after.

We continued our signalling, picking up first the Brigade Station and then the Division, but they were quite annoyed at our delay in not calling up before. Lucky for us we were able to call up at all!

A further interruption occurred about 2.00am when the Boche spotted the Brigade lamp and immediately put down a salvo of shells round it. We never saw their light again that night, and heard later that a shell fragment had broken the lens, and two men were wounded. So ended an interesting test of our emergency visual positions, and we turned in about 3.00am – quite ready.

27.08.15   In the afternoon Corporal McKay and Lance Corporal Hampson were out on the daylight shift. They got sick of doing nothing and – just like Hampson, of whom I shall have more to say – he and McKay had a stroll round in the daylight in No Man's Land. They found a sniper's hole in a shell crater out in No Man's Land. It had been recently occupied for there were rations – biscuits, meat, chocolate, tobacco and a newspaper.

We had been worried by a sniper from that direction for some nights, but could not locate him definitely. However here was his Post – and there was a clear trodden track through the long grass from the Boche trench to this hole, clearly indicating constant use.

Leaving a couple of men to watch this hole and deal with any Hun approaching it, Corporal McKay and Lance Corporal Hampson returned to make the report to Captain Waterhouse. McKay had made a sketch of the situation. In conjunction with the Skipper, a plan was made to cover this Post that evening by a patrol.

At last there seemed a chance of realising our ambition – a real live juicy fat Boche!

The Skipper telephoned me to let me know the latest news.

Everyone wanted to go out. But a selection was necessary. Latter and Kemp took charge with Corporal McKay, Corporal Hoyle, Lance Corporal Hampson, and Private Ronksley; and I was a hanger on. The plan of action was this:

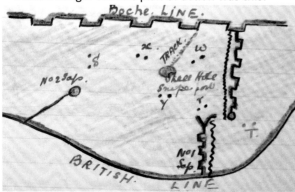

1. McKay and Lance Corporal Hampson to position W

2. Hoyle and Ronksley to position X

3. Kemp and myself to position Y

4. Positions S and T were to be Covering Posts for protection from flank attack.

The orders were for Post W to allow any Boche to pass them and occupy the shell hole, then, immediately the Boche had occupied, to challenge them – which was dangerous as they were near the Boche sap head; but a party was sent from our N° 1 Sap to draw their attention at Post T.

Post X was to close in behind the shell hole to prevent retreat of the Boche, whereupon I was to go to Post X and Kemp to Post W.

The Boche came out as expected, but, instead of two as we expected, four came out and moved to their position. McKay challenged. But there was no response from the Boche. So he closed in behind them, Hoyle also closing in, while Kemp and I separated. Then there was rapid movement by the Boche. A shot was fired, quickly followed by several more – intense excitement once again!

I got to Ronksley who fired and hit a Boche – there was a loud explosion – whereupon Ronksley very humorously remarked, "Eh Sir, I never thought as 'ow a Boche went off wi' a pop like yon fellow when I 'it 'im."

Then we crept forward and heard another Boche moaning, while two others, the third and fourth, ran off and got clear. On examining the shell hole we found two Boche near it, both hit. One was dead – or practically so – the other was hit in the arm and making an awful commotion. Hampson and Ronksley were very funny with this fellow, threatening all kinds of things if he didn't get a move on towards our Line. The other man we carried in – he was an awful mess; Ronksley had hit a bomb he was carrying round his neck – the bomb exploded on the Boche's chest and simply blew his chest and lungs open – this man was dead.

When we were coming in Corporal Hoyle – after his strenuous ten days of patrolling and watching, and the final excitement of this melee – temporarily lost his reason – but recovered in a few days.

The stretcher bearers came for our Prize Boche. I rushed down to HQ to break the good news and warn Thompson of the Boche coming down. Latter also came down with the Boche.

We had a time with the wounded Boche – he would shout and make an awful row, and when we offered him morphia he imagined we were trying to poison him. However, he took some Brandy and eventually the morphia. Thompson decided to take the Boche's arm off, so I started to help him – some dirty business after being on patrol and all the excitement.

Thompson talked to the Hun and found out he was a butcher from Mannheim. He was married and had two children. And he was continuously talking about his wife. Eventually he quietened down and we sent him off to the Casualty Clearing Station.

The dead Boche was also brought down. We wanted to get his identity disc and eventually I managed to extricate a part of it from his lung. His name was WERNER ALBERT, BAVARIAN REGIMENT. He was only 18.

We got his papers from his pocket and found a letter to his mother half-finished, in which he had written just prior to coming out on this his last patrol, "I have been ordered to go on patrol. I will finish this when I return …" The letter was never finished. This boy was an Unteroffizier. If you were to go to Aveluy Military Cemetery near Albert you would see this boy's grave with a neat cross made by our prisoners.[113]

Kemp got a very nice Boche automatic pistol and we also got a Boche bayonet which today hangs in the Officers' Mess at the Bury Drill Hall, as a souvenir of the first Boche captured by the 2/5th Lancashire Fusiliers.[114]

When all was over, I – like the Boche – felt very groggy for an hour or two, after fighting and operating etc.

28.08.15   Today we were to be relieved in the Line after a 15 days' tour. The weather had been glorious almost all the time. We had been able to take our meals out in the open under the trees in the wood. It really was glorious, and – except for occasional short Hates by the Hun – it was like a picnic.

HQ, "W" Company, "X" Company, and "Y" Company, were to proceed to billets in Aveluy after relief. "Z" Company were to proceed to Post Donnet, in Support to the 1/8th Liverpool Irish, who would relieve the 1/4th King's Own Royal Lancasters, then holding the Right Battalion Sector of our Brigade Front.

Owing to shortage of troops on the British Front at this time, each Battalion was compelled to hold long Fronts. The Left Sector Front was about 2000 yards, as a result of which the Front Line Battalion could not find their own Supports and had a company of the Reserve or Support Battalion in support. That was the reason for "Z" Company going to Post Donnet, and it meant that "Z" Company would probably do five weeks in trenches without a break; which, after their strenuous time of the past 15 days, was a bit heavy. However "Z" Company were always cheery under Ken Waterhouse, Joe Hedley, and the rest.

It was a stifling hot day, which at about 8.15pm began to cloud over, with every indication of a heavy storm, probably thunder.

At about 8.30pm the heavens seemed to literally burst – rain came down in torrents, and it thundered and lightened. The lightning in the middle of a dense wood was almost blinding, and the echoing roar of the thunder peals almost terrifying. The Boche suddenly took it into his head to have a share in the upheaval. Whether it was that he wished to try and outdo Nature in her efforts, or that the thunder and lightning was an indication of his famous Hymn of Hate "Gott strafe England", I cannot say – but he certainly added to the unpleasantness of the night.

On reaching Aveluy, not very far away from the Line – still, far enough to feel the strain of the Front Line partially removed – I was soon asleep. I was thoroughly tired out after the past 15 days, which had been rather a strenuous tour with numerous mini-adventures to relieve the monotony of trench warfare.

---

[113] Norman visited this grave later in the War, on 21st August 1917 – see the passage giving an account of the visit which is set out in the *Afterword* on pages 277-278. The Battalion War Diary describes the man as "*Under Officer W. Alber of the 121st Reserve Regiment, XIII Corps*". The website of Volksbund Deutsche Kriegsgräberfürsorge has a record of a Werner Alber, born on 18th July 1898 at Ravensburg. He is described as a private on the website, but as the website also records his death as having occurred on 27th August 1915 at Authuille, it must be the same man. Assuming that it is the same man, he is now buried at the German Military Cemetery at Rancourt, and was in fact only just 17 when he died, not 18.

[114] This bayonet is no longer displayed in the Drill Hall, and its whereabouts are not known.

Aveluy, Martinsart, Senlis and Aveluy again
29th August 1915 to 4th November 1915

29.08.15   Welcome to Aveluy.

A brief description of Aveluy might be interesting here.

It was a small village about three quarters of an hour's march from the Line.

The main road ran West to East from Albert (Bouzincourt) through the village, where it branched into a triangle, the roads meeting again near the bridge to Crucifix Corner, a well known place – probably as well known as any point in the Somme District. Here the road branched to the North to Authuille, Mesnil, and Thiepval, and on to the Ancre Valley road up to Achiet-le-Grand. The other branch went South East over the crest of the hill to La Boiselle, where it cut the main Albert to Bapaume road [see also the map on page 66].

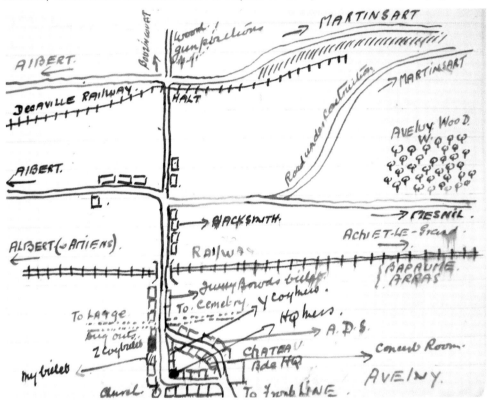

The village itself had a normal population of only about 500 inhabitants. The houses were fair. There was a church and a few Chateaux with very fine grounds and stables. On either side of the road running from the bridge to Crucifix Corner the land was flooded, due to the fact that, when the Germans attacked over this ground in September 1914, they cut the river bank when they were driven back by the French, and flooded the valley for several miles.

John Minden, the regimental pet, standing in flood water, probably near Aveluy; see the plan on page 75

The village at this time was not badly damaged, though the village was subjected to shell fire occasionally, and a few houses had been razed to the ground.[115]

There were one or two shops, several estaminets, and a blacksmith's shop. The Civilian Cemetery was very prettily situated and the British Cemetery was sited adjacent to it. We were able to get a very good supply of fresh fruit – plums, peaches, pears, bananas, and good vegetables – at reasonable prices.

The Doctor and I had a jolly good billet over a shop – quite a nice cosy room, and very clean. We could see the Support Line trenches across the valley.

On 29th August I slept until 8.30am, got up, had a good hot bath, a complete change, and a fresh uniform – and felt really civilised again. I got down to breakfast at about 9.30am, and

The Ancre marshes in front of Aveluy (this photograph was taken in 1916 when Aveluy was in ruins); see the plan on page 75

enjoyed bacon and eggs. The weather had picked up again, and it was a glorious sunny morning with a nice cool breeze. I had an Active Service haircut, and felt A1 after it.

I went out with Peak[116] to see the Right Sector Line in front of La Boiselle, which was very wet from the previous night's storm.

We sent up a board to the Front Line painted "RIGA" to be put out in front of our barbed wire to annoy the Boche. He simply riddled the thing with bullets – more than he could do to Riga,[117] for he was compelled to evacuate it.

I began to really think there might be a chance of leave home.

Waddicar souvenired a nice brass candle stick for me – very useful.

30.08.15   We spent the day cleaning up and getting the men dry from the previous night's soaking.

---

[115] See the the similar observation onpage 70 regarding lack of damage in the diary entry for 31st July 1915, and the footnote there.

[116] Also referred to as "Peake".

[117] The Battle of the Gulf of Riga was a naval operation of the German High Seas Fleet against the Russian Baltic Fleet in the Gulf of Riga in the Baltic Sea in August 1915. The German fleet had set out to destroy the Russian fleet, but failed to achieve this objective, and were obliged to retreat.

The HQ Mess was in quite a nice house with a good room for a Mess Room. We soon made it quite cosy and put up our usual array of pictures.

31.08.15 The Colonel lent me his horse and Noton borrowed the CO's second horse. We had a glorious ride over the country to Bouzincourt, through Martinsart and Martinsart Wood, and then across the fields to call on Jimmy Bowd at the Transport Lines. It was glorious, and really a nice change from the trenches. We arrived back for lunch.
Occasionally I used to borrow Captain Waterhouse's horse, "Sandy Mac", a nice horse, which had a very peculiar action and ran in three-quarter time, but was quite an easy beast to ride. We used to call him the Rocking Horse. He was a chestnut with four white fetlocks. Newhouse, the Skipper's groom, knew how to look after him and always turned "Sandy Mac" out very clean and well groomed. The leathers and saddlery were beautiful.
In the afternoon our Gunners shelled the Boche hard, and he retaliated, putting shell on the cross roads up the village. One of our men was on traffic control duty up there and the concussion of the shell-burst a few feet from him blew him right across the road. I was too near to be really comfortable, but neither of us was hit – luckily.[ix]

02.09.15 In the evening I was asked to go up to Post Donnet to have dinner with "Z" Company. I hadn't seen the Skipper or Uncle Joe for several days. I asked the CO whether I might go up and he gave consent. It was lucky I had taken the precaution of asking permission as things turned out. I found "Z" Company as cheery as ever. They were quite comfortably fixed up in the Support Line with good dug outs, but they were having rather a strenuous time finding working parties, and occasional bursts of shelling; however, no damage was done. We had quite a good evening, and a very nice little dinner, the menu of which was as follows:
Beef, beans, carrots, potatoes
Stewed fruit
Cheese, coffee, pears, peaches, plums
Waterhouse broke some news to me during the evening. It was rumoured that Captain Hartley Goldsmith was leaving the Battalion, which would mean a vacancy in the command of "W" Company. It was suggested that Joe Hedley would take over "W" Company, thus leaving Captain Waterhouse without a 2nd in Command. He seemed very keen that I should go to him for the job. I was very bucked that he had asked me, and there was no one I would rather go to than the Skipper, although I was very keen on my signalling and liked living at HQ – they were such a cheery crowd – so that, if the matter developed, I felt rather undecided whether to accept Ken's offer – provided the CO gave his consent. However, for the time it was all conjecture.
After our chat we settled down to a game of bridge, as we were only in Support. "Z" Company never played cards in the Front Line – the Skipper was very strict about this point. At about 10.20pm we were just thinking of turning in. I had decided to stay the night at "Z" Company HQ. However, I got a call to the telephone. The message ran: "Lieutenant Hall will report immediately to the Colonel at the Crucifix Corner – very urgent." Damn! Just my expression. What did it mean – what was the matter? Everything seemed quite peaceful. However, I picked up my revolver and hurried off at the double.

I decided to go down the road instead of the trench – it was quicker. It only took me a few minutes to cover the three quarters of a mile to the Crucifix. When I got there, there was not a soul was in sight. My first thought was that someone was pulling my leg, so I walked down towards the village, as the CO was nowhere about, thinking I might meet him.

Very soon I met "W" Company's leading platoon with Gray. "Hello, what's the trouble, Gray – bit of a bother on – have you seen the CO?" "Yes, he's down by the bridge."

All the men looked decidedly like business in full kit.

Then I met Kemp looking very excited with his bombers. "Where are you off to, Kemp, with your suicide club?" "Oh, the Boche has attacked at Authuille Wood, and we're off to do the devils in."

"Get away," I said, "Why, I've just come down from Post Donnet, and it's perfectly quiet and peaceful – not a shot being fired."

A few yards further down I met the CO (Colonel Shirley) at last.

I saluted. "Any orders for me, Sir?"

"Yes, Hall – the Boche have attacked from Thiepval. We are to go up in Reserve to support the Right Sector of the Left Brigade. Your Signallers will occupy their Alarm Posts as laid down – Battalion HQ will be as for Alarm Positions. You proceed there and collect reports from OC Companies when they are in position. "Z" Company will take instructions from OC Right Battalion, Left Sector."

I just remarked to the CO that all was quiet when I came down from "Z" Company, and said, "I suppose it's a test?" He smiled and said, "Yes!", but added that I mustn't tell anyone.

My HQ Signallers didn't turn up, so I had to get in touch with Brigade HQ with a flash lamp. Also my telephone wire from Alarm to HQ wouldn't work. The CO wanted to know why, so I replied, "Just been destroyed by a shell, Sir." (Liar!) – But one has to use one's initiative in an emergency.

The Battalion got into position quite satisfactorily, the test was considered quite creditable, and the order was sent round by runner to OC Companies to stand down. Didn't the men curse – having turned out of bed and no fun for their trouble, as they put it.

I was six Signallers deficient. Where were they? Possibly they had gone to the Front Line Visual Station near the Indian Post described in the entry relating to August 25th, in which case they might experience the same trouble that I had had a few nights previous to this. I told the CO I would go up there and see – it was about 2 miles; however, he wouldn't allow me to go alone, and insisted on coming with me, in spite of my assurance that I should be quite alright alone, although I must admit that I was quite pleased to have company. When I got in view of the Post I tried to get an answer with my flash light – without success. So we went right up to the Post, were challenged by the Indian Sentry, and had almost the same unpleasant experience I had before. However the CO managed to speak enough Hindustani[118] (!!) to satisfy the Post who we were and what we wanted. But there were no Signallers – so we went back to Aveluy, where we found my men. They had been up to the Indian Post, signalled to Brigade for three quarters of an hour – watched by the Indians – and then they managed to get away. So I cursed them soundly

---

[118] Lieutenant Colonel Shirley had been born in India in 1868, to a father who was practising as a barrister in Madras.

for not complying with my instructions for Alarm Posts, which had been issued immediately we came to the village. So we turned in at about 2.00am, quite tired, and my night out with "Z" Company had been somewhat spoilt.

03.09.15   The weather was very unsettled. Peak,[119] the Brigade Signalling Officer, came down and had dinner with us at Battalion HQ. We had a good game of bridge and played the gramophone. We went up for tea with a fellow belonging to the 1st City of Aberdeen Battery Royal Field Artillery 15 pounder. They were very excited as they expected to get the new 18 pounder any day.
We were invited to go up to the opening shoot when the new gun arrived.

04.09.15   "Z" Company came down from Post Donnet to billets in Aveluy. We packed up our kits onto the Transport, which came down from Bouzincourt to Aveluy, and took our kits and stores etc. to Martinsart.
The Battalion paraded at 4.30pm and moved to Martinsart, about 3 miles, arriving at 5.30pm. The Doctor and I joined at a room again, at the farm where the Orderly Room and HQ details were billeted.
It was rather a cold room with a tiled floor, which Waddicar assiduously scrubbed, and eventually discovered that the tiles were red.
I slept on a stretcher with my valise on the top. It made quite a comfortable bed.

05.09.15   I rode over to Bouzincourt to get the money from the Field Cashier. I took "John Minden" with me. He was very fond of going out with me and dearly loved to follow a horse over the fields. He was very obedient and intelligent. I almost taught him to signal in the Morse Code by wagging his tail!
I managed to get hold of two rather nice souvenirs:
German shell (nose) fuse which I had made into an inkstand;
77mm shell fuse made into a cigarette lighter.
I was quite excited, wondering whether a parcel of Japanese Kisses (Arques Cakes[120]) would arrive by the mail in time for afternoon tea.
Almost all the officers went out for a ride. They looked like a riding school turning out. I was much too lazy after my morning ride – so took life easily.

06.09.15   It was a glorious day. The men were out on working parties most days while we were up at Martinsart. They got a big day of it from 7.00am until about 6.30pm. They had to march about 6 miles to the Line, then dig all day, and come back after their hard day's work. But they were very fit and in good spirits.
We arranged a Mounted Gymkhana at Bouzincourt, on the high ground between Bouzincourt and Martinsart.
The show started at about 2.30pm. We could see the trenches from the ground, and it seemed quite strange to be having an afternoon of that nature within view of the Hun. But what did we care? In fact we had quite forgotten there were such people as the Boche for the time being. The events at the gymkhana were:

---

[119] Also referred to as "Peake".
[120] See the diary entry for 21st to 30th June 1915 for why they were called Arques cakes.

1st event

Ride 200 yards, dismount, take an apple from a bucket of water with your teeth, mount, ride back, still holding the apple in your teeth. My horse went back riderless.

2nd event

Ride 200 yards, dismount, thread a needle, light a cigarette, and ride back.

3rd event

Musical chairs round a circle made of flags. At various intervals there were posts with caps on. When the music stopped – the music, by the way, being a concertina – you had to take a cap off a pole. The one who didn't get a cap was out. Major Milnes won.

4th event

Ride in and out of tall poles without touching the poles, using the left hand only for guiding and controlling the horse. The one who did it in the shortest time won, two seconds being added for each contact with a post.

5th event

One mile cross country race – horses.

6th event

Half mile race on mules.

Major Milnes got a mule which bucked at both ends at once. He was very amusing. Kemp's mule insisted on taking him through a hedge.

We had afternoon tea under the trees and altogether had a very amusing afternoon. Joe Hedley and Little Barwood[121] were especially funny as bookies.

I was sixth on the list for leave; I was quite excited – it was due in about 10 weeks' time.

I had dinner with the Skipper and Joe Hedley, quite a good evening as usual.

I was keeping very fit and thoroughly enjoying the life.

07.09.15 to 09.09.15	The weather was glorious. During this week we carried on with the usual billet life, training in the mornings, bathing the Battalion etc. In the afternoons we usually had a ride. We went into Albert a few times, the chief item of news being an increase in the leave allotment.
10.09.15	In the afternoon I went to call on Major Boon D85 Battery 4.5" howitzers. Major Boon was a very fine soldier, and an exceedingly nice man. He had fought through the Mons Retreat, Le Cateau, and the Aisne Battles. He won the DSO and MVO. All his officers were excellent fellows. We went down to see his guns firing, the Battery position being just off the Martinsart to Mesnil Road, near the Cemetery, and on the Decauville Railway,[122] quite

---

[121] This is the last mention of Lieutenant A.V. Barwood until 18th February 1917, when Norman went to Fountains Abbey with him while they were both on Home Service in Ripon. He was with "B" Company of the 2/5th Lancashire Fusiliers when they first landed in France on 3rd May 1915, but is not otherwise mentioned as being with the 2/5th Lancashire Fusiliers apart from here, though there is a photograph of him with Duckworth, Hartington and Barnsdale, probably taken in September 1915, on page 65 (in which he is markedly smaller than the others, hence, presumably, the nickname "Little"). It is not clear what happened to him, but he was not one of the seven original officers referred to as still being with the 2/5th Lancashire Fusiliers in the diary entry for 21st to 26th August 1916. On 30th June 1918 he is referred to as *"late of the 2/5th Lancashire Fusiliers"*; at that time he was a Rail Transport Officer at Gézaincourt, and was travelling with Norman on No 26 Ambulance Train having had an unspecified accident.

[122] See footnote 112 on page 84; see also the plan on page 66.

a good position. The Gun Pits were dug into the hedges, and well camouflaged from enemy aeroplane observation. He did a shoot for me, the observations being carried out by a forward observing officer who was in an Observation Post in the Front Line and in telephone communication with his Battery. All the ranging and correction for fire was controlled by the forward officer.

It was most interesting to see the charges being put into the cartridge cases. The charges look like small life belts and are numbered from 1 to 5. They contain the propellant charge. The number used varies according to the type of trajectory the shell is to travel, i.e. whether a flat trajectory or at a steep angle of descent. The greater the number of charges employed the greater the muzzle velocity of the shell, and the flatter the trajectory. We were shooting on the MouquetFarm (this position was famous later for very heavy fighting in the 1916 Somme Offensive, and was a tough nut to crack).

We had a very exciting incident during the afternoon. The gun is brought into the loading position and then clamped in the firing position. The gun was placed in the firing position but evidently <u>not</u> clamped, the result being that – when the striker came forward – the shell, in travelling down the barrel, tipped the barrel; thus, instead of the shell whizzing over the bank directly in front of the Battery position, it struck the bank and burst. Many shell fragments blew back with tremendous force over the gun. Luckily we were behind the shrapnel shield – otherwise I might not be writing this diary.[x] Fortunately no-one was hurt – but we were all a little surprised and shaken for a few minutes.

Goldsmith left the Battalion and was attached to the District Office of the RE at Divisional HQ at Senlis.[123] Consequently Captain Hedley left "Z" Company and took over command of "W" Company, thus leaving Ken Waterhouse without a 2nd in Command.

11.09.15   We went into the Line again – the Aveluy Wood Sector. We had the same old wooden huts – Doctor Thompson decided it was like going home (nearly!). The Doctor had a busy time going up, as there were one or two casualties on the way up, and only turned in at 1.30am. We relieved the 1/4th Loyal North Lancashires.

We built a new Mess Room[124] – quite a posh wooden hut with steel girder roofing, having a double air space roof as an extra bursting cushion for shells, then about 8 feet of loose earth on top – whizz-bang-proof only.[125] Still, it was weather-proof, and we hoped Fritz wasn't going to throw quite all Krupps'[126] works at us at once. The Mess Room had a jolly nice fire place, which our Battalion bricksetter – one Private Bradly – made in one of his sober periods. Fancy being able to sit in front of a real fire grate with a real fire of coal in

---

[123] This is the last reference to Captain G. Hartley Goldsmith in the diary, apart from in the diary entry for 8th/9th January 1916, q.v. He was with "A" Company of the 2/5th Lancashire Fusiliers when they first landed in France on 3rd May 1915, having first reported to the Drill Hall in Bury on 12th September 1914, and applied for a commission in the 5th Reserve Lancashire Fusiliers. He has featured frequently in the diary up to this point, especially during the period of training in England (where Norman says that he, Kenneth Waterhouse, Barnsdale, Norman, and Norman's brother, George, all sat together at Mess at Southport – see the diary entry for 8th November to 13th December 1914), and as one of the competition fishermen in France in June 1915, then being in the trenches the first time the 2/5th Lancashire Fusiliers were really under fire on 18th July 1915.
[124] See the diary entry for 22nd August 1915 for how the decision to build this Mess Room at Battalion HQ, known as Post Lesdos, came about, and the entry for the first part of December 1915 on pages 126-7 for its later decline. See also the visit on 21st August 1917 mentioned in the *Afterword* on page 278.
[125] Whizz-bang was army slang for a type of high velocity shell, usually the 77mm type.
[126] Krupps was a German arms manufacturer.

the trenches. Glorious! Where did we get the fire place? Well, some house in the village had one missing. That's all! But what a jar leaving a nice fire to go out at night round the Line.

13.09.15   Thompson brought a mouth organ up the Line with him – probably it was made by our "friend" the Hun across the way. Anyway, it kept the MO quiet. This particular evening he practised very energetically in our dug out. He played any old thing – including hymn "tunes". Rather an amusing incident occurred. My Signallers were having a concert over the phone. First one station would sing a song, then another would add their turn, giving a recitation. Eventually, with difficulty, I persuaded Thompson to give them an instrumental solo on the mouth organ. This was greatly appreciated. Then he gave a Scottish Song.

At last I really had to stop this improper use of a field telephone and I spoke to my HQ Signallers on the matter. Their reply was that there was some B —— Scotchman singing – or, if he wasn't a Scotchman, he was a jolly good imitation. Thompson was very amused at the latter idea, for he was a very broad Glasgow Scotchman. From this he was often known as the "Imitation Scotchman".

So after a cup of bivouac cocoa and a dip into the contents of a parcel from home, I retired to sleep at 11.15pm – hoping not to wake in "a fitful dream".

14.09.15   Nothing exciting happened in the next few days – the same old watching and waiting –
to   expecting. The same old trenches. Stand to morning and evening. Yards and yards of
18.09.15   barbed wire put out, and yet it never seemed thick enough. Patrols, working parties, ration parties – and so the days went on.

I wrote to Bill (my sister, Kathleen) and ordered Packers to send her a Lancashire Fusiliers' brooch for her 18th birthday.

Effie

19.09.15   I got a great surprise. I heard from my brother, George, with the following remark, "Dear Jim, I have found another sister-in-law for you to tease in the future." And I wondered whether I ever should tease her!

Effie (my future sister-in-law) enclosed a postcard and we started from that day to correspond.

I was just longing to see George's Ideal Girl – and I must say I wondered and puzzled in my mind to imagine what she would be like.

I was very busy, re-wiring the HQ Signals Office, labelling all wires with wooden labels and numbers, separating Infantry lines from Artillery lines. I made several switch boards with French cartridge cases and bullets. I got a fine specimen of a German 77mm shell fuse from Corporal Nuttall.

I practically decided to give up the Signalling Officer's job and to go to Kenneth Waterhouse as 2nd in Command of "Z" Company. Colonel Shirley recommended me to the General for promotion to Captain. I was rewarded for all the hard work on Signals, leaving the Section in a very efficient state – due entirely to the hard work of the fellows.

Major Milnes went on leave. We did miss him.

I turned in at 12.15am for a few hours' rest.

20.09.15   We were making preparations for relief in the Line.

21.09.15 to 24.09.15	On September 21st we marched via Aveluy and Bouzincourt to Senlis, about 6 miles from the Line, arriving at about 2.30am. On September 23rd I ceased to be a Signalling Officer with HQ, and went to "Z" Company as 2nd in Command to Waterhouse. Waddicar went with me to "Z" Company. We had quite good billets on Warloy Road. I was busy getting in touch with the Company.

We decided that I should be entirely responsible for the "Q" side of the Company, i.e. I should look after the rationing, clothing, equipment, ammunition, rifles, and billeting, while Waterhouse concentrated on the "A" side, i.e. the training, routine orders, operations, trench discipline, and organisation. Also I was to understudy Waterhouse in the above duties, and we further developed our company organisation by arranging a scheme by which all officers understudied their immediate senior. Latter and Kenderdine were to work with me. Each Sergeant was to learn Company Sergeant Major and Company Quartermaster Sergeant's work, Corporals were to learn Sergeant's duties, and senior privates to understudy junior NCOs.

The object of this was to ensure that the Company ran satisfactorily in spite of casualties.

Billet improvement for our men was one of our pet hobbies, every effort being made to provide recreation rooms when at rest.

While at Senlis this tour Colonel Shirley took a photograph of each Company officer and also one of the Battalion HQ officers.

On September 23rd, we could hear the distant Rumble of <u>Very</u> Heavy

Capt L.H. Blay. Jimmy Bowd
a.n.

This may have been one of the photographs taken by Lieutenant Colonel Shirley at Senlis. See also pages 65 and 112.

Gun Fire from the North. A heavy bombardment, such as the preparatory bombardment of enemy defences for the "Loos Show" (which this was), sounds like one continuous rumble, and miles away one can see the reflection of the gun flashes in the sky – resembling constant lightning, or the flash of an electric car.

For some weeks past we had been making preparations on the sector North of Albert, between La Boiselle and Thiepval, where the Ancre valley runs up through Mesnil, Hamel and onto Grandcourt. Along this Front we had constructed underground trenches (tunnels) from our Front Line into and under No Man's Land.

These tunnels were wide enough for two men to walk along together. The exit into No Man's Land was concealed by having a movable door covered with sods on its upper surface, so that it was not evident to the Boche that such communication existed.

The object was to be able to move the Battalion quickly into No Man's Land, under cover. They would then climb out of the tunnels and form up in fighting formation in the open. All our Brigade, including the Scottish Rifles, had worked very hard on these tunnels. Working parties were found by the units in Support and Reserve. About 10 men worked on each tunnel – digging the faces, propping, and carrying away the excavated earth and

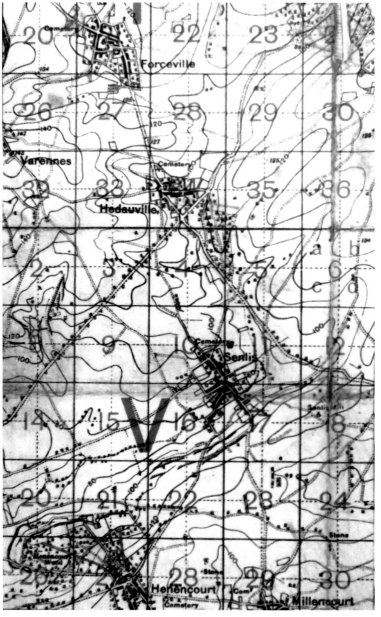

chalk. Eight hour shifts were worked – constantly. The difficulty was the removal and disposal of the excavated material, which had to be deposited, and then covered, to avoid any new earth being seen by the Boche. This was a constant trouble in all digging and mining operations. However the work was completed before the Fateful Day – September 25th. From that day all leave was stopped on account of the "Loos Show". We were preparing to go to the trenches again, and we were warned to take up as little kit as possible. But in the end we were left in our peaceful little village of Senlis.

During these few days in Senlis we had a Route March on awful roads – it had been raining for about three days. We started from Senlis, across the Warloy to Hédauville road, then on to Forceville, North West to Acheux, this being the most advanced Railhead for the Northern Sector of the Somme Front (British portion). At Acheux we struck North East towards Beaussart, and then cut across temporary military roads to Englebelmer, from there to Martinsart, Bouzincourt, and back home. It rained practically the whole way. We also had two test Gas attacks and one Flammenwerfer[127] test. This was most unpleasant – lying on the bottom of a trench with a huge flame of burning oil sweeping over our heads. We got very hot and one fellow lost his nerve in the middle of the show and yelled out as if he was mad. To save accidents he was quickly quietened by a sharp blow on the head.

The principle of these Flammenwerfers is interesting. The apparatus consists of two cylinders, one containing nitrogen gas under high pressure, the other containing a mixture of oil and paraffin or petrol. The two cylinders are connected, and the nitrogen is allowed to flow from the cylinder into the oil container, which is about ¾ full. Thus the annular space above the oil is filled with nitrogen under pressure. The valves are then closed, and the gas-holder disconnected.

Attached to the oil container is a flexible tube fitted with a jet having a small orifice and automatic lighter. This part of the apparatus can be carried by one man. He creeps out of his trenches, across No Man's Land to within about 40 yards of the hostile Line, and then opens the stop-cock from the container to the tube. The nitrogen, being free to expand, forces the liquid oil up the tube, and it is forced through the small orifice as a fine spray – which is ignited by the automatic lighter. Thus a huge flame is produced.

I shall not describe the Gas cylinder here or the apparatus for Gas attacks, as I propose to devote a section of my diary to the Development of Weapons as used in trench warfare.[128]

25.09.15 to 03.10.15	We left Senlis on September 25th at about 4.00pm, and marched via Bouzincourt, Albert and Aveluy to our old Front Line in front of Authuille, my first tour in the Line with "Z" Company. I knew most of their work, but certain points were fresh to me; however, these I soon dropped into.

We were a very cheery Company.

We were holding exactly the same Line as described above in the entries relating to the period August 14th to August 28th, so all our men knew it thoroughly.

"Z" Company now consisted of Captain K. Waterhouse, myself, 2nd Lieutenant Kemp, 2nd Lieutenant Latter,[129] 2nd Lieutenant Moffatt, and 2nd Lieutenant Kenderdine, Joe Hedley having gone to "W" Company.

---

[127] Flame throwers.

[128] In fact, there is no specific section devoted to the development of weapons, but mention of new weapons as they were developed is interspersed in the text.

[129] This is the last mention of 2nd Lieutenant J.C. Latter (whose full name was John Cecil Latter) until 18th February 1917, when Norman went to Fountains Abbey with him while in Ripon when he (Norman) was on Home Service recovering from being wounded. They also went for dinner together at the Majestic in Ripon on 17th March 1917. After Norman had returned to France and been posted to the 1/5th Lancashire Fusiliers in June 1917 they again met up in September 1917, at which time Latter had rejoined the 2/5th Lancashire Fusiliers. Up until this point in the diary (September 1915) Latter has featured quite frequently, having been one of the original officers to have come out to France with "D" Company of the 2/5th Lancashire Fusiliers on 3rd May 1915, the first time he is mentioned in the diary, although in his own private papers in the Imperial War Museum (see below) he records that he was gazetted to the 5th Lancashire Fusiliers as 2nd Lieutenant on 23rd December 1914, and that he joined up in Southport on 30th December 1914. Norman got to know him well when he (Norman) joined "D" Company's Mess from 9th May 1915 until they finished their training at Arques on 8th July 1915. He is mentioned as being *"quite a musician"* on the piano of the Mayor and Mayoress at Arques, which possibly gave him his nickname "Ludwig", after Beethoven (a nickname which Norman uses when writing about

The "Loos Show" was anything but a success – in fact it was a decided failure, as few of the objectives were taken.

Certainly our people took the Hohenzollern Redoubt – in itself a fine piece of work, and a very difficult objective. But the idea was to take Lille, thus driving this flank on the North back Eastward, which would have necessitated a big withdrawal of the German Line right down to the Somme in order for them to be immune from enfilade fire.

We were quite prepared to advance on a small scale North of Albert and thereby harass the Boche.

But we were called upon to co-operate, consequently this tour in the Line did not prove particularly exciting. The first half of our tour was very wet, and, as our trenches were in clay, we got more than our share of mud-larking. Sometimes we were literally knee deep in thick slimy liquid mud. Pumps were useless. Waterhouse's scheme to occupy the high ground never developed, and, during the period from August 1st, the Boche had worked hard, and constructed a very formidable Strong Point – Leipsig Redoubt – on the very ground we had tried to keep him off. This Strong Point proved a constant trouble to us. The Boche had several large Trench Mortars safely tucked away in the Redoubt. His Minenwerfers,[130] aerial torpedoes,[131] and Rifle Grenades fired from this defence work were a constant menace to us.

The most annoying part was that we had no counter Trench Artillery to worry him with, also our Rifle Grenades had a limiting range of 120 yards approximately, and, as the Hun was 350 to 400 yards away, we were unable to worry him. After considerable annoyance we eventually arranged with Major Boon's Battery to worry them. By a system of strict observation and listening we were able to fire two rounds 4.5 inch howitzer shells for each "Tock Emma"[132] he poofed off at us. This quietened him somewhat. Also we arranged periodic "strafes" on this point, at least once a day, but at different times, thus hoping to catch the Boche napping. Our action certainly made the Hun think twice about worrying our little home.

---

him in 1921 - see below). He is also mentioned as making *"chevaux de frise"* on 18th July 1915 , being a *"crack shot"* ratting in August 1915 (page 78), and frequently commanding patrols or raids in No Man's Land (see the diary entries for 14th to 19th August 1915 on page 81 and 27th August 1915 on page 86). It is not clear what happened to him after this, but he is not listed as one of the officers of "Z" Company by 24th April 1916, nor was he one of the seven original officers referred to as being still with the 2/5th Lancashire Fusiliers in the diary entry for 21st to 26th August 1916. In *At Ypres with Best-Dunkley* Thomas Floyd mentions that he was wounded in 1916, and rejoined the 2/5th Lancashire Fusiliers at the Western Front in August 1917. There is a photograph of him with Norman, Kenneth Waterhouse, Hedley, Kemp, Simon, and the Mayor and Mayoress of Arques on page 52, taken between 20th May 1915 and 8th July 1915. After the War, as mentioned in the *Afterword* on page 309, Latter (along with Norman and others) was chosen to represent the 2/5th Lancashire Fusiliers at the unveiling of the Givenchy Memorial to the 55th Division on 15th May 1921, at which time he is referred to as Captain J.C. Latter MC (having been awarded the MC when Adjutant to the 2/5th Lancashire Fusiliers in an action near St Julien on 20th September 1917 in the 3rd Battle of Ypres, a fuller description of which is given in *The History of the Lancashire Fusiliers 1914-1918*, mentioned below, pages 230-235). Norman spent most of his time with Latter on this trip, including having breakfast at Latter's parents' home in London on 14th May 1921. Some of the photographs of the trip pasted into the diary show Captain Latter, including one in front of the actual unveiling of the Memorial, reproduced on page 309. Latter must have remained in the Army as a regular soldier after the end of the First World War, or re-enlisted in the Second World War, as he eventually reached the rank of Major General. In 1949 he published *The History of the Lancashire Fusiliers 1914-1918*, a history of the Regiment's service during the First World War in two volumes, compilation of the records for which had been begun by Captain G.C. Hutchinson (referred to in the book as Major G.C. Hutchinson). Some of his papers are in the Imperial War Museum, Catalogue nos. 12265 and PC1213, covering a period in France and Italy from September 1917 to December 1917, and including photographs from a visit to the Western Front area of France in 1920.

[130] Mine launchers.

[131] Torpedoes dropped from aeroplanes.

[132] Army slang for Trench Mortars, derived from telecommunications language – "Toc" for "T", and "Emma" for "M".

Our snipers also devoted a considerable amount of time to a suspicious mound on this work (a suspected Observation Post).

So that, at any rate, I think we made the Boche keep at rest, and his head below ground level.

04.10.15   After a week in the Line we came out to Aveluy Village as Battalion in Brigade Reserve. Our men were billeted in a huge barn and our officers' billet was across the road in a house. Kenderdine and I joined at a room. We had wooden beds with rabbit wire stretched on the frame – quite cosy. We took the front room for our Mess, and, taken all round, were quite cosy.

05.10.15   Waddicar was simply splendid – doing all kinds of useful odd jobs, from cooking to making temporary furniture out of ration boxes. I enjoyed a splendid hot bath. The men were rather badly off for baths. We decided something might be done to improve the conditions of living, and a scheme was under consideration for making some baths. I was chosen to tackle this job. The scheme also brought in a "billet repair scheme".

At this time we were sleeping on straw in farm barns. The barns themselves were in bad repair, through lack of attention (the male population being away on service). The first thing to do was to repair holes in the roofs, then to repair the holes in the plaster inside, and thirdly to make beds out of the timbers and stretch wire across them. Roughly one platoon, 30 to 40 men, were billeted in a barn.

The other work in hand was to erect a bath house, where 30 men could have a hot bath in an hour, and get a complete change of clothing, and also have their uniforms ironed to try and stamp out the lice – a great trouble in trench warfare, especially in trenches taken over from the French, who seemed to be decidedly dirty.

I had a return rendered from the companies showing the number of tradesmen under the following heads:

Bricklayers

Joiners and Carpenters

Plasterers

Slaters

Plumbers

I got a very efficient squad of men – about 20 – who were keen on the work. They were excused all other duties, which rather appealed to them.

Sergeant Nicols of the 8th Argylls was sent to me as permanent works foreman.

He and I made a survey of the billets in the village – available accommodation and the repairs required. Then we indented through the usual channels for free timber, dressed timber, canvas, wire, nails, cement etc.

A fatigue party of 25 men came to me daily to work along with my trained men, and so we started out.

Bricks and slates were collected from buildings destroyed by shell fire. The plastering of the walls was quite an experiment. The barn walls in most of the French villages were made of skeleton timber filled in with a mud paste made from sand, cement and straw and stucco.

My mixture served the purpose quite well. Inside the week we had made 300 beds and repaired most of our billets. The men worked exceedingly well – of course we had no union officials to regulate our rate of work or pay.

We also made considerable progress with the Bath House. I was given a farm on the banks of the River Ancre, opposite the Chateau at Aveluy. This farm had two huge barns and about three outhouses. The plan was roughly as under – (not to scale):

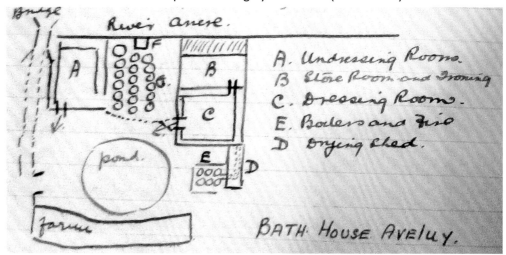

The arrangement of the Bath House when completed was as follows:

Barn with seats – where the party undressed, tied their uniform and boots in a bundle, and fastened their identity disc on the bundle.

The floor was bricked and filled in with cement, 30 huge washing (low) tubs were put in, with trench boarding between rows of tubs.

Barn divided in two by wooden partitions. Half was a store room with shelves for shirts, vests, underpants, socks, towels, ironing tables.

Dressing room with seats and boarded floor.

Small outhouse, through which flue from fire ran, fitted with racks, used as a drying room for gum thigh boots.

Range of six copper boilers set in a brick stand, with fire under boilers.

Pump from the river.

The system of working was this: The Company bathing provided two men as stokers, four men to carry water from pump to boilers, two men to pump, four men to iron clothes. We had a permanent storekeeper (a man unfit for the Line).

Each man drew his hot water from the boilers in biscuit tins (28lbs[133]) with lids removed and wire handles with wood grips fitted.

When 30 men came down to the baths they undressed in A and each man bundled his clothes in two bundles:

Uniforms and boots;

Dirty clothes.

When they had bathed, their clothes were handed back to them, and they took them to

---

[133] 28 pounds, which is 12.72 kilograms.

C, handed their Bundle N° 1 into B for ironing, and drew a clean garment in exchange for each dirty one.

We also had a couple of proper foot baths fitted up in separate cabins for officers' bath accommodation. These were really quite posh bathrooms with seats, clothes hooks, looking glass etc.

In addition to these conveniences, I erected a small wooden shed at Crucifix Corner, just at the entrance to the Communication Trench leading up the La Boiselle road. In this hut we sold hot coffee, soup, chocolate, cigarettes, notepaper, matches, boot laces, buttons, and other odd useful accessories. This proved a great asset to the men, and incidentally quite a profitable concern. All our <u>own</u> men derived direct benefit from the profits as they were divided amongst the Companies each month for extra messing.

08.10.15   I took a working party up to the trenches in front of Aveluy Wood to work on sap heads, mining. We left at 4.00am, working a four hour shift.

Going up to the Line across the open from the Aveluy to Authuille road into the wood we were held up by the Boche Machine Gun fire. The Hun was apparently having a morning Hate which took the form of sweeping the approaches to the Line by indirect Machine Gun fire. We lay down and took whatever cover we could, and fortunately no one was hit.

I went to bed as soon as I got back, and slept until one o'clock.

Captain David L. Gray

In the evening we had a little dinner party – Joe Hedley, Gray, and two Scotch fellows, Captain Harvey from the Seaforth Highlanders, and Captain Gray from the 6th Scottish Rifles. We had quite a cheery evening, singing etc., and bridge. I quite forgot myself and dressed up as a Scotchman, also seemed to rather amuse the Mess by imitating Formby, and relating a few tales about old John [i.e. Lieutenant Colonel John Hall] and incidents in the Line. Gray and Harvey argued about the relative merits of the Lowlander against the Highlander, and I am afraid that the argument became more boisterous in proportion to the amount of their national beverage which they had consumed, until it developed into a scrap, with chairs, glasses, and bottles being literally flung about the place, until our Mess looked as if a shell had dropped into it. This lasted until about 2.30am when Gray and Captain Harvey shook hands and agreed that they were both jolly good fellows as they were both Lowlanders having been born in Wishaw near Glasgow.[134] Eventually we got rid of these cheery Scotchmen and we retired to bed.

---

[134] The photograph of Captain Gray is from a newspaper cutting pasted at the end of Volume 2 of the diaries, entitled *A Bombing Hero*, with the following caption: "*Capt. David L. Gray, of the 6th Scottish Rifles, mentioned in General French's dispatches for gallantry in the field. He led a party of bombers, who succeeded in taking several lines of German trenches. In the counter-attack the officer and his party were cut off for 48 hours, subsequently escaping in a marvellous manner back to their lines. Son of a well-known Motherwell man, his uncle is David Gray, of Luggie fame.*" The final words may refer to a poem entitled *The Luggie*, which was written by a David Gray (1823-1861), son of a weaver from Merkland near Glasgow, based on memories of his early life and the stream (the Luggie) which flows through Merkland.

09.10.15 We tried to improve our Mess. I made a hat rack and a notice board.

Several Expeditionary Force Canteens began to operate in existing buildings in the villages in our area – quite a useful idea. I bought a splendid pair of fur gloves – rabbit fur, I think. They cost 14 francs.

Colonel Shirley accused me of getting very thin. I suggested I needed a change of air in England. Conversation was abruptly changed.

There was a Battalion concert in an estaminet opposite to the Chateau which was Brigade HQ in Aveluy – quite a good show.

11.10.15 I had a ride over on "Sandy Mac", Waterhouse's horse, to get money from the Field Cashier at Bouzincourt. Doctor Thompson went with me. We had quite a jolly ride.

A SOLDIERS' ENTERTAINMENT.

Writing from "Somewhere in France," on the 9th inst., Regimental Sergt.-Major T. J. Crawford says:—Will you allow me through your paper to let the people of Bury, Heywood, and Radcliffe know how the boys enjoy themselves when out of the trenches? On Thursday evening a concert was held under the chairmanship of C.S.M. Aspinall, and was attended by a good many of our officers, including Lieut. Col. Shirley (commanding), Major Milnes, Captains Waterhouse, Hedley, Gillenders (chaplain), and Lieut. Thompson (medical officer). The programme was thoroughly appreciated by all ranks. After the artistes had been thanked for their services, the concert was brought to a close with the hearty singing of "Auld lang syne," accompanied by the gramophone. The accompanists were Sergt. Cooke, Lance-crpl. Hulton, and Sergt.-Major Crawford. Programme:—Recitation, "Play the game," Lieut.-Col. Shirley; gramophone selection; song, "Humours of the old church choir," Private Jackson; song, "Take them home to father every night," Bandsman Wood; whistling solo, "Poet and peasant," Drummer Scotting; humorous selection, "Farms," Lance-crpl. Brooks; gramophone selection; song, "Same as my feyther," Lieut. Harker; song, "Where my caravan has rested," Sergt.-Major Crawford; song, "Lancashire Fusiliers," Sergt. Watts; song, "Mountains of Mourne," Lieut. Noton; gramophone selection; song, "We 'ad 'em," Lance-crpl. Brooks; whistling solo, "Ragtime dixie," Drummer Scotting; song, "Thora," Pte. Jackson; song, selected, Bandsman Wood; "Auld lang syne"; "The King."

12.10.15 to 04.11.15 Leave started again in mid-October, two officers per week. My turn was due on November 5th, the same date as Captain Hedley's.

Details of this part of my life in France are not very definite. I remember that in this period the Boche very rudely broke the window of our Mess in the dug out by dropping a Trench Mortar just at our back door. Dirty Dog!

Other than that, things had settled down to an "unexhilarating but salutary routine", as Ian Hay describes it in his book *The First Hundred Thousand*; he sums up the life exactly under the heading *The Trivial Round*.

Each dawn and evening we "stood to arms" and peered morosely over the parapet watching the distant trench line grow more plainly visible and gradually fade away into the night. In between was the monotony of cleaning rifles, of ration parties, of working parties etc.

Artillery on both sides had their daily Hates, not at each other, so their respective hostile infantry casualties were few; but the ones and twos added up.

Such things as flank attacks as described by Napoleon were out of the question, for there was one huge Army stretching from the Alps to the North Sea.

Surprise attacks on a scale large enough to make any material impression on the enemy were well nigh impossible, in view of the efficiency of our Intelligence Department, aeroplane reconnaissance, dispatch work, and telephone communication.

For the specialist – the Sniper, the Intelligence Officer, the Signalling Officer, the Machine Gunner or the Bombing Officer – life had its variety.

Machine Gunners planned schemes for indirect fire on cross roads, approaches used by the enemy etc., anything to make him as uncomfortable as possible. Freddy Harker thoroughly enjoyed strafing the Huns in this way.

Of course, he never knew whether his many calculations had really given him the correct range, or whether he hit his target or not. One indication of success in this way was given by the Hun trying to locate our Machine Guns by his Artillery Retaliation.

Then again Kemp or Kenderdine, Noton or Waterhouse would go out with a bombing party in conjunction with the other members of the Battalion Suicide Club – Sergeant Cadden, Lance Corporal Hampson, Corporal Lord, Sergeant Watson, or other kindred spirits.

These parties could be seen in the daytime, looking anxiously at trench maps and aeroplane photos of the Boche Line, and filling khaki apron-like articles with numerous pockets with bombs – for we had got small quantities of a new interesting toy delivered to us, in the form of the N° 5 Mills hand grenade.[135] Night arrives, calm and still, with a moon just resting on the horizon, and everyone hoping it will hide itself sooner or later behind a cloud; the party steals up a sap and climbs out into the grass. They are lost to view as they move forward towards the enemy Line, making a bee-line for their objective, a suspected sap head in front of the Hun Line. Their progress is arrested by sounds of digging in front. The party halts temporarily, while one of them moves forward in advance of the rest to investigate. As he raises himself up on his knees, a chance star shell bursts near him – he remains quite still, and by the light is able to see several Boche digging at the sap head. The flare light having died out, he returns to report to the party, who form round the sap in the form of a crescent – about 20 yards away from the sap head. The first bomb is thrown at the sap, followed in quick succession by several more. A shattering roar, a hail of shrapnel, several flashes – a cloud of smoke – shouting and groaning; then a succession of flare lights from the Boche trench – a burst of enemy rifle fire – and the zip zip of Machine Gun bullets. Meanwhile, Kemp and his party are lying on the ground, breathing hard, their brows wet with perspiration, awaiting their opportunity to return to our Line.

About half an hour later they return, and tumble into our sap to report the results of their labour to many anxious watchers.

The party indulge in a rum ration, and anxiously enquire whether the mail has come up. The OC of the party retires to make his "Patrol Report", which is forwarded in due course to Divisional HQ, who some days later publish an extract in the Divisional Summary of Operations as follows:

"*On the night of October 11th at 9.00pm a small party of the 2/5th Lancashire Fusiliers under 2nd Lieutenant Kemp bombed a suspected sap head at A12 d.o.2. Loud groans were heard indicating that some casualties were inflicted on the enemy. The enemy retaliated with rifle fire and Machine Guns. Our party returned safely without casualties.*"

Each side seemed to delight in Artillery Practice, which at times we considered should be limited to, say, 10 rounds per gun, the general opinion being that life would go on much more smoothly without the inconveniences of Black Marias,[136] Coal Boxes,[137] Tock Emmas,[138] and whizz-bangs;[139] or, as one of my men very aptly put the question of gun

---

[135] The first hand grenades widely issued to the British Army; developed by William Mills based on an earlier Belgian design, they were first put into service in May 1915.

[136] A type of heavy German High Explosive shell, so called because of the black smoke that it produced when exploding.

[137] Another type of heavy German shell, usually 5.9 inch, again named after the black smoke emitted on exploding.

[138] Army slang for Trench Mortars – see footnote 132 on page 100.

[139] Army slang for a type of high velocity shell, usually the 77mm type.

fire one day when a huge shell burst uncomfortably near him, "You know, Sir, what annoys me about these 'ere German Gunners is that I expect it's only a little feller as pulls the string what fired that shell, and if I 'ad 'im 'ere ha'd punch his blinking 'ead."

The Machine Gunner, Freddy Harker, and his band of slackers could be most annoying at times. They only had two Machine Guns; by the way these were now Vickers New Guns – quite curiosities, only issued in small doses to each Division, especially the Territorials; Kitchener's[140] darlings at home had to have an adequate supply of these toys to play with on Salisbury Plain before the War Office sent them out to France to be of real practical use.

The Machine Gunner had what he called Battle Rations – especially strong emplacements – or supposed to be strong – only to be used in an emergency. In these positions were wonderful diagrams of ranges, lines of fire etc. – very pretty to look at, but seldom used. In addition one usually found a reasonable part of unexpended portion of the day's ration stowed away in these Posts, and sundry articles of equipment.

When Freddy wanted to fire his guns he either took them to a small trench behind the Front Line and fired over your head, or placed them on the parapet in the Front Line, or else chose your favourite sap head – which you had carefully concealed from the Boche by camouflage. The result was retaliation, but when this came the Machine Gunners would be nicely stowed away in their dug out – usually the deepest in the sector – and an appetising smell of fried bacon and eggs or toasted cheese would be coming out.

Trench Mortars had also come into existence by this time. In the early stages of this weapon, it was scarcely a compliment to be sent to a course of instruction on the wonders of the Trench Mortar, and eventually to be posted to a Trench Mortar battery. Initially it was regarded rather as a damned nuisance than as a useful weapon for trench warfare. Later, as improvements came along, we changed our minds and realised the value of the Plum Pudding, the Stokes Mortar, and the "Flying Pig".[141]

These weapons were usually known as "Tock Emmas".

The first "Tock Emmas" looked rather like a drain-pipe, stuck on legs; the bomb – cylindrical in shape – was put into the pipe and fired from that position. The bomb exploded with a very loud report, made a huge crater, and usually hurt anybody who happened to be near – at least we hoped it did!

No one liked a Trench Mortar in their sector, because to fire it usually caused trouble from the Hun. The position fired from was difficult to conceal owing to the discharge giving a huge flash.

Usually the Trench Mortar Commander chose a position to fire his mortar from which was near a Company HQ or a Platoon HQ which you particularly wished unmolested, or some place as near to the Boche Line as possible so that he could reach the enemy trench – his mortar having a maximum range of about 300 yards, whereas the Boche had mortars capable of fixing 1000 yards correctly.

Often Bodell (164th Brigade Trench Mortar Commander), late 1/8th Liverpool Irish, would select some trench which was of vital importance and to be held at all cost. Consequently

---

[140] See footnote 90 on page 69.
[141] Different types of Trench Mortar, 2 inch, 3.2 inch and 9.45 inch bore respectively. See also the footnotes to the diary entry for the period 2nd to 7th March 1916 on pages 152 and 155.

we didn't want it blowing in by the Huns.

The Trench Mortar fellows – like the Machine Gunners – had a marvellous way of fixing up their pea shooters, firing off about a dozen rounds, picking up their tackle – and clearing off long before the Boche retaliated; so that we got all the presents intended for the Trench Mortar operators, who were probably sound asleep by then.

Everyone anxiously waited all day for the mails to come up at night. These were very regular. In fact you could depend on getting your mail daily at the same hour. If it was half an hour after time you could be sure there wouldn't be any at all that night.

Letters, newspapers, parcels were worth their weight in gold. It was most amusing to see fellows opening their parcels, like a child opening a stocking at Xmas.

We learnt quite a lot about the War from the newspapers!!

Often we would have heated arguments on Government Policy, especially on the advisability of Compulsory Service.[142]

Then the subalterns had the pleasure of daily censoring the letters written by the men of their own platoon. Generally speaking this was a dull and monotonous job, but occasionally it provided food for amusement. Letters for censorship were divided into three classes:

Field Cards

Letters in official green envelopes

Ordinary letters.

Class 1

The first class needs little comment – very convenient to complete in an emergency, yet doubtless they saved many anxious hours of wondering for those at home. This type of card is well known:

"I am quite well"

"I have been admitted to Hospital"

etc.

All one had to do with this missive was to cross out the sentence which did not apply to your particular case, and sign at the foot of the card.

Our men had a great fascination for sending French postcards – the silk embroidered type, most wonderful things!

Class 2

Official green envelopes were in great demand, the demand usually being greater than the supply. Letters enclosed in these envelopes were not liable to censorship regimentally, but were liable to censorship at the Base Censor's office. The sender signed the document to the effect that the contents contained no reference to anything of a military nature, but only contained reference to private and family matters. It was surprising at times how elastically the term "private and family matters" was used.

Occasionally one of these envelopes would be returned from the Base through the usual channels, back to the Battalion with a footnote by the Brigadier to the CO of the Battalion "For your information. Please take necessary action against 403211 Private Jones J.W. and report action taken to this office".

---

[142] This did not come in until January 1916.

Class 3

These were letters left open for censorship by Regimental officers. They were, of course, dealt with confidentially. Nevertheless they often contained very amusing expressions. Often you would find one fellow writing to several girls – to each of whom he swore his fidelity.

The various styles of commencing and closing letters were decidedly numerous and unique in some cases:

"It is with great pleasure that I take up my pen … " Most of the men never saw a pen from one week to another.

"Everyone is in the pink, as it leaves me at present"; "Bill Jones went west last night with a bit of lead through his 'ead."

The men were certainly sincere in their letters and I personally must admit that censoring men's letters helped me a great deal in getting to know my men. Thus one was enabled to get an insight into quite a different side of a man's character, and it was astonishing in some cases to find how thoughtful and thrifty some men were, often the very last men whom you would imagine would think of their homes.

Strangely one seldom heard much complaining, and the majority made light of their hardships and trials, probably to try to re-assure those at home, and help them not to worry. One often came across cases of men requesting their people <u>not</u> to send them parcels out, but to spend the money on little Annie or Baby Joe.

Undoubtedly, as the men got to know their officers, they wrote very freely, feeling that they could trust us to treat their letters as secret correspondence, which <u>we did</u>.

In fact we knew our men, and the type of letter they would write, and, if green envelopes were scarce, we used to tell those fellows we knew were dependable that they could seal up a letter by giving us their word that there was nothing of a military nature enclosed.

Orders on censorship were many and lengthy and had to be read out periodically on parade as reminders.

Of course, we got a few grousers who never failed to make mountains out of mole hills. These particular characters enjoyed using their letters as a medium for airing their grievances before the officers – often because they hadn't a genuine grouse and hadn't the pluck to come and see their Company officers and put their case honestly.

In "Z" Company I may say every effort was made to help the men and make life as pleasant and easy as possible, and each of us was ready to try to set right anything we could, and receive suggestions from the men.

One of our schemes in the Line was to collect orders and money from the men for cigarettes which the Company Quartermaster Sergeant purchased for them at the Canteens behind the Line, and brought them up with the rations. We felt that we officers got our extras up each day, and there wasn't any reason why the men shouldn't have something done for them in the same way. The scheme certainly worked very well. In fact we had developed the scheme still further, when circumstances permitted, and were beginning to run a small Company Canteen in the Line, as mentioned in the diary entry for October 5th 1915.

When up in the Line for long periods it was necessary to send the men out in parties of, say, 10 to 20 at a time during the day time to have baths. Consequently we were able to guarantee each man a bath and change of clothes once a week even in the Line. Of course there were occasions when the scheme could not be kept up.

As winter was now fast approaching, we were having some very cold and wet weather. Precautions had therefore to be taken to prevent the men getting trench feet and "going sick". We made every effort in this way; for example we had started trench foot treatment, the daily washing of feet in cold water and the rubbing of feet and legs with whale oil. Also we sought to ensure a plentiful supply of <u>hot</u> nourishing food. Each night we used to issue the men with a ration of <u>hot</u> cocoa or soup at midnight, when the shifts changed over duty. At one time we also issued the rum ration at this time; but some of the men seemed to derive more benefit by having their tot of rum 1/64 gallons[143] at "Stand Down" just before they turned in to rest after sunrise or dawn, so we changed our time accordingly for the whole Company.

We always tried to keep a small emergency ration of rum to issue to patrols when they returned from their duty, which often entailed crawling about on wet sodden ground.

Our Routine was approximately:

"Stand to"	1 hour before dawn.
	Clean rifle before "Stand Down"
"Stand down"	½ hour after it came really light
	If foggy double sentries were left on duty while the fog lasted
Breakfast	8.00am
	The men rested after breakfast till dinner
Dinner	1.00pm
Work	1.30pm to 2.30pm
Rest	2.30pm to 4.30pm
Tea	4.30pm
"Stand to "	1 hour before dark – all men on duty

Gas helmets were tested daily.

"Practice Actions" for the following emergencies were tested:

Action in case of Bombardment

Action in case of Gas attack

Action in case of Enemy attack

Action in case of Bombing Raid by enemy

Action in case of above, on Companies on either flank

The many other duties of the trenches took a considerable amount of time and thought. A few of these are enumerated below:

Ration Parties

Carrying Parties for RE material for trench construction etc.

Sanitary Duties

Planning of Schemes of work

---

[143] Approximately 70 millilitres.

Planning of Schemes to worry the Hun

Inspection of Lines, dug outs, rifles, guns, stores, ammunition, bombs, rockets, flare lights, vermorel[144] sprayers etc.

The Platoon Commanders had their reports to make to the OC Company, who in turn made a compilation report to Battalion HQ. These consisted of:

Strength Returns

Dispositions – Sentry Posts, dug outs etc. with maps

Casualty Returns

Patrol Reports

Situation Reports

Work Reports

RE Indents

Trench Store Returns

Consequently there was a great deal to be done in a day.

Before coming out of the Line we used to have kit and clothing inspections so that indents could be submitted to the Quartermaster a few days before we arrived in billets; this enabled the Quartermaster to get his stores from the Ordnance ready for the men when they came out into billets.

During this period two rather amusing incidents occurred in the Line.

I was on duty one calm, clear, peaceful night, with scarcely a sound, except perhaps a very occasional bullet, or the sound of gun fire in the distance, to relieve the almost distressing quietness, when I heard a bullet – or rather a rifle – fired from one of our Posts. I located the Post and rushed down to the spot, knowing it to be a place which had very little field of fire on account of dead ground in front, and a position which could be approached on the edge of the wire to within 20 yards, without the Boche being observed. I imagined the Boche had crept up silently to our wire and surprised the Post. One Eckersley, a rather dull individual of about 45, was on Sentry Duty. I asked him what he was firing at, and at the same time jumped on to the fire step and looked over. I couldn't see a sign of any living thing. Then old Eckersley replied, "I'm firing at yon feller coming o'er yon 'ill wi' a lamp." I looked in the direction indicated and couldn't refrain from laughing, much to Eckersley's disgust – "It's no laughing matter, Sir – what I says is reet enough." My reply was, "Just you wait a few minutes and you'll have a shock." I was right – the moon was raising her lamp above, and Eckersley in his excitement and fidelity to duty had shot the moon. After this he was always known as "the man who shot the moon".

Little incidents such as this certainly relieved the monotony of what was otherwise a very serious business.

The weather was simply the last word. Rain! Rain! Mud! Mud! Ankle deep, knee deep, waist deep, water in many places.

During one very wet night I was on duty and walking down the trench. I passed a dug out where two of my men were getting what shelter from the rain they could. They had just come off sentry wet through, and their dug out was about 3 or 4 inches deep in mud on the floor. As I passed they were scooping out the mud with their entrenching tools and

---

[144] A sprayer used to neutralise contamination caused by chlorine gas.

trying to get down to some dry earth, which I assumed they would cover with dry sand bags (contrary to orders) and eventually settle down to sleep, making the best of a bad job.

As I passed I heard one fellow say to his pal: "Eh Bill, I'm fed up with this b ——— war; I'll tell thee what it is – I've walked 'arf of bloomin' France and t'other bloomin' arf I've put in b ——— sand bags". His pal tried to cheer him up and replied "Eh, mon, that's nought. Why, when't bloomin' war is o'er, you'll 'ave to start empt'ing these 'ere sand bags, pile 'em in bundles of ten and send 'em back th'ordiance."

A tour round the Line on such a night was a bit wet, but full of exciting incidents – slipping here – falling there – calculated to drain the dregs from anybody's vocabulary. The duckboards floated about. Sometimes you stepped on one end, and then either the other end came up and hit you, or you slipped off into the mud, or the falling duckboard made a fountain of mud and muddy water. If you put your hand on to the side of the trench to steady yourself, the sides were all slimy, squelchy mud, which your hand dived into and consequently even the cuff of your shirt, as well as your jacket, became caked with slimy mud.

Such nights as this a man on sentry had an awful time, drenched through, and when he came off duty where had he to go? A dug out usually several inches in water with a layer of mud below; all this had to be scooped out before he could attempt to lie down, and yet he seldom groused. On one particular pouring wet night (October 25th), when everyone was soaked through and cold, and a bitter North East wind was blowing, the Skipper decided that "Perhaps we were fairly loyal to be living a life like we were". Waterhouse was certainly a good sort. He always seemed so cool, just at the right moment.

My dug out – A lay of the trenches
What is this slimy dismal hole
Where oft I'm lurking like a mole
And cursing Germans heart and soul?
My Dug out.
Where is it that beneath the floor
The water's rising more and more
And where the roof's a broken door?
My Dug out.
Where is it that I try to sleep
Betwixt at arms, when up I leap
And dash through water four feet deep?
My Dug out.
Where is it that I catch a chill
And lose my only quinine pill
And probably remain until
I'm dug out?
My Dug out.

The Innocent Abroad.
Out since Mons: "Well, what sort of a night 'ave yer 'ad?"
Novice (but persistent optimist): "Oh, alright. 'Ad to get out and rest a bit now and again."

Above: A cartoon and poem by Captain Bruce Bairnsfather, who trained as both soldier and artist, and served with the Royal Warwickshire Regiment on the Western Front from 1914-1915. He suffered shell shock and hearing loss during the 2nd Battle of Ypres and returned to England, where he began drawing cartoons for a magazine called *The Bystander*. These were popular with both serving troops and people at home, and were subsequently collected together in a series of volumes called *Fragments from France*. Norman pasted five of Bruce Bairnsfather's cartoons into his diary; three others appear on pages 134 and 182.

Can one wonder that, after about 14 days of life such as the poem and drawing on the previous page illustrates, we were glad to leave the Line in front of Authuille Wood and return to rest billets in our old village, Aveluy.

Then people at home wondered why rum rations were issued to the troops, and some old cranks in Parliament wanted to stop the issue of rum.

On Wednesday November 3rd 1915, I was feeling particularly cheery as leave had started again, and Joe Hedley and I were due to go on leave on Friday November 5th. Consequently we weren't over keen on going up to the Line with working parties between November 3rd and 5th, and every odd shell that came into the village put the wind up us much more than usual – if that were possible.

On the night of November 3rd one additional officer's leave was granted to the Battalion, and this went to Gray. So we looked like being a very cheery party. Each of us had a few small souvenirs, but one of Joe Hedley's calls for special comment. Well, it wasn't a small souvenir, in fact it was decidedly bulky! It was a Boche Trench Mortar bomb of the oil drum type about 2 feet 6 inches high by 1 foot in diameter, filled with High Explosive and any old bits of scrap iron, rusty nails, gramophone pins etc. apparently not required in Germany. The history of the bomb was briefly: one afternoon during the last tour in the Line the Boche put a few of these old "oil drums" on to Joe's Company Line. One dropped in No Man's Land without exploding. The same night Long Waterhouse, Joe and a couple of kindred spirits went out to look for the Dud and found it, brought it in, and detached the time fuse and detonator, and so it came into Joe's possession. Immediately we came out of the Line, the bomb was sent over to Jimmy Bowd at the Quartermaster's store at Bouzincourt for safe custody, marked "To be called for JWH".

Left to right: Lieutenant Colonel H.J. Shirley, Lieutenant R.N. Thompson RAMC (behind), Major H.N. Milnes, and Captain G.C. Hutchinson. This was probably taken at Senlis in September 1915 with Lieutenant Colonel Shirley's camera – see page 97.

CHAPTER 9
First Leave to England
5th November 1915 to 14th November 1915

05.11.15   On the morning of November 5th, I was busy erecting a Coffee Tavern at Crucifix Corner, Aveluy, which I wanted to complete before going on leave.[145]

Naturally our little party were feeling <u>very</u> cheery. We had quite an enjoyable dinner at "Z" Company HQ, during which time many notes were made regarding purchases which were to be made for the Mess in the way of cutlery, pans, primus stoves etc. and sundry personal requirements for fellows in the Mess.

Waddicar had been extremely busy trying to make my cleanest uniform as respectable as possible to travel home in.

It was about 9.00pm on Friday when Hedley, Gray and myself, loaded with valises, haversacks, burberries[146] etc., left "Z" Company HQ, Aveluy.

As it was night we decided to take the direct route to Bouzincourt, which route was marked "NOT TO BE USED BY TROOPS IN DAYTIME, UNDER OBSERVATION". As we started out a couple of shells landed on the village and a Boche Machine Gun dropped a few rounds of indirect fire into the streets. Almost by instinct all three of us quickened our pace, with the feeling that we wanted to get clear before any accidents happened.

As we mounted the high ground West of Aveluy we could hear the Machine Guns occasionally having a burst of fire in the Line, and see the Very lights[147] lighting up the sky brilliantly for a few seconds and then dying out again. What a glorious feeling it was to think that we were leaving that life for a whole week, the first time since May – six months – it seemed an age – and, moreover, we were actually going to England – Home. Words cannot express the feeling – only those who were fortunate enough to experience it can appreciate it, in its true aspect.

Bouzincourt was about 3 miles from Aveluy, and we arrived at Jimmy Bowd's billet there at about 10.00pm. Jimmy Bowd and Abbotts[148] were both out, so we made ourselves quite at home, and had a chat and some supper.

There was only one room at this billet (Abbotts slept out in the village). Joe decided to occupy Jimmy's bed, so Gray and I pulled some chairs together by the fire, and collected a few blankets. This was easy – trust an old Quartermaster for having a few blankets to spare.

We had to be off early the next morning, Saturday. We had previously arranged for the Maltese Cart[149] to turn out at 4.00am to take us down to the Railhead.

Sleep wasn't a great success that night! What with wondering about home, whether the

---

[145] See the diary entry for 5th October 1915 and page 108.

[146] See the footnote to the diary entry for 31st July 1915.

[147] These were flares, fired from a breech-loaded single shot pistol, developed by an American Naval Officer called Edward Wilson Very.

[148] Lieutenant W. Abbotts was Transport Officer with the 2/5th Lancashire Fusiliers when they first landed in France on 3rd May 1915, but this is the last mention of him in the diary. It is not clear what happened to him, but by 16th February 1916 Lieutenant G.H.A. Humble of the Notts and Derby Regiment, who was first attached to the Battalion in France on 23rd August 1915, is referred to as Transport Officer.

[149] See footnote 40 on page 37.

boat would sail, or leave might be stopped at the last minute etc.

Jimmy Bowd arrived back at about 2.30am, having dined well but none too wisely with some old pal of his in Albert. He was delighted that Joe had his bed, and eventually slept on the tile floor. 3.15am, the time for us to get up, came along at last, but it seemed ages.

06.11.15   After shaving, and a brush up and wash, we had a jolly good breakfast, and then climbed into the Maltese Cart (without springs). It was a bitterly cold morning. But what did we care? Of course, it was dark, and there was a slight drizzle. The Very lights were still lighting up the sky – but it was a quiet night. Yet, as one looked across the country, one realised that as far as the eye could see, aye and hundreds of miles beyond, were lines and lines of trenches inhabited by human beings, a proportion of whom at that moment were staring into inky blackness, yet alert, ready to wound, to kill, at a flash. And this was war, and yet, because of this Outpost Line, the Advanced Guard of our Army – the foremost protection of France – of England – we were able to leave it all for a little while and return to those whom we loved. Those at home, by virtue of this Line of defence, held all at costs under the severest conditions, were able to live in safety and carry on their work – their lives – in a more or less normal way.

On our drive down we soon crossed the main Albert to Doullens road, a typical National Road of France, with its poplar trees stretching for miles.

We soon passed through Millencourt, but to all outward appearances there wasn't a living soul in the place. Yet how different would the scene have changed in a few minutes had the Alarm been given. Leaving Millencourt behind we came to Laviéville, about 3 kilometres further South West. Occasionally we glanced at our watches, as our train was due to leave Méricourt at 6.00am. We had allowed two hours to cover about 12 miles, but we couldn't miss that train of all trains – the Leave Train.

Soon we crossed the Albert – Amiens – Bapaume road – a road in pre-war days famous for the Gordon Bennett Motor Trials[150] – and coming down to Ribemont we were then in the Ancre Valley.

Thirty minutes' ride from here brought us to Méricourt Station at 5.40am. It was still dark, but in the glow of the station yard flares could be seen little groups of men in various garbs, sheepskin coats, great coats, blankets, all looking cold and rubbing their hands to keep warm, for many had been there several hours; others were taking advantage of a YMCA hut nearby, and enjoying hot coffee or tea.

After reporting to the Railway Transport Officer, having our Leave Warrants stamped, and signing our names, we waited patiently for the train.

There is always a feeling of anxiety in waiting for any train, but the anxiety is especially intense when the train in question is a Leave Train.

Eventually we heard the whistle of the old French engine, and the familiar escape of the steam as she came up the incline into Méricourt Station.

Perhaps it is incorrect to say that the noises on these French trains were familiar, for it was three and a half months since I had been near a train.

---

[150] The Gordon Bennett Races were first run from Paris to Lyons in 1900; this race was for a trophy provided by the newspaper owner James Gordon Bennett of the New York Herald to help promote the motor industry. It was an open road race until 1903.

Méricourt is only a small country village in Peace time, but, since the British Army moved down to the Somme Front, it had become quite a busy place. Many new sidings had been put up and sheds erected for Ordnance Stores and Supply Depots, for this village station was now the main advance Railhead for the British Front, stretching from Thiepval to Bray, i.e. the Front South of the River Ancre. So much for Méricourt this time – we shall visit her again many times.[151]

Here we are – in the train – going on leave at last! At least we are off to Havre! Leave is always a gamble – one never knows when or where on the journey some counter-orders may be received, either postponing or cancelling leave.

It was still dark when we started off, but "forewarned is forearmed", and Joe Hedley, with his usual attention to detail, produced a couple of candles; these were put on the window ledge, there being no gas or electric lamps in the carriage. It had been a First Class carriage once! But 13 months of war in constant use by troops had rather taken the varnish off in places. Hedley, Gray, and I settled down for a long tedious journey. Huddled up in our respective corners, with our fleece-lined burberries[152] and air pillows, we tried to sleep. But in vain! The human body may be absolutely tired out – but an excited brain will not rest. So it was with us.

After about one and a half hours' journey from Méricourt we arrived at Amiens. Like all big stations – for Amiens is an important junction on the main line from Calais to Paris – it looked cold and cheerless at 8.00am in the morning. We had half an hour's wait here. So the four of us cleared off to the Refreshment Room and got coffee and rolls. That room was just full of sleepy, dirty, war worn soldiers, all either going on leave or returning from *"Permission"*, as the French soldier calls it. It wasn't difficult to discriminate between the "Goers" and the "Returners" by the facial expressions.

There were all Regiments represented, both French and English, or British. I don't think there were any British Colonials, for only the 1st Canadian Division were in France then, and they were up North. "Digger Jim", the Australian contingent, was still in Egypt or the Dardanelles. Whether French or British, they all resembled Italian Organ Grinders rather than soldiers. It was all very interesting – but our time was short.

So we got hold of a luncheon basket each, which consisted of chicken, ham, bread, cheese, biscuits, salad fruit and wine, for three shillings and sixpence (four francs) – quite cheap in war time. Then we bought our morning papers, the *Daily Mail*, also the *Strand* or similar magazines. This really made it seem as if we were getting back to civilisation once more. At 8.30am we steamed out of Amiens. It was now quite light and promised to turn out a glorious day.

It seemed strange to look across the open country and see fields and houses, instead of earthworks, trenches, and ruins. The countryside looked quite nice, and autumn tints were still to be seen in sheltered woods.

We had plenty of time to admire the view on our passage to Havre. One fellow thought that God must have made "Leave Trains", for it says in the Bible that "*God made all creeping things*".

---

[151] See the diary entries for 15th July 1916 through to September 1916.
[152] See footnote 94 on page 72.

When we arrived at Montérolier-Buchy we had a half hour stop to give the engine a drink. This was quite an out of the way place, but there was a YMCA Canteen run by voluntary lady helpers, and very nice girls they were. Of course it was splendid to see real live English girls again. We thoroughly enjoyed some sandwiches and coffee, and got some chocolate and cigarettes.

We left here at about 4.30pm. It was dark again and we had been on the train 10 hours. We were really feeling very tired and stiff, to say nothing of dirty. By 6.30pm we were in Rouen, but it was too dark to see anything of the city. We still had at least two hours' journey to Havre. It got quite chilly in spite of there being six of us in the carriage and all smoking like chimneys. We reached Harfleur – about 4 miles outside Havre – at 8.30pm, but it took some time to get down to the docks. The train ran right through to the Quay. Running down to the Quay over dock railways is bad enough at any time, but in a French train, much the worse for wear – it was the last word in jolting and squeaking.

One very typical incident on the way down, passing through any place with houses, was to see the French kiddies on the Railway Embankments, running along with the train calling out in one chorus.

"Souvenir, Bully-Beef, Biscuits!"

At last we arrived alongside the Quay.

It was cold, with a strong fresh breeze from the sea. Our ship was alongside, the RMS *Connaught*,[153] Holyhead to Dublin Service.

Joe Hedley was in charge of the Divisional party, so he had to see them aboard. He went off to collect his men, while Gray and myself went on board with Lieutenant Colonel Chadwick (RAMC), with whom we had been playing bridge on the train. Joe very kindly lent me his "Boche Trench Mortar Bomb Souvenir" to carry onto the ship. Feeling a bit guilty I wrapped it under my burberry[154] and boldly walked aboard.

Colonel Chadwick, it turned out, was CO of the ship, so he very kindly asked us to join him in his reserved cabin. Eventually Joe came aboard. We were all ready for a jolly good wash, shave, and brush up. This over, we each gathered up a life belt for use in case the old Hun did his dirty work with a torpedo, and we started from Havre at 10.15pm. Feeling hungry and thirsty we all went down to the Saloon and had a jolly good meal.

We were now actually crossing over to England – Southampton. As our ship was fast we were due in at 6.00am. So we turned in for a few hours' rest, arranging to be wakened in time to see Southampton Water as we sailed up.

07.11.15   We picked up a pilot at the entrance to Spithead. It was a dull grey misty morning, but not so thick as to have slowed us down. As we sailed up Southampton Water it came light, and we could just see Netley Hospital and a few Hospital Ships riding at anchor. After picking up our second pilot we ran into a thick mist and went dead slow, and eventually stopped, and – much to our surprise – the anchor was lowered. It was now 8 o'clock.

Half an hour, an hour, one and a half hours passed, and no sign of the fog lifting. Everyone had been very patient up till now, and then, as time crept on, many began to wonder whether we should be able to get home that night, as it was a Sunday. Every minute of

---

[153] See the photograph and footnote on page 142.
[154] See footnote 94 on page 72.

leave was precious, but in these days when one only got six days, it was more than annoying to be held up in a fog, so near our port of arrival.

Many attempts were made to persuade the pilot to risk moving on, and it was proposed to make him a substantial offer by collecting from the fellows on board, but it was no use. The pilot knew his job and wasn't risking 2000 lives for any amount of money.

At about 10 o'clock things looked better, and at last the mist lifted in a few seconds to show what a perilous position we were really in; only a matter of 150 to 200 yards ahead was a huge sand bank, but we had missed it and our leave boat was saved from running aground.

We were soon at the Docks now, and very quickly got off the boat. I managed to get off one of the first with Gray, but as Joe was going to Cheltenham direct he was not in a great hurry. Gray and I got the first train up to London and arrived at about 12.45pm. I went straight across Town from Waterloo to St Pancras, and had a jolly good wash and shave at the Hotel.

Being rather a mess, and having had a long journey of about 30 hours, I certainly looked grimy and somewhat war weary. I remember going down the hall at the Hotel – a tiled hall – and my nailed boots seeming to make an awful clatter, and people sitting about in their morning coats etc. looking as if they wondered what on earth had blown in. However I didn't care. I got a jolly good lunch and caught the 2 o'clock train to Manchester, arriving home at 8.45pm in time for supper. Jack, Kathleen, Mary and Jack Ashworth met me. Words fail me to describe my feelings on reaching home.

08.11.15 to 12.11.15	I have no record of how I spent my time on leave, except that I remember that it was a very busy time rushing round to see everyone, and I couldn't possibly fit in all my invitations.
13.11.15	It suffices to say that I more than enjoyed every minute of my visit, and Saturday came round all too quickly.

I left Bury on the 8.20pm train, changing into my field boots at Bolton Street Station in Bury, for they had been sent on from Manchester and had not been delivered in time. I caught the 9.20am train from Manchester Central Station to London. Naturally it wasn't by any means pleasant leaving everyone and going back to the Trenches and the War! In fact it was a thought which gave me a cold shudder down the spine and a nasty plum stone feeling about the throttle.

Still it had to be done cheerily. One thing helped me on my journey to London. George had promised to bring Effie up from Stubbington to see me and, as I hadn't seen her before, I was very keen on seeing what 'Erb had picked up for a future wife, and, incidentally, my future sister-in-law.

Just my luck some old trucks ran off the line somewhere near Derby and we had to go a round about way which made us about an hour late. The hills in Derbyshire looked beautiful – they were covered with snow.

George and Effie met me at St Pancras at 2.05pm and we went straight to the Regent Palace for a chat. I remember feeling as if I had known Effie for years. My train was due to leave Waterloo at 4.00pm so we hadn't long. George and Effie came over with me to Waterloo, where we met Joe Hedley, and George just had time to have a word with him.

The scene on Waterloo Station was one which will always be remembered. A train load of khaki clad figures of all Regiments in the British Army, little knots of people standing outside carriage doors, fathers, mothers, sisters, brothers, wives, all bidding Fond Farewells and wishing "Good Luck". One thought came into my mind, "How many of these fellows would come home again?" Luckily "the future was all unknown". Then the last minute – last seconds – came – with the porter's "Take your seats please". Joe and I had already taken ours – a corner each!

Then the Guard's whistle blew, and the train pulled out to the accompaniment of a farewell cheer from everyone on the platform. I wonder who felt the sadder, those in the train, or those left behind as they walked out of the station. For many things I was glad my "Au Revoirs" were over, and so ended seven days' leave.

The journey down to Southampton was uneventful. No one said very much.

We sailed at about 7.30pm on the Isle of Man boat, SS *Empress Queen*.[155] It seemed strange to see her on a job like that, but it gave one a homely feeling, although I must say I should have preferred crossing to Douglas rather than Havre.

I stayed on deck while we sailed down Southampton Water to Spithead. As we sailed down Spithead we passed a Hospital Ship, with her broad green band of electric lights, and a huge red cross in electric lights amidships. How peaceful she looked, but one could hardly imagine that her passengers were quite as peaceful.

SS *Empress Queen*

Still they were coming home – Blighty.[156] Gradually the lights of England grew dimmer and dimmer until they seemed to go out altogether. Such was the case for some who saw them! Then I went down and joined Joe and Gray. We had a jolly good dinner and then settled down on the Saloon floor for a sleep.

14.11.15   I wakened up at about 3.00am feeling very stiff and cold. I got up and went down to get some hot coffee, and to order some sandwiches to take along on the train with us. I managed to get some coffee for Joe and Gray also, which they were very glad of. One of the stewards claimed acquaintance with me, so I seized the opportunity and persuaded him to get me some bottles of Bass ready with the sandwiches – a couple of bob (shillings) did the trick. But I never said a word to Joe and Gray, just slipped them into my pack, which was already fairly full.

We got into Havre at about 3.30am. But there was no train; we walked up to the station and it was very cold and pouring with rain, so we all lay down in a huge shed till about 6.00am. Then we got into the train and tried to warm things up by lighting several candles. I soon fell asleep and never noticed the train had started, in fact it was 8.30am – and light – when I wakened. It was an awful morning, and we had a broken window in the carriage. We traversed the same route as the week before. We had breakfast at Montérolier-Buchy and managed to get some boiled eggs and coffee. The same girls were there and very cheery in spite of the heavy work and long hours.

To pass the time we talked and compared notes about our leaves, also we played bridge. Then lunch time came and Joe and Gray were very fed up because they thought we hadn't

---

[155] SS *Empress Queen*, a paddle steamer launched in 1897, was chartered as a troop ship in February 1915; on 1st February 1916, when returning to Southampton from Le Havre in bad weather with poor visibility, she ran aground off Bembridge on the Isle of Wight; the 1300 troops and crew on board were safely taken off, but she was pounded by the ensuing storm to such an extent that she was unsalvageable.

[156] Blighty is slang for "Britain" or "home", and is derived from Hindustani "bilayati", meaning "foreign land".

anything to eat. However I produced the sandwiches which delighted them ever so much. Then Joe said he would give five pounds for a bottle of Bass. So I said, "Well Joe – hand over the money and the Bass is yours." Naturally he thought I was pulling his leg, but when I did produce six real live bottles of Bass, both Joe's and Gray's faces were a treat to behold. They might have been going on leave and not coming back, they looked so cheery. Anyway we enjoyed them.

The train travelled so slowly at times that fellows got out and walked alongside to stretch their legs.

We reached Amiens at about 7.00pm. It was <u>very</u> cold and freezing keenly, and I really appreciated my new fleece-lined burberry.[157] We arrived at Méricourt at about 8.45pm. It seemed no time since we had left it. The Mess Cart was waiting for us. The Battalions were out of the Line still, and the driver, Mills, had some wonderful rumours. The Division was to move, probably to Egypt. This afterwards proved to be merely a Transport Line fairy tale – quite a common occurrence.

We had quite a long ride – worse luck! – as the roads were certainly getting worse for wear, and we were half lying down, so got quite cramped. However, we passed through Dernancourt, Buire, Méaulte, Albert, Aveluy to Martinsart.

The Front seemed peaceful enough, except for the momentary illuminations of a Very light. We arrived at "Z" Company HQ at 10.00pm. Everyone seemed very glad to see us back and naturally wanted to know all the news, and how things were going in the old Country. So each of us related our doings, and our impressions of the conditions in England. Briefly my impression was this:

The Country was normal, and it did not seem to have really developed the necessary enthusiasm for the War. By that I mean the General Public did not seem to have realised that the Empire's very existence depended upon the War result – that it was either Germany or the Allies who were to govern the World, that it was a struggle between Civilisation and Militarism of the very worst type – Prussianism. Instead of setting their teeth and either joining the forces or mobilising the industry of the Country to produce war materials, they were all fighting amongst themselves – strikes in vital industries were prevalent.

The Government were still frightened of the people. It was obvious to those at the Front that the War was going to be a long job and a costly one, not only financially, but in lives. So far we hadn't made a single offensive action with success. Loos had failed. We were only holding our ground, and that under tremendous strain because we had neither men, guns, nor ammunition to deal an effective blow at the German. Yet at home they were still holding on to the Voluntary Service system, when it was evident that a system of Compulsory Service was the only way to win the War.

The Government were frightened of the British workman – who was, even at this time, getting wages out of all proportion. They were frightened of internal trouble with the British workman if his liberty and freedom of action were interfered with.

This was the beginning of the serious Labour troubles which lasted through the War and after the Armistice.

Lord Derby introduced a scheme of Registration for Service[158] – undoubtedly a wonderful scheme for the times, but – as of old – the "willing horse" got all the collar work.

The General Public didn't seem to care what happened – they took the War as a game, instead of a Life and Death matter.

---

[157] See footnote 94 on page 72.
[158] See footnote 11 on page 20.

Certainly there was a lot of sorrow and sadness that we had suffered, but nothing like we should have to do. Yet people couldn't see that daily on all Fronts lives were being sacrificed without any results being achieved and with the Army getting weaker.

We in the 51st Division were just looking forward to receiving 18 pounder Field Guns – we had had to be content with the 15 pounders used in South Africa up till now.

England seemed mad on amusements. Why? Because the people were making big wages and getting just what they demanded. Charlie Chaplin seemed of far more importance nationally than fighting the Hun. Conscription was quite a secondary consideration.

The Country seemed full of khaki, but these were Kitchener's Army[159] who had been in training for months. Surely they were ready to come out and do their whack? Evidently someone knew when and where to use Reserves.

One thought did buck one up – viz. knowing that so far we had held the Hun; England and our homes were safe except for occasional raids by the Boche, and our people were not driven from the firesides as the French and Belgians had been. This was something!

We in France felt we should most certainly win, but we were sure that it would take certainly two years and tremendous sacrifices.

Some people smiled when I made a statement that the Hun would raid England by aeroplanes in the daytime before long. But he did it, and pretty effectively.

Well, to return to "Z" Company's billet in Martinsart, it was just an ordinary French farm, owned by ordinary French peasants who were chiefly women, children and old men, for France had long ago been forced to realise that Conscription was her very security. Naturally her geographical position demanded such a Protective Policy, and in consequence all her manhood of military age were on service. But those who remained had stout hearts and patience. Seldom did they show any real antagonism towards our soldiers, though we took possession of their farms, their stables, their granaries, and their fields. Certainly they were paid for accommodating troops, but one often wondered whether English people under similar conditions would have been so kindly disposed towards French soldiers billeted upon them. Why, we heard of many cases in England where troops had anything but a friendly reception.

The people where we were were exceedingly kind, and the children were quite bright, and happy little friends of ours – one little girl about 12 years of age was a special friend of the Skipper.

Naturally we were anxious to know what the Battalion were doing and what our future movements were to be.

We soon learnt that the "Egypt Story" was all rot, and that we were to move up to the trenches on Tuesday November 16th, but to a new sector, further North than before, directly opposite Thiepval, and running up to the marshes near Beaumont-Hamel. We were to relieve the 155th Brigade, one of the Scottish Brigades.

So much for our leave and return to duty.

We retired to our beds that night very tired and soon dropped away to sleep in our valises. But what a difference from the few nights of comfort on leave made.

Still there was the next leave to look forward to now.

---

[159] See footnote 90 on page 69.

CHAPTER 10
Martinsart, Thiepval Wood and Authuille Wood
15th November 1915 to 1st January 1916

15.11.15   We wakened up to find a heavy fall of snow.

The Battalion was on working parties up the Line; it was very heavy work to walk about 6 miles in heavy snow, dig all day, and return to barns for the night.

A party had been arranged to go to see the Divisional Theatre Party which had just started at Senlis, where a very cosy theatre had been erected in a barn. Motor buses came for us to Martinsart at about 6.00pm, and we went to Senlis via Aveluy, Albert, and Bouzincourt. We had great fun en route both going and coming.

Ainscow had joined the Battalion while I was away.[160]

16.11.15   We made preparations to move up to the Line. When the Battalion paraded at about
to   4.00pm they really looked a splendid sight, all in sheepskin coats.
27.11.15   Our orders were to move slowly as we had a long tramp. We passed through Aveluy, past Crucifix Corner, along to Authuille and Authuille Wood.

Our Battalion were on the Left Sector of the Brigade Front, with the 1/4th Loyal North Lancashires on our right, the 1/8th Liverpool Irish in Support, and the 1/4th King's Own Royal Lancasters in Reserve in Authuille village.

The order of our Battalion was, from right to left, "Z" Company (Hammer Head Corner Right), "W" Company, and "Y" Company with the left resting on Peterhead, with "X" Company being in Reserve.

The Front Line ran right on the edge of Thiepval Wood, with an inspection trench running parallel to the Front Line proper, and about 10 yards to the rear. We had a very big frontage. "Z" Company had nearly 700 yards of Front to cover with only 70 men, and one of Freddy Harker's Machine Guns, which were now Vickers (these were quite good).

The weather was terrible – snow drifts and storms with strong North East winds.

The relief was quite satisfactory except for the bad weather – the snow having turned to rain, with accompanying <u>mud</u>.

Fortunately the trenches in this part were dug in solid chalk, which was comparatively clean, and the water could be swept away into sump holes.

Waterhouse had quite a nice little dug out, but Kenderdine, Moffatt (Cecil), and I had rather damp ones and very cold, sort of chalk caves. Kenders (Charlie Chaplin) and I joined at a dug out. It was fairly good with two beds, fairly shell-proof, at any rate to a whizz-bang,[161] unless one came from the right flank, in which case, being a Boche, it was quite probable that it would come right in without knocking. We had no door, only a ground sheet hung down.

We had two large dug outs for the men, and several small ones.

Our Mess was away from the Skipper's dug out, and was dug about 20 feet down in solid chalk, very cold. It had a nice dripping roof, and we hadn't any fire. We had a very nasty bit

---

[160] Ainscow had been left behind in Bury in April 1915 when Norman joined the 2/5th Lancashire Fusiliers as Signals Officer at the eleventh hour before their departure for Bury – see the diary entry for 19th April 1915.
[161] Army slang for a type of high velocity shell, usually the 77mm type.

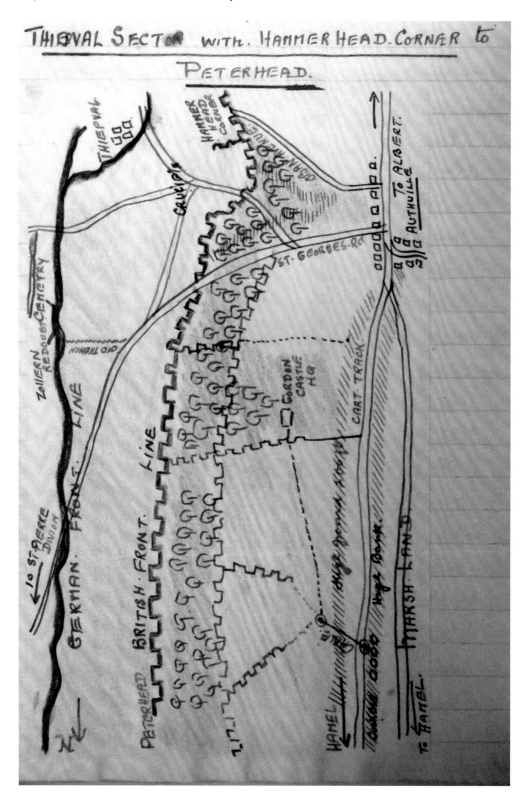

THIEVAL SECTOR WITH. HAMMER HEAD. CORNER to PETERHEAD.

of Line on our right, running round a re-entrant into our Line and across a valley, with a
<u>thick</u> wood on the Right Post, and a sap running out at Hammer Head Corner towards the

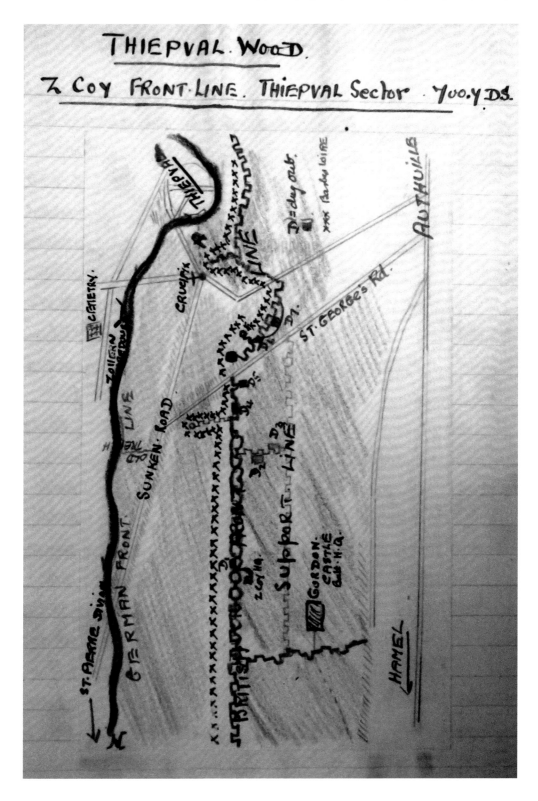

five cross roads at the Crucifix Corner just South West of Thiepval village, which stood on a hill and overlooked our Line in this part; also it was uncomfortably near, about 250 yards away, just in convenient range for German Trench Mortars, and the old Hun didn't forget to take advantage of his position. We had some very unpleasant "strafes" from that quarter, also the Crucifix cross roads provided many an evening's entertainment, fortunately without many casualties to us.

We had a main road running right through our Line, St George's Road. It had high banks on either side and this also necessitated a constant scheme of patrol and observation in No Man's Land.

Our chief danger point was the valley on our right, which ran down to Authuille, and had to be specially watched, for it offered a very favourable point of attack for the Boche – the occupation of which would have practically isolated our Battalion.

Governing this valley the Boche had a very strong fortification known as "Zollern Redoubt", which also acted as a very strong flank guard on the North side of Thiepval. This Redoubt proved a very formidable obstacle in the Somme Offensive in 1916.

This sector can certainly be described as an interesting sector; certainly it had many points which required careful watching.

A sunken road ran right across No Man's Land, the Thiepval – Authuille – St-Pierre-Divion road. Patrols had to deal with this with care and thought, for it was an ideal place for the Hun or ourselves to lie in wait for hostile parties. Whoever got in position first had a great advantage.

Running from this road to the German Front Line was an old disused Communication Trench. We had one or two patrol encounters in the vicinity.

The Crucifix Corner, opposite "Z" Company's Right Flank, and about 200 yards into No Man's Land, was also a favourite spot for encountering the Hun. He seemed to have an underground approach to this from Thiepval village, for, no matter how carefully we watched all the approaches to it, he seemed able to get men there.

One road running down from the village always had our thought at night, for we kept several Fixed Rifles trained on it, thus a constant fire was kept on this approach throughout the hours of darkness.

Without doubt it was hard work on this sector – we had such a big frontage and few men, and we endeavoured to establish a complete command over No Man's Land by constant patrolling.

I had rather an interesting time trying to tap German telephone communications. I took out a party including two Signallers, Sergeant Nuttall and Green. We tried placing a series of earth pins in the ground inside the German wire. These pins were all connected together by insulated wire and a main lead was taken back towards our Line, and a telephone was attached. We hoped to pick up the German messages by induction. At first we did not meet with any success. This, we concluded, was due to the fact that we were not near enough to the German Signal Station. We tried several nights moving our position along the German barbed wire each night, and staying out for about four hours each night.

We did pick up some Morse signals in one place – they were regular but faint. The conclusion of our experiment was that it would be possible to detect enemy signals in this way, but a transformer would be necessary to multiply the current or waves coming through by induction. A report was made to this effect to Division, but the usual reply came back "Transformers not available". About two years later, in 1917, a similar idea was used to interrupt enemy telephone messages, with considerable success.

Luckily, during this work we had no unpleasant encounters with the Hun, though, of course, we always had a covering party with us. The chief trouble was lying out there in the cold, wet ground hour after hour.

The long nights were very trying, about 16 hours of darkness – hours of constant strain, of uncertainty, and watching.

Kenderdine and I had a very cheery time one night up the old Communication Trench in No Man's Land. I found an old telephone wire and was following it up, tapping it at intervals with the telephone, in hopes of it being still connected to the German wires. No luck! But the old Boche nearly got us – appearing on the top of the trench. He fired a few shots, but our flank guards were quite alert and we put up a fight for a few minutes.[xi] We drove the Hun off, but we didn't bag one.

"W" Company did some useful patrolling on our left – especially Long Waterhouse and Noton. Noton had really done some very useful reconnaissance. One night he went over to the Boche trench to inspect their wire and brought back some interesting specimens of the Boche wire and some screw pickets, the type which were used by our people in the First Somme Battle, and from then onwards. They were made in various lengths and were much easier to handle than wooden posts, the driving in of which with a huge maul made a resounding noise and often drew fire, also it was slow. Noton was awarded the MC for continuous good work, the first honour to the Battalion.[162]

About 50 yards behind the Boche Second Line, and opposite to "Z" Company, was Thiepval Cemetery. It was on a road, and a Communication Trench ran close by it. For some reason or other the Hun used to get out of this trench and walk – or more often run – across about 15 yards of open ground into the Cemetery, usually at about 7.00am to 8.00am every morning, and also at about 12.00 noon. We imagined he was going for rations. We had a very good Sniping Post in "Z" Company's Line, and one fellow, Grange, used to watch this spot very carefully. He was a good shot, and, as the range was about 700 yards with a telescopic rifle, it was a good mark. Grange claimed at least one per day – this I rather doubt, but I am confident that we certainly hit some Boche, and after about a week they stopped using this open short cut – a good indication?

Hot food (which was very necessary, because, although the weather had improved considerably by Sunday November 21st, and was fine and dry, it was still frosty, and very cold) was brought up by rather an interesting method to this Line. We sent our ration parties down as usual to the cookers. The Field Kitchens were situated in a valley about 800 yards behind the Front Line [see the sketch plan on page 122]. They were protected from shell fire by a high steep bank 200 feet high. An endless cable working on a pulley was slung from the top of the cliff down to the cookers, and the large dixies were hooked on to the cable and hoisted up, then the dixies were carried about 600 yards to our Company HQ. Occasionally a dixie was not securely fastened on to the hooks and the contents were spilt on the way up – consequently short rations for that meal.

On November 23rd Waddicar, my servant, was taken ill and I sent him down to the MO after much talk, and very much against his wish. However, it proved later to be the only thing to do, as he had appendicitis and was sent over to England quickly for an operation. On November 29th I had a letter from him from Rouen saying he was off to England, so I should have to get someone else. I was very sorry to lose him. He had been with me since the beginning, and was a hard worker and very willing.

---

[162] The Battalion did not learn of this award until 2nd July 1916 – see the diary entry for that date.

On November 26th I managed to have a really good night's rest. I came off duty at 10.45pm and slept till 8.00am, a bit of luck! Only disturbed by a rat who kept crawling over my face, quite friendly intentions no doubt, but most annoying.

28.11.15 It was a glorious morning – sunny and frosty. We made preparations for relief. I went out of the Line early to do the billeting in Martinsart. I took out the billeting party at about 3.00pm – quite a nice walk down to Authuille, across the marshes, and over the Albert – Aveluy – Bapaume railway, which had barricades and breastworks built across it, with dug outs in the railway banks.

We walked along the Martinsart to Hamel road and got to Martinsart at about 5.30pm. Billeting was easy, as we had been there before, so HQ and each Company took over the same billets. I expected the Battalion back from the Line at about 10.00pm. I got the cookers going at about 8.30pm; they came away from the Line early so as to have a meal ready for the men on arrival. Our Mess things were late, so I had some difficulty in getting a meal ready for "Z" Company Mess. The post arrived, and it saved the situation, for I had a very useful parcel. Consequently we had oxtail soup, sausages, mashed potatoes and fruit. We finished at about 11.00pm. I had got braziers and good fires going in all the men's barns and a huge fire in our billet. It was quite a treat to sit round the fire, after days of bitter cold in the Line.

29.11.15 The frost turned to rain, and made everywhere an awful mess.
to I had an idea at this time of transferring to the Chemical Corps, but didn't like to leave all
05.12.15 my pals in the 2/5th Lancashire Fusiliers.
We had several interplatoon football matches while we were out of the Line this time. I was also able to visit a couple of old friends of the Manchester Pals, the 22nd Manchesters, Eric Oldham at Englebelmer and Walter Cornall at Mesnil. They were also both able to visit me at Martinsart for dinner. Eric's Battalion had just arrived from England. Walter seemed very well and cheerful, in spite of having rather a heavy time.

On Tuesday November 30th I went to Pierrots at Senlis with Dr Thompson, Young, and Kemp. It was Kenderdine's birthday so we made a special effort at dinner on our return, and had:

Sardines on Toast
Mock Turtle Soup
Curried Mutton, Roast Beef
Carrots – Peas – Roast Potatoes
Pears, Toasted Cheese
Coffee

We had several interplatoon football matches while we were out of the Line this time. Moffatt turned out to be quite a good player, and Kenderdine was very funny. The Officers played the Sergeants one day and Joe Hedley kept goal.

06.12.15 On Sunday December 6th we went into the Line again. It was very wet, and the trenches
to were nearly flooded, over the knees in water in some places, especially near Hammer
17.12.15 Head Corner.
We went back to our old sector for a few days near Authuille Wood, with Company HQ in Oban Avenue. Our beautiful HQ which we had spent so much time building in September

had been badly neglected and had about 6 inches of mud all over the floor. The Seaforths had been in occupation. Really these Scotchmen were the limit. However, a few solid hours' work the next day made things more homely again.[163]

The trenches were simply a quagmire. It took two hours to get round our Line; parts were almost impassable. We were on clay. Ugh! Gum thigh boots were absolutely necessary. I got so much mud on my burberry[164] round the bottom, I couldn't do anything with it, so cut a strip off about 9 inches wide and made a short waterproof, which proved very useful. The thaw after the keen frost made the sides of the trenches crack, and crumble, and fall in. The pumps were in constant use, but seemed to make very little difference, the water collected as fast as it was pumped away. Digging was almost impossible, although we did continue a big job which was on hand – making some new deep dug outs.

It was absolutely impossible to keep clean. One hardly liked to send parties down the Communication Trench to Authuille with petrol tins for water – it was quite sufficient to bring up rations and drinking water. Consequently we were all glad to get out of the Line on Thursday, December 9th and back to our billets at Martinsart, where we got hot baths and a change of clothing – the first real wash for five days; and we were soaked to the skin – in fact the mud actually found its way through the skin.

I got a rotten chill on my inside and developed a minor type of dysentery which gave me a very unpleasant time for the next few weeks.

The weather was so bad about this period that we were doing four days in the Line and four days out. It was very hard work, and the marching to and from the Line was hardly enjoyable. Really we never seemed to be dry.

On our last trip up the Line during this period we had more Kitchener's Army[165] in for instruction – rather a nuisance as we had to keep moving in and out to make room for them. They came up first by platoons, then companies, then I suppose they cleared off to take a sector over on their own. We got the 18th Division and the 11th Borderers – who I believe came from Whitehaven District and Carlisle. They were fine fellows physically, but very slow witted.

On Thursday December 17th we came out of the Line. It was too wet even for the Gunners to uncover their guns to fire.

19.12.15   We received warning orders for the Line. This meant that we should spend Xmas Day in the trenches, and probably New Year's Day also. At last we had a fine sunny winter's day – quite a welcome change.

The bright weather made good visibility, and consequently both our Gunners and the Boche Gunners got busy again. Fine weather always meant target practice and registering of points.

21.12.15   I went up with Manse Evans to take over the trenches in the Thiepval Sector in the morning. I was feeling very rotten and really not fit to go up, but Waterhouse was due to go on leave, so I had to take over the Company when he went.

We were to relieve the 9th Borderers (Kitchener's Army). I knew the sector quite well, so

---

[163] See the diary entry for 11th September 1915 for the construction of this HQ.
[164] See footnote 94 on page 72.
[165] See footnote 90 on page 69.

there were no special difficulties. I was almost done in when I arrived at the Front Line, but rested a short time and then went round the Line to see if there was anything fresh. Corporal Stevens as usual checked off the stores.

We went into Kenderdine's old dug out and there I met one or two of the officers, three besides the Major. We returned to the Mess and had just started lunch when I heard a couple of "Minnies"[166] burst in the Front Line. A few seconds later a man came down to see where Mr ———— was, as his dug out was blown in. The roof of this particular home was about 10 feet thick, made of huge tree trunks.

We immediately went off to the scene of the commotion. It was an awful mess, and all the trench was blown in as well. We soon found that one officer and his servant were under the debris, at least everyone said so, and certainly we had left three officers and one servant there only about 10 minutes before.[xii] The OC of the Company, a Major, got the wind up most horribly – he hadn't even seen a casualty before, let alone a trench and dug out blown in. It was their first real tour in the Line. The Major fellow was very keen to fill the whole job in with earth.

Luckily I had seen accidents like this before, and I insisted on trying to dig the fellows out. The Major was very reluctant to let us carry on and work in the daylight, as we were in full view of the Boche, in fact a Boche Sniper had already got his eye on the place. At last I lost my temper and told the Major that I was going to do the job, as the fellows might possibly be alive even though buried, and every minute was valuable. He was nearly off his head by then. But I threatened to put him under arrest for "Neglect of Duty" and eventually sent him away with one of his officers. Then I got four Border fellows, picks and spades (not "Picts and Scots"), and we started.

In about 20 minutes we came to the officer's leg. So we carefully lifted logs and earth and managed to get the poor chap out. He was alive and conscious, but badly shaken, and in pain with a broken leg and probably his ribs either badly crushed or broken. We sent him off on a stretcher to the Aid Post. We continued our digging for his servant, and after about four hours' hard work, under intermittent rifle fire from a rude Boche Sniper, we eventually found parts of a body. We collected as much of the poor boy as we could find, and the remains were buried in Authuille Cemetery.[167] Anyway we certainly saved one life by our trouble.

But personally I felt about fit to die on the spot. The Battalion were some hours before they came up – at about 9.00pm – so I got a sleep before they arrived.

23.12.15   We soon took over the Line and settled in. Kenderdine took duty until midnight, and we decided to join at my old dug out. It was a filthy wet night, simply coming down in sheets. Kenders was wet through when he turned in. I had slung some ground sheets up in the roof of the dug out to catch the water which was coming through. Poor old Kenders, very tired, had just settled down on the bed, when I was passing the dug out and heard loud – and not altogether Parliamentary – language issuing therefrom, so went to investigate. The weight of water had got too heavy for the ground sheets and had broken the supports, with the result that the whole flood came down on Charlie Chaplin (Kenderdine), and he was again soaked through, including his blankets.

---

[166] Minenwerfers, a type of Trench Mortar.
[167] In fact it was the 15th Battalion Highland Light Infantry that the 2/5th Lancashire Fusiliers relieved. Their War Diary shows that the officer who was injured was Lieutenant D.S. Dickson, and the man who died was Private A. Watson, Service no 13091, aged 35, husband of Margaret Watson of Bridgeton, Glasgow. He is buried in Authuille Military Cemetery, reference B.71.

Noton crocked up about this time and unfortunately had to go to Hospital on January 5th 1916, and later to England. He had done some very useful work and was greatly missed by the Battalion, and especially "W" Company.

24.12.15 Captain Waterhouse went on leave. We were sorry not to have him with us for Christmas, but were pleased that he was able to go home to his wife. At this time I took over the Company. We had received a Special Order of the Day from Sir Douglas Haig who had taken over command from Lord French on December 15th. The order was to this effect:
There was to be no fraternising between the Germans and ourselves, troops in the Front Line were to be extra vigilant, and the GOC in Chief desired that troops should be especially active with small raids and worry the Boche during the Christmas period. He relied on all troops to carry out the spirit of this order.[168]
As a result "Z" Company got a job of work to do. Four Trench Mortars were brought up to our Front Line to fire on the Crucifix Corner. A pre-arranged 10 minutes' strafe had been arranged with the 15 pounder and 4.5 inch howitzers to shell an area round the Crucifix. This was all timed to commence at 6.00pm. 2nd Lieutenant C.H. Moffatt was to take out a party of 12 men, and, immediately the barrage lifted, he was to rush the Crucifix and capture any Boche who were there, also to report the result of the shoot. It had previously been reported by Moffatt that, for several nights prior to this, the Boche was holding the cross roads and Crucifix with a strong standing patrol.
Some difference of opinion came up between Colonel Shirley and myself as to the best line of approach to the place. We had reconnoitred the ground many times and knew every inch of it, and I wished to approach it from Hammer Head Sap, because it was quite near to the Crucifix, and gave Moffatt's party only a short distance to go, thus enabling them to reach the point of attack before the Boche would expect any attack. However, the Colonel insisted on approaching the Crucifix from the North side. As we expected, by the time Moffatt reached his objective, the Hun had reinforced his standing patrol so that it numbered about 40 men; consequently Moffatt's party came under heavy rifle, Machine Gun, and bomb fire.
They only escaped receiving heavy casualties by having a thorough knowledge of the ground, and were thus enabled to take advantage of what little natural cover there was. We suffered two casualties – luckily both slight wounds.
We had not succeeded in our object. So I arranged with Harker to bring enfilade Machine Gun fire on to the Crucifix Corner from the left, and with the Liverpool Irish to enfilade the same place from the right. Kenderdine took out a new patrol from Hammer Head Sap and made a frontal attack under cover of our fire. He did not get any prisoners, but the Boche vacated the position and had several casualties. Both Moffatt and Kenderdine showed pluck and initiative in this little Show. It was all over by 9.00pm.
I wakened up in my dug out at about 9.30pm – very dazed. I couldn't imagine what had happened. However, it wasn't anything to worry about – merely that I had been carried in from the trench unconscious. I soon felt better.
At about 10.00pm we received a report from "W" Company that Lieutenant Long Waterhouse had taken a patrol out to reconnoitre the St-Pierre-Divion road. I was alone at the time, so went out to warn the Company of the above patrol. I had scarcely got to the Front Line when I heard explosions of bombs and rifle cracks. I didn't know what was

---

[168] This reflects back to the famous fraternisation between the troops over Christmas 1914.

happening and, as we were holding the Line very thinly, I decided not to run any risks and gave the order to "Stand to". I thought that possibly Waterhouse had met a party of Boche in No Man's Land, who were intending to make a surprise raid on us. We couldn't fire, because we didn't know precisely where "Long Un's" party were.

Quite a number of bombs were thrown, and there was a certain amount of shouting – both in English and German. We couldn't fire any Very lights[168] for fear of giving the position of our patrol away. Then we distinctly saw figures running and all quietened down again.

What had actually happened was that the Boche had got out on to the sunken road early and was lying in wait for any patrol we sent out. They – the Hun – allowed our party to approach within a few yards of the road before they threw any bombs. They certainly completely surprised our party, and were in much greater numbers. Waterhouse thought there were two separate Hun parties of about 10 to 15 men each. One party fired first, and drew fire from our little patrol of one officer and five other ranks. Immediately they replied, they were fired on from the other flank, and the Boche appeared to be outflanking "W" Company's patrol. Three of our fellows were hit. Long Waterhouse immediately picked up one fellow and carried him in to our trench, under fire all the time, leaving Corporal N. Howarth to fight the Boche, who were running away; also Howarth was guarding two wounded fellows – he himself being wounded also. Waterhouse went back and carried another fellow back to our Line, and again returned to help Howarth to get the third man in. One man was missing, and Waterhouse thought he might have been badly hit, and was quite near where they were surprised. Lieutenant Waterhouse and Corporal Howarth made a thorough search of all the ground, but failed to find the missing man. Waterhouse was very badly shaken, but luckily not wounded. He was <u>very</u> bothered at losing one of his men, and at daybreak on Xmas morning he again went out to search for this fellow, spending a considerable amount of time in No Man's Land in broad daylight, but without success.

Lieutenant Waterhouse and Corporal Howarth showed great coolness in this small fight, and Waterhouse certainly carried two men (wounded) into our Line in the face of heavy fire, and a much greater force of the enemy than we had. He was deservedly recommended for his bravery, but we were all sorry that he did not receive a well-earned honour. Corporal Howarth was awarded the DCM for his work, and well deserved it.

Lieutenant Waterhouse – who had had a very strenuous time in the Line under exceptionally bad weather conditions – went to Hospital with "'flu" on January 4th 1916, and generally jiggered up, proceeding to the South of France for a well-earned rest.[170]

Things quietened down a bit towards 12.30am, so I decided I must go and have a lie down for half an hour. I had had very little food for several days and we had had an exciting evening's entertainment.

I went to my dug out and got some brandy and lay down. Soon afterwards my Company Sergeant Major (Howard) came in to report something, and, being Xmas Eve, he just had

---

[169] These were flares, fired from a breech-loaded single shot pistol, developed by an American Naval Officer called Edward Wilson Very.

[170] Some weeks later they received word that the missing man had been taken prisoner and had died of his wounds. Waterhouse stayed in the South of France until mid-March 1916 – see the diary entry for 16th March 1916. Corporal N. Howarth, Service no 201241, was promoted to Company Sergeant Major. He died aged 30 on 17th June 1917, as a result of a punishing march the day before from Millam to Westbécourt, in sweltering conditions and in full kit, described by Thomas Floyd in *At Ypres with Best-Dunkley*. The Battalion War Diary says that he "*remained on the march until completely exhausted and as a result died the following day in No 10 Stationary Hospital*". Company Sergeant Major Howarth DCM was the husband of Ethel Howarth of Montrose, and is buried at Longuenesse (St Omer) Souvenir Cemetery, reference IV.C.34.

a drink or two with me. He was a great fellow and always at the right place when there was any trouble. He made a remark in passing in his blunt rather crude way that he didn't know what we were going to do. To use his own words: "Why, the 'ole B —— Company's going melancholy – all because they're int' bloomin' trenches for Christmas. Why, it's t'only place to wish the Boche a Happy Christmas, and I think we've done it tonight." "Very well, Howard. Come along, we'll have a walk round the Line, and just have a chat with the boys to cheer them up a bit. Bring the rum ration along." So we went.

But I never got right round that night – for the second time in the evening Howard very kindly carried me to my dug out and put me on my bed.

25.12.15   I wakened up at about 6.00am, and felt much better. I had a jolly good wash and shave. I went round the Line. Kenders and Moffatt were both out, and as cheery as usual. I sent in my usual reports and then had breakfast.

It didn't feel a bit like Christmas Day, and naturally I often wondered about them all at home. It rained during the morning. I got a message from HQ to say that our Artillery would shell various points of the German defences starting at 1.30pm. Thiepval village was included. We were evidently going to deliver a few Christmas presents to the Hun – made specially for him in England. The thing that pleased us most about the shoot was the fact that 8 inch guns were to fire into Thiepval. This was certainly a Christmas Day surprise – and a very welcome one – for we had only had 4.5 inch and 4.7 inch Naval Guns up until now. At last England had actually made some decent sized guns and we were going to give the Boche a sample of what he had given us for some time, without any reply from our side.

Our Christmas Day lunch was a poor do, as the ration was short – fancy, on Christmas Day of all days – so we had to be content with bully beef. How about this compared with Turkey or Goose!! Also the mails didn't arrive so we didn't get any Christmas Cards. I kept a look out for Father Christmas – but I don't think he knew where the trenches were – at least he didn't arrive!

Kenders, Moffatt and I went round and told the men about the 8 inch guns, and we anxiously waited for 1.30pm. Then they started. We all stood on the fire step to watch. The first shell didn't do any damage. But the second big fellow got a direct hit on a house in Thiepval, and the men all cheered with delight. It really was great to feel we were letting the Hun have it in the neck. Meanwhile the 18 pounders, or "pant splitters", as Bloy always called them, devoted their attention to the German Front and Support Line. This went on for two hours without a stop; and no retaliation. Then the Hun started, and he gave us quite as much in return. Fortunately he was about 30 yards over our heads, so didn't hit anybody. When this started I had gone to my dug out to send a report off. Luckily the CO wanted me on the 'phone so I went to the Signallers' dug out near mine to speak to Colonel Shirley. What luck he wanted me just at that particular moment, for while I was out of my dug out he dropped a shell right on my little home which came through the roof at one corner and burst inside. Just one of those many "might have beens". I found the nose cap of this shell and kept it as a souvenir – the only present I got from the Boche. He also very unkindly hit a tree which fell right across the path to my home, and, not content with that, blew in my private latrine.[xiii]

He really gave us a very rapid half hour. Can people imagine that in England this day people had been singing "Peace on Earth – goodwill to men"? There didn't seem much of that spirit with us.

The rest of the day passed quietly.

28.12.15   We managed to have a Christmas pudding for dinner – one sent out from home – and it was excellent.

I had now got a new servant to replace Waddicar – Private John Edward Ashton from Heywood. He was a cotton spinner by trade, rather a rough diamond to start with, but he was very sound, very hard working, and a fine chap. He was thoroughly conscientious and made a very excellent servant.

Kenderdine was about due for leave, so this meant that Moffatt and I would be alone. There were rumours that we were to go right away from the forward areas after this tour in the Line, and we were about ready for a rest and to be out of the shelled areas. We had been in the forward areas since June, and, although we hadn't in this time been in any big Show, yet we had done some good hard work, with constant patrolling, and the watching and waiting and anxiety was beginning to have its effect on us all. Also we had been exposed to very severe weather for the past six weeks.

I was about as weak as a kitten with about three weeks of either trench fever or dysentery in a mild form.

I had another narrow escape one night during this tour.

When I was walking round the Line, the Boche sent a few "Minnies"[171] over on our right, near where he blew the dug out in on December 21st. I went down to see whether everyone was alright. As I approached a Post of Sergeant Smith's platoon, I heard the familiar "puff" of a "Tock Emma"[172] and looked into the sky for the spark trail. It was clearly visible and seemed to be coming straight for us. They always did! Then we heard the whirr-whirr-whirr of the bomb only a few yards away. We took cover in the bottom of the trench. We heard the thing drop quite near and waited, what seemed to us like hours, in reality probably a couple of seconds, then Crump! Crack! A terrific deafening explosion – followed by a shower of earth, stones, mud, and bits of steel or iron. For a few moments we were deafened and stupefied, and not quite certain whether we were hit. Howarth and Barlow were on the Post at the time. Barlow was very badly shaken but not wounded. Howarth was quite speechless, and, when he regained his speech, he started to cry and sob like a baby – I was sure that he was a shell shock case – but he was sent off duty and was soon himself. I felt very unnerved for an hour or two, but soon recovered.[xiv]

30.12.15   I had many presents for Xmas from all kinds of friends and relations. When the mail did arrive, it was some mail. Our Battalion alone had about 30 mail bags. What must it have meant for the Expeditionary Force?

31.12.15   It was a very wet day.

Kenderdine and Major Milnes went on leave. The Skipper was not expected back until January 4th. We were to go out of the Line any day, so the Colonel wanted to bag a real live Boche to send to the Divisional General as a New Year's present, so a raid was planned for this night.

There were four parties, and it was to be carried out opposite to "Y" Company's Line with Bloy, Young, Ainscow, Evans and Duckworth. About 40 men were detailed, but not all from "Y" Company; "Z" Company sent 12 men.

They really made quite a joke of it, and blacked their faces with burnt cork and turned

---

[171] Minenwerfers, a type of Trench Mortar.
[172] Army slang for Trench Mortars – see footnote 132 on page 100.

their coats inside out. Really they looked more like "Pace Eggers"[173] than soldiers.

10 o'clock was the time chosen. All the Battalion "Stood to arms", to be ready for a counter raid by the Boche.

Ainscow was the wit of the party, and to explain this a tale was told about him.

The Brigadier, General Edwards, issued an order that all officers would carry revolvers in the Front Line at all times. Ainscow was on duty one morning and the General met him. Noticing that Ainscow had no revolver he asked him what he thought orders were issued for. In fact the Brigadier got quite annoyed. Ainscow explained that he had left his revolver in his dug out by mistake, but would attend to it immediately.

A day or two later General Edwards again met Ainscow in the Front Line and remarked, "I see that you have your revolver today, Ainscow", to which Ainscow replied in his quite characteristic manner, "Yes, Sir, and do you know, I've taken the precaution to load it."

So much for Ainscow – who was a great fellow, and had a mania for losing things, revolvers especially, on patrol.

Well the raiding party started out about 9.00pm, full of beans, and determined to get a real, juicy fat Hans. They got up to the Boche wire in four parties, moving in single file in this formation:

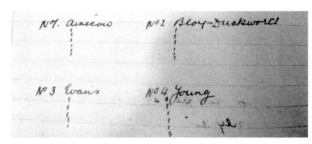

To start with Ainscow spotted a German Sentry Post and proposed rushing it, but found the wire too thick. They could hear the Boche talking quite distinctly, and he was busy firing Very lights about every few minutes. So our people waited till the next light went up, marked the spot, and then Ainscow ordered each man in his party to throw one bomb at the Post. They <u>were</u> thrown, and each exploded. "Shrieks and groans were heard" – so Ainscow's report said – so possibly at least one Boche was hit. We hoped so!

Then the Boche came out, and Ainscow and Bloy's parties had a hand to hand scrap.

It was evident that it was impossible to get into the Boche Line without first destroying his wire, so our people had to withdraw, and only just in time, for our fellows had just got back when a heavy burst of rifle and Machine Gun fire swept No Man's Land. The Boche was not captured, but they had some good fun.

Ainscow dropped his steel helmet[174] on the road and it rang out like an alarm bell. He also lost yet another revolver and very funnily remarked "Do you know I've lost my revolver –

---

[173] Pace-Eggers were groups of fantastically dressed 'mummers', complete with blackened faces, wearing animal skins and festooned with ribbons and streamers, who traditionally performed to villages at Easter. The Bury Pace Eggers were a particularly well known group of this type.

[174] The classic image of the First World War British Tommy wearing a steel helmet belies the fact that this helmet was introduced in place of the Field Service cap only part way through the War; this is the first reference to a steel helmet in the diary. Later, in the diary entry for 4th to 6th April 1916 on page 169, Norman refers to an issue of steel helmets and the difficulty of persuading the men to wear them at first. Later in the diary Norman gives accounts of individuals being saved, and not saved, by their steel helmets, but overall his conclusion was that they did save lives. Norman also refers to Captain William Tickler's "tin hat" being struck by lightning in a thunderstorm at Gommecourt on 29th July 1917 – see *Endnotes*.

I think I'll have a walk out when it comes daylight and look for it" – but he left it for someone else to find!

Thompson, the Medical Officer, also "stood by" all the time – expecting many casualties. Nobody was hurt – the MO was out of work.[175]

A rather strange thing happened at about 11.55pm – rapid Machine Gun fire was heard in the far distance somewhere South. It gradually grew louder and was evidently travelling North, until it came into the sector on our right. We didn't know what was happening, but turned everyone out to take up "Battle Positions". We couldn't see any Boche attacking but our fellows got the fever and took up the fire, and they did fire – two of my fellows, Clare and Greenwood, were having a competition who could get off the most rounds. They fired fully a thousand rounds. Then the next Battalion on our left took up the fire – the 2nd East Lancashires – and so it travelled into the 6th Division Area and away along their Front towards Hébuterne.

The Boche retaliated. Howard and I did a tour round our Line, and, in crossing George Street from one trench to another, we had a very sticky passage, as the Boche had a Machine Gun trained on to the open bit. Howard and I had to lie down in the road for cover, with bullets spitting all round. How we missed being hit was a miracle.[xv]

Another strange thing happened at about midnight; the Bell of the village church was rung – probably the first time since the beginning of the War.

01.01.16   After midnight, everyone was ringing up on the telephone and wishing one another "Bonne Chance". Officers from the 2nd Inniskilling Fusiliers reconnoitred our Line, preparatory to taking over the next day.

The New Submarine Danger
" They'll be torpedoin' us if we stick 'ere much longer, Bill"

The Communication Trench
PROBLEM—Whether to walk along the top and risk it, or do another mile of this

---

[175] According to the account of this raid in *The History of the Lancashire Fusiliers 1914-1918* by Major General J.C. Latter Ainscow received a slight wound to his hand during this raid. Also in that account it is mentioned that Sergeant W. Cadden received the DCM for his work in this raid; Norman records that they heard that the medal had been awarded to Sergeant Cadden on 2nd July 1916 – see the diary entry for that day.

CHAPTER 11
Baizeux, St Gratien, Rainneville, St Sauveur, Métigny and Longpré
2nd January 1916 to 2nd February 1916

02.01.16   We were relieved by the 2nd Inniskilling Fusiliers at about 7. 00pm. It was a pitch black night and raining. We were quite ready to go out of the trenches. We had been up for 14 days, without having our clothes off, and no really decent wash. Also our feet were very sore with wearing gum boots. Most of the men's boots were in <u>very</u> bad condition. We marched out of the Line down to Authuille, which was as busy as Piccadilly Circus, simply packed with troops and Transport. The 51st Division was moving out and the 32nd Division was coming in. Marching through Aveluy we halted for the first time. We should have blocked the roads if we had halted before, but it was a good stretch. The men enjoyed a smoke. They were all wonderfully cheery, in spite of having had a very hard time the last two months. They were marching through Albert to the then popular song *"We are the Fus–il-iars"*. Each company was moving independently and by platoons. When we got clear of Albert on the Millencourt road we halted for half an hour's rest. Here we formed up as a Battalion. The cookers had been sent ahead to prepare tea. Luckily I had "Sandy Mac", or I scarcely think I should have got to our destination. I had been marching up to this point about 6 miles.

We continued our march to Hénencourt and on to our destination Baizeux, where we arrived at 2.30am. The men were very tired but "Z" Company had no men out or absent when we arrived. Moffatt and I eventually found our billet, a very nice room with a clean bed, but we were such an awful mess and hadn't our valises, and we didn't like to use such luxury, so we covered the bed with a rug, half undressed, covered ourselves with our burberries,[176] and slept like tops.

03.01.16   Ashton woke us at about 8.30am and we thought it was about 10.00am. We were still very tired. However up we got and went to see the men get their breakfast, then returned to our billet for ours. We received orders to move at 12.00 noon. We inspected the men and there was the usual feet washing and blister pricking. The men turned out on parade at 11.45am looking very clean considering. Here we formed Column of Route with the rest of the Brigade, leaving Baizeux at 12.30pm. We marched past General Edwards – he was decidedly livery. It was a hard march but fortunately only about 7½ miles to St Gratien, where we arrived at 2.45pm.

Quite a large number fell out on the march, but rejoined us later. We got our valises here, but couldn't manage a bath, so decided to hang on to our dirty things till we got to a fixed halt. We turned in early that day, and had a jolly good night's rest.

04.01.16   We left St Gratien at 11.15am and marched to Rainneville, 2½ miles, arriving at 12.30pm. The Germans had been through Rainneville when they took Amiens in September 1914. We got quite good billets for our Company. Moffatt and I had a very good billet, and we decided to take things quietly. Both of us had a jolly good hot bath and complete change

---

[176] See footnote 94 on page 72.

of clothing. It was glorious – the first time we had had our clothes off since December 20th. After a very good dinner we censored the men's letters – some accumulation there was. We expected to stay here for at least a fortnight. It was quite a nice village and only about 4 miles from Amiens. It seemed too good to be true. However we were fully 20 miles from the Line and clear away from shell fire and the sounds of war. It was a relief! A new Padre came to our Battalion – Captain Davenport.

Waterhouse returned from leave and I handed over the Company to him. We gave the NCOs and men of our Company a little Christmas Gift – a match box case.

05.01.16 In the morning I rode to Fiesselles via Bertangles, and got the money to pay the men. I met Peak,[177] Signalling Officer, whom I had first met when I was Signalling Officer in 1915, but I couldn't go with him, as I had the money to pay the men.

We got a great shock – at 11.45pm we received very sudden and unexpected orders that we were to move from Rainneville at 7.45am the next day, where to we didn't know. But our first stop was to be St Sauveur.

Jimmy Bowd was in a terrible state at Rainneville; in loading up at Thiepval Wood he had lost 150 waterproof capes – personally I think he was overloaded and somebody dumped them. Anyway a "Court of Enquiry" settled the business. Also the Battalion Dispatch Box was lost – this contained the duplicate forms of the War Diary and many other important papers. So far as I know it was never found.

06.01.16 The Military Service Bill was brought up in Parliament for the first time.

Manse Evans went to Hospital with "'flu".

At 7.45am the Brigade marched to St Sauveur, which is on the Somme North West of Amiens. My few days' rest had bucked me up a bit, but I was still not fit.

Joe Hedley and Bloy marched off with us, but left us after about a mile, and proceeded to Amiens en route for England on leave.

We passed through Coisy, where the 1/4th King's Own Royal Lancasters joined us. We arrived at St Sauveur, 8½ miles away, at about 1.00pm. There were no billets ready for us, but we soon found billets, and eventually the Skipper, Moffatt and I had a very nice omelette at an estaminet, and eventually the Skipper and I found a very excellent billet in quite a nice house. We had a bathroom opening out from our bedroom, and a very nice cosy bed. St Sauveur seemed quite a nice little town and really civilised, with electric light in the streets. There were many troops here, and it was impossible to find billets for Company Messes so it was quickly arranged to have a Battalion Mess in an estaminet. This proved very successful and we had quite a cheery evening.

Jimmy Bowd had taken on rather a full cargo and he was ragged by everyone. Waterhouse and I had a very excellent rest that night, and a bath next morning. It was fortunate, for we had a big day in front of us.

07.01.16 We paraded at 10.30am, and left St Sauveur at about 11.40am. I took up my old spot in the rear of "Z" Company, Waterhouse taking "Sandy Mac". We crossed the Somme, and

---

[177] Also referred to as "Peake"; see the diary entry for 25th August 1915 for the first meeting with him.

the Abbeville to Amiens railway, to Breilly. Then, taking the main Amiens to Abbeville road, we passed through Picquigny to Soues. It rained heavily all the time. We had our usual 10 minutes halts each hour. At Soues we had lunch. The men's dinners were a bit late as the cooks could not keep the fires lighted on the march.

Most of us had a nice steak and chips at an estaminet. I am afraid I wasn't in great form, having been quite bad on the march.

When we started off again I rode "Sandy Mac" for about 3 miles and very glad I was to have a lift. Then I marched the rest of the way through Le Quesnoy-sur-Airaines and Laleu to Métigny, where we arrived at 5.30pm, after about 18 miles in full kit. We had covered about 50 miles from the trenches, so we were now right away, and "back area wallers".[178]

We got some excellent billets for our Company. We bought some new straw, settled the men in, and saw to their dinners, which they were more than ready for by now. Then we turned in to our own billet, a very nice large farm house with two nice bedrooms, a good kitchen for our own use, and a very cosy Mess Room.

I was just about "<u>done</u>" – the last few miles of the march were most trying, keeping the men going. One or two fellows fell out, but they did extremely well. Jolly glad I was to get to bed that night, I felt <u>really ill</u> and had a very rotten night.

The 154th Brigade, consisting of the

1/4th King's Own Royal Lancasters

1/8th King's Liverpool Regiment (Irish)

1/4th Loyal North Lancashires

2/5th Lancashire Fusiliers

had now left the famous 51st Division (Highland) and proceeded to a concentration area prior to the formation, or re-formation, of the 55th Division – the West Lancashires.

We were sorry to leave our friends, the Scotchmen, but, at the same time, very pleased to be brought back to join our Lancashire Comrades. The 2/5th Lancashire Fusiliers were an East Lancashire Battalion, but we retained our position in the Brigade.

So from now onwards we are in the 55th Division and the 164th Infantry Brigade.

The Battalions composing the 55th Division (formed on January 3rd 1916) had all seen War Service, and might reasonably be termed seasoned troops. The Divisional Headquarters were at Hallencourt, about 15 miles South East of Abbeville. Most of the Battalions had been serving with Regular Army Brigades. The 1/10th Liverpool Scottish embarked for France in October 1914 and the remaining Battalions in the early months of 1915.

The various Battalions had taken part and given full evidence of their capabilities in the Battles of Hill 60, St Eloi, 2nd Battle of Ypres, Hooge, Festubert and Loos. The Esprit de Corps and morale were excellent, and it was evident that in the small French villages around Hallencourt was the material of a first rate fighting force.

Major General H.S. Jeudwine was appointed to command the Division. *"No General was ever more devoted to a Division, and no Division ever more devoted to its General."*[179]

---

[178] "Waller" or "wallah" is army slang based on a Hindustani word, meaning a person with a particular role.

[179] This quotation comes from a book entitled *The Story of 55th (West Lancashire) Division 1916-1919* by the Reverend J.O. Coop; Reverend Coop attended the unveiling of the Memorial to the 55th Division at Givenchy on 15th May 1921, at which Norman represented the 2/5th Lancashire Fusiliers (see the *Afterword*, pages 308-310).

The command of the 164th Infantry Brigade was as follows:

Brigadier General G.T.C. Edwards CB

Brigade Major Captain V.A. Jackson DSO

Staff Captain J. Fisher, King's Own Royal Lancasters

08.01.16 and 09.01.16	We gave the Company a thorough rest. We had kit inspections, including clothing, boots etc. We needed refitting <u>very</u> badly. We also had a complete medical inspection. We improved the billets, and generally tried to make our men more comfortable.

The caretaker of the house we were billeted at was a bit awkward at first. He had been badly treated by some Canadian Troops previously. However, as usual, the 2/5th Lancashire Fusiliers soon made friends and he was really quite reasonable, in fact couldn't do enough for us.

He ran the adjoining farm and had a plentiful supply of vegetables, eggs, butter, chickens, geese, and turkeys. As we hadn't had our Christmas Dinner in the trenches, we arranged for several seasonable things. We gave the men an excellent Xmas dinner. Leach, the Company Cook, along with Hargreaves and Jim Longat, really excelled themselves.

I retired to bed early – under doctor's orders; I was threatened with the Hospital, but I didn't want that, so really made an effort to pull myself together, and took advantage of the place to take things quietly. I really felt like leave, but had some little time to wait, as several people seemed to think they had prior claims; Hutchinson, Goldsmith,[180] Jimmy Bowd were before me.

We heard that the Germans attacked the trenches we had just left, the night after we were relieved.[xvi] Luckily the 2nd Battalion Inniskillings were about double our strength and were Regular Troops. So the Boche got a surprise no doubt, and the attack was easily repulsed – but our people had heavy casualties for a small Show.

Poor old "John Minden" was beginning to take an interest in life again. He didn't enjoy being on the move any more than the rest of us.

10.01.16	I had a day in bed. Hutty excelled himself by riding on his horse full tilt into a piece of barbed wire and came a terrific "purler". He damaged his nose and lip, which was thicker than anything on earth – so the MO said. Otherwise all was quiet on our Front.

11.01.16	We arranged our "Z" Company Mess Xmas Dinner, and asked in a few special pals.

Gray, Doctor Thompson, Ainscow, Humble, Waterhouse, Moffatt, and myself sat down to the dinner, which was excellent. Kenderdine returned from leave just before we had finished. The menu was:

Hors d'oeuvres, Soup

Turkey, Sausage, Vegetables

Xmas Pudding, Mince Pies, Fruit, Raisins etc.

Coffee, Liqueurs

I didn't do much in the dinner line, as I was on light food. What a blow!!

---

[180] This reference to Goldsmith is odd, as he had left the Battalion and moved to Divisional HQ on 10th September 1915 (see the diary entry for that date).

16.01.16   Waterhouse went to the IIIrd Army Infantry School at Flixecourt for a course of instruction. I took over command of "Z" Company, so also took over the Skipper's bedroom, which was quite nice. It was a glorious day.

17.01.16   I was feeling almost fit again. I had to be – there was plenty of work to do.
I took over "Sandy Mac", the Skipper's horse. I had now got quite accustomed to riding and thoroughly enjoyed it.
Leave was extended to eight days starting on Thursday for our Unit.
Ainscow and I went into Le Quesnoy-sur-Airaines for dinner and had quite a cheery time. I found "Scoff" a very genial companion.

18.01.16   I had quite a nice ride over to Le Quesnoy-sur-Airaines to see the 22nd Manchesters. They were still out of the Line, only having done four days in the trenches since they came out in November. Walter Cornall was limping about with a stick, having sprained his ankle. Eric Oldham was also laid up with a damaged kneecap from football.

19.01.16   Major Milnes, Hedley, Bloy, Thompson, and I found some jumps in a field, and we all took our horses round. The MO's and the Major's were the only ones that were any use.

20.01.16   We received orders to move to another village about 5 miles distant, Longpré. We moved off at 11.30am. The boots were still in a very bad state, but we had tremendous difficulty in getting new ones. Many of the men were almost walking on their socks. About half way we encountered opposition – the Brigadier; we had to perform antics for him, in the way of a deployment. He imagined the Battalion had suddenly come under shell fire and made us adopt Artillery Formations, then we had to make a Battalion attack on a wood, which was occupied and had to be cleared before we could proceed, quite an interesting scheme. Then we had food and proceeded to Longpré, arriving at about 4.45pm.
Longpré was a quaint place, quite civilised. It was on the main line from Boulogne to Amiens. Paris Boat Trains used to pass through, and even the Church Bell used to ring for service.
"Z" Company got quite good billets, and our Company Mess was excellent, a very nice room, also I had a splendid bedroom. The MO was billeted with a French Doctor's wife. HQ had quite a nice place near the station.

21.01.16   Kenders, the Padre, the MO and I had drinks at the Hotel de France.
I felt very groggy again at night.

22.01.16   I was feeling decidedly groggy and did not get up. I sent for the Doctor, who prescribed lead and opium pills.
Kenders took the Company for a March Past, a Divisional Inspection by Lieutenant General the Earl of Cavan.

23.01.16   There was a church service in "Y" Company billets in the afternoon. Kenderdine and I rode over to Le Quesnoy-sur-Airaines, about 6 miles away, to see Eric Oldham and Walter Cornall again.

24.01.16   We did training in the morning. We encouraged the men to take an active interest in sports – football, Cross Country running, boxing, concerts, anything to find outside interests for them, the only way to keep the fellows cheery.

At an event held in an estaminet in Longpré, Thompson sang *"We all walked into the shop"* and shocked the Padre, and also sang the *"The Wedding of Sandy McNab"*. Colonel Shirley also recited.[181]

25.01.16   The MO had an exciting time at the mobile Veterinary Station with his mare, getting her clipped. She broke the machine and nearly killed the fellow working it.

We had quite an interesting little evening, rather unique for Active Service.

Our Machine Gun Section, Lieutenant Freddy Harker, 2nd Lieutenant Hartington,[182] and their men had proceeded to Bettencourt to join the Brigade Machine Gun Company, which had just been formed. Kenders and I walked over the tops to Le Quesnoy-sur-Airaines village. We did some shopping there, had afternoon tea, then, feeling tired, we made enquiries about a motor for hire. We eventually found one, and, after some difficulty, we started off in a great style. Our driver was a fat Frenchman who wore a huge fur coat. We had a very cheery evening with Freddy and his crowd, and left at about 9.45pm, walking home – 1½ miles.

26.01.16   At 7.30am we took the Company to the baths, 3 miles away, and gave them clean clothes. Kenderdine took a party of 20 men from "Z" Company to Pont-Remy, which was a Railhead. He was to carry out some detraining arrangements for the 46th Division (North Midland Territorial Forces Division), who had been to Marseilles – or, rather, the correct version was: The Division was hurriedly put under orders for Egypt, taken to Marseilles and equipped for Egypt. Two Brigades sailed for Alexandria and reached that port. The third Brigade was ready to sail when counter orders were wired for the first two Brigades to return to France. "Here's not to reason why, here's but to do, and die"; someone had bungled. The 46th Division were never meant to go to Egypt at all. So they returned, and that was why Kenders and half my family were at Pont-Remy near Abbeville, and Moffatt and I were once more doing the work.

27.01.16   I was busy all day. I paid the men at 6.00pm. It looked pretty hopeless for my leave as I couldn't possibly leave the Company with Moffatt. He was very good, but hadn't sufficient experience.

---

[181] Lieutenant Colonel Shirley also performed *Play the Game* at a Battalion concert on 9th October 1915 at Aveluy (see the newspaper cutting relating to the diary entry for that date).

[182] 2nd Lieutenant John Ernest Hartington had been a fellow pupil with Norman at Bury Grammar School. He would have been four years his junior, and perhaps Norman did not realise that he had been at school with him, as he refers, in the unedited version of the diary, to *"first"* meeting him in Southport on 16th April 1915. He was with "B" Company of the 2/5th Lancashire Fusiliers when they first landed in France on 3rd May 1915, and is mentioned in the unedited version of the diary as participating in one of the *"bathing parades"* at Arques (see page 53). There is a photograph of him with Duckworth, Barwood and Barnsdale, probably taken in September 1915, on page 65. He ceased to be an officer with the 2/5th Lancashire Fusiliers on moving to the Machine Gun Company, and is not mentioned again in the diary. He was awarded the MC for an action near Delville Wood on 27th September 1916. On 12th July 1917 at Ypres he was hit by a piece of 4.5 inch shrapnel when an ammunition dump in his vicinity was hit by a German shell, and died the following day. Aged 21 when he died, he was the son of George A. and Mona Gertrude Hartington of Heywood, and is buried at Lijssenthoek Military Cemetery, West-Vlaanderen, Belgium, reference XIII.A.1. His promotion from 2nd Lieutenant to Lieutenant was gazetted posthumously on 4th August 1917.

The MO went to Amiens by motor lorry and brought back 8 barrels of beer for the Regimental Canteen.

A Naval Airman (Royal Naval Air Service) had to come down with his aeroplane about 2 miles away – engine trouble. We sent out a guard from "Z" Company, one NCO and three men. The pilot came to live at HQ Mess, and his mechanic was billeted in Longpré. Everyone was hoping to get a fly round when the aeroplane was fixed up, but no luck – not even the CO. I took my Company out for a Route March to see the aeroplane, as very few of the men had seen one close to.

28.01.16   Foden Wagons (steam wagons) were on duty. There was a "Lice Hunt" in the Battalion's blankets; in other words, the blankets were stoved.

29.01.16   We had testing of Gas helmets – the old flannel sand bag type with mica eyepieces – and a Gas demonstration.

30.01.16   There was great excitement, as the King's Own Royal Lancasters got orders to move, no one knew where; we all thought "back to the Land".

We had a very fine lecture on Esprit de Corps and morale by Colonel Kentish, Commandant of the IIIrd Army School, Flixecourt. Major Milnes went on an Artillery Course.

The "Skipper" came over from the IIIrd Army Corps for the week-end. Flixecourt was only about 6 miles away, so I sent Newhouse with "Sandy Mac". I was very glad to have a chat about the Company with the Skipper.

31.01.16   I rode to Pont-Remy with Humble to see Kenders, and, incidentally, pay his men (about a 12 mile ride). They were working very hard, day and night, unloading Battalion Transports etc.

01.02.16   I was feeling quite bucked as my leave was at last in sight. I was about ready for a change of air and occupation, having had a very rotten time since Xmas.

02.02.16   Kenderdine returned with his party from Pont-Remy. He had done exceedingly well and was especially thanked for his good work by the GOC of the 46th Division, a feather in Kenders' cap, also in the cap of the 2/5th Lancashire Fusiliers, and, lastly, that of "Z" Company.

I received my Leave Warrant and handed over the Company to Kenders.

Lieutenant T.H.G. Kenderdine, nicknamed Kenders or Charlie Chaplin

03.02.16   It was a glorious morning. I went down to the station at Longpré at about 9.30am, and trained to Havre by the same route as November 5th, arriving at Havre at about 9.00pm. We had to detrain at Gare du Nord as one of the bridges on the docks was broken, so the train couldn't get on to the Quay Station. I marched down with the troops. It was blowing a regular gale when we got to the ship, RMS *Caesarea*, a London and South Western Boat, formerly on the Southampton to Channel Island Service. By skilful tipping I managed to get a very nice cabin to myself with a comfortable bunk. I was clicked for the job of Duty Officer (worse luck!). It consisted of two hours' duty from 10.00pm to 12.00 midnight, inspecting Submarine Guards etc. Everyone was issued with life belts before we moved away. At about 10.15pm I got a message to report to the Captain of the ship – he told me that it was impossible for us to sail that night – too rough!

I reported to the OC of the Ship and then went back to the Captain's Cabin by invitation. I had supper with him, and an interesting chat about his doings. The ship had been on patrol duty in the North Sea since November 1914, and she had had some exciting adventures. I retired to my cabin at about 12.30am, and slept very well.

04.02.16   I had tea in bed at 8.00am, and breakfast in the Saloon at 9.00am. Then orders came that
to   we were to leave the ship as we shouldn't sail until evening. I went down to the Rest Camp
12.02.16   at the West end of the Docks, signed on there, and received orders to be at the ship at 6.00pm. We reported at the ship at 7.00pm, got our passes endorsed, and dated forward one day. We left Havre at 12.15am on our old ship, RMS *Connaught*,[183] and had a good

passage, arriving at Southampton at 8.30am, London at 10.30am, and Bury at 4.50pm. Bill and Mary[184] met me. I had a really great time on leave and saw most people I wanted to see, went to some shows, and celebrated Mother's birthday on February 8th; but the time was all too short – Saturday soon arrived. Still I had done pretty well.

RMS *Connaught*

On February 12th I left Bury to catch the 9.20am train from Manchester – it was just as rotten as ever going back from leave. It was some consolation to know that I was meeting George in London (I had missed him on the way home). He met me at St Pancras, and we went to the Regent Palace, had a stroll round Regent's Park, Piccadilly etc. I left for Waterloo at 2.30pm to catch the 4.00pm train to Southampton, and we left Southampton at about 7.00pm, had a

---

[183] RMS *Connaught* was the ship in which Norman had crossed the Channel on the way to his previous leave in England in November 1915 – see the diary entry for 6th November 1915. Launched in 1897, she was torpedoed and sunk on 3rd March 1917 while returning to Southampton from Le Havre with only crew on board; three crew members were lost.
[184] Kathleen and Mary, Norman's sisters.

good passage, and arrived at Havre at 1.00am. I walked up to Gare du Nord, left there at about 4.30am, and slept most of the way – I felt rather fed up, but heaps better for the change.

At this time the Military Service Act had come into operation in England, Scotland, and Wales. While I was away, on Friday February 4th, the Battalion moved from Longpré to Beaumetz (13 miles). There was no food for anyone from 7.00am until 3.00pm. Colonel Shirley and Hutty wanted the Brigadier's blood. The Brigadier got it in the neck from the Divisional Commander a couple of days later. Meanwhile, on February 5th the Battalion moved to Le Meillard, arriving at 11.15am. Major Milnes returned from his course.

On February 8th the MO gave a demonstration of the use of a vermorel sprayer[185] to "Z" Company, who were dashing about a field in Gas helmets. The MO's demonstrations were always a joke. Kenders and Moffatt were running the Company. It was rumoured that we were to take over trenches near Arras.

There was an outbreak of "'flu", the result of salubrious Longpré. On February 9th the MO went raging and ramping down to "Z" Company, who had 24 men sick in billets. On February 10th, Captain Davenport, the Padre, had a temperature of 103°, and was singing a mixture of the 119th Psalm and *"I'm the Guy"*; he was packed off to Hospital.

13.02.16   I got up to Longpré and asked for the 55th Division, and was told to go on to the Doullens section of the train to Fienvillers-Candas.

The train left for Doullens at 6.30pm, passing through Flixecourt, the home of the IIIrd Army Infantry School, and arriving at Fienvillers-Candas at about 8.00pm. I interviewed the Rail Transport Officer, a blighter! He knew nothing – didn't want to – about the movements of the 55th Division. I walked to the Royal Flying Corps HQ to try to get a tender to run me out to my Battalion to try to find them. No luck! I trailed back to the station, and on to Fienvillers, about 2½ miles. I found the 55th Division's Supply Column, and went to their Mess to find out the location of our people. The Major was very decent, and invited me to have some food – and I was quite ready! He was very apologetic because he couldn't find a car to send me out in.

I discovered that the Battalion were about 5 miles away at Le Meillard. I went through Bernaville, Autheux, and Boisbergues. Eventually I arrived at Le Meillard, and the first farm I came to happened to be my Company billet. It was then about 11.00pm. I found a very good billet and everyone was very cheery.

GRAND-MEILLARD, par Bernaville (Somme)

Waterhouse returned from the IIIrd Army Infantry School, and took over command of "Z" Company again.

Captain Hartley, the IIIrd Army Infantry School Chemical Adviser, lectured to the Battalion.

---

[185] A sprayer used to neutralise contamination caused by chlorine gas.

14.02.16 We had Company Training in the morning, incorporating slight changes in organisation and methods as a result of the Skipper's course at the IIIrd Army Infantry School.

It was wet and cold all day.

There was great excitement at about 9.00pm – a fire at HQ's billet. The Fire Bugle sounded. All the Battalion turned out, but were soon dismissed.

We were under orders to move towards the trenches again.

15.02.16 The Battalion paraded at 9.00am, and marched through Doullens, and along the Doullens to Arras road to Halloy – 12 miles. It was raining the whole time, and we were forced to have long unnecessary halts, as many troops were on the move. The men were billeted in huts just at the West end of Halloy.

About 16 of us slept on the floor or desks in the village school. We had a Battalion Mess in a small estaminet with a splendid fire – hardly wanted to leave it. Having no valises we just used our wet burberries[186] as covering during the night, and wakened up many times, cold and stiff.

We now knew we were going to relieve a French Division – the 88th French Division. The British Front was being extended – or, rather, we were taking over the Arras Salient and joining up with the Northerly boundary of the British Somme Front. This was on account of the contemplated attack on Verdun by the Huns. Consequently the British Front now extended from Ypres to Bray on the Somme.

16.02.16 We left Halloy early in the morning, at 9.00am. There was a strong cold wind blowing, with blinding sleet and rain. We marched through Grenas and Mondicourt, and along the main Arras to Doullens road to Saulty L'Arbret, where there were many French troops – Infantry, Transport and Artillery. We left the main road here and marched to Saulty-Sombrin, and on to Barly, a frightfully cold march We were absolutely soaked through when we arrived at about 1.30pm. "Y" and "Z" Company were billeted in French huts – quite good when we got them cleaned.

The men were very wet. We had some difficulty in purchasing some new straw for them, but eventually managed it. Then the cooks couldn't get water. It had to be brought by water-cart, which was quite a problem, and necessitated careful using. However, the fellows all enjoyed their dinner, and having settled them down we decided to find our own billets. They were about five minutes' walk away in the village.

We saw a Regiment of French Cyclists march out; they looked wonderfully clean and smart as they marched out of Barly, headed by their Regimental Colours and Band.

"X" Company Mess was in a very nice clean farm house quite near. Waterhouse, Kenderdine and I joined at one room with a stone floor – very cold! Moffatt, and Humble, our Transport Officer, lived with us. Our Mess owner was Monsieur E. Willerval, Rue de Sombrin, Barly.

The Willervals were exceedingly kind to us. We were the first British troops they had seen, so consequently they made quite a fuss of us. They made us hot coffee and omelettes on arrival, and dried all our wet clothes. The family consisted of the grand'mère (an old lady of 84), a father, mother, and two daughters. The only son was on service.

---

[186] See footnote 94 on page 72.

The old grandmother was a bit frightened when we entered. The reason was that she couldn't see very well, and couldn't tell the difference between our uniforms and German uniforms, but she knew we weren't French.

Twice in her life the Germans had occupied Barly – first the Prussians in 1870, and then the Germans for a few days early in the present War. Poor old dame, she was constantly running to the window and saying, "Les Allemands – ils viennent!" "The Germans are coming!"

However we treated her as any British officers would, and she soon was quite friendly.

Seldom did I meet such thoroughly kind, genuine, French people as the Willervals.

17.02.16 to 23.02.16	We were now in the VIIth Corps, commanded by Sir T.D. D'Oyly Snow.[187] We were in Divisional Reserve, still out of the Line, but not very far from it. There was a mixture of French and British troops in the area, as relief of the French was not quite complete. Heavy fighting against the French at Verdun began on Tuesday February 22nd.

There was some talk of Waterhouse leaving us again – I was very fed up about it. We had only had him for about six days in all since December 24th.

On Thursday February 17th, we had Company Training – Bayonet Fighting, Platoons in Attack, and Covering. Waterhouse certainly brought some splendid ideas back from the IIIrd Army Infantry School. Everyone was made keen on training bombers and Rifle Grenadiers.

Other than that, nothing much happened during these few days – football, lectures, the Royal Artillery Band from Portsmouth playing in the grounds of the Chateau at Barly. On Saturday February 19th Waterhouse, Hedley and I walked to Avesnes-le-Comte, a village about 5 miles away, and had lunch there – quite a busy little country town with some good shops.

On Sunday February 20th, bombs were dropped by a Boche Taube[188] on Barly and the villages round, but no damage was done. There was a spy scare in Barly.

The news from England was as follows:

Lighting restrictions became very important on account of German Zeppelin Raids;

Major Kay went to command the 4/5th Lancashire Fusiliers. Very bad luck![189]

Personally I was feeling quite fit again.

24.02.16	Major Barnsdale, Captain Bloy, Major Milnes, Captain Hedley and I walked from Barly to the Front Line. We were taking over a new Line from the French, or it would actually have already been taken over by some of our Division. We went through Barly, Gouy-en-Artois, Monchiet, Beaumetz, and Rivière to the Front Line trenches in front of Blairville Wood. It was about 13 miles to the Front Line, and there was a blinding blizzard the whole way.

---

[187] Grandfather of the broadcasters, Peter Snow and Jon Snow, and great-grandfather of Peter's son, also a broadcaster, Dan Snow.

[188] German for "aeroplane".

[189] The last mention of Major Kay (who had been at Southport while Norman was there, from October 1914 to April 1915) is in the entry for 9th to 10th August 1915 in the original diary, where Norman reports that they heard that "*Major Kay went back to Bury – finished as a soldier*", which suggests that he had retired, but, assuming that this is the same Major Kay, he was presumably recalled to command the 4/5th Lancashire Fusiliers; as for whether it was bad luck for the 4/5th Lancashire Fusiliers or for Major Kay, Norman does not say, but as he "*got on very well with Major Kay*" (see the diary entry for 11th January 1915 to 4th April 1915) presumably it was the latter.

We couldn't see much of the new Line when we got there – we could scarcely see across No Man's Land, and the trenches were literally full of snow and drifts, several feet deep in places. We got up to Blamont village and quarry, and got as much information about the Line as usual both from the tactical and supply standpoint. We returned to Bretencourt, found an old – or, rather, shell-damaged – house, lit a huge fire, made some tea, and had our lunch.

We started back at about 3.00pm, and stopped at Beaumetz for some coffee. We arrived back at Barly fagged out, blue with cold, and wet through; 26 miles in a snow storm is no pleasant occupation. However, after a hot bath and a change of clothes, I thoroughly enjoyed my dinner, and slept like a top from 10.00pm until 8.00am.

25.02.16   There was still snow and frost. Waterhouse went to the IIIrd Army Infantry School again.

26.02.16   Colonel Shirley went to Hospital at Barly with "'flu".

The Battalion made preparations in the morning to move towards the trenches. We were to go into Brigade Reserve at Bretencourt. We had trouble with 3199 Private Briggs – the result was an FGCM.

We marched off at about 3.30pm via Gouy and Monchiet to Beaumetz. The main line from Doullens to Arras passed through Beaumetz. This line was well guarded by a strong, well wired trench system, with some very wonderful dug outs made in the railway embankment. Beaumetz was on high ground, and from here we had to march by platoons at 200 yards distance, as we were now within range of German Guns. It was lucky that we did spread out, for immediately we crossed the railway we could see shells bursting almost every 50 yards down the road. Either the Boche knew we were relieving, or he saw troops moving, or it was just one of his daily "strafing" times. Anyway we had a sticky passage. Luckily I moved my Company off the road. One shell dropped within a few yards of my leading platoon, which the MO and I were accompanying. We all lay flat, and got nothing worse than well splashed with snow, water, and mud – no casualties.[xvii] Rivière, our destination, was about 2 miles away. When we arrived, there was a terrific commotion of troops and Transport – it was two hours before we got into our billets. "Z" Company, for once, were lucky, as our billets were in the village itself, so we got our men settled down comparatively early. They were really quite good, empty houses in many cases. Our officers' billet was quite a nice small house. There were only three of us sharing it, Kenderdine, Moffatt and myself, as OC of the Company. Company Sergeant Major Howard and Company Quartermaster Sergeant Davenport had a nice billet and Company store room.

"Y" Company were at Bretencourt, "X" Company were in Reserve at Blamont Quarry about 1½ miles away, and "W" Company were in Reserve at La Sucrerie, Wailly, about 1½ miles away. So we were fairly well scattered.

27.02.16   We reconnoitred the approaches to the Front Line so as to be able to move up in the event of attack, and also reconnoitred the Village Line, our *"line de résistance"* in the event of attack. I called to see Uncle Joe, Gray etc. for lunch at the Sugar Factory. It was quite a long walk round but very enjoyable, as it was a nice morning and there was not much doing in the way of "Flying Pigs"[190] etc.

The 55th Division had now got properly organised as a Division and had completed the relief of the 88th French Division in the Bretencourt to Wailly Sector, South of Arras. *"They immediately began to make their presence felt, to harass the enemy as much as possible, to keep him ever upon the alert, to lose no opportunity of inflicting casualties upon him. These were the first methods drilled into us in the 55th Division, and the enemy was not slow in learning to appreciate them."*[191]

28.02.16   A thaw set in, and made everything very wet and muddy, but it was much warmer and we got some sunshine. The first signs of spring seemed to be appearing. The birds were actually singing again. Although out of the Line we went up to the trenches, as there was quite a lot of work to be done in keeping the trenches in repair, and improving them, especially after frost, which always caused trouble.

I had a very cheery birthday,[192] with quite a number of very nice parcels and letters. I had a real English afternoon tea, with toast, Japanese Kisses (Arques cakes[193]) etc.

It was fairly quiet in this part except for occasional gun fire, chiefly our Artillery registering. Of course, the French certainly seemed to like to live in peace and quiet, rather than aggravate the Boche. We, on the contrary, played a worrying game, and always tried to gain supremacy over No Man's Land by constant patrolling, also by shelling the approaches to the Boche Line. Perhaps it was a game of bluff, but the dull monotony of trench life called for active minor operations in view of future action.

Rather an unfortunate accident occurred to one of my men, 1567 Private Howarth, C. He and Sergeant Wild[194] were detonating N° 5 Mills hand grenades[195] in the Brigade Bomb Store at Bretencourt. The lever retaining pin broke on one bomb and slipped the lever, thus discharging the bomb, which luckily was heard. Howarth, in attempting to get this box out to save the store, came in for the explosion and got rather badly riddled in the seat of his trousers – he went to Hospital.

29.02.16   Private Bennison[196] of Southport fame went home, time expired. I mention this because I had had a lot of trouble with Bennison since the early days, but I was very pleased when, during dinner, Ashton, my servant, announced Private Bennison, saying that "he just wanted to say goodbye to me before he went to England, and wish me good luck, and hoped I had no ill feelings towards him, even if he had been a lot of trouble at times". So long as he was sober he was a good fellow, but on his "on days" there was no dealing with him at all.

---

190 A type of Trench Mortar. See the footnote to the diary entry for 2nd to 7th March 1916 on page 155.
191 Norman does not say where this quotation comes from.
192 This would have been Norman's 24th birthday.
193 See the diary entry for 21st to 30th June 1915 for why they were called Arques cakes.
194 Norman mentions that a Sergeant Wild *"late of Z Company"* was an instructor in bombing at Ripon in January 1917 when he (Norman) was on Home Service there, which very probably was this man.
195 See footnote 135 on page 105.
196 See the diary entry for 20th May 1915 for Bennison getting drunk.

CHAPTER 13
Rivière, Blairville and Monchiet
1st March 1916 to 15th March 1916

01.03.16   I went up to reconnoitre the Front Line trenches at 10.00am, preparatory to relieving the 1/4[197] Loyal North Lancashires, "D" Company (Captain Renard), whom we got to know well, as we took turns to man this part of the Line. I got full particulars of the disposition in the Line, information about rations, water, cooking supplies, accommodation, the German trenches, the habits of the Boche, danger points etc. A relief in a new Line always required special foresight and careful planning. I found the Line fairly good, but requiring a tremendous lot of work. Being of French construction it was, as usual, practically devoid of traverses.[197] The dug outs were moderate. The French usually thought more about their accommodation and less of their protection from a tactical respect. This, of course, was contrary to the correct attitude. Protection from fire first, then fighting positions, then wire!!! Then living accommodation came as the luxuries.

I made all my dispositions, allotting men to Posts ready to take over.

As the approaches to the Line were under cover from view from the Boche it was possible to carry out a daylight relief, a great advantage.

We marched off from Rivière at about 3.00pm and moved via Bretencourt, past the Sugar Factory, up Clean Street (Sap 26). This was a long Communication Trench (1¼ miles). The trench was boarded all the way. The sides of the trench were well revetted with rabbit wire (fine netting) or brushwood, supported by overhead frames. At this time Clean Street wasn't particularly clean, for the recent thaw had caused a lot of water to accumulate.

We arrived in the Front Line at about 4.15pm, and the relief went very smoothly. The Loyal North Lancashires were clear by about 5.00pm, and we had time to get the men fixed up before dark came.

We always "Stood to" in Battle Positions immediately we took over. Then I went down the whole of my Company Line to ensure that each man knew his position and various particulars about his Post.

I let each Post "Stand Down", once I was satisfied.

My previous reconnaissance of the Line enabled me to make out a very good work programme, and to start off with it the same night. I will describe this programme in more detail below.

I went down to HQ Mess for a farewell dinner for the MO, Lieutenant Thompson, who was to leave us very shortly (on March 8th), to go home to England, or perhaps I should say Scotland, as he came from Glasgow. We all regretted this – he was a splendid fellow. Captain Levine took over duties as Medical Officer.

02.03.16
to
07.03.16   We were busy improving our Company Line, but our progress was hampered considerably as we had a very heavy fall of snow. It was frightfully cold and we had a regular blizzard intermittently for three days. It was so bad that we had to shorten our time of trench duty from 12 hours to 6 hours, which was quite long enough for a man to be exposed. This

---

[197] A zig-zag formed in a trench by means of a protrusion into it constructed of earth and sand bags, designed to reduce the risk of an entire trench being blown in or overrun by the enemy.

meant that, for a Three Man Sentry Post, each man did one hour on and two off, and had only two hours in six actually on sentry.

We took advantage of the bad weather to strengthen our barbed wire entanglements very considerably, but – to ensure the Hun wasn't doing the same – we patrolled No Man's Land and the Hun wire constantly throughout the night. This was very trying work as the ground was so cold and wet.

Freddy Harker went to Hospital.

The Germans shelled fairly heavily, but we had no casualties.

I will now give a brief description of the Battalion Line in this sector, and our Company Line, and will also give a general description of our armaments and strategies at this time. The Divisional Dispositions were as shown in the diagram on the left.

Bretencourt to Blairville was an interesting sector, for, in the early days of the War, in September 1914, heavy fighting had taken place here, when the Germans made a desperate attempt to capture the city of Arras. This sector was

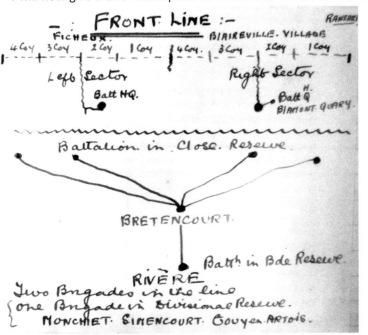

about 5 miles South West of Arras, which itself is in the valley of a small river called the Crinchon. We were actually on the Rising Ground, the Boche, in his retirements of the above date, having finally chosen the commanding High Ground for his main Line of Defence, and from which he had not moved, in spite of several attempts made by the French to drive him out, without success.

Originally the Boche held the Front Line held by us, but was driven back on to the crest. Attempts to capture the crest from him failed again and again.

French Colonial Troops – Turcos – from Algeria had made the last attempt in September 1915, and the concentration of German fire was so severe that they were compelled to withdraw to their original Line, leaving many casualties, and, as a matter of fact, the remains of these poor fellows were still out in No Man's Land, even in February 1916 – we found many indications of this during our patrolling.[198]

The Battalion Line was held at this time from right to left by "W", "X", "Y", "Z" Companies. "Z" Company had a long stretch of Line ["Z" Company's portion of the Front Line was as shown on page 151].

---

[198] See the diary entry for 19th March 1916.

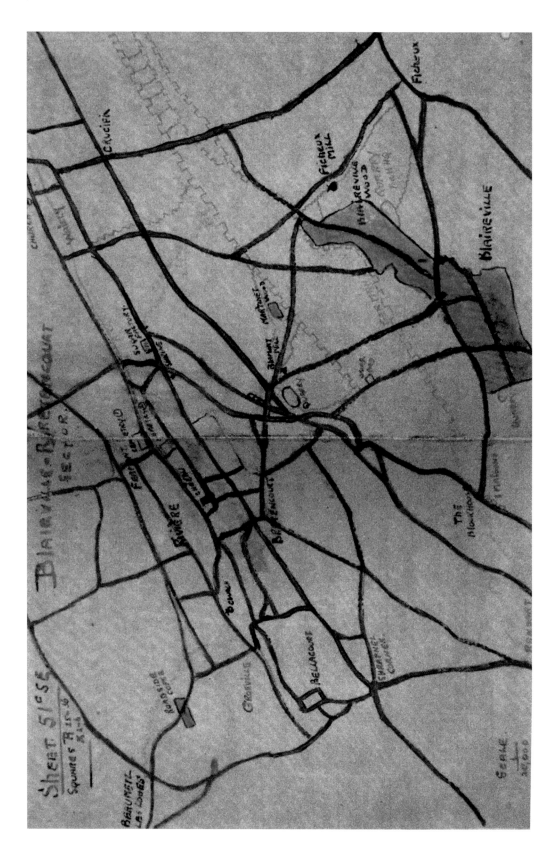

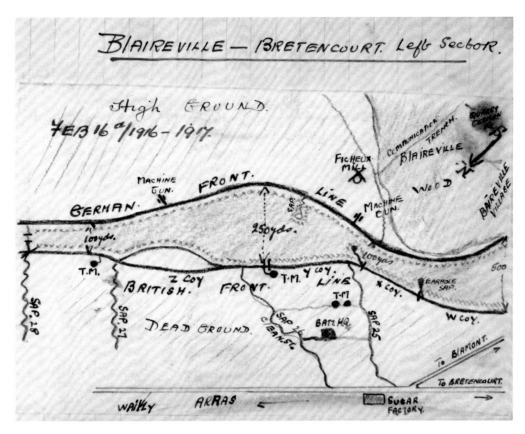

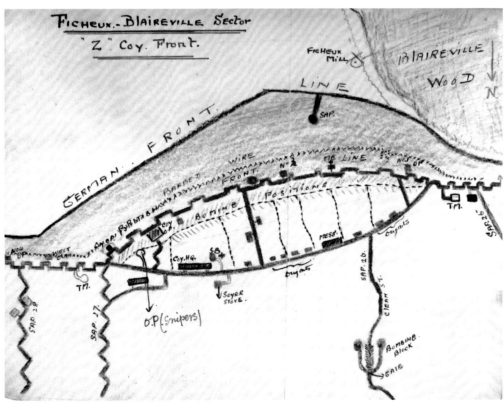

The distance between the Lines varied considerably. On the right it was about 500 yards across No Man's Land, then the trenches converged until they were about 100 yards apart; our Line kept fairly straight here, but a re-entrant in the Boche Line made the distance across No Man's Land about 250 yards, then it became narrow down to about 100 yards again, and the next Battalion on our left had no place where the trenches were more than 100 yards apart; in many places the distance was even less. Here the Germans had been driven back, and their old Communication Trenches from our Front Line (their old Front Line) to the German present Front Line (their old Second Line) ran across No Man's Land. These Communication Trenches had blocks constructed in them by ourselves and the Boche, in some places these blocks being only 15 to 30 yards apart. In reality they formed a series of duplicate saps from our Line and the Boche Line.

They were most uncomfortable Posts to hold, and each was in easy bombing distance of the other, which often meant times of danger and excitement. From my Company Line on "The Loop" I could see into all the saps, and could easily distinguish Boche in their sap heads. For this reason I had two Sniper's Posts constructed in my Line, which were used incessantly for firing onto these Boche, and making them keep their heads down. By this means we were able to help the Battalion on our left – usually the 1/5th or 1/6th King's Liverpool Regiment (Colonel Harrison's troops).

Generally speaking this sector was quiet, except for constant patrolling, which we did to get command of No Man's Land. We also tried several of our new toys – West Guns,[199] Stokes Trench Mortars,[200] Rifle Grenades, and Fixed Rifles.

The Right Sector was if anything less strenuous than the Left Sector, because the trenches were much further apart, consequently there was less worry from Trench Artillery by Trench Mortars, Rifle Grenades etc.

The Right Sector was chiefly in a chalk strata and was consequently much drier, but the trenches were much wider, and not so deep.

The Left Sector was in a soft clay soil and on lower ground, and was therefore much wetter and required more trench upkeep.

In our early days on this Front it was awful, with snow, rain, and mud, but later, in May and June, it was glorious.

Blairville Wood and the village were quite a picture to look upon from our Front Line.

My Company Line in this Sector was very interesting. When we first took it over it had been badly neglected by the French. The trenches were very wide and shallow, and practically devoid of traverses,[201] except for a few fascines built up – these are kind of baskets made of brushwood and filled with loose earth. They are practically useless even for rifle bullets, and no use against even small shells. Consequently we set to work to deepen, narrow, and traverse our Company Line. It took a tremendous amount of hard work. We also drained our trenches and made a brick gully at the bottom with several sump pits, lined with bricks. These pits were large enough to take a trench pump, so that, when they filled with water, we lowered the pump into the sump, and pumped the water out. We also put trench boards down the whole length. This all took a great deal of time, but fully repaid us, for, while some Companies were living in mud and water, we were comparatively dry.

---

[199] See the full description of these on page 155 and for the position see the plan on page 151.
[200] This was a 3.2 inch bore Trench Mortar designed by Sir Wilfred Stokes KBE in January 1915; it remained in use until the Second World War.
[201] See the footnote to the diary entry for 1st March 1916.

In fact, in conjunction with "D" Company of the 1/4th Loyal North Lancashires, we constructed a really fine piece of Line; it was considered a really good piece of work, so good in fact that the Divisional Commander, General Jeudwine, ordered officers to come to see what could be done in the way of trench repair and upkeep.

I had organised a Pioneer Section in my Company at Waterhouse's suggestion. This Pioneer Section consisted of 12 men, trained in pairs on special duties of trench construction.

> (a) Wiring – rapid wiring – apron fence system.
> (b) Traverse building – sand bag or wire frames filled in with loose earth.
> (c) Trench revetting – wire frames, brushwood, hurdles, or utilisation of any convenient material.
> (d) Tunnelling and dug out construction – I had several miners who were extremely useful for this section.
> (e) Flooring for trenches, laying trench boards – two joiners took this work.
> (f) Trench drainage, sanitation – I gave this work to my stretcher bearers because they did no trench Sentry Duty.

The system of working the Pioneer Section was to select the particular job on hand under sections (a) to (f) above, explain what was required to the two specialists who controlled the work, and give them sufficient men from the platoon in whose section of the Line the work was to be done. In this way each platoon was working on its own Line and improving it for their own advantage.

It was always better to let the men work in their own section of Line rather than on some other platoon's section. They took a great interest because they reaped the benefit of their own labours.

The system worked excellently, and we worked on a regular Work Timetable, so that the men knew what hours they had for work, and what time they had for rest.

Occasionally, of course, something cropped up which upset the regular programme, but generally things worked out well, and we were a very happy family in "Z" Company.

For rations we allocated so many men from each platoon to go down to the Ration Dump or Cookhouse in the trench at HQ.

A Duty Roster for ration parties was kept – thus every man got his share of this duty, which often had to come out of rest periods.

Corporal Stevens acted as Trench Company Quartermaster Sergeant. He always took the party down, and was responsible for issuing the rations to each Platoon Commander. He did his work <u>most</u> satisfactorily.

In addition we got sign posts made which we put up to indicate:

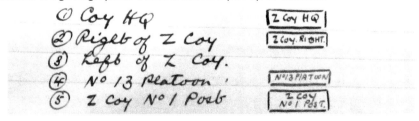

These were put up in prominent positions on the Fire Bays.

In addition the Divisional Front was divided into sections.

Each Battalion had a letter – or, rather, each Battalion Front had a letter – e.g. A, a big white letter on a Black Board put up in a visible position behind the trenches, facing the rear, so that the Gunners could see the boards from their rear Observation Posts.

The Divisional Front was measured out in distances of 25 yards – each section of 25 yards being numbered in succession, e.g. 40/41. These numbers were painted on a small board and fixed in the trench.

This was for rapid communication with the Gunners in the event of our Line being shelled, so that we could immediately telephone to the Gunners and inform them exactly what point of our Line was being shelled. They usually retaliated to points opposite to us, which quietened the Hun.

For instance the message would read *"Am being shelled with 5.9 inch at D 40/42 – retaliate"*. This I mention because it shows how the importance of co-operation between the Infantry and the Artillery was developing on a systematic basis.

In addition we had a system of Retaliation. This consisted in firing on certain points which we knew would annoy the Boche, e.g. Ficheux Mill, Dumps, Blairville Quarry (which we knew was a German Brigade HQ). These were all lettered and numbered R, R2, R3, etc.

A message "R2" meant that you wanted Artillery to fire on R2 in reply to fire from the Boche on some of our tender spots. This usually silenced him.

The most effective way of quietening him was to try to locate the position of the hostile Battery firing.

This was done by several methods:

Sound bearing i.e. judging the direction from which the sound of the guns firing came from, judged from two points wide apart in our Line, and taking bearings on the direction. Then, tracing the bearings on the map until their point of intersection gave an approximate position of the German Battery.

Possibly the aeroplanes might have spotted a Battery firing near this place, and photographed the position from the air, so that it could be fairly accurately fixed. Then the guns would open fire on this Battery and make things a bit uncomfortable for the Hun Gunners.

Another method – at night – was to mark the position or direction of gun flashes from our Line and trace back on the map.

The second method was especially useful in spotting the position of Boche Machine Guns or Trench Mortars, which, of course, were firing at much shorter ranges, although for this reason the Boche (and likewise ourselves) were very clever at concealing the flashes.

One of our dodges was to hang sand bags in front of our Machine Guns so that the bullets passed through the screen but – so to speak – absorbed the flash.

Cross Machine Gun fire is more difficult to spot than direct frontal fire.

For Trench Mortars we used to fire Very lights[202] a second or so prior to the Mortar, so that a bright light was visible as compared with a small flash.

Each platoon had a specially strong protected Sentry Post made with steel girders etc. These were for occupation under heavy bombardment.

---

[202] These were flares, fired from a breech-loaded single shot pistol, developed by an American Naval Officer called Edward Wilson Very.

There was also an excellent Observation Post (OP) for the OC of the Company, which was in telephone communication with Battalion HQ. As mentioned above, we had two excellent Sniper's Posts which had very fine fields of fire, and also gave very fine observation along the whole of my Front.

The special characteristic of the Line was the double trench as shown in my sketches [on page 151]. It was built on the bank of a sunken road, the rear trench being on the road, hence there was high ground between the two trenches. This was very useful as we could move about in safety in the Second Line. Also we had a system of "Counter-Attack" in the event of the Boche making a surprise Bombing Raid. Everyone had a definite position to occupy on this ground behind our Front Line and above. From there bombs could be very easily thrown into the trench, also it gave a commanding position over No Man's Land, to prevent other Boche reinforcing the Raiding Party. Enfilading Positions were good and we were in easy range of the Boche with Rifle Grenades, Trench Mortars, and West Guns.[203]

I had two Heavy Trench Mortars of 9.45 inches, Plum Pudding Bombs, in my Line.[204] The West Gun or West Bomb Thrower was a new idea for firing N° 5 Mills hand grenades,[205] but it was not a success. It was very heavy to move about, and once its position was

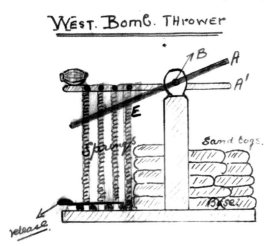

observed by the Boche he gave it a bad time with Rifle Grenades and Counter Trench Mortars. It consisted of a large square wooden base about 5 feet square with a vertical post in the centre. To this post was pivoted a lever which was attached to springs. The springs at E on the diagram (left) were compressed by two men pressing down the lever A^1 to position A. The bomb was then placed on the end of the lever and then, by means of the foot release, the lever flew up and threw the bomb.

We had wiring parties out nearly every night, and considerably strengthened our entanglements.

The Company HQ dug out was quite good and in a central position in the Second Line.

It was a deep dug out and lined with wood. It had a wooden bedstead, and also an iron one. Next to it was the Signallers' dug out and telephone, then the Company Sergeant Major's (Howard's) and – through it – a long dug out accommodating five men.

We had a very good dug out for a Company Mess with a dug out opening out of it for a Kitchen and Servants' Quarters.

Moffatt and Kenderine slept in the Mess with Evans. "Y" Company had bad officers' accommodation, so Evans fed and slept with us.

The Boche were making many Bombing Raids along the British Front; consequently the

---

[203] The West Spring Gun, otherwise known as the West Bomb Thrower, was powered by 24 springs, and more akin to a catapult or ballista than a gun, as shown by Norman's diagram. It was designed by Captain Allen West, and brought into service in 1915, but lasted only until 1916, being cumbersome, unpredictable, and dangerous to operate.
[204] "Flying Pig" was generally the nick-name used for a heavy 9.45 inch bore Trench Mortar, while the term "Plum Pudding Bomb" was normally used to refer to 2 inch bore Mortars, so perhaps Norman means that he had both.
[205] See footnote 135 on page 105.

Higher Powers were very keen on Defence, and Schemes of Counter Action. We had our Communication Trenches well protected in case the Boche drove us out of our Front Line. Our main Communication Trench, Sap 26, Clean Street, had a very fine bombing block, [as shown in the diagram on the right and the plan on page 151].

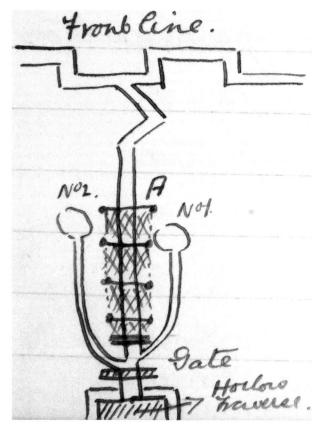

The place chosen was about 50 yards down the trench from our Front Line, and was on a straight stretch about 30 yards long.

Two Arrow Head Trenches were made on the Communication Trench, which was covered by a wire netting cage. A strong gate of wire netting was erected, behind which was a hollow traverse,[206] large enough for two men and a Machine Gun. If the Boche came down this trench two bombers would occupy each Arrow Head and two Machine Gunners would occupy the hollow traverse, the gate being closed in front of the junction of the Communication Trench and the Arrow Heads.

As the Boche came down the Communication Trench and got into the net, bombs would be thrown by No.1 and No.2 Posts, which would fall through the cage – but it was very difficult to throw one out of the cage. Also the Machine Gun would open fire up the Communication Trench and give the Hun a happy (!) few seconds.

Other small points of organisation in this Line included:

(a) Company Small Arms Ammunition Stores, Company Bomb Store.

(b) Platoon Small Arms Ammunition Stores.

(c) Platoon Bomb Stores.

(d) Gas Gongs – old shell cases for each Sentry Post. Also compressed Air Gas Horns for giving warning of Cloud Gas attack – Strombus Horns.[207]

Our Artillery Co-operation was also improved.

(i) Various Coloured Rockets were used for giving warning of a German Infantry attack.

(ii) Special Code Words for testing the efficiency of our covering Batteries were instituted.

---

[206] See the footnote to the diary entry for 1st March 1916.

[207] Cylinders of compressed air operated these horns, which are named after the Latin generic name for marine gastropods such as conches (which can also be used to make a trumpet sound).

Tests were given by Company Commanders.

The time allowed for the Battery to get into action was one minute, this time being reckoned from the time the message was handed into the Company Signal Office in the Line to the first shell coming over.

Inability to comply with the test meant trouble for the Battery concerned.

Efficiency and preparedness was our motto. The Boche would most certainly have found our Line a hard nut to crack.

We had our schemes to meet

> (i) Heavy Bombardment
> (ii) Infantry attack
> (iii) Cloud Gas attack
> (iv) Surprise Raids

and we constantly practised the Company in these actions.

Hot food was a difficulty as the trenches were so bad for traffic. I managed to get up a Soyer Stove (a big boiler),[208] and we made an emplacement for this in the Second Line. I also got a cook up, so that we were able to make hot soup or coffee, cocoa, or tea during the night. This was very much appreciated.

We were taking all possible precautions against Trench Feet and frostbite. Every man washed his feet daily in cold water, then rubbed his feet and legs with whale oil thoroughly for 10 minutes. When possible we got dry socks for the men, but it was difficult. Luckily about this time Mother sent me a parcel of 20 pairs, and Mrs Spencer Mossfield sent me 100 pairs. These were a god-send! As the MO said, "Really I don't know what keeps the men in the trenches alive at all; snow, mud, and misery. Bad enough at HQ dug out which leaks like a sieve."

Rather a strange incident happened to me in the Line during this tour.

One morning, at about 6.00am, Captain J.G. Dill DSO (Leinster Regiment), 2nd General Staff Officer, 55th Division, came up to my Line to consider the advisability of putting some Machine Gun Positions on my left to enfilade the Front of the 1/6th Liverpools on our left. The field of fire was excellent, and we could support them very well. We selected the positions, and he left at about 8.00am.

During the same morning, at about 10.30am, two officers and a private came into my Line. One officer had a steel helmet[209] and an old raincoat, but no rank badges. The other had a Staff Field Service cap with a red band – but not one of the three had any Regimental Badges visible.

The officer with the steel helmet stopped me and asked about some Machine Gun Positions, how many were going to be made, where they were to be built, and their fire direction. I didn't know this man and never gave information to unknown people in my Line. I pretended to know nothing about this scheme, whereupon he said, "That is absurd."

My reply to this remark was, "Who are you?"

"Really, Boy, don't you know me? Why, I'm Brigadier General Duncan, commanding the 165th Infantry Brigade."

---

[208] A spirit stove invented by Alexis Soyer, first used in the Crimean War in the 19th Century. For the position of this stove see the plan on page 151.
[209] See footnote 174 on page 133.

I apologised, but still I didn't know him, and told him nothing.

He got rather annoyed, and then said, "Do I look particularly like a Boche?"

"Well, Sir, I've seen some very good looking Boche!"

This quite amused the gentleman!

He realised I wasn't going to tell him anything, and said he would go, and come again some other time.

"Sorry, Sir, but you can't leave my Line until I have satisfied myself who you are."

"Come now, Boy, you can't keep me here, I've plenty to do. This is my Brigade Major, Captain Newton, and this boy is my runner."

I examined the runner's pay book, the particulars in which agreed with those given me by the General.

Then I asked him to come to my dug out and I would telephone my Brigade. He quite agreed and the confirmation was satisfactory. He was Brigadier General F.J. Duncan CMG DSO (Royal Scots) later (in 1918) Major General.

So, after a drink and a chat about the Machine Gun Positions, he left me with my apologies.

A day or two after this incident he came round the Line with Major General Jeudwine, Divisional Commander, and, remembering me, he turned to the General and said, "Oh, this is the boy who put me under arrest the other morning, Sir."

The Divisional General was quite pleased and said that I was quite right to arrest General Duncan – he was a very suspicious looking character!!!

THE DISTINGUISHING BADGES OF THE DIVISION

On the 30th March, 1916, an order was issued directing that distinguishing badges of coloured material were to be worn by all ranks just below the collar at the back of the S.D. jacket.

The badges worn by Battalions are shown below.

164th INFANTRY BRIGADE.

1/4th King's Own R. Lancs. Regt.

1/8th King's Liverpool Regt.

2/5th Lancs. Fusiliers.

1/4th Loyal N. Lancs. Regt.

Shortly before he left on the morning of March 8th Thompson came up to say "Good Bye" to me. As he says in his diary: "Went to say Good Bye to Hall, away down in the bottom of a hole in the ground."[210] My Company HQ certainly was deep down in the earth, but it was a splendid place, very deep, well lined with wood, quite dry, but very cold.

08.03.16 We were relieved in the evening at 4.00pm, by "D" Company, 1/4th Loyal North Lancashires. Then we proceeded via Bretencourt and Rivière, up the Communication Trench to Beaumetz, and arrived at Monchiet at about 9.00pm. It was a glorious moonlight night.We found quite a good hut camp, with small Armstrong Huts[211] for the officers.
The men were all tired out and soon settled down to a good feed.
Captain Waterhouse returned from his additional course at Flixecourt, and we went along to our Company Mess in the village, only a few minutes' walk from the camp.
I was <u>very</u> tired and, after a short chat with the Skipper, I turned in, but I just lay down as I was in my clothes and slept soundly until 9.45am on March 9th. The Skipper and I had no beds here, so we used stretchers – quite comfortable!

10.03.16 Germany declared war on Portugal. Germany was well advised not to try to have Portugal on her side![212]

---

[210] This is the last mention in the diary of Lieutenant R.N. Thompson, RAMC, MO as being with the 2/5th Lancashire Fusiliers in France. He had accompanied them as MO when they first landed in France on 3rd May 1915, at which stage Norman said of him that *"he turned out to be a great fellow"*. He had mentioned a 2nd Lieutenant R.N. Thompson as being with the 5th Reserve Battalion in Southport in November 1914, who is likely to be the same man, in view of having the same initials. Up to this point in the diary he has featured frequently; for example, he *"wakened up in great spirits and did balancing tricks"* after the first proper sleep in France on 5th May 1915, he went with Norman for a day trip to Ypres from Arques in May 1915 (this last is not actually mentioned in any of the diary entries for May 1915, but is mentioned in a later diary entry for August 1917, when Norman is about to go into action at Ypres for the first time), and he also went round the Saintoyen glass works with Norman while at Arques. In August and September 1915, while at Aveluy, he shared a dug out with Norman; the Kirchner pictures that they put up on the walls of their dug out (see the diary entry for 1st August 1915 on page 73 and footnote 96) are likely to have been Dr Thompson's (in contrast to the photographs, which Norman expressly says were his own), and he appears to have spoken good German so as to be able to communicate with the German butcher from Mannheim whose arm he amputated on 27th August 1915. He was a broad Scot from Glasgow, and played the mouth organ and sang, according to the diary entries for 13th September 1915 and 24th January 1916 (on the latter occasion shocking the Padre by his choice of song). He is mentioned as enjoying a ride from Aveluy to Bouzincourt with Norman on 11th October 1915, and as being one of the only two successfully to ride over a course of jumps on 19th January 1916, but of his demonstrations for training purposes Norman says these *"were always a joke"* (this relating specifically to a demonstration of a vermorel sprayer on 8th February 1916). There is a photograph of him with Lieutenant Colonel H.J. Shirley, Major H.N. Milnes, and Captain G.C. Hutchinson on page 112, on the reverse of which photograph he is described as *"Capt R.N. Thompson"*.
[211] Small, collapsible British army huts made from canvas.
[212] In Norman's opinion, reflecting the opinion of many of his colleagues, Portuguese soldiers were unreliable. His diary entry for 8th February 1918 when he was servng in the La Bassée sector reads as follows:
We had the Portuguese on our left in this sector. They only had one Corps – Praise God! That was enough of that sort. They were "no use", and that sums them up. In fact they were a nuisance and a responsibility, because they were unreliable, and we never knew what they would do in the event of trouble. Circumstances made this mistrust still worse, for everyone was talking of the coming Spring Offensive of the Boche. Naturally no one knew where or when his attack would be launched, but, as a precaution, one of the first duties of the Battalion in Reserve was to reconnoitre the defences behind the Portuguese Front and the approaches to their Line. The instructions were perfectly definite, and were these:

11.03.16   I was very pleased to have the Skipper once again as OC of "Z" Company. I paid the men, fitted clothing etc.

12.03.16   It was a glorious day, sunny, and much warmer. After Church Parade at 10.30am I went out with a digging party. We were making some bombing trenches just outside the village for training purposes.

There was a "Z" Company concert, then several of us went over to Gouy, where the Divisional HQ was, some considerable distance from the Line.

There was an excellent Canteen and Baths here. Captain Percy Rothband (cousin of Lieutenant B.H. Rothband of "Y" Company) managed the Divisional Canteen, Divisional Baths, Theatre Party, Cinema, Barber's Shop and Fish and Chip Saloon.

There was also an excellent Officers' Club at Gouy, in two large Army Huts, very nicely decorated and furnished with settees and tables for cards and writing, and with about a dozen cubicles equipped as bedrooms, also a very nice lounge and dining room, where you could get breakfast, lunch, afternoon tea or dinner. There was also an excellent bar, and you could get hot baths. Every convenience was there, and the whole organisation was really well done, and wonderfully run. The whole place was a god-send, and fully appreciated by us when we came out of the trenches.

We went to the Divisional Concert Party there, at which there were several ladies. The Divisional General brought them down. We had an excellent evening's entertainment, and then we all walked back from Gouy.

"In the event of our allies, the Portuguese, vacating the Front Line in the event of enemy attack, the Battalion in Brigade Reserve to the Left Sub-sector will take up defensive positions (here followed detailed directions as to the dispositions) and will counter-attack the enemy immediately. Commanding Officers, and all officers of the Reserve Battalion will reconnoitre these positions within two hours of taking over Brigade Reserve billets; further troops will actually take up their positions as opportunity offers."

Our respect for the Portuguese was no better than anyone else's; in fact the Army as a whole had no use for the "Pork and Beans" [Portuguese], so much so that GHQ considered it necessary to circulate a memorandum, the exact words of which were:

"In future, the Portuguese will be known as, and spoken of, as 'our Gallant Allies' and not 'Those B —— Portuguese', as seems to have become too general."

                                                                                                Signed
                                                                                                Haig

Whilst Acting Adjutant, I actually saw this circular memorandum myself.

In his diary entry for 19th February 1918 he adds:

The forthcoming German Offensive was always in our minds, and one of our duties in Corps Reserve was to be in a state of readiness to move on short notice to reinforce any part of the 1st Corps Front – and, in particular, one Infantry Brigade with one Machine Gun Company to be in readiness to reinforce the Portuguese on the left of the Corps Front. Buses were always ready to transport this Emergency Brigade. Actually, on February 25th to 26th, the 126th Brigade were moved in to Support behind the Portuguese at Vieille-Chapelle to La Couture, after a heavy bombardment of their Lines; however, nothing more serious than a raid was attempted, and the Brigade was withdrawn. I mention this in support of my previous statement regarding the Portuguese.

CHAPTER 14
Blairville, Blamont Quarry and Monchiet
16th March 1916 to 9th April 1916

16.03.16 We took over the same line of trenches as on our last tour, on the left of the Blairville Sector. The Skipper and I lived together at Company HQ. Kenderdine, Moffatt and Manse Evans (who was still living with us) slept (sometimes!) at the Mess.

The trenches were much drier, and the hedges were beginning to break out. The Battalion hadn't had many casualties, but a winter in the Line had weakened our strength considerably. We had very few cases of trench feet.

We took over a couple of kittens as trench stores.

Waterhouse (Long Un) returned to the Battalion at Monchiet and rejoined "W" Company – he had been to Nice since Christmas recovering from "'flu" – Lucky Chap![213]

Rumours had reached Bury that our Battalion had been mixed up in the Verdun Show, which was raging fast and furious. The rumour was quite unfounded as the Battalion had never been anywhere near that place.

17.03.16 Brigadier General G.T.G. Edwards CB was on leave at this time. During his absence, Lieutenant Colonel F.M. Charleton DSO was commanding the Brigade. He was a fine soldier, a strict disciplinarian, brave, perhaps too brave, but a lover of eye-wash. For instance, when going round our Line one morning, I met him in the trench. After asking me several questions he said, "Ever thought of cleaning your Gas Gongs?"

"What with, Sir?"

"Why, metal polish."

"No, Sir, we never dreamt of such a thing."

"You had better try it, and see it is done by tomorrow."

"Very good, Sir."

I immediately went to the telephone and spoke to Captain V.A. Jackson DSO, Brigade Major, and asked him if he had any metal polish.

"What the devil do you want metal polish for in trenches?"

"We don't, but Colonel Charleton says we have to clean our Gas Gongs."

"Oh, does he? Well, tell him from me there isn't any."

Anyway we did clean them, but with sand and water.

18.03.16 Now that Captain Waterhouse was back, it left me more time to go on evening parties, patrols etc.

I had often wanted to reconnoitre the Boche sap near Ficheux Mill, opposite "Z" Company's section of the Line, shown in the sketches of this Front in the description of the Blairville trenches [on page 151].

Corporal Mc Kay, Sergeant Street, and Lance Corporal Hampson had reconnoitred it but I wanted to see it for myself.

So I took Lance Corporal Hampson and Private Ronksley. It was a glorious evening and

---

[213] See the diary entry for 24th December 1915.

bright moonlight – the same old moon! – too bright in fact. We had to move slowly and keep low, but we managed to get to the sap. It was very strongly wired. By the sounds, it was occupied by at least three men. We tried to find out whether we could get into the sap, surprise the Boche and possibly capture a real live juicy fat one, but no luck, so we contented ourselves by throwing one bomb each into the sap head. They burst quite nicely, but we didn't wait on this occasion to find out what damage was done, but made for our trench. The return journey was nothing like so peaceful as the outward trip, for the Boche evidently thought that we were making a raid and immediately opened fire wildly on No Man's Land. Hampson, Ronksley and I took cover in a shell hole until the storm of bullets abated, and then cleared for our Line – feeling very hot and somewhat excited – however we were all three safe.

Both Hampson and Ronksley were splendid fellows on patrol, very calm.

19.03.16   It was a glorious spring Sunday morning.

The Boche were rather rude during the day. At about noon he put over quite a number of 5.9 inch shells on our Line, also on Clean Street, and he also put several shells into the Sugar Factory, where our cookers were. There were always a lot of men about here, fetching rations, also RE material. One man was killed and several wounded. We didn't see any Boche aeroplane over who could have observed any special movement on this particular day. Moffatt and I had a little walk out over No Man's Land in the evening. While we were out on patrol, we came across some dead Turcos, French Colonial chaps. At first when we saw these figures we thought it was a Boche patrol. They didn't move so we crept towards them, and got rather a fright when "several rats ran in front of us". On examination the figures proved to be dead Turcos, who must have been there since September 1915. Of course they were all decayed and chiefly bone. Round one of them was a brass trumpet which I carefully removed and took back with me. It really was in good condition and the open end was wrapped in a duster. I kept this in my valise and later brought it home.

20.03.16   It was a quiet day. Moffatt and Kenderdine, encouraged by the Skipper, started a Rifle Grenade and West Gun[214] strafe, in co-operation with the 9.45 inch Trench Mortars. We gave the Boche a busy time for half an hour – of course he retaliated, but, except for moving one or two sand bags, the Hun didn't damage us, and for all we knew we didn't hurt him.

21.03.16   General Edwards had returned from leave, and came round the Line, starting with "Z" Company.

It was the usual procedure.

"You're wanted on the telephone, Sir."

Waterhouse being busy, I answered it.

Hutty at the other end.

"That you, Hall?"

"Yes."

"Oh, thought I would let you know the General is on his way up to your Line. See that

---

[214] See the footnote to the diary entry for the period 2nd to 7th March 1916 on page 152 and the fuller description of a West Bomb Thrower on page 155.

everyone is doing their job."

"Oh, that's alright, Sir, they always are in "Z" Company."

General Edwards arrived, and seemed in quite a cheery mood. Waterhouse and I accompanied him round the Line. He always had a weakness for putting Questions and Problems to the Sentries. He came to Private Smith.

The General: "Let me look through your periscope, my man."

Smith: "Oh aye, tha' can look thr't periscope if ti wants."

The General, looking through the periscope, "I can see six Germans coming over No Man's Land. What are you going to do? Quick!"

Smith (quite calm) "Hey up, let's 'ave a look fur mysell."

So the General moved away for Smith to have a look.

Smith looked through his periscope, carefully turned it to right and then to left, scanning No Man's Land, then, not the least bit excited, turned to General Edwards and said, "Nay, Sir, I dern't think yer can see any Germans."

General Edwards moved on round the next traverse[215] very quickly and just reeled in laughter. It certainly was very funny!

So we walked on past each Sentry Post with the usual report from the Sentry coming smartly to attention (sometimes!) followed by "Nº 2 Post, 13 Platoon, all correct, Sir."

So he passed on.

In the afternoon I went over to see Joe Chamberlain, "D" Company of the Liverpool Irish at Blamont Quarry. We were to relieve them there in Reserve to the 1/4th King's Own Royal Lancasters the next day. I took over dispositions, duties, work programmes etc.

22.03.16   We moved over in the afternoon to relieve "D" Company of the 1/8th Liverpool Irish, at Blamont Quarry Post. It was not very far to go. The men were in dug outs in the Third Line – Cavalry Trench it was called. It was a wide trench and had been used by the French for taking rations, ammunition etc. up to the Front Line on mules. The men were fairly comfortable. A few HQ men lived in the same house as we did. At one time it had been an estaminet at the corner of four roads on the Bretencourt to Blairville Road – in fact there were the remains of several houses nearby and also on the high ground nearer the Front Line was the remains of a windmill.

It wasn't safe to occupy the ground floor rooms in these places, so we used the cellars as our Company HQ. The Signallers, Company Sergeant Major, servants and runners occupied another cellar. It was quite a good place, fairly safe with an arched roof. There were several beds, a table, and chairs, but it was very cold. The only means of getting warm was by a brazier, and this usually smoked so badly we were almost suffocated. Still, it was a cheery little home – but very cold.

Our role was in Support to the 1/4th King's Own Royal Lancasters, so that we took our orders direct from the OC of that Battalion, Lieutenant Colonel Charleton, or his 2nd in Command, Major Caddy – who was some character!

I reconnoitred the Support Line – Martinet Wood, Ransart Road, Blamont. It was a poor Line – plenty of work to be done on it.

---

[215] See the footnote to the diary entry for 1st March 1916.

Naturally we had our Battle Positions allotted in the Reserve Line, and, as our Company was the only immediate Reserve, we held a long Line.

We had no permanent Sentry Posts to furnish, only Gas Guards on dug outs when the men were asleep, so that our Company was at the disposal of the OC of the King's Own Royal Lancasters for work, and he didn't forget to find our fellows plenty to do. This consisted chiefly in trench repairs, but the thaw after the continual snow had caused a lot of damage, and, in consequence, it was day and night work, draining the trenches which were flooded, revetting, wiring the Support Line, and making the Second Line a defensive position. This Line had been practically untouched by the French – who seemed to rely on Providence, or the Goodwill of the Boche, rather than on their own initiative, to make their defence works strong.

So my old motto "Get to work" came in quite well.

Major Caddy worried the life out of poor Skipper, always wanting to know whether our parties for the next day would be at full strength, how many hours they had worked, and what they had done.

I really believe he thought our men were like bacteria and could split their own kind at the rate of hundreds per second.

Eventually the Skipper had words with Colonel Charleton, and told him he expected too much from our men, that they were only human, and couldn't do more than 24 hours' work a day.

One redeeming feature of this tour was that leave started again. It had been closed on account of the Verdun Show, which was still going strong.

We did rather well for rations these days in our Company, possibly due to the fact that the Battalion Butcher was on our Company strength, hence the Company Meat and Bacon ration was good. We even got Kidneys for breakfast.

Jokingly I used to say to the Butcher, "No Kidneys, No Pay!"

24.03.16 We had another fall of snow, and more frost. I got Kippers from home, and very good they were too! I was a witness on an FGCM at Bretencourt. Bretencourt was only a short distance from Blamont.

There was a road leading up to our Company HQ from the village, which the limbers[216] used to come right up at night, for our Company and for the King's Own Royal Lancasters. The Communication Trench to the village ran down this road at the side, and sometimes it was a very unhealthy place, especially at night. In addition the Boche could fire on the road from his Line by Machine Gun indirect fire – so it was called! But it was quite direct enough for my liking.

The Quarry quite near our Company HQ, and also Battalion HQ for the King's Own Royal Lancasters, was a very unhealthy place at times. One night during our tour the Boche gave us a pukker[217] heavy bombardment, so much so that we quite expected that he was coming over to raid us, but he didn't. Anyway Colonel Charleton decided that the Quarry was no place for a Battalion HQ, and decided to move to some old dug outs in the sunken road about a quarter of a mile away.

---

[216] See footnote 39 on page 37.
[217] Pukker (more normally spelt pukka or pucca) is slang for "proper", derived from the Hindustani for "cooked" or "ripe".

25.03.16   The brothers Moffatt went on leave. They left the trenches in the early evening. It was an awful night – snowing and blowing.

The Allies held a big Conference in Paris. It was evident that something would have to be done to relieve the tremendous pressure of the German Attack on the French at Verdun. This Conference was the first indication that there was Dirty Work in the wind for the British troops on the Western Front.

A French officer was staying with the King's Own Royal Lancasters for liaison duty. He had recently returned from Verdun, and gave us some very interesting and vivid accounts of the fighting at Fort Douaumont. Our sector naturally seemed quite a health resort to him.

28.03.16   We went into the Front Line trenches in front of the Blairville Wood. A re-arrangement of the Front Line Sectors had been made. All Battalions were to take a smaller frontage and move along to the Right – South. By this new scheme three Battalions were in the Line and found their own Reserve. This meant that "Z" Company went on the right flank of the Battalion Front, and the order was "Z", "W", "X", "Y". This new Company Line was fairly good, but as usual needed a great deal of improvement.

We were much further from the Boche; it was about 400 yards across No Man's Land. This was an advantage, as we were less liable to be worried by German Rifle Grenades and Trench Mortar Bombs. On the contrary we were more liable to shelling. The Boche Trenches were dug in front of Blairville Village and Wood, which stood out prominently on high ground. There was a valley between our Front Line and theirs, and our Front Line was on a reverse slope.

The Line was dug through solid chalk and the trenches were not very deep. In some places you could easily walk along and see over the top. After months of occupation the chalk had fallen and widened the trenches to about 7 feet in places. We had two very long saps running out into No Man's Land, Liverpool Sap and Derby Sap. These we found were very badly protected by wire; in fact, the whole Front was very thinly wired. Consequently we had to put up a great deal of barbed wire on my Company Front at night.

The dug out accommodation was not good, and the approaches to the Line were poor. We therefore decided to devote our attention to the work as follows:

        1. Wiring our Front

        2. Improving fire positions

        3. Deepening and narrowing trenches.

The Company HQ dug out was also a very poor place when we took over, but we set to work on this and made an excellent place with a Mess Room and Sleeping Quarters opening from it. But this took time, and was continued by our old friends "D" Company of the 1/4th Loyal North Lancashires. Digging in this area, through chalk, or a mixture of chalk and flint, was very difficult and slow. We concentrated our attention in the day time to improving dug outs inside the trenches, so that the chalk could be carried away at night.[218]

It was essential for us to continue to have the control over No Man's Land, undoubtedly the best means of keeping the Boche from our Lines. This entailed constant patrols at night.

---

[218] The work in this area, i.e. in the area of Liverpool and Derby Saps, is described again in the entries in the original diary for 26th May 1916 onwards, and some details from the description in those later entries have been included here.

Joe Hedley's Company was on our left, and we saw more of him in the trenches this tour than we had done for some time.

The Liverpool Irish were on our right with Captain Chamberlain, Lieutenant Mahon, Baxter, and Johnny Gordon.

They were a cheery crowd and we worked well together.

In order to ensure co-operation between the Battalions in the Line, our Right Post exchanged positions with the Left Post of the Liverpool Irish, consequently there was an overlapping and touch was maintained.

Mahon was a particularly aggressive individual who simply revelled in patrolling. But he had rather a weakness for getting his patrols into two parties and on one or two nights he had scraps with his own men with bombs – not exactly an ideal method.

We had rather long tours of duty as Moffatt was on leave, so that there were only three officers in the Company; the Skipper, Kenderdine, and myself.

So we came to the end of March. The Boche had developed other methods of warfare to some considerable extent. He had got his Submarine Campaign on shipping in full swing, also his Zeppelin and aeroplane attacks on England.

Raids during this month (March):

    A. Zeppelin

        Two raids, L15 destroyed in the Thames, her and crew captured.

    B. Aeroplane

        Two raids.

    C. Attacks on Shipping

        HMS *Primula*

        HMS *Coquet* and destroyer sunk

        HMS *Fauvette* sunk

        Dutch Liner *Tubantia* sunk

        Dutch Liner *Palembang* sunk

        British Liner *Minneapolis* sunk

        British Liner *Sussex* torpedoed in Channel

        Hospital Ship *Portugal* sunk

01.04.16   It was a glorious afternoon. I sat in the trenches during the afternoon writing a letter. I was off duty, and things were quiet. Very heavy shelling could be heard in the distance, like the rumble of distant thunder. I had had a period of duty during this tour from 2.00am to 8.00am, quite nice, with glorious sunrises. Spring seemed to be really coming at last. The trees were breaking out, and the birds singing – where on earth they found places to build their nests seems a mystery. Blairville Wood began to look really glorious, with the red-tiled roofs of the few remaining houses on the edge of the wood and village. Most of these, we knew, were used as Observation Posts or Machine Gun Posts by the Germans, but we left them religiously alone for future attention on a more opportune occasion.

Our troubles of the previous spring were soon to start. The grass in No Man's Land was beginning to grow, which interfered with the view from our covered Observation Posts, and had to be cut down by parties sent out at night with scythes and bill hooks.

02.04.16   We were relieved by "D" Company of the 1/4th Loyal North Lancashires in the evening, at about 7.00pm. The relief passed off without any misfortunes, and we started off for Monchiet. It was a perfect night.

We went through Bretencourt, Rivière and Beaumetz. We had to wait some considerable time to cross the main Arras to Doullens road on account of long Columns of motor wagons taking up the nightly supply of rations, ammunition, RE material etc. This main road is the Route Nationale N° 25. It is a fine, wide road, lined with tall poplars. In the day time it was under observation from the Boche, but only occasionally did he fire his long range guns on the target. We reached Monchiet at about 10.00pm, and occupied the hut camp again. It was very close marching back from the Line, especially as it was uphill practically the whole way. We were quite ready for bed when we turned in after 16 days in the Line. It felt splendid to get into a suit of pyjamas again, and sleep in comfort between blankets in my valise.

03.04.16   I revelled in a hot bath. What !!!

I had Kippers for breakfast, and sent some over to Joe Hedley, who also appreciated them.

04.04.16   Our routine in Monchiet consisted in work in the morning, with the afternoon off.
to
06.04.16   There seemed to be a vertical breeze up in the Higher Commands, and a passion for making rear Defence Lines known as the Corps Line. One of our jobs while in Monchiet was digging, wiring and improving these rear Lines of Defence. One of these Lines ran on the South East side of the Arras to Doullens road and railway, and was a very important defensive position in the event of the Boche making an attempt to break through at any time. It was well dug, with good dug outs and Machine Gun Posts. This Line was quite 2½ miles as the crow flies behind the Front Line, and was to be held at all costs. It certainly was a <u>very</u> important position both tactically and strategically.

The Second Corps Line was really a Switch from the Main Corps Line of Defence and was known as the Wanquetin or Gouy Switch. This Line was only in its infancy at this time. A section of it ran quite near our camp at Monchiet and cut the Monchiet to Gouy road. This was the work we were chiefly engaged upon. Although very many hard hours of work were put in on these trenches behind the Line, it is interesting to note that they were never used as a defensive Line, as our Show at Messines in 1917 drove the Boche many miles East of this Line, and, even in 1918, when he again made his most wonderful attack – never to be forgotten – yet he never got as far back as this Line.

Our training consisted in Musketry, Bayonet Fighting, Close Order Drill, Defence against Gas, Bombing, and Lewis Gun Training.

A slight alteration in the Gas helmet had now taken place. We still had the Flannel Helmet like a bag fitting over the head and tucked inside the jacket, but the mica eye-pieces were replaced by glass eye-pieces. Whereas the mica eye-window was in one piece, the glass eye-windows were separate, one for each eye, and set in metallic rims.

A further improvement was made in the helmet. The flannel was made double thickness,

and an india-rubber valve was fitted, the action of the helmet being to inhale the air which had passed through the flannel which was soaked in chemicals. This air after passing through the lungs was exhaled through the mouth and out through the valve, which was only an outlet valve.

The Chlorine Gas was absorbed by the Sodium Hyposulphite solution and Glycerin (to keep the flannel moist) in which the helmet was soaked. It was quite sufficient protection against Chlorine even in fairly heavy concentration, but was a very uncomfortable thing to wear, and <u>very</u> hot.

The Germans had now started mixing Phosgene, a very poisonous gas, and certainly difficult to detect. The action on the men varied. Sometimes its toxic action was almost instantaneous, whereas in other cases the effects would not develop for several hours, when a man might suddenly collapse without any apparent cause.

Some means of protection had therefore to be sought. This was not difficult, for, by adding an alkaline solution of Hexamine to the previous solution before soaking the flannel, a fairly efficient absorbent liquid was obtained for both Chlorine and Phosgene. So the Boche was once again foiled with his Gas attacks.

Gas Casualties were chiefly due to men failing to get their helmets on quickly enough, or to faulty helmets. The greatest care had to be taken in inspecting the helmets most minutely, and frequently.

Thanks to hard work on the part of Chemical Experts at home, and to the Manufacturers, helmets were easily obtained in sufficient quantities, both for new issues and replacements of damaged helmets.

Yet another device had been instigated by the Hun, "Lachrymatory Gas" or "Tear Gas", because it made us cry. The effect of this new gas was irritating rather than toxic. The result was to put a man out of action temporarily, for a few days, but seldom had any serious effects on his constitution. For protection against Tear Gas we had eye-screens or masks issued, made with flannel and mica eye-pieces.

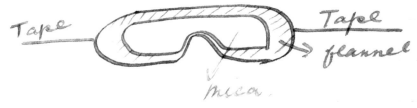

These were <u>not</u> really efficient, for the Boche seldom used Chlorine or Phosgene Gas alone or Lachrymatory Gas alone, more often a mixture of the two.

Fellows often put on only the Tear Gas mask, and consequently breathed in Chlorine or Phosgene Gas, thereby becoming Gas Casualties.

The masks were therefore very soon considered useless and were all called in, the order being that "Gas helmets would be worn for protection against Gas (i.e. Chlorine or Phosgene Gas) or Tear Gas".

"Tear Gas" even in these days was used by the Boche chiefly against our Battery Positions. For this he had to fire it over in shells. The shells contained, in addition to the ordinary bursting charge, a cylinder of glass, which cylinder held the chemical which had the property of producing eye irritation.

Sometimes the glass cylinders contained the chemical substance in the form of liquid, sometimes it was a solid, but in each case the ultimate action was the same, namely the bursting charge developed sufficient heat to vapourise the solid or liquid.

The substances used for this purpose were Brom Acetone, Sodo Acetone and others. So much for our protection against Boche Asphyxiating Gas.

While at Monchiet we had an issue of steel helmets.[219] These were anything but popular. They felt heavy and uncomfortable after the soft Field Service cap, and it was only by being especially stout about the wearing of steel helmets that the men eventually got used to them, and as time went on fully appreciated their protective value against shrapnel.

Personally I detested them intensely, but I am confident that they really were the means of saving thousands of lives.

We hadn't anything like one per man, and hadn't yet used them, except an odd one or two, in the Line.

07.04.16   I took "Z" Company over to Gouy on a working party.

Our officers played the 1/8th Liverpool Irish at football, and won 5-1. We had Ward, Gordon, and Chamberlain to tea.

Captain Waterhouse had been selected as an Instructor at a School of Instruction to be started by the 55th Division. This School was for junior officers – Platoon Commanders and NCOs, especially Junior NCOs, Corporals and Lance-Corporals. It was to be at Gouy-en-Artois, a nice country village, where our Divisional Headquarters was stationed.

Our work in connection with this School was to erect Armstrong Huts[220] and tents. We left at 8.00am, and arrived at Gouy at about 9.00am, where we reported to an RE Officer, whose name was Parkinson. We got our task detailed and the fellows set to work in real earnest. During the morning I was chatting with Parkinson, who was rather tall, slightly built, shrewd, thin, sharp-featured, with a yellowish skin, and his hair turning grey, his eyes being rather deeply set. He had been in the 1st Volunteer Battalion Lancashire Fusiliers[221] about 20 years before, after which he went out to British Columbia and settled there. On the outbreak of war, he came over with the 1st Canadian Divisional Engineers, and was then attached to VIth Corps HQ.

We worked all day and really made a tremendous change in the orchard, quite altering the appearance by erecting huts, tents, etc., amongst the trees. Half my Company dug about 300 yards of trenches.

When 5.30pm came I considered my men had done a very good day's work. When I suggested taking them back, Parkinson got quite annoyed. However, at 6.00pm I marched my Company back to Monchiet, where we arrived at 7.00pm. Eleven hours' work in hot sun, when you are nominally "In Rest" or Reserve, struck me as a fair day's work.

08.04.16   It was a glorious morning – quite hot. Cecil and Leslie Moffatt arrived back from leave. In the afternoon we had Battalion Sports in a field behind the village.

---

[219] See the diary entry for 31st December 1915 for the first mention of steel helmets in the diary, also footnote 174 on page 133.

[220] Small, collapsible British army huts made from canvas.

[221] In 1908 this Battalion became the 5th Battalion Lancashire Fusiliers (Territorial Force).

We had several events:

1. 100 yards Flat Race
2. Bomb Throwing
3. Sack Race
4. Three legged Race
5. 880 yards Cross Country
6. Slow bicycle (chiefly to get the Signallers' bicycles clean)
7. Tug of War – Company Teams
8. Relay Race – Platoon Teams

They were quite a success, and the Battalion was very interested in the events.

"Z" Company won the Tug of War after a great struggle with "W" Company, Joe Hedley's Company. "W" Company were much heavier than our team but "Z" Company stuck to it to the bitter end, and won by sheer determination. Company Sergeant Major Howard was very funny coaching our Company team.

Long Waterhouse won the Bomb Throwing.

Lance Corporal O'Donnell ran very well in the 100 yards – he really was a crack sprinter.

In the evening the Divisional Concert Party came over from Gouy and gave us a very good show in one of our large huts, where we rigged up a stage. The electric lighting was generated from one of the portable lighting sets belonging to the Divisional Signal Company.

09.04.16   Again it was a glorious morning. After Church Parade we had a walk and gathered some glorious wild daffodils, primroses, etc. for our Mess.

In the afternoon we had arranged a "Great Football Match" against the 2nd Battalion Lancashire Fusiliers, who were in the 4th Division, holding the trenches round Monchy, Foncquevilliers, and Hébuterne. Their team drove over in style in General Service Wagons[222] from Forceville.

The 55th Division Band came from Gouy and played selections during the afternoon.

Many of the officers and men of the 2nd Battalion came over to watch the game, which was very exciting. The 2/5th Lancashire Fusiliers managed to inflict a heavy defeat on the Line Battalion, winning by 6-2. After the match both teams had a jolly good feed. A large quantity of beer had been obtained for the men. Then the Divisional Concert Party came over specially to put on a show for us.

This was the first time we had really met the Line Battalion – it was a great day!

---

[222] See the footnote to the diary entry for 1st May 1915.

CHAPTER 15
Blairville, Rivière, Blairville again, and Monchiet
10th April 1916 to 13th May 1916

10.04.16   Captain Waterhouse left the Battalion to take over duties as Instructor at the 55th Divisional School at Gouy. We went to the Line and occupied our old position in the Blairville Left Sector.

11.04.16 to 13.04.16   We had the usual trench routine of wiring, patrols etc. We found several weak points in the parapets, and decided to strengthen these at night.
We were rather short-handed, as there were only three officers in the Company, Kenderdine, Moffatt and myself, which made it very hard work. I was doing an ordinary tour of duty as well as having the usual daily reports to render, and, as a result, I was on duty practically day and night, and getting very little sleep.

14.04.16   It was another glorious morning. At about 8.45am I was making a tour of my Company Line prior to turning in for breakfast (and, incidentally, a sleep, after practically two days without any) when I passed Private Schofield in the trench near the Company Observation Post. He was working in a Fire Bay repairing the parapet. I had a chat with him about the work and told him that he had better leave it until it was dark, as I was afraid he was under observation from the Boche (only about 250 yards away), and might get sniped.
I left him, and had scarcely gone 50 yards down the trench when Maxwell[223] came running after me – he looked as green as grass and just gasped, "Schofield is shot in the head, Sir."
I could scarcely credit this, but returned to the place I had left him only a few minutes before. Maxwell was right, Schofield had a bullet through his steel helmet[224] and right through his head, the back being practically blown out. Poor boy, he was dead.[225] I was very upset, and perhaps more so as I had only warned him a few minutes previously. In addition, I was dog tired and almost too tired to eat. Breakfast was out of the question – I couldn't face it.
Schofield was an exceedingly nice fellow; quiet, unassuming, but always doing his job whether on sentry, patrol, or work, a "Brave Soldier", efficient and thoroughly reliable.
Such an incident as this brought home to each and all of us "The Sadness of War – the Cruelty", and the uncertainty of it all. One almost became a Fatalist, for no one could know from one minute to the next what might happen.
Schofield was only 22 years old and his home was at 20, Scholes Street, Elton, Bury.
Work had to go on in spite of Casualties.

---

[223] Nick-named "Fido", also Company Sergeant Major Howard's batman, as mentioned in the diary entry for 24th June 1916.
[224] See footnote 174 on page 133, and the diary entry for 4th to 6th April 1916, only a few days previously on page 169, which refers to the fact that up until then steel helmets were only occasionally worn in the Line, and that a new issue of steel helmets was received at that time, perhaps one of those that Private Schofield was wearing, although on this occasion it unfortunately did not save his life.
[225] Norman spells the name "Scholfield", but the Commonwealth War Graves Commission's record has the spelling "Schofield", and gives the date of death as 15th April 1916, rather than 14th April 1916; also the age is given as 24, rather than 22. John Schofield, Service no 2921, was the son of Walter and Mary A. Schofield, and is buried at Le Fermont Military Cemetery, Rivière, reference 1.B.9. The cemetery and his headstone are pictured on page 176.

15.04.16   The Boche had an unexpected Hate on our Line at about noon with 5.9 inch and 77mm shells. He gave us a very sticky half hour, and there were several direct hits on my Line. I think he was trying to find the positions of our Trench Mortars, which had been doing some rather useful shooting. He made rather a mess of Clean Street, Sap 26, our main Communication Trench.

In the afternoon the Skipper came over from Gouy to see us in the Line. As usual we were all delighted to see him, and get a few useful suggestions. He went round to see the Company before leaving. The Skipper really loved his men in "Z" Company, and undoubtedly had their interests at heart. He was very upset about Schofield.

Schofield's remains were interred at midnight at Bretencourt/Rivière Cemetery. Major Milnes, Captain G.C. Hutchinson, and 2nd Lieutenant Moffatt attended the funeral. I couldn't go myself as we were in the Line.

17.04.16   Lieutenant Bodell, Trench Mortar Officer, came up to fix a Trench Mortar in my Line. He wanted a point near to the Boche Line, and chose a position in my Line near a small overhead screen at the junction of five trenches.[226] I refused to allow him to fire from here, because, should the Boche retaliate and get a direct hit on the position – which was highly probable – my communication would be disorganised. I selected another position for Bodell to play about with his new toy.

There was method in this project, as the 1/8th Liverpool Irish on our right were making a raid on the Boche trenches this night, and the scheme was for our people to send out one or two active patrols on our Front, and put up a Trench Mortar and Rifle Grenade barrage on the Boche Line to attract their attention to our point, so as to try to bluff them that we were going to make a raid on our sector, thus enabling the Irish to make a successful surprise raid.

Lieutenant Gardiner also came up to my Line, in order to register on the Boche Line prior to the raid. He, like most Gunners, was a cheery fellow, always out for a bit of sport.

A Machine Gun in the Boche Line had been giving us some trouble for a few nights, so we decided to register on this target.

It was quite a definite emplacement. I bet Gardiner he wouldn't hit it in twenty shots. He guaranteed to hit it in six. After careful (!) reference to maps, calculation of range, and the many corrections necessary for accurate (!) shooting, he gave the orders so characteristic of the Gunners:

"No 1 Gun, Stand to ... Hello, that you, Jim? Shake your receiver, can't hear a bloomin' word ... Aye – that's better ... Hello! Range 3,540 yards – Q.4.a.30.40. One round – "

"No 1 Gun ready, Sir"

"No 1 Gun, Fire!"

And No 1 Gun did Fire! The Shell burst finely – but behind our parapets – and Gardiner, myself and his Signaller got very nicely splashed with shrapnel and dirt.

After increasing the range and repeating, the second shell burst still further behind our

---

[226] Shown in the sketches of this front in the description of the Blairville trenches on page 151.

trench. This happened with four shells. I pulled Gardiner's leg and he said, "Oh, it's this rotten American ammunition – you never can tell where it is going."

I suggested that he checked his range. He did, and found he had under-ranged by 200 yards. The next shot was much better, about 50 yards short, and to the left of the Machine Gun emplacement.

More orders were issued:

"N° 1 Gun increase 25 yards, one-oh minutes right."

This nearly did the trick for the shell was a beauty, a splendid burst – just striking the bank below the emplacement.

Little shoots like this helped to pass an hour or two on a nice afternoon, and were really quite interesting.

Night came. Everyone was very interested in the raid to be carried out by the 1/8th Liverpool Irish, as it was the first raid on a large scale to be made by the 55th Division since its formation. Specially trained volunteers were selected to carry out the scheme, all details having been carefully planned and practised previously. The plan was to cut several roads through the Boche wire, then the raiders in three small parties were to enter the Boche trench, and inflict as much damage as possible on the Hun in 10 minutes. There had been an earlier raid on the night of April 16th, but they had been delayed in cutting the wire by a Boche working party, and also because the wire proved to be thicker than had been reported by reconnoitring patrols, hence the cutting was more difficult. This preliminary work could not be completed before dawn on April 17th, so the raid was postponed until the night of the 17th.

On the night in question, April 17th, the weather was perfect – bright moonlight followed later by sufficient clouds to conceal movement. A box protective barrage had been put down around the spot raided on the previous night, and then, at midnight, the raiding party went out. The Boche had apparently not noticed that the wire had been cut the previous night, and consequently the wire cutting party was able to set to work on completing what they had started, which was by no means easy and was a task calling for a considerable amount of nerve – lying on one's back in the enemy's wire not 30 yards from his Sentry Posts and cutting through his barbed wire.

To drown the sound of the wire cutting a heavy Machine Gun barrage was kept up on either flank. Also we sent out several patrols to throw bombs and attract the enemy's attention away from the point of attack. Then, at a given signal, the Artillery opened fire, and the Storming Party entered the Boche trench. Every man knew his job, whether he was a bomber, a Lewis Gunner, a ladder carrier, detailed to escort prisoners, or carry wounded back to our Line. The party was divided into two sections:

1. Under Lieutenant Mahon
2. Under 2nd Lieutenant Baxter.

Their object was to work to right and left along the Boche trench.

Telephone wires were immediately cut, and the first sentry was shot by Lieutenant Mahon. All the enemy seen were killed, three dug outs were heavily bombed, and a Grenade Store was blown up. From prisoners captured later, it was ascertained that no fewer than 56 Germans had been killed, and considerable damage had been done to their trenches and dug outs.

All the party returned safely except the officer leading the Left Party, Lieutenant Baxter. He showed great gallantry, resources, and coolness in leadership. He was the last man to leave the Boche trench, but was never seen again. He was awarded a posthumous Victoria Cross for this Action.[227]

It was a most successful raid and a good illustration of what can be done by good leadership, forethought, discipline, and courage with determination.

19.04.16 We came out of the Line at about 10.30pm, relieved by the 1/4th Loyal North Lancashires. It was a pouring wet night. We marched to Rivière to billets. After fixing up the men, and seeing that they got a good hot meal and a rum ration, I turned in to a nice bed, _very_ tired after 10 days of strenuous work and very little sleep.

20.04.16 Kemp rejoined the Battalion,[228] and took over duties as Bombing Officer again. He did not rejoin "Z" Company, but was attached to HQ Company – a new scheme – and lived with Battalion HQ. He brought word that Packman was probably coming back to us.

Bretencourt and Rivière were very prettily situated villages. It was difficult to say where one village ended and the other started. A small valley ran between the two villages and the River Crinchon really divided them.

Interesting events were happening in Ireland at this time – the Irish Rebellion began. The Germans attempted to land arms in Ireland. Sir Roger Casement[229] was arrested.

The weather improved considerably and everything was really looking quite spring-like.

21.04.16 Nothing particular happened. The Padre held a voluntary service.

22.04.16 I went down to HQ Mess for the evening. The "Card Sharpers" were playing cards. I ran Major Milnes' Gramophone. He had a large selection of records.

23.04.16 It was a glorious warm day. Kenders and I were all alone for lunch.

24.04.16 Several new officers joined the Battalion.

2nd Lieutenant Ronald	"Y" Company
2nd Lieutenant Petrie	"W" Company
2nd Lieutenant Coats	"X" Company
2nd Lieutenant Waugh	"Z" Company
2nd Lieutenant Murray	"Y" Company
2nd Lieutenant Frew	"W" Company
2nd Lieutenant Wolfe	"Y" Company
2nd Lieutenant Nicholson	"X" Company

In the afternoon I rode over to Monchiet with Uncle Joe to see our team play the 1/8th Liverpool Irish. The Skipper came over from Gouy, and met us at the match. It was a good game but the 2/5th Lancashire Fusiliers lost for the first time in France, 0-1.

---

[227] Lieutenant Edward Felix Baxter VC of the 8th Battalion King's Liverpool Regiment, the son of Charles and Beatrice Baxter of Hartlebury, Worcestershire, was aged 30 when he died, and is buried at Fillièvres British Cemetery, reference A.10.

[228] Norman Kemp has not been mentioned in the diary since an outing to Pierrots in Senlis on 30th November 1915. Later in the diary it becomes clear that he suffered an accident while attending a course on bombing, and a piece of bomb had lodged in his hand; it may be that this is what accounted for the absence from which he was returning; see the diary entry for 1st June 1916 on page 185.

[229] One of the leaders of the Easter Rising in Ireland.

Joe, the Skipper and I had tea with Captain Chamberlain and Ward at the billets of "D" Company, 1/8th Liverpool Irish, and a very cheery time we had. We went back to Bretencourt for dinner – we couldn't be away long as we were in Reserve.

26.04.16   We relieved "D" Company of the 1/4th Loyal North Lancashires in the Left Sector, Blairville, with new dispositions.

The Skipper was still away at the Divisional School, so I was carrying on as OC of "Z" Company. We had now four officers, including myself. As mentioned above, we had a new officer, 2nd Lieutenant Waugh, from the Royal Scots. He didn't seem any great shakes on first acquaintance. He looked like a bookie or jockey, and had a cheery habit of giving boxes of matches away, advertising his profession, "*Waugh – Volunteer Arms – some place near Edinburgh*". However, we decided that time would show.

27.04.16   We were having glorious weather.

News of interesting events reached us from Egypt and Mesopotamia. General Townshend was in a very tight corner at Kut-el-Amara. Also Martial Law was proclaimed in Ireland.

29.04.16   General Townshend was compelled to surrender to the Turks at Kut-el-Amara.[230]

30.04.16   Rather an amusing notice appeared outside the Boche Trenches at daybreak. It was printed in huge letters on a length of canvas – 20 yards long.
"*KUT-EL-AMARA IS OVER 13,000 PRISONERS*"
Captain Bloy's Company tried to pinch this the same night, but some care had to be taken as the Boche had a trick of putting out notices, flags etc. with bombs tied to them, arranged to detonate immediately the article was touched. Bloy's party did not succeed in getting the notice over to our Line.

However we did get our own back to some extent by taking a gramophone down Earhole Sap and playing "*Puppchen*", the march the Germans were supposed to have marched into Brussels to. We had two Lewis Guns trained on the Boche parapet. When the Boche heard the tune, they cheered, which was a signal for our Lewis Guns to sweep their parapet with bullets. It is extremely probable that several Boche cheered for their last time on that occasion.

Incidents like this helped to relieve the monotony of trench warfare.

01.05.16   A patrol of mine was sent out under Sergeant Street with Lance Corporal Brooks and two men. They went out at 8.30pm from the right of my Company Line, with instructions to reconnoitre one or two suspicious looking diggings that we had noticed in the Boche wire during the day. Their orders were to return at 11.00pm, but to come in by a way through the wire on the left of my Line, the reason being that it was a very clear night, and I thought the Boche might wait for our patrol returning on the right. I arranged to keep a look out at 11.00pm on the left, and to go out to meet Sergeant Street's party.

---

[230] Kut-el-Amara had been besieged by the Turks since 17th December 1915. According to the Battalion War Diary this notice appeared on 2nd May 1916, and the account given of the British response was: "*We retaliated with 'WER HUSSTE SEINE PERISCOPEN IN SÄCKEN VERHÖLLEN?'*" as the "*Enemy had recently wrapped his periscopes in sandbags owing to great number broken by our snipers.*"

It was a fairly quiet night, apart from a few rifle shots being fired. At 10.30pm I was in the Front Line listening for Sergeant Street's party. At 10.40pm I heard someone on our wire on the left, and immediately rushed down to the "Gap in the Wire", and got out of the trench. I saw no one, but I heard movement. I challenged, but got no reply. I then heard a sound of running but I did not fire as our patrol was due in, and I thought it must be Sergeant Street. I went back through the wire. A Very light[231] was fired by the Boche which fell in our wire on the right of my Company. It was immediately followed by a rifle shot. When I got into the trench, one of my men rushed down to tell me that the patrol was coming in on the right. A few seconds later Sergeant Street came in – he was very upset and told me that Lance Corporal Brooks was shot in the head, and stuck in the wire.

Lance Corporal Hampson, with his everlasting pluck, volunteered to help me to get Brooks in, then 2nd Lieutenant Moffatt came along, and we were soon joined also by Private Smith and A. Howarth, my Company stretcher bearers.

We went to the spot and found Lance Corporal Brooks – hit through the head and stuck in the wire. We had great difficulty in getting him through the wire. He was dead.[232] Then

the Boche threw up several Very lights and spotted us, immediately opening rifle fire. The bullets were <u>very</u> near – too near to be pleasant, and, as Brooks was certainly killed, I ordered the party to withdraw to our trench to avoid further casualties.[xviii]

Later in the night Moffatt with the stretcher bearers did get Brooks in, but it was no easy task, and anything but a pleasant one.

His body was taken down to the Aid Post and interred in the Cemetery at Bretencourt, near Private Schofield, who was killed on the last tour in this sector.[233]

Lance Corporal Brooks was a very good fellow, and a very promising NCO; he was only 21, and lived with his widowed mother at Booth Street, Tottington.

Losing my men was always a great sorrow to me.

This photograph of Le Fermont Military Cemetery taken in 2018 shows Private Brooks' gravestone in the foreground, with Private Schofield's immediately behind (to the left in the photograph).

02.05.16   Today I had completed one year's service in France.

---

[231] These were flares, fired from a breech-loaded single shot pistol, developed by an American Naval Officer called Edward Wilson Very.

[232] Lance Corporal Harry Brooks, Service no 2950, son of Jane Chadwick (formerly Brooks) of 193, Booth Street, Tottington, and the late William Brooks, is recorded in the Commonwealth War Graves Commission's records as having died on 29th April 1916; he is buried at Le Fermont Military Cemetery, Rivière, reference I.A.9. He is also mentioned as having performed two songs, *Farms* and *We 'ad 'em*, at a Battalion concert on 9th October 1915 at Aveluy (see the newspaper cutting relating to the diary entry for that date).

[233] See the diary entry for 14th April 1916.

04.05.16   A strange incident happened in the evening at about 9.00pm. Someone came to my dug out and reported that Private Porter was killed. I went at once to the Sentry Post he was on – and found Porter alive, and not even wounded, but he had had a very narrow escape. He was stunned and very frightened. While he was on sentry a bullet had hit him on the steel helmet,[234] but luckily had not penetrated the helmet, only dinted it. The blow had certainly unnerved Porter – he was only a boy of about 17 – but a nice lad with a chubby rosy face and always a smile. He had been very upset when Schofield and Brooks were killed, as they were all friends. I relieved Porter from duty and put him on light duty for two or three days.

05.05.16   On Friday May 5th we were relieved in the Line and proceeded to billets in Monchiet.
to   The men were rather fed up as leave to Bury and Radcliffe had been stopped on account
09.05.16   of an outbreak of smallpox.

    During this period we were busy training most mornings, when we didn't go out on working parties, chiefly digging the rear defence trenches known as the Corps Line. Our particular piece at the time was between Beaumetz-lès-Loges and Gouy, either on the Line immediately in front of – to the East of – the Arras to Doullens railway, or on the Gouy Switch from this line.

    We received a visit from the Skipper (still instructing at the Divisional School at Gouy) on May 7th, and the following day we went over at his invitation to a lecture at the Divisional School. We also went to a dinner there on the evening of May 9th – Waterhouse was President of the Mess at Gouy.

    The weather was glorious, and hot.

10.05.16   We had a good trip on a London Motor Omnibus to Givenchy-le-Noble to see a demonstration of destruction of barbed wire entanglements.

    We left Gouy-en-Artois at 9.00am. We went via Avesnes-le-Comte and Noyelles to Givenchy-le-Noble. It was a very fine morning and we had a cheery run. I was with Major Potter who was from Bolton and was 2nd in Command of the 1/5th Loyal North Lancashires. It was rather amusing on these trips, especially if you are riding on the top of the bus. As the Signal Companies do not always put their signal wires over roads quite high enough, there is a constant danger of getting one in the neck, unless you are ready to duck. We seemed to spend most of our journey ducking. Another thing – the trees overhang the roads very often, and, unless you are on the alert, it is quite common to get your faces nicely scratched with tree boughs.

    On arrival at Givenchy-le-Noble we found a very distinguished company present, including two Army Commanders, General Rawlinson and General Allenby, several Corps Commanders, such as General D'Oyly Snow[235] and Lord Cavan; also Divisional Generals were fairly common, for example Major General Jeudwine and Major General Strickland, and Brigadiers were mere nobodies. But my old friend Brigadier General Duncan spotted me. He was all dressed up with his red tabs etc. and, coming across, greeted me, "Good morning, Hall. You see I am allowed in these High Societies."

    As usual on these stunts, things were not quite ready when we arrived. However we soon

---

[234] See footnote 174 on page 133.
[235] See the footnote to the diary entry for 17th to 23rd February 1916

found out the reason – the REs were running the show!! The idea was to demonstrate a new method of destroying barbed wire entanglements, and at the same time to make a suitably covered approach to the enemy Line.[236] A barbed wire entanglement about 40 yards square was made, and 30 yards away from the edge of it was made a hole about 4 feet wide, 6 feet long, and 6 feet deep.

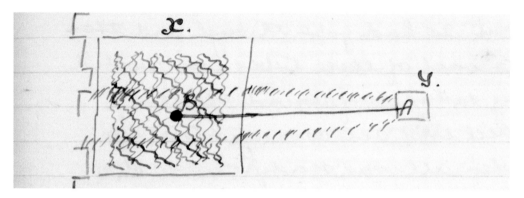

A solid bar with a cutting edge on one end was then driven horizontally in the ground about 5 feet below ground level and towards the wire. This knife was then driven inch by inch into the ground until it was completely in, when a second, but hollow, pipe was attached to the first bar, and this in turn was driven in by means of a ratchet pile-driver. Each of these tubes was about 6 feet long and, as one was driven in, so a third etc. was attached until about 20 feet had gone through, and then into each of these tubes was pushed long cartridges of amitol explosive, which were all connected together. When all was ready, to the last cartridge of amitol were connected two electric wire leads, which were run back about 200 yards, and connected to a switch. Everyone got clear of the barbed wire, and the pressing of the switch caused a tremendous explosion – a huge column of earth was thrown into the air about 100 feet. When this had subsided we went to examine the damage. The whole of the wire was broken – literally shattered into threads – scarcely a piece larger than a foot remaining; also a trench had been made from the hole A, through the wire, and up to the trench beyond, about 8 feet wide by 8 feet deep. It was marvellous, and all done in about two hours.

The idea was that such a scheme might be used by our raiding parties to create a surprise, destroy wire, and give a covered approach for the raiding party.

The idea was excellent, but its use was very limited and could only be applied in a loose sub-soil – in any place with chalk or flint it was useless.

However we all thoroughly enjoyed the show. I was lucky to get there as there were only very few officers below the rank of Brigadier present.

We returned to Avesnes and had lunch there, then back to Gouy where I had tea with the Skipper and arrived back at Monchiet at about 7.00pm.

---

[236] This was a method of creating an explosion underground from a distance, first devised in 1912 by Captain R.L. McClintock while attached to the Madras Sappers and Miners unit of the Indian Army at Bangalore in India. Hence the device was named a "Bangalore Torpedo", a name which Norman himself uses in reminiscing about this demonstration when writing about his return to Givenchy-le-Noble on 13th August 1917.

CHAPTER 16
Blairville and Bretencourt
14th May 1916 to 25th May 1916

14.05.16
to
18.05.16

We took *over the Front Line again on May 14th. I was now the Right Company of our Battalion, with "W" Company (Joe Hedley, Gray and Long Waterhouse) on our left. Cecil Moffatt and I were carrying on on our own in "Z" Company at this time, Kenders being on a course at the Divisional School at Gouy, and Waugh having crocked up when the first bullet came over. He had wonderful ideas of the intensity of shell fire! Soon after this he was sent away to the Divisional School.

Our Battalion Frontage was extended to the South, and we now included the Osier Bed on our Front. The "Osier Bed" was a collection of rush-like plants about 4 feet high. It was a rather large bed about 50 yards square, and was in No Man's Land. It was naturally a fine place for collecting patrols under cover prior to making a small raid on the enemy trench. The Boche had connected it up to their main Front Line by a trench, consequently they could approach it with safety at all times, by day and night. We had to crawl out to it in day time, which was rather a dangerous undertaking, but necessary, in order to prevent the Boche making a permanent work there – there were indications that he was attempting to do this.

Many were the minor patrol scraps with rifle and bomb that our people took part in at this place, well known to many troops who occupied that sector.

It was rather a long way across No Man's Land on this sector. In the centre it was about 500 yards, so there was plenty of room to have a stroll out on patrol at night, although it was decidedly wet in the long grass.

Rather an interesting report was circulated to Battalions:

The Germans have organised a special Company for raiding our trenches. Each man of this enemy Company is specially trained in his own duties, as bomber, rifle man, carrier, dug out bomber, etc. They are raiding our trenches every 10 days, and at intervals of miles along our Front. Between each raid this special Company go right away from the Line for special training, and have special rations. They are reported to be exceedingly good troops and very efficient. They are known as the "Travelling Circus".

Such was the gist of the document circulated to us.

We were specially ordered to take all necessary steps to organise our defence in the Line to combat enemy raids.

Consequently we made out Company schemes – "Action to be taken in the event of an Enemy Raid".

This scheme was actually practised daily in the trenches so that everyone knew exactly what he must be prepared to do on hearing the "Alarm Siren".

Bombing Parties were all detailed to bomb the enemy out, should he get into our trench.

Machine Guns were detailed to bring enfilading fire to bear on No Man's Land so as to prevent:

   (a) Reinforcements, Small Arms Ammunition, bombs etc. being sent to the Raiders; and
   (b) Them retiring.

The Artillery were to co-operate by dropping a barrage along the front of the enemy trench to bring about a similar result to the Machine Guns.

Brigade constantly tried to put the wind up us by sending wires that "Extra vigilance must be exercised tonight, it is expected that the Circus will visit this sector".

For my part, I believed that the only way to protect one's Line from surprise was by having the mastery of No Man's Land, so that the enemy could not possibly move there without our knowledge. To this end therefore we had patrols constantly out in No Man's Land from shortly after sunset to dawn. This meant hard work; even when it was quiet it was nerve racking, and by no means pleasant in all kinds of weather. But the men willingly carried out their duties, well knowing that it was for their own protection and that of their pals. The morale of the troops was excellent, and some really funny incidents occurred.

I decided to adopt a surprise scheme for animals of the Circus if they came to visit us; I pushed out 75% of my sentry groups into No Man's Land 200 yards in front of our main Line. Here my fellows lay out through the night ready for the old Hun if he came our way. One of the principles of war is the element of surprise. It was my intention to surprise the Travelling Circus in No Man's Land, inflict many casualties on it before it realised what had happened, and, if necessary, withdraw to our <u>Front</u> Line under the cover of fire provided by the men left behind to hold it. We did this for three nights and nothing happened.

Of course, all my men knew about the Travelling Circus.

One night, when going round my Posts in No Man's Land, I asked our sentry if he had anything to report. He replied, "Eh, a've bin fur sturring into black all neet but a 'anna sin nought o' any white elephants or lions yet, Sir."

We also built special protected Posts so that, if the raid was preceded by a sudden bombardment of our Line, at least one sentry group per platoon could remain on duty in comparative safety.

Our dug out accommodation in this part of the Line was by no means good, at least from the point of view of protection from shell fire; also, we had one or two big dug outs in which perhaps 20 men lived, so that consequently one shell might make the whole lot casualties.

To get over this danger, we made "Shell Shelter Slits" off our Communication Trenches to accommodate 6 to 10 men. These Shell Shelter Slits were just deep narrow circular trenches dug in semi-circles off the Communication Trenches. We had several of these off each Communication Trench, thereby splitting up the Company into small groups during bombardment.

Immediately heavy shelling started Section Commanders took their own men to their allotted positions. On the barrage lifting or ceasing, they immediately left their Shelters and took up their allotted Posts in the Front Line ready to meet an enemy infantry attack. These positions were also practised daily:

(a) Take cover as for Enemy Bombardment

(b) Stand to Alarm Posts

These Shell Shelter Slits were also made to act as Assembly Trenches in the event of a big attack being made by us.

I have drawn a sketch showing Shell Shelter Slits on the next page.

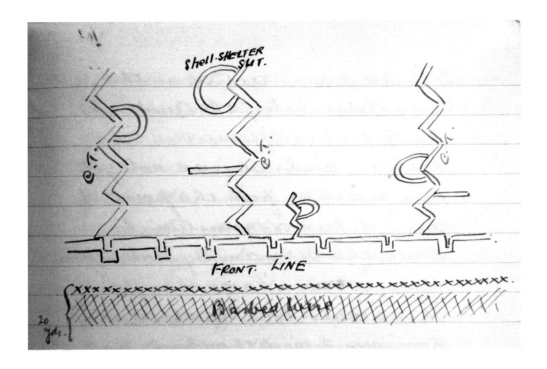

Spring Offensive 1916 was on everyone's lips, but no one knew where it was to be made. But made it had to be, for things were, to say the least of it, not going too well with the Allies. The Boche were still pressing the French very hard at Verdun. They were also active on the Vimy Ridge Sector, and the Austrians had started their offensive in the Trentino, but we were not yet in a position from the point of view of men or munitions to draw the Germans by making an offensive on a large enough scale.

19.05.16   "Z" Company were relieved by "D" Company of the 1/4th Loyal North Lancashires at 9.15pm. We marched via Blamont Trench Windmill on Blairville Road to Blamont village, and thence to Bretencourt. The Battalion HQ and "W" and "Y" Companies went to Rivière, which was just across the valley of the River Crinchon. "Z" Company were ordered to occupy the Village Line. This system of trenches formed the defensive line of the village of Bretencourt. It consisted of three main Strong Points on the South East side of the village. These Strong Points were connected with each other by Communication Trenches, which were made through the houses and across the village streets.
Many of the houses on the Boche side were specially strengthened by reinforced concrete and sand bags, and were converted into Machine Gun Posts. The Village Line was a strong position, with an excellent field of fire overlooking Blamont village. I established my Company HQ in the village, and about 50 yards to the rear of the main centre Strong Post. After seeing that my Platoon Commanders understood their positions and orders in the event of an attack, I turned in at about 2.00am.

21.05.16   It was a glorious morning – everywhere looked splendid. It was just getting light when I turned out at 4.45am, having enjoyed nearly three hours' sleep in my clothes, being too tired to get undressed.

I went round the platoons. Everyone seemed in good spirits, but very tired. But the birds singing and the sun shining very soon bucked everyone up. I was busy all morning making work schemes for improving the Village Defences, by digging, making Lewis Gun Posts, and wiring.

In the afternoon I took things gently, sleeping in the orchard of my billet.

It was a pretty little village. Practically every house had had a garden and a small orchard in Peace times, but the houses in many cases were razed to the ground by shell fire. The outstanding feature was the green – the whole village seemed hidden in trees, blossoms, and, in spite of the War and man's attempt to destroy everything, the fruit trees were in full blossom, the flowers in the gardens were in bloom, and seemed if possible more beautiful than usual. We had no difficulty in providing our larder with food. We got fresh gooseberries and rhubarb – as much as we wanted.

We were luckily spared from any great troubles from the Hun. Each day he gave us a few shells, just to let us know that he had our welfare on his mind. But it was a fairly peaceful life for a few days, although we were fully occupied with working parties, either on the Reserve Line or Village Defence. At night we provided parties for the REs – as usual carrying up wire, posts, sand bags, timber, steel girders etc. to the Front Line.

One or two nights we had to send special parties up to a section of the Front Line to repair some part which had been blown in by Trench Mortar or shell fire during the day. So our days and nights were spent. We had no definite hours, no definite time for finishing work, and some days we worked almost day and night – but <u>we</u> had no strikes!!

In spite of shells, minnes, rain, mud

24.05.16   I went with Kenders to have dinner with the Skipper at the Divisional School at Gouy. It was a pouring wet afternoon when we started.

We went up the Communication Trench from Rivière to Beaumetz, then by road to Gouy – about 6 miles.

We went to the Divisional Canteen at Gouy to buy some mess stores, and we also had a haircut and shampoo, then had a very cheery evening with Waterhouse, and got back at about 11.30pm.

"The Spirit of our Troops is Excellent."

CHAPTER 17
Blairville, Simencourt and Dainville
26th May 1916 to 28th June 1916

26.05.16
to
30.05.16
We moved up to the Front Line on May 26th, and took over from "D" Company of the 1/4th Loyal North Lancashires on the sector which included Liverpool and Derby Saps. I had the 1/8th Liverpool Irish on my right, with Joe Chamberlain, Ward and Johnny Gordon, all splendid fellows.

We continued the work on the dug outs started by ourselves in March.[237]

"Y" Company were on the left of the Battalion Line, and held a portion of Line which ran quite close to the Boche Line, being about 100 yards from it, near the edge of Blairville Wood, at the North West Corner, overlooked by the Elephant, or Ficheux Mill. They made several bold attempts to pinch some Boche from one of his saps there, without success. They were constantly worrying the Hun with patrols, Trench Mortars etc. They were in a more suitable position than the other companies, being much nearer to the Boche.

Blairville Village

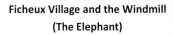

Ficheux Village and the Windmill
(The Elephant)

---

[237] In the original diary it says that the work here had been commenced in May, but the first entry describing being positioned in the sector with Liverpool and Derby Saps in it, and beginning work on improving the dug outs in that area, is that for 28th March 1916.

On Saturday May 27th I received word from the Division that I had been promoted Temporary Captain. I felt that this was some reward for my work of the past five months, during which time I had been commanding "Z" Company, as Captain Waterhouse had been away at the IIIrd Army School at Flixecourt twice, and then as Instructor at the 55th Divisional School at Gouy.

[The original note regarding the temporary promotion is pictured on the right and reads:

~~Lieut.~~ Captain Hall.

Application for your temporary promotion to rank of Captain has been approved. Divisional Commander approves of your assuming badges of this rank in anticipation of London Gazette. C.D.S Circular Memo 384 (Instructions for Promotion of Officers) is forwarded for your information with reference to Sect. iii para.5. G.C.Hutchinson Captain Adj[utan]t. 2/5 Lan[cashire] Fus[iliers] 26.5.16]

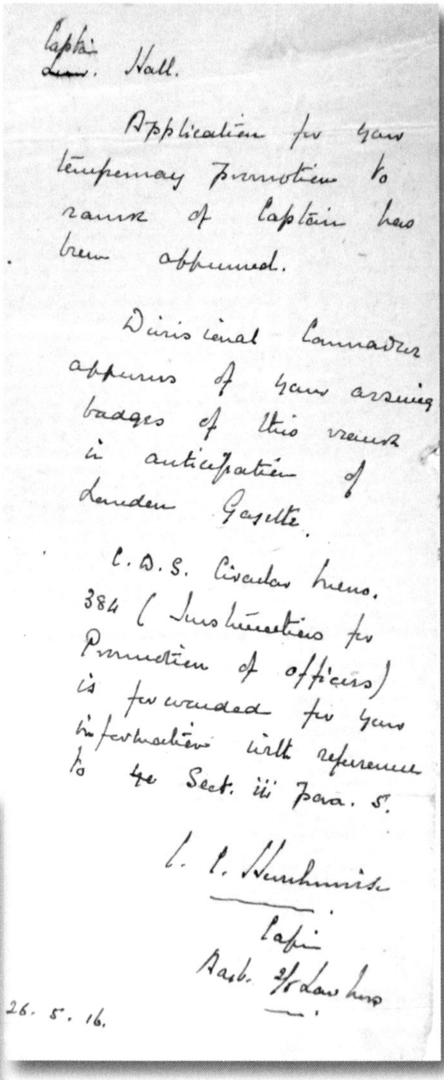

I also got a note from the Skipper in reference to my promotion.

[The text of the note from Captain Waterhouse (pictured above) reads:

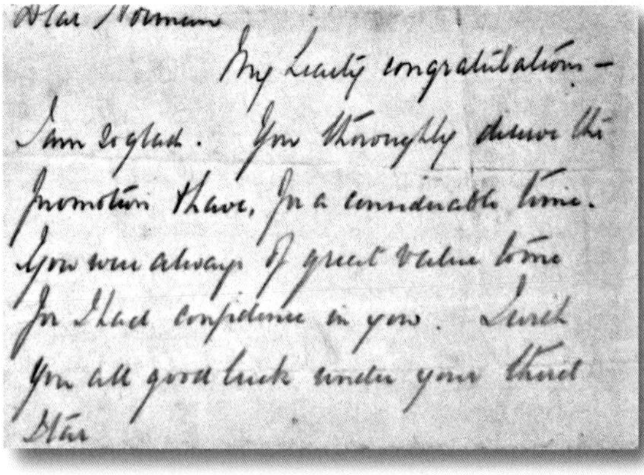

Dear Norman,

My hearty congratulations – I am so glad. You thoroughly deserve the promotion, and have for a considerable time. You were always of great value to me for I had confidence in you. I wish you all good luck under your third star.]

Special mention should be made here of the hard work done by all ranks, and specially for the organisation of covering parties and wiring parties by 2nd Lieutenant Cecil Moffatt and Kenderdine. Mention might also be made here of the good work done by the other companies: "W" Company (Gray and Long Waterhouse), "X" Company (S.L. Moffatt, and Fryer, Sniper Officer), and "Y" Company (Captain Bloy, Evans, Ainscow, Young, Sergeant Major Burns, and Sergeant Cadden).

01.06.16
to
15.06.16

There was nothing of special interest to report in our trenches during this period, just occasional shelling and Machine Gun fire. "W" and "X" Company were troubled a bit with Trench Mortars. Luckily my Line was not troubled with these war luxuries – possibly we were out of range. We were just carrying on digging, wiring, patrolling, watching and waiting. A very tedious nerve straining duty, because one never knew from one minute to the next what might happen; one minute perfect quiet, and the War seemed miles away, the next Hell let loose.

During the evening of June 1st "John Minden", our regimental pet, called to see me at about 10.00pm. Hearing a dog bark outside my dug out, I went out and found him. He was all alone, having come up from Battalion HQ; he made himself quite happy on my bed in the Company HQ, and slept there all night. I sent him down next morning to Battalion HQ under escort, and charged him on AF. B 252 – "Leaving his Post without permission".

Lieutenant J.B. Packman rejoined the Battalion at about the beginning of June, having left us a few days after we landed in France in May 1915. He was posted to "Z" Company.

Meanwhile, 2nd Lieutenant Norman Kemp[238] had to leave us again, and proceed to Hospital. Some time before this, while on a Bombing Course, he had a bombing accident and got a small piece of bomb in his hand. The wound had opened out again and blood poisoning set in it. He was sent to England. He was a great loss to the Battalion for he was a very sound, brave, energetic officer.

One of our troubles was the shortage of officers. After Kemp left, there was only Kenderdine, C.H. Moffatt, Packman and myself in "Z" Company. I then lost Moffatt temporarily, as he went on a Bayonet Fighting Course, which left only Kenders and Packman. Kenderdine was an excellent fellow. Luckily, the same day as Cecil Moffatt left, 2nd Lieutenant G.G.A. Kerr, 3/9th Middlesex, joined the Battalion, and was posted to "Z" Company. Kerr had been in Malaya before the War, rubber planting. He seemed to be quite a nice fellow, very keen, and a hard worker. He turned out to be A.1. when he found his feet. On June 15th E.A. Elson, also 3/9th Middlesex, who was another rather useful fellow, also joined "Z" Company.

2nd Lieutenant E.Y. Saxby, 3/9th Middlesex, and 2nd Lieutenant W.H. Weller, 4/4th Queen's Royal West Surreys, also joined the Battalion and were posted to "W" Company at about this time.

Major Milnes and the Skipper went on leave early in June, returning on June 12th. I was living in hopes that my turn was not far distant. What a hope!

On his return the Skipper sent us some very nice asparagus to the Line – some luxury in the trenches!

Meanwhile, to our great surprise and disappointment, Major Milnes was ordered to proceed to the Divisional School at Gouy as an Instructor.

Officers, NCOs, and men alike were all sorry to lose the Major. He was one of those people who do such a lot in a quiet unassuming way, yet are always busy. The 2/5th Lancashire Fusiliers owed a very great deal to Major Milnes. His very presence, whether on parade or in the Mess, seemed to alter the whole atmosphere. However we hoped that our loss

---

[238] See the footnote to the diary entry for 20th April 1916.

would be his gain, and that we should soon have him back.

The Army is a strange organisation. One can never solve their puzzles and method. "Man as well as God moves in a mysterious way, his wonders to perform."[239]

Major C.J.B. Bridgewater had joined the Battalion in May as 2nd in Command. He came from the 6th Inniskilling Dragoons, a typical Cavalry Officer. He was a fine big man, and exceedingly genial. He seemed quite new to Infantry methods when he joined us, but he was a capable officer and very quickly fell into our ways.

Lieutenant R. Grace, Army Service Corps, had also joined the Battalion in May, and was appointed Transport Officer. Grace was a very nice fellow, frightfully keen on his job and efficient. He also was strange to Regimental Duties, but he luckily took over a Transport Section which had become very efficient as a result of their experience in France.

At about this time the Brigade Horse Show was held at Simencourt, where our Transport Lines were. The Batttalion did quite well, and slightly better than other Battalions in the Brigade, taking first prize for "Travelling Kitchen", and two second prizes – "Pack Mule" and "Pack Horse".

It was also about this time that all Corps, Divisional and Brigade, went mad on "Spit and Polish" in Transport. Consequently the Quartermaster suddenly became busy ordering paint – General Service Grey – and metal polish, saddle soap etc. for cleaning General Service Limbers[240] and saddlery. Oil was in great demand for polishing up limbers, and there is no doubt that this mania for cleaning did a great deal in raising and maintaining the morale and Esprit de Corps of the Battalions. Perhaps on first thought it seemed foolish to make such a fuss on Active Service – it wasn't fighting. But while on service it is necessary to keep up an individual's pride. Also cleanliness in everything, both personal and material, keeps men fit. Everyone has experienced the feeling of a good hot bath or wash after a hard day's work. The prevention of sickness, and the prevention of despondency, was the object in view.

On June 1st there were constant rumours all day of a great Sea Battle in the North Sea. Such expressions as "German Grand Fleet completely annihilated" came through.

As we were in the Front Line, news had to travel some distance before we heard it. Consequently there was every probability that the story grew in wonder by the time we heard it. Anyway this battle was a fact. It was the Great Battle of Jutland.

On June 5th we heard of the sinking of the HMS *Hampshire*, with Lord Kitchener on board, proceeding to Russia – a Tremendous Shock, and loss to the Country, especially at such critical times – just at a time when the great Volunteer Army which Kitchener had done so much to raise was going to assert itself, and he would have seen some results of his efforts.[241]

Such a thing made one imagine and realise that anything is possible in war. The great question was, "Who is able to take up the work of Lord Kitchener? Is there anyone capable enough?" When a man is dead you <u>have</u> to do without him. Someone must rise to the occasion, take up the reins, and drive the Coach. So it was in this case.

The Battalion was very keen to make a raid on the Boche. The spirit of revenge seemed to

---

[239] *"God moves in a mysterious way, his wonders to perform"* is a line from a hymn written by William Cowper in 1773.
[240] See footnote 39 on page 37.
[241] See footnote 90 on page 69.

have risen in everyone, and we really wanted to get at the Hun. Things were not looking any too rosy on the Western Front. A Great Allied Conference was held in London on June 9th, and it was evident that something big would have to be done by the British to relieve the pressure on the French at Verdun. We were now in a better position to make a big push than hitherto. We had many new well trained Kitchener Army Divisions out now, and, though they were inexperienced, yet they were excellent troops, as they proved themselves when put to the test.

We were getting many more guns out now of all calibres. Our troops had been delayed, there is no doubt, because Britain had had many calls upon her resources. She had a big Army in England to equip, and, in addition, she had tremendous calls on her equipment, guns, Army etc. and munitions from other Countries – France, Belgium, Russia, Italy. What England had done since August 1914 was simply marvellous.

The Russians at this time were moving, and were meeting with success, taking many prisoners and German material and stores. The Italians were preparing for a big offensive against the Austrians. But the French were having a hard time in Verdun, and our Mesopotamia Expedition was not going too well. For some months past great preparations had been being made on our British Front on the Somme and Ancre. We saw little of it, because we were North of the Zone, but the concentration of troops, munitions, erection of railways, roads etc. was well on its way from Monchy to Bray.

GHQ were literally crying out for information about the Boche, wanting to know which units were holding the various sectors; hence it was essential to raid his trenches to capture prisoners for identification purposes.

For this reason, on our Front at Blairville, Captain Bloy, Captain Hutchinson, Lieutenant Young, and Ainscow organised a Special Raiding Party, who were all volunteers, consisting of 56 NCOs and men. This party left the trenches and proceeded to Rivière for special training in raids. The method, time and location was kept very secret. Every detail received the minutest attention, and each individual knew precisely what his job would be.

Aeroplane photographs were taken of the sector of the German Line selected for this minor operation, which was to be on the North West Corner of Blairville Wood. Trenches were dug on the ground at Rivière, which was an exact copy to scale as the German trenches to be raided, a plan having been made from the aeroplane photographs.

Previous reconnaissances of this Line had provided valuable information as to the location of enemy Sentry Posts, Machine Gun Posts etc.

The original intention was that this raid should be just a single raid by our Battalion alone, that it should be a silent raid without any Artillery Co-operation, unless required to cover our withdrawal. Bloy and Hutchinson were especially keen on the Surprise Scheme, the idea being to go out the previous night, and cut lines through the enemy wire, then to concentrate on the enemy wire, and to rush his trench, to bomb, shoot, kill, take prisoners, and return in about 10 minutes. However, when all plans were made, and the party thoroughly conversant with their job, the Division decided it could not take place as arranged. Bigger events were anticipated South of us on the Somme and Ancre Front at an early date. Corps HQ ordered our Division to make several raids simultaneously on a date to be fixed.

Our Division's Scheme was to be a "bluff" in conjunction with the big offensive, the object being to make the Boche believe that this was a minor operation to be followed by a big attack on this sector, thus either

(a) drawing troops from the German lines South to reinforce our immediate enemy; or

(b) preventing the Boche from sending his Reserves from opposite to us further South.

We also wished to try and find out what his strength in men, Machine Guns, and Artillery was on our Front, and, by annoying him, we hoped that he would reveal this in his retaliation. It was also decided that <u>gas</u> should be used, and also smoke screens.

Consequently while our "Specialist Suicide Club" was rehearsing in Rivière, we were making the necessary preparations in the Line.

15.06.16
and
16.06.16
In preparation for the operations already referred to, on June 15th I had a visit from an officer of the Special Brigade RE (Chemical Corps), and two NCOs. I had previously received an order marked "VERY SECRET" from Battalion HQ, to the effect that Gas cylinders would be placed in my trench in the next few days. The trench would be prepared to receive them, this work to be carried out by the Battalion Reserve, the 1/4th King's Own Royal Lancasters Reserve troops, under the direction of Special Brigade RE Officers. This work consisted in digging away my fire steps to a depth of 3 feet 6 inches, and placing wooden framed fire steps over these pits. It was a big job, but practically the whole of my trench was reconstructed during the next few days. The working parties worked continuously in shifts, day and night. By June 17th all was completed. I then received orders that the Gas cylinders – which were to be spoken of as "water jars" – would be carried up by the Reserve Battalions on the nights of June 17th and 18th. Everything was to be done in secret and in silence. Only sufficient men were to be kept in the trench to furnish one Post per platoon. The Company Commander was to be on duty day and night from the time of receipt of the order until further instructions were issued. One officer could be used in addition to relieve the OC of the Company while he wrote reports, dealt with messages, and during meal times. All our Gas helmets were specially sprayed and inspected twice daily; these precautions were taken in case the Boche got to know of the Scheme and put down a heavy barrage on our Line and burst the Gas cylinders, thus liberating concentrated Chlorine and Phosgene – for that was what the "water jars" contained.[242]

On June 16th it rained all day. We had the constant stress of working parties in my Line, digging, sawing, hammering etc. My trench became a perfect shambles from having been a clean well-kept Line.

17.06.16
At about 8.00pm the procession arrived, long lines of dull dim figures, slowly moving under their heavy loads, and through the slimy mud and lime which stuck to the boots like dough to a baker's hands, thus making it still more difficult. They came up in parties of 50, carrying 25 Gas cylinders. Two men carried each cylinder, which was slung on a pole rested on the shoulders. They had carried these cylinders about 2½ miles up long Communication Trenches full of mud and water, and the men themselves were wet to the skin. No wonder they cursed the War. So the procession went on all night long, the same men making perhaps

---

[242] In *The History of the Lancashire Fusiliers 1914-1918* by Major General J.C. Latter it is said that the gas was euphemistically called "*the accessory*", and that term is used in a report appended to the Battalion War Diary. The term "*water jars*" is not mentioned.

three or four journeys during the night. The cylinders were put into the pits below the fire steps in batteries of 10, 15, or 20. When a battery was complete, the cylinders were covered with sand bags to protect them, leaving only the valves ready for use. My sector and Uncle Joe Hedley's sector seemed to be the chief trenches selected for gas discharge.[243]

The Boche let us carry on in comparative peace except for a few shells, some aerial torpedoes and some Tock Emmas.[244] Fortunately "Y" Company secured his pet annoyance this evening – they were about 700 yards to my left. The night passed without accident – no casualties. But it was an anxious and trying time, living in a trench with hundreds of cylinders of liquid Chlorine.

18.06.16   Daylight broke with a glorious summer feeling in the air, and a hot sun. The birds away back in Martinet Wood[245] – where Gray and Long Waterhouse had often gone with me to search for birds' eggs – were almost bursting their throats with joy.

The Red Poppies – thousands of them shaking the dew from their petals in the early morning – all looked so beautiful against the green. Though weary – dog tired – this glorious morning made me thank God to be alive.

2nd Lieutenant Waugh – who had rejoined from the Divisional School – had got a very bad vertical breeze up the previous night. I found him in my dug out sitting gazing blankly at a candle – and shivering like a leaf. He said he was ill – perhaps he was – but I wasn't in a very sympathetic mood. I decided to send him down to see the MO. Private Wilde,[246] Moffatt's servant, went with him. What happened to him from that moment I don't know!! But he never returned to the Battalion.[246] However a good exchange – Cecil Moffatt came back from his course. He was a tower of strength to me, a real spark of life and cheer to all of us, absolutely loved by the men, always so cheerful and willing, never grumbling, no matter what unpleasant job he was detailed to do. He had a very funny way of saying, "Jolly little war this, ain't it?"

2nd Lieutenant H.H. Andrews, 3/9th Middlesex, joined the Battalion, and was appointed Signalling Officer. On the top of all my odd jobs and lack of sleep – having now been in the Front Line for 21 days – I was asked to try to instruct Andrews in the routine of Signalling Officer's duties, having done the job myself. I did my best, but couldn't give as much time to Andrews as I should have liked.

Practically all day we were worried by shelling – Tock Emmas.[244] Luckily the Hun concentrated on our Communication Trenches more than the Front Line trenches. Probably he had spotted our new digging of Assembly Trenches and Shell Shelter Slits – which were very difficult to camouflage on account of the white chalk. "Z" Company had no casualties, but "W"

---

[243] The Divisional War Diary records that 1898 gas cylinders were placed across eight bays.

[244] Army slang for Trench Mortars – see footnote 132 on page 100.

[245] This wood has been mentioned only in the diary entry for 22nd March 1916, with no mention of birds' eggs.

[246] Norman also spells the surname "Wild".

[247] There is a slight lack of clarity in the diary with regard to the sequence of events in relation to Waugh. He is described as *"having crocked up when the first bullet came over"* in the diary entry for 14th to 19th May 1916, but it is then mentioned that he went to the Divisional School at Gouy, so the inference must be that he was subsequently deemed fit enough to attend that course. This description of Waugh having to be sent down from the Line on 18th June 1916 is both vivid and specifically dated, so presumably is accurate, and the inference must be that Waugh either *"crocked up"* twice, or at least that he was so badly affected by his nerves as to be virtually no use from almost as soon as he arrived, despite managing to attend the course.

Company (Uncle Joe's Company) had a few wounded. During the day Moffatt and I rigged up several Fixed Rifles set on Boche Communication Trenches and exposed points in his Line. We wanted to worry him during the next night by keeping a constant fire, one shot every half minute through the night. Joe Hedley worked in conjunction with us.

The day passed once again, then the dark came with its long procession of men with more and more "water jars". They came all night. I was getting fed up with the damned things. By 1.00am the carrying of "water jars" was completed.

Moffatt and Kerr went out on patrol, and returned to report that a large Boche working party were out wiring in front of his trench. As Moffatt said, "It's really a glorious target, the chance of a life time." This was at about 11.30pm. What could I do? My trench was full of men and Gas cylinders, and I had instructions not to annoy the Boche until the "water jars" were all in position, for fear of drawing retaliation.

At 1.00am Moffatt went into No Man's Land again and reported that the Boche was still working.

We found the position of this wiring party on my map, and decided to put some of England's best munitions on the market, or, as one fellow put it, "Deliver the goods as ordered". I went to my telephone, and called Battery C 275 18 pounder. I couldn't get an answer, and every minute was precious as we were keeping the Hun waiting. After 30 minutes I at last got a reply, and played hell with the Gunner Officer on duty. Then I reported:

"Enemy wiring party working on wire at x 34 d 5.2 to x 34 d 5.7. Open fire immediately. There are about 150 men working. You can't miss them."

"Right ho! I'll give them four rounds of Battery fire." That meant four guns firing simultaneously four times, 16 rounds in all, 18 pounder shrapnel shells. In addition we fired our Lewis Guns (two), and one Machine Gun.

The guns fired! The shells burst right in the Brown!

What actual casualties the Boche had we never knew. But it was a good Show for us!

After this I was still on duty, but just about done to the world. Scarcely knowing where I was, and almost walking in my sleep, I stopped, leant against a post, and – I confess – the next thing I knew was Sergeant Dixon coming to me saying, "Excuse me, Sir, N° 14 Platoon all correct taking over from Corporal Hewitt." I felt absolutely ashamed of myself. Asleep on duty! On Active Service, in the Front Line – probably only about two minutes. But asleep! Perhaps I may excuse myself to some extent, as it was 22 days since I had had my clothes off properly, and 48 hours since I had had any sleep.

We didn't mind work, long hours, discomfort – provided we kept the Hun where he was until a favourable time came to have a good biff at him and drive him back to Germany. The chance of a Blow at him wasn't far off, but we didn't know the exact date of the offensive or Big Push.

19.06.16   At 3.00am, I received Operation Orders for relief at 8.30am the same day, and at the same time received orders that the "Special Vigilance Period" for "water jars" was over. I don't think I ever felt so pleased to see Walmersley and Henderson – the two Battalion runners who brought these messages.

Having issued orders for relief to my Platoon Commanders, Company Sergeant Major and Company Quartermaster Sergeant – Howard and Davenport respectively – I made a final tour of the Line prior to turning in to try to have a few hours' rest before moving out of the Line.

A very amusing incident occurred during my round of Posts. I came to one Sentry Post. One of the fellows, Relief N° 1, said, "When's that there Travellin' Circus coming a visiting us, Sir?"

I couldn't really say.

"Well, I don't care so much if it do come. How far did yer say it wer to Garmin trenches?"

"500 yards."

"And how far fer 'ere to t'village?"

"800 yards."

"Well, tha con tek it fur me – ther b'aint be no Boche livin' as can gi' me 500 yards start in 800 yards."

So I turned in to my dug out, had some food and a drink, lay down on my wire bed, pulled my burberry[248] over me and, well, I remember nothing until Ashton came to waken me at 6.00am. It was broad daylight – I had been asleep about three hours.

From that moment we were busy getting ready to move out, with parties carrying stores down to the dump where the General Service Limbers[249] would collect our loads for transport to our billeting area.

An officer of the "X" Liverpools had come up in advance to take over dispositions and trench stores etc. and at 8.30am we were relieved. It was a glorious morning – hot sun.

All my men were quite ready to go out of the Line. They were tired out and needed a proper sleep very badly – just as we officers did.

We marched out via Blamont Trench, Blamont Mill, Blamont village, Bretencourt, Rivière, and up the Communication Trench to Beaumetz, as the road was under observation by day, and we were not over keen on drawing shell fire unnecessarily. From Beaumetz we moved by platoons at 250 yards' distance to about a mile outside Simencourt, our billeting area and destination. I believe that Major J. Barnsdale was Town Major of Simencourt at this time for some reason or other.

The Band met us outside the village. The Band had been reformed – this was the first time we had had the drums since Southport in 1915.

To hear drums and bugles again bucked me up, and, although weary, we marched into the village in good form.

Lieutenant B. Best-Dunkley had now joined the Battalion, and was appointed Adjutant, in succession to Captain G.C. Hutchinson.[250]

The Battalion Transport had taken part in another Horse Show, this time the Divisional

---

[248] See footnote 94 on page 72.

[249] See footnote 39 on page 37.

[250] Norman has not actually mentioned previously that Captain G.C. Hutchinson had been appointed Adjutant; the diary entry for 14th to 19th August 1915 is to the effect that Captain L.H. Bloy took over duties as Adjutant when Captain Jeffreys left the Battalion, and performed the duties well, and Captain L.H. Bloy is referred to as Adjutant in the newspaper report quoted in the diary entry for 28th June 1916, and in the newspaper report quoted in the *Obituaries* section with reference to Captain Bloy. The Battalion War Diary's entry for 8th September 1915 records: "*Captain G.C. Hutchinson to take over duties as Adjutant, Captain L.H. Bloy to command "Y" Company vice Captain G.C. Hutchinson*", which explains why Lieutenant Best-Dunkley was taking over the role from Hutchinson rather than Bloy. In any event, the diary entry for 4th to 12th February 1916, which records that "*Colonel Shirley and Hutty wanted the Brigadier's blood*" for failing to ensure that the troops were fed between 7.00am and 3.00pm while on the march, would be more consistent with Captain Hutchinson being a Staff Officer rather than one of four Company Commanders, while the fact that the diary entry for 30th April 1916 refers to "*Captain Bloy's Company*" as trying to steal the insulting notice about the Kut-el-Amara defeat from the Germans would be difficult to square with Captain Bloy also being Adjutant.

Competition, and had done very well, coming out second in the 55th Division, winning:

1st Prize in "Pack Pony"

3rd Prize in "Field Cooker"

4th Prize "Pack Mule"

1st Prize "Officer's Charger" (Major Milnes)

1st Prize "Jumping" (Lieutenant Grace, Transport Officer)

On arrival at Simencourt we had good billets.

Two more officers joined the 2/5th Lancashire Fusiliers:

2nd Lieutenant H.K. Forrester 4/4th, Queen's Royal West Surreys, posted to "Z" Company.

2nd Lieutenant R. Walker, Artists' Rifles, attached temporarily to run an NCOs' Class of Instruction, posted to "Y" Company.

20.06.16   We spent all day cleaning up, with Bathing Parades etc. We thoroughly enjoyed our first night's rest and real sleep in bed after three weeks in the trenches. The men were very tired, but, as usual, Company Quartermaster Sergeant Davenport had got a move on with indents to the Quartermaster, Lieutenant Bowd, to replace deficiencies.

21.06.16   Lieutenant Colonel Shirley was evacuated to Hospital and eventually to England – sick. This was the last we saw of him with the Battalion, worse luck. He had done a great deal for the Battalion since May 1915. He had worked very hard, too hard, and in consequence had rather racked himself up.[251]

Major C.H.J. Bridgewater took over command of the Battalion.

I rode over to Dainville with Uncle Joe to reconnoitre the area. Dainville was a village about 3 miles from Simencourt, and about 2 miles from that famous old city of Arras. We had tea at a little estaminet near the station at Dainville, and in the evening went over to see Waterhouse.

---

[251] Lieutenant Colonel H.J. Shirley had been a medical doctor before the War, and went on to transfer to the RAMC in 1917, becoming CO of a Military Hospital in Malta, then MO to a Transport Division of the Royal Army Service Corps. After the War he returned to his practice as an anaesthetist in London. He had been born in India in 1868 to a father who was a barrister in Madras, and thus he was able to communicate in Hindustani with some Indian troops who challenged him and Norman on 2nd September 1915. His birth name was Herbert Johan Scharlieb, but he changed it by deed poll in 1914. At that time his mother, Dr Mary Scharlieb, was a well-known gynaecologist practising at the Royal Free Hospital in London. He is more than once mentioned as being particularly concerned and anxious to help if his men were injured, presumably because of his medical background (for example when Lieutenant Hill was shot on 13th July 1915, and when Captain Simon was killed on 17th August 1915). He had two horses with him at the front (see the diary entries for 14th and 31st August 1915, when Norman was able to borrow one of them), and he brought an Airedale terrier (John Minden) out with him on his return from home leave in August 1915. He was a photographer, taking a photograph of *"the Column"* on 8th July 1915, and photographs of *"each Company officer and also one of the Battalion HQ officers"* in September 1915, and performed at concerts (see the diary entries for 9th October 1915 and 24th January 1916). He visited Norman in hospital in London in the autumn of 1916, and Norman also visited him in London when well enough to get out and about. He also mentions having tea with him, presumably at his house, on the afternoon of 19th July 1919, after the Victory March. In the diary entry for 11th July 1915 Norman writes: *"The Colonel suddenly took it into his head always to address me as 'This Boy'. We got on quite well together ..."*, and it was he who recommended Norman for promotion to Captain (see the diary entry for 19th September 1915). There is a photograph of Lieutenant Colonel Shirley on page 58 sitting on a chair smoking a pipe in a trench, and also a photograph of him with Lieutenant R.N. Thompson, Major H.N. Milnes, and Captain G.C. Hutchinson on page 112.

22.06.16   The Battalion marched to Dainville near Arras (still in the VIth Corps area), where we were billeted. Dainville was quite an ordinary kind of French village, rather straggling, but we had quite good billets. "Z" Company were billeted on the Eastern edge of the village, about 15 minutes' walk from Battalion HQ, on the main Arras to Doullens road – Route Nationale N° 25. "Z" Company's HQ was in an estaminet at a cross roads in the village. My Company Sergeant Major Howard and Company Quartermaster Sergeant Davenport lived in the next house. All the platoons were fairly near, with "Y" Company HQ just across the road from our place.

23.06.16   We were training and finding working parties on Artillery Gun Pits.
In the afternoon I rode into Arras and had a good look round. It was not too healthy, with occasional heavy shells landing on the main streets. Practically everyone was living in cellars and the place was very badly damaged. The city only a mere ghost of its former self, for Arras was a beautiful city in pre-war days, and an important Railway Centre. The majority of the large buildings were destroyed, the Hotel de Ville and Railway Station being very badly damaged by shell fire.

Arras Hotel de Ville photographed in 2018

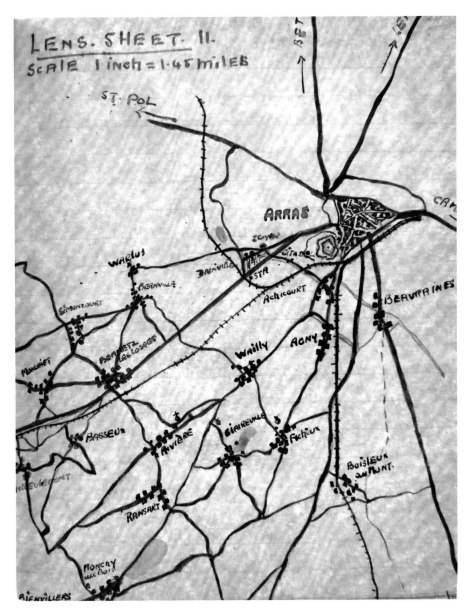

24.06.16   I was busy all day on an FGCM. The President was Major Bridgewater, while the Members were the VIth Corps FGCM Officer, Captain Merriman (later Lord Justice Merriman), Captain Widdows MC of the 1/4th Loyal North Lancashires, Captain J. Chamberlain of the 1/8th Liverpool Irish, and myself. This court sat for two and a half days. We had seven big cases to deal with, all Desertion Cases – rather an unpleasant job. Still, one amusing incident occurred: the Court was sworn in as usual, then, when the accused were asked whether they had any objection to be tried by this Court, not one of them raised any objection to the President or Members, save for four soldiers who were Americans enlisted in the Liverpool Irish; they did a beautiful "about turn", turned their backs on the Court, and in one voice, as though by word of command, said, "I guess we're not going to be tried by this Court unless the American Consul is here"; to which the President replied, "I guess you will be tried by this Court whether the American Consul is here or he isn't. March the accused out, Sergeant."

We got through the seven cases and made our Finding – whatever that was!

In the evening I went to "X" Company HQ for dinner with Captain W. Duckworth, Lieutenant Fryer, 2nd Lieutenant A.D.G.O. Kerr, 2nd Lieutenant S.L. Moffatt, and Petrie. We had just started soup when Company Sergeant Major Ashworth rushed in to tell me that one of my Company billets had been hit by a shell, and there were several wounded. I left my soup – rushed off down the village street, and found a crowd round my own billet,[xix] and an ambulance coming up the road. I forced my way through the crowd to find Lieutenant G.H.A. Humble (Notts and Derby),[252] Company Sergeant Major Howard, Private Maxwell or "Fido" (Company Sergeant Major Howard's batman), Private Wilcock and Private Jebb (Lewis Gunners), all wounded badly.

Company Sergeant Major Howard was wonderfully cheery, although badly hit, and, when I asked him if I could do anything for him, he replied, "Eh, I wouldn't 'ave cared a damn if it hadn't been a hanti-haircraft shell."

The truth of the matter was, a Boche Taube[253] had come over, our Anti-Aircraft Guns had engaged him, and one of their shells, instead of bursting in the air, had misfired, come down with the usual terrific whizz and buzzing sound, and burst on contact with the ground.

We got them all away at once in the ambulance. This was a great loss to "Z" Company, more especially losing my Company Sergeant Major. Poor old Howard, he really looked as if he was finished. This was the man who in November 1914 fell out on the flank of N° 3 Company when Colonel John Hall was asking for Service NCOs. Corporal J. Howard and Corporal Ashworth (who had rushed to tell me of the incident) fell out together.[254]

Company Sergeant Major Howard originally belonged to the 4th King's Own Royal Lancasters, the IVth Foot, or, as he always preferred to designate that Famous Regiment, "the 4th o' King's". He was a jolly good soldier. He had spared no energy to try to make "Z" Company an efficient Company.

He was a typical soldier – he knew every trick of the trade, but he was sound. In or out of the Line, he was always a soldier, especially in the Line, and more especially when there was any extra work or shelling to be faced.

---

[252] Lieutenant G.H.A. Humble of the Notts and Derby Regiment was first attached to the 2/5th Lancashire Fusiliers on 23rd August 1916. He was originally posted to "W" Company, but at some time before 16th February 1916 must have replaced Lieutenant Abbotts as Transport Officer (see the diary entry for that date, at which stage Lieutenant Humble was sharing accommodation with Norman, Kenneth Waterhouse, Kenderdine, and Cecil Moffatt at the Willervals at Barly). This is the last mention of him in the diary, apart from when the Willervals were grieved to learn that he had been wounded on 10th July 1916, when the 2/5th Lancashire Fusiliers returned to Barly; it is not clear whether he ever returned to Active Service.

[253] German for "aeroplane".

[254] Joe Howard first came to Norman's attention on 7th November 1914 (see the diary entry for that date); in the original version of the diary entry for 24th June 1916 Norman has put "*Sept 1914*", but he must mean November 1914. Howard then features in the diary quite frequently, for example out on patrol with Norman in August 1915, touring the Line with him in December 1915 (including carrying him to his dug out on a couple of occasions when he passed out and enjoying a drink with him on Christmas Eve), and coaching "Z" Company in a Tug of War on 8th April 1916. Norman met him again at Ripon in January 1917 while he himself was recovering from being wounded, but Howard did not accompany him on his return to France in June 1917, much to the regret of both men. In describing that parting Norman describes him as "*a man for whom I always had, and shall have always, a great regard*".

We had been through some mixed times together. Captain Waterhouse and Captain Hedley – in fact, all "Z" Company Officers – thought more than can be expressed in words of Howard. Like everyone else he had his peculiarities, his little Howardisms, for example, his little squeaky voice saying "Aye Aye, to be sure" and "Yes! Certainly", two of his favourite expressions. We were all delighted to hear from Howard from Hospital to say that he was getting on well. He was like a second "Peter Pan" – never seemed any older even after five years of war.

25.06.16   An unfortunate bombing accident happened at Rivière to the Special Raiding Party while training, resulting in 3498 Sergeant Higgins ("X" Company), 2809 Sergeant J. Street ("Z" Company), and four others being wounded. The prompt action of 2522 Private Greenwood ("X" Company), who picked up and threw away a bomb, undoubtedly saved several casualties.

26.06.16   Some genius of the Higher Command invented the wonderful "Alert" position for Gas helmets. Instead of carrying the Flannel PH[255] Helmet in its satchel slung over the right shoulder, when the wind was dangerous i.e. blowing from the Boche, the helmet had to be taken from its satchel and container, and pinned to the shirt on the chest.
The coat (jacket) was then just pulled loosely over the helmet and the top buttons left undone. The object of carrying the helmet as described was for immediate adjustment over the head when gas was sent over – saving several seconds in drawing the helmet from its satchel. It was a good idea, but – my hat – rotten to wear; it felt like a poultice on your chest, especially in this hot June weather.
Captain Bloy, Captain G.C. Hutchinson, and Lieutenants Young and Ainscow came from Rivière to see us prior to the raid.
Ainscow and Hutty were very cheery, but the other two rather less confident, in fact despondent. In fact Bloy and Young insisted on saying "Good Bye" before leaving. Bloy actually said to me "Good luck, old chap, I don't think we shall see each other again". We wished the four of them "Bonne Chance!" and they returned to Rivière.

27.06.16   Captain J.W. Hedley left the Battalion to take over duties as Instructor at the Infantry Base Depot N° 1 Training Camp at Étaples, the famous Bull Ring which all troops knew and hated. He was very fed up at leaving us, just as we were also all sorry to lose "Uncle Joe", as we all called him.
The Western Front was just one seething mass of troops, guns, munitions, and the increased activity of our aeroplanes was very marked. The Boche made attempt after attempt to get over our back areas to observe what preparations we were making, but our Flying Corps were at last finding their feet and more than holding their own.
The Artillery were especially active. The preparatory bombardment on the Somme Front from Hébuterne to Bray had begun in earnest. Day and night there could be heard a distinct rumble of heavy gun fire, as our Gunners were shelling the forward German trench systems and back areas systematically. By night the flashes of the guns could be seen

---

[255] Phenate-hexamine.

reflected in the sky – like distant lightning in a heavy storm.

The guns in our area had also been shelling all day as a preliminary to the operation to be conducted at Blairville. Near my billet in an orchard there was a Battery of 60 pounder guns. They had been firing all day. During the night the Boche tried to find this Battery and retaliated with one of his counter Batteries. He was firing quite big stuff into the village, especially down near our cross roads and billets.

At about 1.30am I thought that things were getting too hot. I got up, put my coat and gum boots on, and went to turn out the men into their cellars. As I left my billet several shells burst quite close enough to be very unpleasant, bits whizzed past me, and I fairly went like a hare down the street. We got the men under cover and were kept there for two hours. On returning to my billet in the dawn light, it looked strange. On entering my room – Lord, What a mess! Broken furniture – bricks – everywhere covered in a red dust; a shell had come through the window, and burst in the room near my bed.

It was lucky I had gone to see if the men were alright, or I myself mightn't have written these words. My Sam Browne Belt, which was hanging behind my bed, had a nice piece of shrapnel stuck in it near the buckle.[xx]

Earlier in the evening we had received orders to detail NCOs and men to replace the casualties on the Raiding Party. I couldn't replace Sergeant Street. But I had to detail Private J. Clare – he was one of my best bombers. It was very much against my personal wish that I had to send him to join the party, but in war unpleasant duties have to be done, in spite of sentiment, and so Private Clare joined the party at Rivière on the night of the 27th June.

24.06.16 to 28.06.16   On the morning of Saturday June 24th the Operation Orders for the Raid were at last received. On that day a heavy bombardment of the German trenches was carried out, and lanes 20 yards wide were cut in the enemy's wire, one lane being allotted to each party; on Sunday June 25th a systematic bombardment of enemy trenches and billets was carried out, and it was arranged that, on the first day on which the wind was favourable, a gas cloud and smoke cloud was to be discharged, under cover of which the Infantry Raiding Parties would advance, and enter the German trench at intervals along the Divisional Front at Blairville. On Sunday June 25th and Monday June 26th the wind was unfavourable, so that only the Artillery programme was carried out. On Tuesday June 27th the wind was good, at midday. The Infantry Parties were ordered to take up their positions in the Line. However, rain set in, and continued all night. At 6.00am on Wednesday June 28th the troops returned to their billets.

During the day on June 28th, the weather cleared. The Infantry Parties again took up their allotted positions, and at 5.00pm gas was discharged.[256] At 5.35pm the Infantry went over the sand bags.

Unfortunately, partly due to the strength of the wind, and partly on account of the contour of the ground – which created local currents – the gas did not carry across No Man's Land

---

[256] A report in the Divisional War Diary is to the effect that discharge of the gas ceased at 5.25pm as planned, but in *The History of the Lancashire Fusiliers 1914-1918* by Major General J.C. Latter it is said that gas *"actually was pouring out for at least ten minutes longer, as all the Royal Engineers in charge of it became casualties before they could turn off the taps of the cylinders."*

sufficiently, but blew along No Man's Land instead. The Boche spotted this, had time to give the Alarm, and immediately opened a <u>heavy</u> fire with Artillery and Machine Guns as the Infantry began to advance.

The two Parties on our right failed to reach the enemy's Lines, but the 2/5th Lancashire Fusiliers Party succeeded in entering the enemy's trench and inflicting considerable loss on the enemy.

It was impossible to carry out the set programme (as so often happens in attacks), as the German trenches were found to be very strongly held, the Boche being practically shoulder to shoulder.

Dug outs were systematically bombed, telephone wires were cut, and very useful bayonet work was accomplished, inflicting severe losses on the Hun.

Captain Hutchinson, though badly wounded in crossing No Man's Land, continued to direct operations,[257] and, when the raid was over, collected several wounded men, and, by cutting a way through the wire, helped the men to regain our trench.

Captain Bloy led the Raiding Party with great gallantry, and, throughout the training, inspired much confidence and Esprit de Corps into men.[258] His loss was very deeply felt by all ranks.

It was generally felt that Lieutenant M.H. Young, in charge of N° 3 Raiding Party, could not have shown greater dash and energy. He was putting in some splendid work when he fell, mortally wounded, after killing a German officer.

2nd Lieutenant H.M. Ainscow, after establishing a bombing block in one of the enemy Communication Trenches,[259] was last seen chasing some Boche towards Berlin. Unfortunately he was wounded and taken prisoner.[260]

Every man of the four officers and 56 other ranks was a hero. We lost some fine fellows that day.

Lance Corporal Hampson ("Z" Company) was very funny; he was a small sturdy fellow about 5 feet 2 inches – he seemed to pick particularly big, fat, and juicy Boche to deal with, and, just before he was wounded, was seen chasing a hefty fellow down the trench, trying to bayonet him.

The Battalion received several decorations for this raid. The highest honour a soldier can

---

[257] In *The History of the Lancashire Fusiliers 1914-1918* by Major General J.C. Latter it is said that *"lying in the open he continued to direct the actions of his party and cheer them on … When the retirement began* (he) *crawled back to the British wire, collected some of the wounded in a shell hole and then cut a path for them through the wire under heavy fire."*

[258] In *The History of the Lancashire Fusiliers 1914-1918* by Major General J.C. Latter it is said that he *"was last seen running along the enemy parapet giving orders and using the butt of a rifle on several Germans who were standing on it."*

[259] In *The History of the Lancashire Fusiliers 1914-1918* by Major General J.C. Latter, it is said that *"in trying to establish a block, (he) had shot three Germans with his revolver but had received a nasty wound and was taken prisoner."*

[260] The participation in the Blairville raid is the last time that 2nd Lieutenant Harold Mason Ainscow is mentioned in the diary (apart from when Norman reminisces on return to the location of the Blairville raid on 13th August 1917); he is first mentioned as being the person whose place Norman took when he was instructed to proceed to France with the 2/5th Lancashire Fusiliers in May 1915 (see the diary entry for 19th April 1915), meaning that Ainscow did not proceed to France until November 1915 (see the diary entry for 15th November 1915). Also known as *"Scoff"*, there have been many mentions of him in the diary up to this point, including a description of him as the *"wit of the party"*, prone to losing revolvers while out on patrol (see diary entry for 31st December 1915), and a man whom Norman found to be a *"very genial companion"* (see the diary entry for 17th January 1916). He is commended for his *"good work"* in the diary entry for 26th to 30th May 1916 on page 184. See also the next footnote, from which it appears that he was ordained after the War.

get was awarded to Private J. Hutchinson – the Victoria Cross.[261] A report of the action leading to the award reads as follows:

For great gallantry and bravery when engaged in a raid on the German trenches opposite Ficheux on June 28th, 1916. He bayonetted and shot at least eight Germans and single-handed held the enemy at bay, covering the retirement of his party until they had withdrawn from this trench. It was largely due to his gallantry and initiative that the party was able to withdraw and bring back the wounded men to our trenches.[262]

The following awards were also made:

Captain G.C. Hutchinson, the MC[263]
Sergeant Russ, the DCM[264]
Private J.W. Bennett, MM[265]

---

[261] Private James Hutchinson was born on 9th July 1895 in Radcliffe, Manchester. He went over to France with the 2/5th Lancashire Fusiliers on the same day as Norman, 3rd May 1915. In *The History of the Lancashire Fusiliers 1914-1918* by Major General J.C. Latter it is recorded that this was the *"first (VC) to be gained by a war-time battalion of the Regiment or by any second-line Territorial unit."* It is interesting also to note that between them the Territorial Battalions of the 1/5th and 2/5th Lancashire Fusiliers, with both of whom Norman served, had a remarkable tally of Victoria Crosses, the highest award of any in the British Army. A total of 18 Victoria Crosses were awarded to all Battalions of the Lancashire Fusiliers; of these seven were awarded to the 1/5th Battalion (six for action on the same day in the Lancashire Landing at Gallipoli on 25th April 1915), and three to the 2/5th Battalion. Private Hutchinson was subsequently wounded in the Somme area in about the third week of July, losing an eye. He never went back to France, but became a bombing instructor in Britain. He survived the War, and, like Norman, was one of the four men chosen to form the Colour Party for the 5th Battalion of the Lancashire Fusiliersin the Victory Parade on 19th July 1919; there is a photograph of the Colour Party on page 308. He was also chosen (along with Norman and others) to represent the 2/5th Lancashire Fusiliers at the unveiling of the Givenchy Memorial to the 55th Division on 15th May 1921, as mentioned in the *Afterword* on page 309. James Hutchinson died in Torquay on 22nd January 1972. Interestingly, in *The Comprehensive Guide to the Victoria and George Cross*, published online at www.vconline.org.uk, it is reported that *"the funeral was conducted by Reverend Harold Ainsc[r]ow, who had been on the same raid James was awarded the VC and been a POW"*.

[262] The report is pasted into the diary; the citation in the *London Gazette* reads as follows: *"For most conspicuous bravery. During an attack on the enemy's position this soldier was the leading man, and, entering their trench, shot two sentries and cleared two traverses. After our object had been gained and retirement ordered, Private Hutchinson, on his own initiative, undertook the dangerous task of covering the retirement, and he did this with such gallantry and determination that the wounded were removed into safety. During all this time the gallant soldier was exposed to fierce fire from machine-guns and rifles at close quarters."*

[263] The participation in the Blairville raid is the last time that Captain Geoffrey C. Hutchinson is mentioned in the diary (apart from when Norman reminisces on return to the location of the Blairville raid on 13th August 1917, and again when visiting the Aveluy area on 21st August 1917 – see the *Afterword*, page 277-278); he was with "C" Company of the 2/5th Lancashire Fusiliers when they first landed in France on 3rd May 1916, having joined the Lancashire Fusiliers at almost the same time as Norman (see the diary entry for 4th September 1914). He was also known as "Hutty", and there have been many mentions of him and his exploits up to this point in the diary, for example *"being in great form on the unofficial bathing parades"* at Arques in May 1915, including riding a bicycle down a board into the canal (page 53), being engaged in sniping on 16th August 1915 when Captain Simon (who was spotting for him) was killed (page 78), and on 10th January 1916 *"riding on his horse full tilt into a piece of barbed wire and [coming] a terrific 'purler'"* (page 138). He served as Adjutant to the Battalion from 8th September 1915 until Best-Dunkley took over in June 1916 – see footnote 250 to the diary entry for 19th June 1916 on page 191. There is a photograph of him on page 112 with Lieutenant Colonel H.J. Shirley, Lieutenant R.N. Thompson, and Major H.N. Milnes, on the reverse of which is written *"Capt. G.C. Hutchinson, later MC, later 1950 MP KC, later 1952 Knighted, QC"*. He began the task of collecting and sorting records with a view to compiling a history of the Lancashire Fusiliers throughout the War. For some reason he did not write the history, but it was completed and published by J.C. Latter (by then Major General J.C. Latter) in 1949. In the book's Preface, in connection with his having performed the task of collecting together the papers, he is described as "Captain G.C. Hutchinson, later Major G.C. Hutchinson".

[264] In *The History of the Lancashire Fusiliers 1914-1918* by Major General J.C. Latter this was for *"crossing the open several times under fire and bringing in a number of wounded, including Captain Hutchinson."*

[265] In *The History of the Lancashire Fusiliers 1914-1918* by Major General J.C. Latter it is said that this was for *"inflicting loss on the enemy and bringing back wounded."* The award was presented to Private Bennett on 15th January 1917 at Ripon while Norman was on Home Service there (see the *Afterword*, page 273).

The following casualties I remember:

Captain L.H. Bloy[266] and Lieutenant M.H.Young were killed.[267]
Signallers J. Manock[268] and J. Turner were killed.[269]
Private J. Clare ("Z" Company) and Lance Corporal Hampson ("Z" Company) were wounded.

A later newspaper report read as follows:

Captain and Adjutant L.H. Bloy, Lancashire Fusiliers, who had been missing since last June, is now reported to have died of wounds as a prisoner of war on June 29th 1916, aged 24 years. He received his commission in September, 1914, and early in 1915 was promoted lieutenant. He went to the Front in May and saw some severe fighting. He was formerly a student at the Victoria University, Manchester. Lieutenant Ainscow, who was with him, and is now a prisoner of war, gives this account of his death:
"Everyone had left the German trench except Captain Bloy and myself. As I got out and was making my way back to our lines, Lieutenant Young was lying on the ground moaning 'I'm done, Ainscow.' I seized him at once by the belt and was dragging him through the German wire when a trench mortar knocked me down on the spot. When I came to myself a corporal told me Mr. Young had died, also Captain Bloy. I fancy Young's wounds were in the abdomen."[270]

---

[266] Captain Laurence Henry Bloy, son of William Henry and Emma Bloy of Wigan, died aged 23, and is buried at Fillièvres British Cemetery, reference B.1. He was with "B" Company of the 2/5th Lancashire Fusiliers when they first landed in France on 3rd May 1915, having joined the Lancashire Fusiliers as an officer in or about September 1914 (see the diary entry for 12th September 1914). He has featured frequently in the diary both when in training in England (for example, Norman says that he "*always used to excel in the cake line – eating about a dozen daily*" at Thom's Café in Southport — page 29), and after they arrived in France, where he is remembered inter alia for christening the 18 pounder guns "*pant splitters*" (see the diary entry for 25th December 1915), and on 30th April 1916 is recorded as having led a party through No Man's Land to try to capture a 20 yard length of canvas erected by the Germans in front of their Line, on which they had written "*Kut-el-Amara is over 13,000 prisoners*", i.e. goading the Allies about the defeat at Kut-el-Amara, and is mentioned for his "*good work*" in the diary entry for 26th to 30th May 1916 on page 184. There is a photograph of Captain Bloy with Lieutenant J. Bowd on page 97. He is said to have taken on the duties of Adjutant on the departure of Captain Jeffreys in August 1915, and to have performed them well (page 83), but, although he is referred to as Adjutant both in the newspaper report quoted here and that quoted in the *Obituaries* section, he was in fact replaced as Adjutant by Captain G.C. Hutchinson on 8th September 1915, as to which see the footnote to the diary entry for 19th June 1916. His promotion from temporary Captain to full Captain, with effect from 1st June 1916, was not gazetted until 4th August 1917, nearly a year after his death. See also *Obituaries*.

[267] Lieutenant Malcolm Henry Young, son of Colonel Pilkington Young and Mrs Young of Whitefield, died aged 23, and is buried at Fillièvres British Cemetery, reference A.1. Malcolm Young is mentioned in the diary entry for 4th September 1914 as having joined the Lancashire Fusiliers in Bury on that day at the same time as Norman. He was with "C" Company of the 2/5th Lancashire Fusiliers when they first landed in France on 3rd May 1915, and has often featured in the diary up to this point; for example, he shared a billet with Norman in Bedford in April 1915, swam in the canal with him near Arques in May 1915 (page 53), and went to Pierrots with him at Senlis, near Martinsart, on 30th November 1915. He participated in an earlier raid on 31st December 1915, and is mentioned for his "*good work*" in the diary entry for 26th to 30th May 1916 on page 184. See also *Obituaries*.

[268] Lance Corporal Joe Manock (spelt "Maynock" by Norman), Service no 200834, is commemorated at the Arras Memorial, Bay 5.

[269] No J. Turner appears in the Battalion War Diary casualty list for this raid or in the Commonwealth War Graves Commission's records as having died on or about 28th June 1916. If a second Signaller died in the raid, it was almost certainly Private Ogden, Service no 1786 (later 200350), who is listed as missing in the Battalion casualty list next to J. Manock. A Private Ogden is listed with J. Turner as a Signaller in the diary entry for 19th April 1915. According to the Commonwealth War Graves Commission's records Francis Ogden, Service no 200350, the brother of John William Ogden of Radcliffe, Manchester, was aged 25 when he died, and is commemorated at the Arras Memorial, Bay 5. If Signaller J. Turner also died in the War, he was John Turner, Service no 3122, son of Jane Turner of Bury, who died aged 27 on 12th September 1916 and is buried at Delville Wood Cemetery, reference XII.H.I, as only two J. Turners landed in France with the 2/5th Lancashire Fusiliers in May 1915, and the other survived the War.

A contemporaneous report read as follows:

On June 28th a daylight raid on a pretentious scale took place. Again the preparations were careful and detailed; gas and smoke were to be discharged on a two mile front, to be followed by raids in no fewer than six different places by parties from the 2/5th Lancashire Fusiliers, 1/4th Loyal North Lancs., and the 1/5th, 1/6th, 1/7th and 1/9th Liverpools. Unfortunately at the crucial moment a change of wind took place and the discharge of gas was only partially successful. In addition the raiding parties were received with heavy rifle and Machine Gun fire, with the result that two of the parties were unable to penetrate the enemy trenches. The remainder, however, were successful, and many of the enemy were killed. The following day the subjoined Special Order of the Day was issued by the Major General Commanding:[271]

"Yesterday six raids on the enemy's trenches were carried out by the 2/5th Lancashire Fusiliers and 1/4th Loyal North Lancashire Regiment, of the 164th Brigade, and by the 1/5th, 1/6th, 1/7th, and 1/9th King's Liverpool Regiments, of the 165th Brigade, assisted by detachments of the Royal Engineers. These raids were carried out in daylight in unaccustomed circumstances, and in the face of very determined opposition. In spite of these obstacles the results aimed at were successfully obtained, and great damage and loss was inflicted on the enemy ...

He wishes to congratulate the Artillery, Medium and Light Trench Mortar Batteries under Captain Bodell on the very efficient and determined Support which they gave to the enterprise, in some cases under circumstances of considerable danger.

He deeply regrets the loss of those who fell, but the spirit shown will have effect on the enemy. When the opportunity comes of avenging their deaths, the Major General commanding the Division is confident that the Division will not forget them."[272]

This raid was typical of many which took place almost daily in trench warfare on one sector or other. The newspapers in Britain used to report such operations:

All quiet on the Western Front. Our troops raided the enemy's trenches, inflicting considerable loss and damage on the enemy. Our troops got back safely and had few casualties.

Consequently the people at home imagined a raid was a mere nothing – a kind of joy ride over to the Boche for the evening.[273]

---

[270] The newspaper report is pasted into the diary.

[271] Major General H.S. Jeudwine.

[272] This report is pasted into the diary, partially completed by Norman in his own handwriting.

[273] In the Divisional War Diary there is a detailed account of this raid and six simultaneous raids by other Battalions. In *The History of the Lancashire Fusiliers 1914-1918* by Major General J.C. Latter it is said that one object of the raids *"was to find out the effects of the gas on the enemy"*, which is confirmed by the Divisional War Diary. Only the 2/5th Lancashire Fusiliers reported seeing dead Germans on their fire step, presumed to have succumbed to the gas; overall it was concluded that *"the effect of the gas was small"*, as most Germans were wearing respirators, or the gas did not reach them. Other objectives of the raids were to learn about the German defences, capture men and machine guns, and destroy enemy equipment. Only one man and one machine gun were captured, but it was thought that significant casualties and damage were inflicted on the enemy. Casualties on the British side were also high, with the 2/5th Lancashire Fusiliers suffering the highest casualties, amounting to about two thirds of the party.

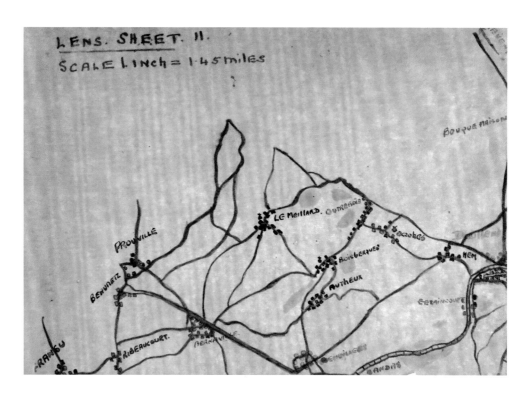

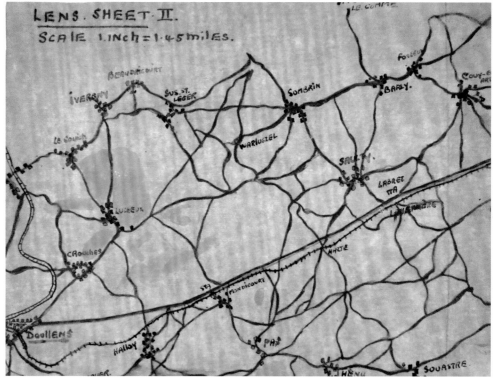

29.06.16 and 30.06.16	Captain Waterhouse returned from the 55th Divisional School, and the Raiding Party – at least, all that remained of the four officers and 56 other ranks, viz 19 other ranks – returned from Rivière to join the Battalion. They were all worn out, and more especially now the excitement was over, and the fellows realised that so many of their pals had been killed or wounded. We were all very proud of the brave way in which they had carried out the raid and for the Honour which they had won for the Regiment and the Battalion; although it was not until some time later that we received the list of honours.

The Divisional General published the Special Order of the Day quoted at the end of the previous chapter.

In consequence of the casualties to officers in the raid, it was necessary to re-adjust somewhat. I was ordered to leave "Z" Company and the Skipper. At first I was ordered to take over "W" Company, Captain Hedley having proceeded to Base. During the night of June 29th orders altered, and I finally took over "Y" Company, whose Company HQ were just across the road from "Z" Company.

No one seemed to know what was going to happen to us. All kinds of rumours were about. We rather expected to move down South, but actually received orders on June 30th to reconnoitre the Front Line South East of Arras at Agny to Achicourt, opposite to Beaurains, which the Boche held.

Each of these villages was very badly damaged by shell fire as a result of constant shelling since the early days of the war.

The Bombardment of the German positions on the Somme got more and more violent, for July 1st was the day selected for the Great Offensive.

In consequence of our Divisional Raids the Boche evidently thought that our Front was a possible sector for a British attack, especially as considerable movement of troops, guns, etc. had been going on in our back areas. So – I suppose on the off chance – he kept up a steady shell fire on our front trench systems.

Our new disposition of Company Commanders was as follows:

"W" Company	Lieutenant G. Gray
"X" Company	2nd Lieutenant S.L. Moffatt
"Y" Company	Captain N. Hall
"Z" Company	Captain K. Waterhouse

The officers in my Company ("Y" Company) were:

Lieutenant B.H. Rothband

Lieutenant M.P. Evans (Lewis Gun Officer)

2nd Lieutenants Walker, Ronald, Wolfe, and Coats

2nd Lieutenant Murray, who had joined "Y" Company in April 1916, went to Trench Mortars, 164th Brigade.

On reconnoitring our respective trenches we found that the Line was fairly good. It was a long way from Dainville, and the Communication Trenches from Agny to the Front Line were the longest I have ever seen – even longer than Clean Street (Sap 26) at Blairville. Also, at first it seemed extremely difficult to get one's bearings.

01.07.16	The Day which had long been waited for by our troops and the impatient people at home had at last come. It was a glorious day, the first <u>big</u> offensive in which our New Army was engaged. But as the 2/5th Lancashire Fusiliers were not engaged in this attack, I have no personal experiences to relate, for we disappointed the Boche on our Front – by not attacking.

At home Sir Roger Casement[274] was tried for High Treason, and sentenced to be shot. Lieutenant Peak,[275] formerly the 154th Brigade Signal Officer (with whom I was quite friendly, having first met him when I was Signalling Officer in 1915), rode over from Souchez, the Labyrinth, North of Arras where the 51st Division – our old Division – were holding the Line. We had quite a cheery evening together.

02.07.16   We had Church Parade near the Church at Dainville. Captain Newman[276] took the service. In the afternoon I took things quietly, sitting in the garden of my billet. There was good visibility, and many planes and Sausages[277] were up.

We heard that 2nd Lieutenant H.H. Noton had got the MC,[278] also Eric Oldham; also Sergeant Cadden had been awarded DCM.[279]

03.07.16   We were busy all day on preparing to move to the Line. We moved at about 8.30pm that evening, via the Arras to Doullens road, to Agny, and through Agny village, a pretty well wooded village in the valley of the Crinchon River. Here the trenches ran right through the streets, but, as it was getting dark, we didn't use them until we were clear of the village.

We got into position at about 12.30 midnight, the relief taking rather longer than usual, owing to the trenches being new to us.

07.07.16 and 08.07.16   At this time Captain K. Waterhouse returned once more to the Divisional School at Gouy-en-Artois. Captain W. Duckworth proceeded to Army School at Flixecourt or Auxi-le-Château. The weather had been very wet, which had hampered operations considerably on the Somme, making it very difficult to bring up the guns and ammunition to support the Infantry.

July 7th was the first day of sunshine, with good visibility – hence the Air Wallers[280] got busy again. Rather an exciting incident happened: four of our planes, in attempting to cross the Boche Line, were driven back by enemy Anti-Aircraft Guns. One of our planes was hit, burst into flame, and crashed – an awful sight. Naturally we all remarked it would be a sudden but horrible death for the pilot and observer, but, strangely enough, when I was in Hospital in London in September 1916, I met a Royal Flying Corps Officer who was in one of the other planes, and he told me that, by a miraculous escape, the pilot of the aeroplane brought down got off with a broken leg and burns, and was still alive and fit.

---

[274] One of the leaders of the Easter Rising in Ireland; in fact he was sentenced to be hanged, rather than shot.

[275] Also referred to as "Peake".

[276] It is not clear when Captain Newman took over as Padre, but Norman describes him as *"one of the very best of fellows"* in the diary entry for 30th July 1916. He probably took over from Captain Davenport, who was last mentioned by name in the diary entry for 10th February 1916, when he was sent to hospital with a temperature of 103°. *"The Padre"* is mentioned as having taken a voluntary service on 21st April 1916, but he is not specifically named.

[277] Observation Balloons – see the photograph on page 47, and the footnote to the diary entry for 17th and 18th August 1916.

[278] The *"first honour to the Battalion"*; see the diary entry for 16th to 27th November 1915.

[279] *The History of the Lancashire Fusiliers 1914-1918* by Major General J. C. Latter records that Sergeant W. Cadden (who has been mentioned a couple of times previously in the diary as doing sterling work in No Man's Land etc. – see the diary entries for 12th October to 4th November 1915 on page 105 and 26th to 30th May 1916 on page 184) was awarded the DCM for his work in the raid on 31st December 1915 (see the diary entry for that day). With Norman and three others he was chosen to represent the 2/5th Lancashire Fusiliers in the unveiling of the Givenchy Memorial to the 55th Division on 15th May 1921, as mentioned in the *Afterword* on page 309.

[280] "Waller" or "wallah" is army slang based on a Hindustani word, meaning a person with a particular role.

This same day, July 7th, there was a COs' Conference at Battalion HQ in Agny village.

At the Conference we were first warned of the probability of an early relief in this sector, the general idea being that we were to move into rest billets and practise an attack, probably a Divisional attack on Blairville. At this Conference I was ordered to take over Command of my dear old "Z" Company again, which I did that same day.

The disposition of the Front Line from left to right (North to South) was "Y", "X", "W" Companies, with "Z" Company in Reserve in the General Service Line as Support to the Battalion.

This was a very long Line, difficult to get along, and in bad repair. As usual there was quite a lot of work to do on the trenches. Our main job in Close Support was to find working parties and ration parties for Front Line Companies.

"Z" Company made their Company HQ with "X" Company. I had one position in Support of each Company in the Front Line, and one platoon at my Company HQ with two Lewis Guns, ready to dispatch to any part of the Line as ordered. This was the disposition as taken over.

"W" Company, on the right of the sector, were in a peculiar position. They held a Line which crossed the Arras to Bapaume railway. The Front Line across the railway, and on either side, was mined by the Boche, who we presumed could blow it up at will. The New Zealand Tunnelling Company were making shafts and counter mines on this sector. The excavated earth – a blue clay mixed with chalk – showed up everywhere, especially at the Shaft Heads. Consequently these mounds, which grew daily, attracted the Boche's attention, who, of course, knew what this meant. So he used to devote considerable attention to the Communication Trench, Front Line, and Shaft Heads. This shelling was most annoying, as it stopped work and made extra work in repairs and upkeep to Communication Trenches.

"W" Company had a very peculiar spot for an HQ, a dug out made in the railway embankment and under the railway – about 50 feet down. It was a regular black hole of Calcutta.[281] There were two entrances, one of which led to the railway itself up an iron ladder. Looking up the railway, there was a breastwork built across about 200 yards up, and 50 yards beyond was a Boche barricade. As the railway was uphill to the Boche, he could look right down the railway. He always had a Machine Gun trained on "W" Company HQ.

There were some wonderful orders for "Action to be taken in event of Enemy blowing up the Front Line" and "Occupation of Crater – duties for consolidation party", and emergency dumps of RE material, picks, shovels, sand bags, pickets, barbed wire etc., were all ready. In view of "W" Company being rather weak, I decided to move my mobile platoon in Reserve to "W" Company's position, as it was an important position to hold on the railway.

The Front Line across the railway – 200 yards – had only about two Sentry Posts. These were relieved every hour, as the strain and isolation was very trying. The idea of weak occupation was to save men in case of the mines being blown by the Boche. We filled in most of the Front Line with barbed wire, used it as an Observation Line, and made our Line of Resistance behind on the higher ground, which was clear of the Mine Danger Zone. The 1/8th Liverpool Irish were on our right. It was a very tedious and lonely job going round Posts on this part of the Line, and, besides, the Communication Trenches were quite knee deep in water. I went round several times with Gray and Long Waterhouse.

---

[281] A stock metaphor derived from an event which took place in Calcutta in 1756, when a large number of British soldiers and civilians were confined in a small prison, and many died from being trampled or suffocation.

09.07.16   A draft of 99 men from East Lancashire joined us in the Line. "Z" Company got about 20 men. I received Operation Orders for relief by the 11th Division, who had come from Egypt and Salonika, and was relieved late in the evening at about 11.45pm.

10.07.16   We moved via Achicourt, Agny and Dainville, then on to Simencourt. It was a long trek, and we arrived at Simencourt at about 5.00am, by which time it was quite light. I slept in the Divisional Canteen with Cecil Moffatt, Evans, Cooper, Forrester, and Kerr. We were very tired and had no valises, so slept in our clothes.

We paraded at 10.00am, and marched via Gouy to Barly, our old billeting area of February 1916, arriving at 12 noon. First we were billeted with "W" Company, making 10 officers together in all, which was too many, so I went to see my old billet owner Madame Willerval[282] at Rue de Sombrin, but she had no accommodation to spare. However, they were very pleased to see us all again. They were very grieved to hear that Lieutenant Humble had been wounded. They gave us a good billet to visit, where we fixed up a Mess, near the Hospital Casualty Clearing Station. There was no sleeping accommodation there, so Jimmy Bowd, the Quartermaster, got us two tents and we pitched them in the orchard of our billet. Moffatt and I joined at one tent, while Packman, Kerr, and Forrester joined at the other. Kenderdine was on leave at this time.

There was another COs' Conference, at which further details were given to us about training for our attack on Blairville. We expected to make it in about a week's time. Things hadn't gone too well North of the Ancre at Gommecourt and Monchy, and it was assumed that our effort would be to try to draw German Reserves onto our Front, thus relieving the pressure for our Divisions on the above sectors.

12.07.16   Madame Willerval was very good to us – she used to send eggs, raspberries, tomatoes,
to   cream, and/or cakes up to our billet almost every day. When we went to pay for them she
16.07.16   was quite annoyed, and wouldn't take a sou.

We were training hard each day. The weather was glorious. Full scale dummy trenches of the Boche Positions were made in an area between Barly and Avesnes. We practised every detail, even to carrying parties, mopping up parties, communications, and consolidation. Each day we did a little more, until everyone got more and more to know their own job.

My job with "Z" Company was a rather – in fact, a very – difficult one. After the First German Line was taken by "X" Company, "W" Company were to cross over it and proceed to the Second Line, take it, and consolidate.

"Z" Company were to follow "W" Company immediately, and, after crossing the First Line, held by "X" Company, we were to change direction Right, and form a defensive flank facing Right and Blairville Wood (the North West edge). The two Communication Trenches leading into the wood were to be cleared for 80 yards, bombing blocks made, and the Communication Trench converted into a fire trench.

Major Bridgewater was very good in his explanations and conduct of the Scheme.

The Divisional General, Brigadier etc. used to come and criticise, and to some tune. We also practised the attack with casualties – taking officers away and letting the next seniors carry on, as has to be done in war. We used to get back to billets at about 5.00pm each day.

On Wednesday July 14th the Divisional Concert Party came over to perform at the Casualty Clearing Station at Barly. I went to the performance. Several Sisters came from the Canadian Hospital at Doullens with McVicker, who had been with us as MO for a short time. After

---

[282] See the diary entry for 16th February 1916 for the previous occasion when Norman stayed with her.

the Concert we all went in and had supper with the staff of Barly Hospital. Then we dropped Waterhouse, who had come over from Gouy, back there en route when we took the Doullens contingent home on a Motor Ambulance. We had great fun – quite a nice change to be able to talk to English Girls again. We landed back at Barly at 1.30am.

The next evening Moffatt, Harker and I went over to Gouy to have dinner with the Skipper. The same day (July 15th) a draft of 92 men arrived, together with three new officers, 2nd Lieutenant S.B. Armstrong, 2nd Lieutenant Griffiths, and 2nd Lieutenant Braedle.

Meanwhile, on July 16th Lieutenant J.B. Packman was sent on a Bayonet Fighting Course at the Divisional School.

17.07.16   There were rumours that the attack on Blairville was to be cancelled, and that we were to move from the VIth Corps area South. Orders were issued that Officers' Kits were again to be cut down in weight to 35lbs.[283] Whenever that figure of "35lbs" cropped up it was always a sure sign of trouble.

I was gazetted Captain with effect from May 8th 1916 [see page 320 - actually the entry in the 7th July 1916 edition of the London Gazette].

18.07.16   We had definite orders to move from the area on July 20th.

19.07.16   I rode "Sandy Mac" to an FGCM at Beaumetz. The Court had to adjourn as the Boche shelled the village and dropped several into the garden of the house we were in.[xxi] I was busy from 10.00am until 5.00pm, but it was rather a boring day.

We had now come to the end of our time on the Blairville – Wailly – Agny Sector. Taken all round, we had had quite a good time.

It had been a period of steady and progressive training for the re-organised Division, in preparation for the more serious days very soon to come. The time had been spent profitably in more ways than one.

The organisation of many details which make for the efficiency of a Division, and the comfort of the troops, had been made. However our time here hadn't been a really peaceful period, as is shown by the Casualty return for the period from February 28th 1916 to July 10th 1916:

Killed, Wounded and Missing:
Officers – 63
Other Ranks – 1047

The Division was finding its feet.

At home one great change had taken place, a change which had a very great effect on the Government of the War. Lloyd George became Secretary of State for War on July 6th 1916.

---

[283] 35 pounds, which is about 16 kilograms.

CHAPTER 19
Beaudricourt, Fienvillers, Journey to the Somme, and Happy Valley
20th July 1916 to 30th July 1916

20.07.16   We got up at 3.30am, struck our tents, and got ready to move. Major J.B. Barnsdale rejoined the Battalion from Simencourt, where he had been Town Major.

It was a glorious morning. We left Barly at about 5.30am, proceeding to Sombrin, Sus-St-Léger, and Beaudricourt, about 8 miles, arriving at about 11.30am. The Band and drums played the Retreat as we marched through the village of Barly. They were getting into good form again. My horse was taken ill during the march, so I marched most of the way. The Divisional School had broken up, as the Division were moving to the Somme Area, and Captain K. Waterhouse again rejoined the Battalion, taking over command of "Z" Company from me.

It was very nice to be right away from the Line and danger areas for shelling.

21.07.16   We left Beaudricourt at 7.00am, and marched via Ivergny, Le Souich, Bouquemaison, Doullens, Hem, Occoches, Outrebois, and Le Quesnel Farm, arriving at Autheux at about 2.30pm – 18 miles.

Quite a number of men fell out on this march. I was detailed to bring up the rear of the Battalion as OC of Stragglers with Sergeant Ramsbottom, the Provost Sergeant.

We got a good billet, and had the usual Feet Inspection etc. Ken Waterhouse and I went to HQ Mess for dinner at a good large farm, and had a cheery evening.

22.07.16   We got up at about 5.30am, and the Battalion left Autheux at about 8.15am. I was still OC of Stragglers. Some job! This time, before we started, the MO sent about 12 men to Hospital. We left about a quarter of an hour after the Battalion. We had two Motor Ambulances detailed to follow about a mile in rear of the Column.

We had quite a short march in front of us this day. We went via Le Meillard (where we had been in billets in February 1916),[284] Bernaville, and Ribeaucourt, arriving at Fransu easily before lunch. We had a quiet afternoon.

23.07.16   We were resting in billets, checking Box Respirators (issued to Machine Gunners only[285]), Smoke Helmets, Small Arms Ammunition, Iron Rations, Field Dressings, Identity Discs etc.

24.07.16   We left Fransu at 4.00pm – marched through Ribeaucourt, Beaumetz, near Prouville, and Bernaville to Fienvillers.

Fienvillers-Candas was a Railhead on the Longpré to Doullens line. The Division were using this Railhead as a concentration centre prior to entraining for the Somme Front. At last it was really definite that we were going to the Somme Area to take our part in the Great Offensive of 1916.

---

[284] 13th to 18th February 1916.

[285] By the spring of 1917 these box respirators, recently introduced at this point as an improvement to the PH helmet (see the diary entry for 26th June 1916 on page 197), were standard issue to all.

We had rotten billets in Fienvillers, but there were so many troops to be accommodated that we were decidedly lucky in getting a roof over our heads. The Skipper stayed with Chamberlain of the 1/8th Liverpool Irish. Moffatt, Forrester and I slept in a very dirty loft at the top of the house – filthy, full of old rubbish and cobwebs. Still it was somewhere!

25.07.16   This was the day of our actual departure for the Somme. We were now in the XIth Corps and the Vth Army – newly created.

We got up at 4.00am, and marched from Fienvillers to Candas Station.

We entrained at about 4.30am. The Divisional Band played cheerful music and various numbers to cheer us on our way. It was early, and after several days' marching we were physically tired, but cheery enough otherwise. We were all ready for the long journey to some Railhead on the Somme, well supplied with rations. I was in the same carriage as Kenneth Waterhouse, Major Milnes, Colonel Bridgewater, Best-Dunkley and Moffatt.

At last the train started at 8.00am – the Band playing our Regimental March. There was a wonderful spirit that morning – we were going to help in the Big Push at last.

The journey wasn't particularly exciting, as I had travelled the same route many times. We went via Domart, Flixecourt, Longpré, and along the Somme Valley to Amiens, using a line which was at this time the main supply route for the Forces operating on the Somme – "one endless stream of trains day and night". Amiens looked just the same as ever – French and English troops returning from leave – perhaps for the last time! We had several meals en route, the card sharpers played cards, and I wrote one or two letters and slept part of the way as usual. Cecil Moffatt was very cheery as usual, and kept the carriage in good spirits. We were now in the heart of the back areas for the Somme Battle. We knew the District well. All the way along the route the roads were thick with Transport, Small Arms Ammunition and other ammunitions, lorries, and hundreds of Motor Ambulances and troops.

At Heilly we saw the large Clearing Stations N° 36 and 49 with their ambulances and Red Cross trains – a hive of work. There were hundreds of soldiers in the Convalescent Camp recovering from minor wounds. These were the men who had made the first attacks on July 1st and the following days.

Just for a moment the thought flashed through my mind, "I wonder how many of us here may be amongst those fellows and when, unless something worse …", then Colonel Bridgewater – perhaps luckily – interrupted my thoughts, "Now then, you fellows, into your harness. Méricourt is the next station."

We detrained at about 3.00pm at Méricourt. We got the Battalion clear of the station, prepared a meal for the men in a field nearby, and then went to the Officers' Club for a few minutes. There was a huge German Prisoner Camp near the station; nasty looking fellows they were – but fine big men, and apparently pleased enough to be in our hands. The men's remarks were rather funny.

"Say, Bill, look at yon Jerrys – if they get mony more o' them, rations is going to be short for our lads."

We were very interested in some 15 inch guns on trucks. Then Ken said, "Come along, Jimmy, about time we got the Company on parade – we're moving off at five you know."

"Right-ho, Skipper."

The Battalion moved off, headed by the Band and drums, via Ribemont, Dernancourt, and Buire to Méaulte. It was a perfect evening as we marched along. The march was full of interest. I had never seen an Army concentrated for a decisive battle before. Everywhere seemed thick with troops and dumps. The Cavalry were all standing by ready to go through when the opportunity came! The woods housed their horses under the green trees, as cover from Aircraft Observation. We were constantly having to squeeze the Column to the roadside to make room for Motor Transport Columns going up the Line. Long Columns of Motor Ambulances were coming down from the forward areas. It was wonderfully organised – there were slow convoys for serious cases, and fast convoys for less serious. There were hundreds of Motor Char-a-bancs full of sitting cases, all as merry as Sand Boys – a motley sight, bandaged and mud-covered, but smiling and singing, in spite of painful wounds, passing encouraging remarks to us.

"It's grand up there – you will have a happy time."

"Now we shan't be long."

"It's a long way to Tipperary, but we ain't downhearted yet."

Many fellows had chalked on the coaches – *"Blighty this way – single journeys only"*.[286]

The British Tommy is a wonderful fellow – it takes a great deal to really damp his spirits.

As we approached Méaulte, our destination, we could see Albert to the North with the ruined church and Virgin – just as we had known it six months before.[287]

The Guards Division were billeted in Méaulte, and consequently our billeting officers had great difficulty in finding billets for our Battalion. We managed to get them under cover, but in awful billets. It seemed rotten. These men, who within a day or two – perhaps sooner – would be going into action, wanted comfortable quarters – but none could be had.

The officers of "Z" Company, Ken Waterhouse, myself, Kenderdine, C.H.Moffatt, Forrester, Packman, and G.G.A. Kerr, joined at two tents in an orchard. We turned in early – tired out after a big day.

26.07.16   We got up at about 7.00am, and tried to find out when we were moving still further forward. Eventually we found out that we were to move about 2.00pm. We spent the morning putting final touches to our organisation. I was ordered to bring up the rear of the Battalion and was given a horse.

We marched out along the Albert to Bray road. It was a clear afternoon as we marched out. Every billet of the Guards seemed to turn out their Quarter Guard to us, and paid the usual Compliments, with the same precision as if they had been on guard at Wellington Barracks in London. Their discipline and turn out was really marvellous.

The aeroplanes were busy this afternoon operating with the Gunners and the Infantry. Many Observation Balloons were to be seen. The country for miles around seemed to be a seething mass of khaki, men, horses, guns, General Service Wagons, and General Service Limbers.[288] We were beyond the area of houses – those that once stood in these areas were mere piles of bricks, overgrown with grass.

Of the troops, some were waiting to go up to the Line for the first time in this Great Battle, others were weary, tired to that extent which cannot be expressed in words, men carrying

---

[286] Blighty is slang for "Britain" or "home", and is derived from Hindustani "bilayati", meaning "foreign land". In the context of a wound, it means a wound bad enough to secure a passage home.

[287] Norman was last in Albert on 2nd January 1916. See also the footnote to the diary entry for 29th July 1915.

[288] See footnotes 39 and 43 on pages 37 and 38.

that battle worn expression on their faces, blood shot eyed, mud-covered clothes, unshaven faces, with just a ground sheet made into a bivouac to live in. There were troops from every corner of the British Empire – Canada, Australia, New Zealand, South Africa – and the British Isles. The guns could be heard in the distance some 5 miles away. The general impression was not one of organisation – but each man amongst these tens of thousands knew what to do when the order came.

We soon reached our destination, our allotted billeting area – just a field.

We passed the Rear Transport Lines of the 30th Division, who had had some terrible fighting at Montauban and Contalmaison – the Manchester Pals.

The Battalion formed up in Mass and were ordered to lie down. Colonel Bridgewater told the officers that we were here at any rate for the night. It was then about 5 o'clock. We were instructed to make all provision to get our men under cover of the same bivouacs of ground sheets etc., see that they had a good meal and report to the Adjutant, Captain Best-Dunkley, when all was arranged.

"Z" Company soon got our fellows housed and fed, and then we looked round for a spot for the officers of the Company. Some old Gun Pits in a railway embankment nearby proved very good.

We set to work with corrugated iron sheets, which we found nearby, ground sheets, a few old boxes etc., and soon we had an excellent Mess – just there out in the open. Ashton, my servant, soon got busy and made us an excellent dinner – about four courses. During dinner Roger Smith of the 16th Manchesters came to see me – he was a Corporal, and we had a cheery hour together. Roger had been having a rough time in Montauban and was full of it, and kept us interested and amused telling his experiences of chasing Boche through houses etc. He had a slight shrapnel wound, but was not going away from the "fun", as he called it. Roger had seen his brother, Alec Smith, and a few days later had heard the reports of Alec being missing. He was very upset. At last he had to go back to his Lines, and this was the last time I saw him, for he also was killed some time later.[289]

We were all undecided where our bedroom was to be. However, we decided that the bank was soft and sloping, so we put on our trench coats and settled down to sleep, just the stars and the sky for shelter. Although it was the end of July, it was quite cold, and at about 2.00am Moffatt, Kenders and I got up and made a fire and some tea, and chatted and smoked.

27.07.16   In the afternoon some tents and bivouacs arrived, to our great joy, so we soon made the men and ourselves more comfortable.

It was a glorious day, very hot, and we were too lazy to do much; besides, I really felt that I might need all my surplus energy in the next few days when we got into the thick of it. There was rather heavy shelling during the night, but we were out of the zone, or, at least, we weren't worried.

---

[289] 2nd Lieutenant Alec Smith, of the 10th Battalion Lancashire Fusiliers, formerly of the 11th (Prince Albert's Own) Hussars, a Cavalry Regiment, died on 8th July 1916, aged 24, and is commemorated at the Thiepval Memorial, Pier and Face 3C and 3D. Sergeant Roger Smith MM, Service no 6683, of the 16th Battalion Manchester Regiment, died on 15th October 1916, aged 26, and is buried at Warlencourt British Cemetery, reference VIII.J.49. They were the sons of William Henry and Annie Sarah Smith of Glossop Derbyshire, formerly of Bury, and were both (like Norman) educated at Bury Grammar School. After leaving school Roger Smith had been a clerk at the Lancashire and Yorkshire Bank, while Alec had been an industrial draughtsman. Both enlisted in September 1914, at about the same time as Norman (see the diary entry for 29th August 1914). Alec, like his brother, initially enlisted as a private, but accepted a commission on transferring to the Lancashire Fusiliers.

28.07.16   The Company and Battalion were engaged in Attack Practice. Our training for the attack was most interesting. Of course, there were no inconveniences like Machine Guns, Shells etc. In the afternoon we had quite an exciting and interesting reconnaissance. Kenneth Waterhouse, Cecil Moffatt, Kerr, and I rode out to Carnoy to reconnoitre the route for our move up to the Line. We got right in amongst the guns. There were hundreds of all Calibres from 15 inch guns on railway trucks to the 18 pounders. Batteries seemed to be massed everywhere – huge dumps of shells. Guns seemed to be firing in every direction. Although there seemed to be a great row, things were really quite quiet at the time. We reached Carnoy without accident, and went to Fricourt across the old British Front Line and German Front Line, and came to Montauban.

The Germans were rather rude and started to fire big shells – 12 inch and 8 inch – back into Carnoy and Montauban. They burst with a terrific crash-crump, and tore up houses and earth, which was shot up into the air to heights of up to 100 feet. It was most terrifying, because each one that came seemed to be coming straight for us; actually they were bursting some 200 yards away, although one huge one made us wish we were rabbits – it burst about 40 yards away, threw up earth, stones, and – oh, everything; and covered us with dirt, while pieces of iron seemed to be flying all around. We just lay flat and hoped for the best. No one was touched.[xxii] We moved on quickly.

We went up to Machine Gun Wood at Maricourt, from which place we had a fine view over the captured ground, also of the heavy shelling on Trônes and Delville Wood, which was still held by the Boche. It was very probable these would be our objective. Our Gunners weren't half plastering the woods. It must have been awful up there. Some days later we found out it was! The ground here was very badly churned up by shell fire from the July 1st Barrage – especially the Boche Front Line. He must have had a terrible time.

We had a fine afternoon; but we realised, as we saw the graveyards etc., what war really meant.

29.07.16   We were training in the morning. In the afternoon Moffatt and I rode down to Bray for a swim. It was a glorious hot day. There were hundreds of troops bathing in the Somme at Bray – French, English, Colonials. The Garde Republicaine Band was playing, though it was only a few miles behind the fighting. But we did enjoy it. Barnsdale and Harker[290] also came.

---

[290] This is the last reference to Lieutenant J.F. Harker (Freddy) in the diary. The first mention of him is when he was with "D" Company of the 2/5th Lancashire Fusiliers when they first landed in France on 3rd May 1915 (having been "*quite ill*" crossing the Channel), and he has featured frequently in the diary in the early days after the Battalion's arrival in France. Norman got to know him well when Norman joined "D" Company's Mess from 9th May 1915 until they finished their training at Arques on 8th July 1915, and mentions him as an adept mimic, perfectly taking off Captain Cummins' expression "*Blast their eyes*" (see the diary entry for 16th May 1915), and a strong man who finished the infamous La Gorgue march on 18th May 1915 "*looking like an Italian Organ Grinder – with a huge waterproof cape thrown over his kit, and carrying about three rifles*". He features also as enjoying bathing in the canal at Arques on 26th May 1915, and the sport of ratting (see the diary entry for 14th to 19th August 1915), and as a man who had considerable cheek, as witness the diary entry for 5th July 1915, which reports that he: "*rode down from Wisques on a horse belonging to an Indian Cavalry Officer. He came down in great style with an Indian Groom – just like Freddy's cheek. He once borrowed a horse in St Omer to ride up to Wisques on and then found it belonged to the CO of the 1st Life Guards. Some cheek!*" It is apparent that after arrival in France he trained as a Machine Gunner (see the diary entry for 21st June to 30th June 1915), and took

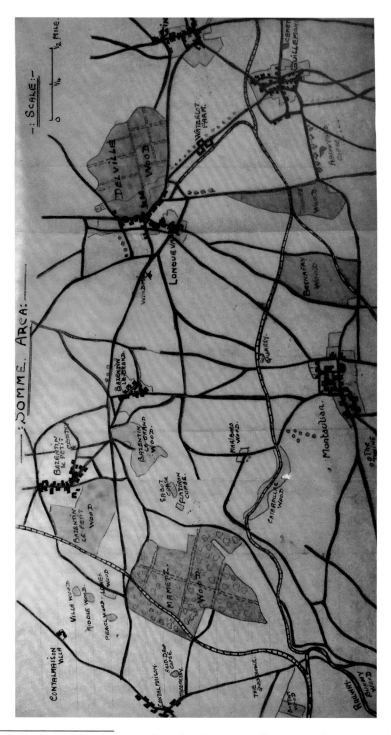

over the role of Machine Gun Officer to the Battalion when Lieutenant Hill was wounded on 13th July 1915; thereafter he is mentioned mostly in the context of firing Machine Guns, apart from performing a song, *Same as my feyther*, at a Battalion concert on 9th October 1915 at Aveluy (see the newspaper cutting relating to the diary entry for that date). He had a spell in hospital according to the diary entry for 2nd to 7th March 1916, but had evidently been discharged by this date. It appears that he is not included as one of the seven original officers still with the Battalion in the diary entry for 21st to 26th August 1916, but the diary entry for 25th January 1916 is to the effect that at that point he and his men joined the Brigade Machine Gun Company, so he was presumably no longer regarded as an officer of the 2/5th Lancashire Fusiliers.

30.07.16   We had a fine Church Parade. The Divisional Band came down to accompany the hymns. Then we had a presentation of DCMs and MMs to some of our fellows. Afterwards the four Battalions marched past Major General Jeudwine – the GOC 55th Division – in Column, Quarter Column and Column of Route. It was a very inspiring Parade. The General told us that we should be in the thick of the fight any day, and he had implicit confidence in us to do well, whatever we had to tackle.

We had a sports meeting to arrange to do something for Minden Day.[291]

The Skipper and I met, and started out for Divisional HQ at the Citadel to arrange with Captain Macready for transport to go to Amiens for beer for the troops for Minden Day. We met Brigadier General Edwards and Captain Jackson, Brigade Major, halfway. They informed us that we should move up the Line that night, so we had better get back to our camp and wait for further orders.

We returned – rather fed up; our Minden Day Sports etc. were off – but we imagined that we might still have some Cross Country sport against the Boche.

When we arrived at Happy Valley everyone was busy striking bivouacs. The Skipper, as usual, was just as cool as if he had been walking down Lord Street to Thom's Café in Southport.

Long Waterhouse[292] had been very rotten for several days, and the MO ordered him to Hospital – much against his will. But it was useless for anyone as ill as he was to think of going up to fight – and fight we should have to this old time.

We had never been in a really big battle before, and when we marched from our camp in Happy Valley at 9.00pm it was pitch black and raining. We didn't know exactly where we were going, but towards Trônes Wood.

The 1/8th Liverpool Irish moved off first, followed by the 1/4th King's Own Royal Lancasters, then ourselves, and later the 1/4th Loyal North Lancashires.

Many were the "Farewells" said that night, and the "Good Wishes", and "Good luck, old thing – see you going over the top".

We officers had all sat down to dinner together – many for the last time. But in war you don't know who will return. Thank heavens! Padre Newman – one of the very best of fellows

---

[291] See the footnote to the diary entry for 1st August 1914.

[292] This is the last time Lieutenant Hugh Waterhouse (Long Waterhouse, or "Long Un") is mentioned in the diary until 18th February 1917, when Norman went to Fountains Abbey with him while they were both on Home Service at Ripon, and later they were stationed together at Scarborough, where on 29th April 1917 they watched a German Submarine firing shells at the port. Long Waterhouse had been with "A" Company of the 2/5th Lancashire Fusiliers when they first landed in France on 3rd May 1915 (the first mention of him in the diary), and up to 30th July 1916 has frequently been mentioned in the diary, for example, cycling ahead of the Column on 6th May 1915 on the first long march after arriving in France, and cycling from Outtersteene to Bailleul with Norman on 15th May 1915, taking part in fishing competitions (see the diary entries for 6th to 12th and 21st to 30th June 1915), and looking for eggs in Martinet Wood (see the diary entry for 18th June 1916). According to the Battalion War Diary he was appointed as Sniper Officer on 17th July 1915, and he excelled as a bomber and on patrol in No Man's Land, and there are many entries relating to this; for example, he is given special credit for his *good work* in this regard in the diary entry for 26th to 30th May 1915 on page 184, and there is an account of him venturing into No Man's Land to salvage a dud German bomb on 3rd November 1915. He was devastated when he lost a man while out on patrol on Christmas Eve 1915, and had a period of absence after this from 4th January 1916 to 16th March 1916, being sent to hospital and then Nice suffering from 'flu and being *"generally jiggered up"* (see the diary entries for 24th December 1915 and 16th March 1916). According to *The History of the Lancashire Fusiliers 1914-1918* by Major General J.C. Latter, in the final action in which any Battalion of the Lancashire Fusiliers was involved, on 10th November 1918 and extending into the morning of 11th November 1918, the objective of which was to capture bridges over the Blaton-Ath Canal and cross over into Ath, Waterhouse, who was by then a captain and CO of "D" Company of the 2/5th Battalion, distinguished himself and was awarded the MC.

was left behind when we marched out. He wasn't supposed to go into these fights, but being a "Man", he wasn't happy away from us all.

He wasn't the type of man who made you feel despondent – he cheered everyone up and had a word of encouragement for all of us.

The march was made rather slowly, by platoons at 200 yards distance, as we were going into the very heat of things this time.

We avoided main roads as far as possible, as these were heavily shelled at night. We went via Bronfray Farm to Carnoy. It was quiet when we started but very soon the guns – ours – started to fire heavily. The flashes of the guns, and the shell bursts reflected against the sky, could be seen for miles. One of our big guns hit a German ammunition dump somewhere behind the Boche Line. The sight was wonderful – like a huge fire shooting out hundreds of little fires. It varied in intensity, sometimes low, then suddenly a flash of flame shot up into the air, followed a few seconds later by a terrific crash. It was fearful, and wonderful.

Our march was like playing follow my leader, "knowing not whither we were going". There was little or no talking amongst us. I wonder what thoughts we had that night – I know mine – but they are mine for ever!

We passed through Maricourt, Carnoy, and Montauban.

At Carnoy we came right into the midst of the Battery Positions. Hundreds of guns were firing – accompanied by the Boom of the big guns, the sharp crack of the 4.5 inch howitzers and 18 pounders, the flashes of the charges at the muzzles, followed by the noise of the shell rushing to its objective on its errand of death to some German. The flashes were so near as we passed the guns that you could feel the heat and the rush of the wind as the shells flew overhead. Each flash lit up the scene of men in all kinds of garbs, some firing so hard, or working so hard at lifting shells, that they wore no jackets or shirts. After the flash followed black darkness, dotted by yellow dots of light, which made it very difficult to see, nay, almost impossible. Then the Boche retaliated on the Batteries – but you never heard the shell come – only saw it burst, and heard the crump–crash, and the bits of shrapnel and shell case flying past. The air literally reeked of burnt High Explosives. But on we went. Skipper and I wondered how many of our fellows would reach the Line. We went about 2 miles until we were clear of the gun positions.

Looking back the whole countryside seemed dotted with tongues of flame. Looking forward one saw the shell bursts, and the Rockets of Red – Green – White, the flare lights. This was a nightly strafe; similar strafes had gone on day and night on this Front for a full month now. The marvel was that anyone remained to tell the experience of it all.

We were lucky that we had very few casualties – one or two cases of shell shock – and no wonder – the strain was terrific. I was literally wet through with excitement – nerve strain it may be called. But in truth <u>Fear</u>. But one dare not show it. What would the men think? This Fear of being marked as a coward needs a lot of fighting against, but it has to be done.

Briqueterie, in Reserve South of Trônes Wood, and Death Valley
31st July 1916 to 7th August 1916

31.07.16   It was by now the early morning of Monday July 31st.

We crossed over battered trenches on to a shell torn road, and over a light railway, also torn up in places. We met troops coming out of the Line who had been relieved. They were worn out. They weren't singing. They had had all their sing taken out of them, for a bit anyway.

Then we halted – we had reached our destination. Thank God, the shelling had slackened considerably, but we could now hear the crack of rifle shots, and the tut-tut-tut of the Machine Guns.

We were in a sunken road which led from the Briqueterie on the Maricourt to Guillemont road to a valley South of Bernafay and Trônes Wood. Along the North side of the road a deep trench had been dug with grooves cut in the walls to hold one or two men.

The Boche started to shell – Colonel Bridgewater ordered us to get into the trench. We did! Very quickly! The shells were dropping on either side of the road, and a few actually on it. The Skipper and I had a very sticky time going down the Company Line to see that our fellows were all in cover. We couldn't get down the trench so had to go on the road. How on earth we missed being killed I don't know.[xxiii] Having settled the men down I took over first duty, while the Skipper, Moffatt, and Kerr went to sleep. I went along to report to Major Milnes at HQ – along the trench. By this time we were tired out. It had been a trying experience, the Preface to our Book so to speak.

01.08.16   When day broke we realised our real position. It was a perfect shambles. There had been
Minden   heavy fighting here only a few days before, and it had been impossible to clear the place
Day[293]

up. Rifles, equipment, steel helmets, Machine Guns, bombs, spades, Lewis Guns, magazines – oh, everything, which only a few days previously had been used; now it was half-buried. Many poor fellows were still unburied. The smell was awful. Never before had I really realised what war – modern civilised war! – really meant. But I knew now!

Still here we were – and it was considered a "good" place. Could it be possible there was anywhere worse? It seemed scarcely credible.

---

[293] See the footnote to the diary entry for 1st August 1914.

The Skipper asked me to see to the men's rations. I soon got the cooks busy making tea and cooking bacon – but what a place! But the fellows were more than ready, and enjoyed their breakfast even in this place!

The Skipper and I then had a walk round – everywhere was the same – Boche and British equipment etc. all over the place.

We came across a huge sand bag Strong Point, and found about 60 men of the Notts and Derby Bantams 25th Division. They had been there five days without food or water, and with no orders what to do. They were nearly mad. We immediately sent word to our Brigade about this party, the remains of a Battalion under one officer. We managed to get them some rations from our men, and then they started off back to find their Division. They were a sorry party.

At about 11 o'clock we received orders to occupy a Reserve trench near the Southern edge of Trônes Wood, looking across Death Valley to Maltz Horn Farm Ridge.

"Y" Company occupied a trench in front of ours. "X" Company were on our left, and "W" Company were in Support at Battalion HQ, still in the sunken road.

It was a glorious morning, hot and sunny – but it didn't help matters. We had no cover and the ground was foul and smelt abominably. We occupied this trench at about 7.00am, and were heavily shelled by 5.9 inch shells soon after occupying it.

We ordered our men to clean rifles and Small Arms Ammunition. At about 10.00am Cecil Moffatt was walking down the trench when the rifle of one of the men – Private "X" – went off accidentally, and the bullet hit Moffatt. I rushed down to do what I could. He was wonderfully brave about it – but in great agony – Poor Cecil – I feared from the first that it would be fatal. I sent him off on a stretcher with Howarth and Turner. Then I went off to "X" Company to tell Leslie, his brother. We wasted no time and caught the stretcher up at the Aid Post, where Moffatt had had his wound dressed – he was quite conscious and quite cheerful. Just as they carried him off to the next collecting station Major Milnes arrived with our Minden Roses, and Cecil was very pleased to take one along with him. Poor fellow. His last words to me were, "I say Skipper – don't let anything happen to "X", it was quite an accident."[294] He reached Corbie Hospital but died the same night.[295]

---

[294] We do not know what, if any, punishment the man who accidentally shot Cecil Moffatt received.

[295] 2nd Lieutenant Cecil Henry Moffatt was the son of George and Georgina Ellen Moffatt. Cecil and his older brother, Leslie, were born in Ireland, but the family later moved to Eccles, Manchester. Both boys went to the Robert Smyth School, Market Harborough, and both initially enlisted with the Manchester Regiment, 16th (1st City) Battalion as privates, before obtaining commissions in the 13th (Reserve) Battalion of the Lancashire Fusiliers. Norman says that the brothers joined the 2/5th Lancashire Fusiliers in France on 23rd August 1915, but it is more likely that it was 11th November 1915, as this is the date of entry into France given on his brother's medal index card. Cecil was found to be "quite good" at football (see the diary entry for 29th November to 5th December 1915), and is mentioned frequently in the context of patrols in No Man's Land, for example on 24th December 1915, 19th March, 1st May, 26th to 30th May (on page 184), and 18th June 1916. In the diary entry for the last date Norman says: "He was a tower of strength to me, a real spark of life and cheer to all of us, absolutely loved by the men, always so cheerful and willing, never grumbling, no matter what unpleasant job he was detailed to do. He had a very funny way of saying, 'Jolly little war this, ain't it?'" He is mentioned specifically for being "cheery" on two other occasions, 25th December 1915 and 25th July 1916. There is a photograph of him on page 232. The Commonwealth War Graves Commission's records give his date at death as 20, which is correct, as his registered birth date is 1 August 1896. However, in his attestation on enlistment on 31st August 1914 he stated his age as 19 years 1 month, in his application for a commission he gave his date of birth as 1st August 1895, and Norman says that he died on his 21st birthday; he may have falsified his age because for privates the minimum age for overseas service, and therefore the advertised minimum age for recruitment into the Battalions formed in 1914, was 19. He is buried at La Neuville British Cemetery, Corbie, reference I.E.46. Norman went through Corbie with the 1/5th Lancashire Fusiliers on 31st July 1917, a year after his death, and his diary entry for that day remembers that his friend was buried there. See also Obituaries.

Cecil Moffatt was one of the bravest, most cheerful, unselfish fellows I ever knew. We had been great pals. His men loved him – we all did. He was a very capable officer. It seemed awful for him to go in this way, and on his 21st birthday. But he will never be forgotten by those of us who have been more fortunate.

But we had our job to do. I went back to the Company, and had to take a party of 200 into Trônes Wood to bury the dead. It was an awful sight, thousands of dead. Many had been there 10 days in hot sun – it is too dreadful, too gruesome, to describe. It seemed a hopeless task to try to identify them before burial. For many it was impossible – they weren't men any more. British and Boche were killed together. We even had to wear our Gas masks to try to breathe more or less fresh air. After six hours' work we were relieved; then back to our littered shambles of a home in the trench. We just lay down on the floor or fire step and tried to sleep.

It was about 6.00pm. All our men tried to sleep, and we were ready. At 9.00pm we stood to for half an hour, and then had an hour's sleep until 10.00pm, when we had to set to work on our trench.

The Boche shelled us heavily until 11.15pm, then rations and our mail came up. At 11.30pm the Skipper told me to try to have a sleep. I was dog tired and feeling a bit rotten after the Burial Work.

British Graves at Trônes Wood

At 12.30am 2nd Lieutenant Forrester came to me, and reported that he was going to make a barbed wire barricade across the road. I was then half asleep on the fire step, and promised to go down to see the job in about an hour. About 20 minutes later the Boche put down a shell barrage of small shells which went off with a peculiar puff, but very little detonation. I immediately suspected gas shells – although I had never heard them before. I went to one which had burst and at once detected that sweet sickly almond smell of Prussic or Phosgenic Acid. At once I rushed down the Line and passed the order for Gas helmets to be worn at once. I warned "Y" Company and "X" Company, and sent a runner to HQ to warn them and "W" Company.

Ashton accompanied me down the Line, and it was fortunate that he did, for at one point a shell burst on the parapet level with me, blew in the trench, and half buried me, so that my arms were pinned. I had been so keen on warning the men of the gas that I hadn't got my own helmet on, and I couldn't get at it. The shell was a gas shell. Ashton at once saw my position, managed to get my helmet from its satchel (for it was the PHG[296] Type – Glass Goggles with Sponge) and put it on for me, then he got a spade and dug me out.[xxiv] Ashton was a marvel, always with me at the critical moments. Then I thought of Forrester and his party, and set off to find him. I found the party but no Forrester. What could have happened? We searched all the ground but couldn't find him, even when it came light later the same day.

---

[296] A refinement on the Phenate-hexamine (PH) Helmet mentioned in the diary entry for 26th June 1916 om page 197.

02.08.16   We searched again for Forrester, but without success. He was reported missing. I wrote to his people. Then, 10 days later, I had a letter from Forrester from Margate. He had been sent there, but remembered nothing until he was told he was at Margate. He was slightly gassed and shell shocked.[297]

In addition we had several men wounded from being hit, and one or two had very bad shell shock.

It was some spot this Trench.

During the morning Private Harrison, one of our Signallers, was buried while asleep – a shell blew the trench in. We managed to dig him out, and luckily he was none the worse, although badly shaken; but after a short rest he carried on with his duty.

Nothing further of interest happened during the day, except the Boche gave us intermittent strafes with "Black Marias", "Coal Boxes"[298] and other pleasant goods from German Munition Works.

The Battalion had now entered a period that for work and thrills easily surpassed anything yet experienced. Here we were right in the middle of a district which was being talked about all over the world; we all felt with pride that the 2/5th Lancashire Fusiliers should be able to do our bit, even if we were just a little bit over anxious that the men should give a good account of themselves. Skipper and I had every confidence in our original men of "Z" Company – men we knew in every way – but it was the new draft, untried, some never having been in action before, that we worried about. It was the biggest thing we had ever been ordered to do. We all had that old Regimental Spirit – the Spirit of Minden and the XXth,[299] and we were still wearing our Roses. Could we but wear them as historically as those before us had done!

On the afternoon of August 2nd I went up with the Skipper from our Reserve Trenches to the Front Line to reconnoitre, prior to taking over the next day. We went via Dead Horse Corner (so called because a poor beast lay on that cross roads – he had been hit by a shell, and there had been no time to bury him). We went up the track through the valley – called Death Valley – leading up to Trônes Wood. It was only too correctly named. There was no doubt which way led up to the trenches – such as they were. Poor fellows – scarcely recognisable as human beings in many cases. Even the RAMC bearer parties had been killed in their attempts to carry down some wounded fellow, but were caught in the barrage. Stretchers were scattered all over the ground.

The Boche, of course, knew every inch of this ground – he had lived here for two years; consequently he had all the approaches absolutely gauged almost to an inch.

We got up to the sunken road running from Maricourt to Guillemont, along the Southern edge of Trônes Wood. The trenches were about 50 to 100 yards from the Eastern side of the wood, and facing Guillemont, which lay about 800 yards further East.

The 1/8th Liverpool Irish were holding this Line, running out to Maltz Horn Farm and Arrow Head Copse.

Eventually we found "D" Company of the 1/8th Liverpool Irish, with Joe Chamberlain, Johnny Gordon, Ward, and Mahon. They were very cheery, but rather weary. The Skipper and I wasted no time in getting the information we wanted. We had no desire to remain in this place any longer than was absolutely necessary. Luckily the evening Hates hadn't

---

[297] Forrester had joined the 2/5th Lancashire Fusiliers in France on 19th June 1916 – see the diary entry for that date.
[298] See footnote 136 and 137 on page 105.
[299] See the footnote to the diary entry for 1st August 1914.

started, so we got through without much excitement. On our return journey the Boche started to shell the valley again so we made a detour through the wood. The Skipper hadn't been in before and wanted to see it – I warned him that it wasn't the ideal spot to go back by, but we went. We saw several Boche Machine Gun Posts and Observation Posts, which our people had recently captured. The Boche Gunners were undoubtedly very brave. They got into these concrete gun emplacements and held on to the last, until they were either killed or captured – thus helping their comrades to get away. They certainly appreciated the full value of rear guard action for delaying their enemy – and did it very efficiently.

**Right: German Communication Trench,
        Death Valley, damaged by shell fire
Below: German gun emplacement**

The emplacements were wonderfully sited to get the maximum field of fire and fire effect.
It was marvellous how our shells had missed some of these Posts, and what a small amount of damage they mostly suffered, even by a direct hit.
Skipper and I then crossed near Bernafay Wood and across some old German Trenches. They weren't really old, for the Boche had only been driven out a few days previously.
Late that evening we received our Operation Orders to relieve the 1/8th Liverpool Irish in the Front Line, Left Sector, directly in front of Trônes Wood. It was intended to make an attack any day on the village of Guillemont. In view of this an Assembly Trench had been dug by the 1/5th Loyal North Lancashires, in front of our present Line and about 400 yards in advance in No Man's Land. The <u>exact</u> Line that the Boche held was unknown.
This Assembly Trench was to be occupied on relief by us and held at all costs. Just "Z" Company's luck – this trench happened to be in front of our particular bit of Line. So we were detailed to find the necessary garrison for it, to consist of Bombing Parties and Lewis Guns; two Lewis Gun teams – each comprising one NCO with six men – and two Bombing Parties of six men each, who, of course, were to act as riflemen also. The scheme was that these men under one officer should form Advanced Posts in front of our main Line. If attacked their orders were to hold on at all costs to this trench – but on no account to withdraw. Some order! Some job! Who was the officer to be!
Kenders was the only experienced officer besides the Skipper and myself. Packman and Armstrong had had very little experience in the Line and it was a very important job.

Kenders' platoon had to guard the railway line on our left.

The Skipper, of course, couldn't go as he was OC of the Company. So I was detailed.

We made our plans on the night of August 2nd. I picked my men, and told them what their work would be. They were all as keen as mustard, and thought it the Pick of the Show. I'm afraid <u>they</u> didn't quite appreciate the position as I did. To be candid I wasn't very up of it, but orders are orders.

The night of August 2nd was rather a breezy

"Kender's bit"

TRÔNES WOOD.   MACHINE-GUN BLOCKHOUSE.

time. There was heavy shelling all night. In fact it got beyond a joke, and I simply longed for the whole thing to cease, if only for a minute or two, just to give my ears a rest. We got most of it on our Support Line, but were fortunate in not having many casualties.

03.08.16   At daybreak on August 3rd, things had quietened down – but we had had a rough night and several fellows went out of their minds. This is worse than a wounded man – you can do nothing for them. One or two people who should have had more sense scarcely helped matters, and did very little to steady the men, who were really fine. Waterhouse as usual was a perfect hero, but he was beginning to show signs of the strain and responsibility. It is no easy task commanding a Company under Battle Conditions. But the Skipper had a marvellous effect on all of us – his very presence even without a word bucked us up. I really believe he never once thought of himself all the time – it was always the men.

The day passed quietly.

The other Companies were in good form. Gray, Rothband, Duckworth (who had rejoined from the Army School), Moffatt S.L., and Cooper were all as merry as could be.

At about 7.00pm we made our final preparations to move up. It wasn't far from Support but the gamble was whether you struck a quiet period to go through Death Valley. At 8.30pm the Battalion moved off by companies. We followed "X" Company, all moving with distances between platoons.

The Skipper and I decided to move our fellows in platoons in single file. When we started off all was quite peaceful, with not a shell – a glorious evening. But the Boche was far too quiet – it was a bad sign, and a certain indication of calm before a storm.

We had scarcely gone 1000 yards when, in the distance, we heard the Boom, Boom, Boom, Boom in rapid succession of German Guns followed almost immediately by the whizz of shells overhead. Whizz Bang! Whizz Bang!

Had the Hun spotted us? He must have done, for we were right in the thick of a heavy shrapnel barrage. The shells were bursting in the air in front of us, about 50 feet up, and all the way up the valley, spreading their death-dealing cone of shrapnel around us. Kicking up the dust! Whizzing past our heads.

The range was perfect – too perfect to be comfortable.

Ken asked me (for we were leading the Company), "What shall we do, take cover or risk?" I was all in favour of pushing on for all we were worth. To lie down there was simply to remain in the danger zone, but by pushing on we might get out of the effective zone, especially as there appeared to be fewer shells further up the valley.

So we just had a word with the men to steady them up a bit – they were a bit inclined to panic at first – and we reached the top of the valley, where we found "X" Company in the sunken road taking cover. I checked off "Z" Company, and found that we had only two casualties, but both fellows were still with us carrying on.

The worst was to come. The Boche now dropped a heavy barrage on our Front Line, Communication Trenches and on our poor old sunken road. It was a terrifically heavy strafe. Each shell as it burst literally lifted the earth bodily – threw it into the air, and covered us with mud and smoke.

What was happening? Were the Boche attacking, or was it just his usual Evening Hymn of Hate? We got our fellows under cover, and I decided to go over to the Front Line to find out what was the cause of all the bother. No Communication Trenches for me – I decided across the open was safer. I climbed up the bank of the road, and then I realised that I was in the open. It was as if the Devil and all his angels had let loose. Every rifle and Machine Gun in France seemed to have suddenly gone mad. Bullets were whizzing about like rain.[xxv]

I didn't half do the hundred in good time across to the Front Line. There I met Chamberlain. I could hardly speak after the run and excitement. Eventually I found out that the Boche had tried to leave his trenches and had got across No Man's Land, but we had stopped him – though a few Boche had actually reached our Line – never to return again. I asked Chamberlain if he wanted any help, as "Z" Company were just behind. "Yes! Good, old chap. I know, I'll take my Company over the top and settle the beggars with the bayonet. When I clear, you come into this trench and hold it."

By the time all was arranged the 1/8th Liverpool Irish – always ready for a fight – had taken off their coats, so as to be able to move better. They were determined to do as many Boche in as possible – and they did. I went back to tell the Skipper, and we moved at once to occupy our trench. We moved by the Communication Trench – but it was almost impassable. It was littered with equipment, telephone wires, and dead – you couldn't help treading on the poor fellows. But there is very little time for sentiment in the heat of an action.

It's too true when you have time to think of it – *"What's a soldier, or even several soldiers? Nothing, and less than nothing in the whole crowd, so we see ourselves lost, drowned, killed, like the few drops of blood that we are, amongst all this flood of men and things."* (Henri Barbusse)

At last we got our fellows in position. The Irish came back, having caught the enemy in the open, and inflicted heavy casualties on them. They only brought back a few prisoners, and reported that the Boche had retired beyond the Line of the new advanced trench. The intensity of shell fire had decreased, so I collected my party for the Advanced Posts.

We didn't know where the exact Line we were to go to was, except that it was somewhere in the direction of the Boche. Neither did we know whether the Huns had really retired, or whether they were still lurking about in shell holes. This all remained to be seen.

I decided to take out a reconnoitring patrol before the main party, so that if we got collared we should only lose a few men and myself. The Skipper gave me a "Cheery Oh!" as we left the trench, and went down the sunken road leading to Guillemont. We had a barrier across this road, and a slightly advanced Lewis Gun and Bombing Post. We climbed over this – then the feeling of doubt – alertness – came. Lance Corporal Sellers and I led the party, with a man on the top of the road. I kept to the side of the road, as the Boche had a Machine Gun trained on it. There were German dug outs dug deep into the bank on either side –

every little niche and crevice seemed to hold a Boche waiting for us. It was pitch black. About 100 yards along we left the road, and went into No Man's Land. It was one mass of shell holes, the ground simply torn up alternately into craters and mounds. Progress was slow, the blackness seemed impenetrable, and you imagined that you could see figures in the darkness. We crawled on our hands and knees – stopping quickly, instinctively, when the Boche put up a flare light. There wasn't much rifle fire, but occasionally a Boche Machine Gun swept the ground. We were relieved to hear this, as it was a good indication that all his men had returned. It seemed miles to that trench, and, when we struck it, it was hardly a trench – it had been taped out, and only just started, so that, even at the deepest place, it was only 2 feet deep, and in many places only a few inches. We traced its entire length for about 600 yards from the Guillemont Road down to the railway, and I selected the positions at the same time for my Sentry Posts. I then decided to try to locate the Boche, but, after half an hour of crawling, I had no information, except that I heard voices about 200 yards away. I returned to the main Line, collected my party, reported to Waterhouse, and then proceeded to occupy the advanced trench. It was now 12.30 midnight.

04.08.16
and
05.08.16

Rations had not arrived, so we had to go without.

My orders were:

1. We were to hold the advanced trench at all costs. This meant that, if the Boche attacked my little band, we were to hold the "Hosts of the Philistines", and were not to withdraw; in fact, we were told to die if necessary.
2. We were to stay out all night and through the next day, and, if possible, Waterhouse would relieve us on the night of August 4th.
3. I was to report every hour during the night to the Skipper as OC of "Z" Company.
4. As the position was secret, during the day we were to keep out of sight, and ensure that no movement was detected.

Imagine lying in a shallow trench between the two Lines – ours and that of the Boche – and between two barrages of shells if firing started – from daybreak at 4.00am until 8.00pm, 16 hours.

I posted my four Group Posts; one on the road, within 20 yards of the road, so that the road, and also the sloping ground to the Boche, was covered by Lewis Gun fire; my Left Post near the railway; and two Posts in between, separated by about 200 yards.

"Z" Company's forward trench

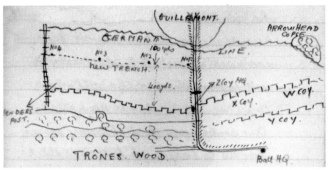

My next move was to really decide where the Boche was, so I took out a small patrol, three men and myself, and carefully reconnoitred the ground in front. I nearly ran into a German Post – I just heard a man cough in time. We lay <u>very</u> flat, and several shots whizzed over us, but did no damage.[xxvi] We located about six similar enemy advanced Posts. By misfortune we got between two of them, and struck the Boche wire, crawled along it, and, by the amount of talking, decided that this was his main Line of Defence – and he was there in considerable numbers, too. But we were few, and we weren't out to fight, only to get information in the orthodox manner – to see without being seen. Our ambitions didn't carry so far as to try to take the Boche trench single-handed, although we had heard stories of men capturing 40 Boche alone. Then I suppose they wakened up!

It was a useful two hours' work. We got back to our isolated trench at about 3.00am. I wanted to report my information to Waterhouse, and was undecided whether to go back or not. But my report was very important, as the Boche's dispositions scarcely indicated "Attack", so I decided that I would go back, and went for all I was worth, handing over the Posts to Sergeant Watts.

Waterhouse was very bucked with our little job of work. I was also quite pleased as my party's rations and water had come up.

Just as I was leaving the Skipper said, "Oh, Jimmy, I've some good news for you. One of the prisoners taken by the Irish reports that the Boche intend to attack on that Front at dawn – the attack is to be preceded by a heavy bombardment and gas shells are to be used. He thought that they would attack at 5.00am, but, when he came away, final orders had not been issued by the Germans."

"In that case, Skipper, I'd better be off back to my lads. Well, Goodbye, Skipper, and jolly good luck if I don't see you again."

"Same to you, old man – the very best, I feel quite safe here with your little crowd in front of us."

"Goodbye, Skipper!"

I came to the conclusion that we were for it before the sun shone again. But it's no use getting excited. I arrived back at my Line, went quickly round my Posts, warned them of the attack, and gave them my final order, "Now then, you fellows; if I can't get round again before the devils come, remember it's 'Fight to the last man'. Good luck!!"

To add to my troubles, when I got to Lance Corporal Dawson, manning my Nº 1 Lewis Gun Post near the road, he reported that he had heard someone on the road. With a thumping heart like a Fog Siren – my head just holding beads of perspiration – I took Private Smith (Pester). Ashton, my servant, wanted to come too but I wouldn't let him. We got on the road, but couldn't hear anybody; then, just on my right, I saw a figure dart into a dug out entrance. Covering him with my revolver, and Smith with a bayonet and a bomb, we rushed the entrance.[xxvii] A Boche rushed out too – I fired somewhere, at anything – a curse followed, and he fell. I had got him in the neck.[300] Smith heaved his bomb into the entrance to make sure if any others were there. The commotion, of course, drew fire from the Boche. Smith and I lay flat in the road for about 10 minutes before returning to our Post (my HQ, with Nº 2 Post, a rifle Post).

It was now 4.00am, and it had been an exciting few minutes. I was jolly glad to be able to

---

[300] This is the second of two occasions in the diary when Norman describes firing directly at an individual and either wounding, or possibly – probably, in this case, as Norman states, presumably on the basis of having ascertained the same, that he had *"got him in the neck"* – killing him. Although Norman here describes his shot as being fired *"somewhere, at anything"*, he must in fact have been a reasonable shot, as his diary entry for 3rd July 1917 records that he tied first with George Horridge in a revolver competition, winning 20 francs. He was also responsible for Musketry training in Bury (see the diary entries for 19th October 1914 and 11th January to 4th April 1915). See also the diary entry for 14th to 19th August 1915 on page 81.

sit down – in fact, I lay down in the trench, and was jolly glad of my brandy flask.

Would the Boche attack? It was like waiting to be hanged. 50 minutes, 40 minutes, 30 minutes, 4.40am, 4.45am. It was now getting fairly light. We could see the village of Guillemont – the battered railway trucks on the siding in the Station, and the new earth of the Boche Line only 100 yards to our direct front.

At 4.45am the Boche Guns started, but at first the shells went well over away back – "Oh, it's alright, those are going well back – on the Batteries probably." Then he started on our Front Line with 5.9 inch, 4.2 inch, 77mm – there scarcely seemed room for them all. Then came a rapid fire of small shells – a peculiar phew-phew-phew!!!! hundreds of them – gas shells. We got our Gas helmets ready.

So far we were alright – very excited watching our front – waiting for the Boche. The Skipper had remembered us, and sent out thousands of rounds of Small Arms Ammunition. 4.50am … 4.55am … five minutes more. Then our guns started in real earnest. We had begun to think that they would never reply. But not half! The Boche Front Line, the Reserve Line, oh, and every Line and in between as well. The Row was terrific – and here we were lying waiting, in between the two barrages, not able to see the Boche Line or our own.

5.00am. Would the Boche come over through that awful fire? The tension was awful – my head nearly burst with a mixture of Fear, and – well – Fear again.

We felt we should be killed by our own shells if the Boche didn't do it.[xxviii] It was awful – unbearable – I prayed for anything to happen to get out of it. But I managed to pull myself together – by saying, "Damn it, you aren't the only one in it, man!"

By 7.00am it was all quiet again except for occasional shells. The Sun came out.

It seemed weeks since the night before at 8.30pm.

Several of my fellows were wounded, but they couldn't be sent back – our orders were: "No movement by day". It seemed awful to have those fellows there – moaning, and even asking to be put out of their misery.

By noon the sun was just pouring down on us. We daren't even sit up – you had to roll over to change your position. We had drunk our water, such as it was, brought up in petrol tins, and tasting of petrol and chloride of lime. My brandy was finished – I couldn't refuse Private Neil, who was hit in the head – even though I knew it was a bad thing.

One or two men wanted to get up and go – but they <u>didn't</u>!

At about 4.30pm in the afternoon our guns opened fire, presumably on the Boche, but their range was short, and we got the full benefit.[xxix] Luckily we had no more casualties – but it was hellish and nothing less.

We were glad to see the evening clouds approaching, and, when it was dark enough, at about 8.30pm, we got up and stretched our legs – but they hardly would stretch.

I sent a runner to the Skipper for stretcher bearers, and asked him to relieve my men. He did, and weren't we thankful. Another officer came out, Lieutenant "X". I showed him my Posts and handed over. He was anything but keen on his job – and I didn't blame him; I'd had enough – too much.

We got back to the main Line, and I posted the men to their platoons again. I had a chat with the Skipper – but I couldn't say much. I was done – the reaction came – the Skipper made me lie down in the trench, and gave me a stiff brandy, and I fell asleep – but only for an hour or so. The old Hun wakened me with his shells. Soon afterwards a message came from Mr "X": "Can I come and see you?" Skipper replied, "Yes."

"X" came. He'd had enough already. It was no use sending him back. What was to be done? Eventually I decided that I would go out again, after I'd had a rest and some food – although the Skipper was very much against it. However, I pulled my socks up, and by about midnight I felt heaps better.

I learnt that 2nd Lieutenant E.H. Fryer, our Sniper Officer, had been killed while observing at Arrow Head Copse. His loss was deeply felt by all of us.[301]

2nd Lieutenant A.D.G.O. Kerr, while setting a fine example of courage, was killed by the same sniper as were several of the men.[302] "W" Company had had a very rough day. So also had "X" Company. Gray, though wounded, carried on for some time but eventually had to go down. Rothband left for Hospital,[303] and Cooper got a slight flesh wound but remained on duty.

2nd Lieutenant S.L. Moffatt had also had an exciting experience with a fighting patrol at Arrow Head Copse, and had the satisfaction of killing several Boche. About 30 Boche had come out to meet him, but with a Lewis Gun and rapid rifle fire his small patrol accounted for most of the Boche party – the remainder rushing off for their lives. This little success was a great morale raiser after spending all day being shelled by an unseen enemy, or, as one fellow said, "I wish I could get at yon feller who fires yon gun, I'll bet he's only a little un."

At about midnight on August 4th, a party of 250 1/5th Royal Lancasters came up to deepen the advanced trench. Soon after we got to work the Boche evidently spotted us and shelled us heavily. Work had to cease – but the Royal Lancasters had about 50 casualties in my little Line. There was almost panic – however we got the wounded away, and I settled down with my new party to another all night and day vigil.

Lieutenant Colonel Bridgewater was wounded, but insisted on remaining on duty. However, he eventually had to go down before morning. Major H.N. Milnes took over command. If anything, we had rather a better time in the advanced trench this night, and all through the day of August 5th, even though we had heavy shelling all day and most of the night. But it wasn't pleasant, and, by the night of August 5th, I was really feeling about ready to die. We were relieved at 9.30pm. Armstrong simply had to relieve me. Packman really wasn't fit. In fact, it was certain he ought to go to Hospital.

Skipper was jolly good when I was relieved – he simply made me have a sleep – but he was just as tired and exhausted as I was. He seemed very anxious and worried – the men were certainly feeling the strain.

06.08.16   It was a glorious morning, accompanied by heavy shelling. The Boche Balloons were up,

---

[301] Lieutenant Eric Hamilton Fryer died on 3rd August 1916, and is commemorated at the Thiepval Memorial, Pier and Face 3C and 3D. Norman refers to him here as a 2nd lieutenant, but on page 196 he refers to him as a lieutenant, as do the Commonwealth War Graves Commission's records. The Battalion War Diary states that he joined the 2/5th Lancashire Fusiliers in France as a 2nd lieutenant on 23rd August 1915.

[302] 2nd Lieutenant Arthur Douglas Garnett Odell Kerr of the 3/10th Middlesex Regiment, the son of Douglas Odell Kerr of Streatham, London, and the late Charlotte Francis Arthur Kerr, was educated at Uppingham School, and was a lance corporal in the London Rifle Brigade before becoming an officer in the Middlesex Regiment. According to the Battalion War Diary he joined the 2/5th Lancashire Fusiliers in France on 27th May 1916. He died on 3rd August 1916, aged 21, and is commemorated at the Thiepval Memorial, Pier and Face 12D and 13B. The Commonwealth War Graves Commission's records state (wrongly) that he was attached to the 1/5th Lancashire Fusiliers.

[303] Lieutenant B.H. Rothband was with "C" Company of the 2/5th Lancashire Fusiliers when they first landed in France on 3rd May 1915, the first mention of him in the diary. This is the last mention of him until 18th February 1917, when Norman went to Fountains Abbey with him while they were both on Home Service at Ripon. The Battalion War Diary states that he left the field owing to shell shock. A diary entry for 5th August 1917 is to the effect that he had to revert to Lieutenant from temporary Captain. His cousin, Percy Rothband, managed the recreational facilities at Gouy (see the diary entry for 12th March 1916).

and so were ours.

I added or – rather deducted – one more life from my "nine cat's lives".[xxx]

The Skipper and I were in a little cut out in the trench. The Boche dropped Two Beauties – 5.9 inch – just in front, which smothered us with earth, and fairly shook the place. Then the next two dropped over. "Come on, Skipper, the old Hun has our home taped." We cleared the trench for about 30 yards, somehow feeling that the next shell would be a direct hit. It was! It dropped right on the very cut out that we had been in. Then we couldn't find Richardson (the Skipper's servant) or Spencer. No one seemed to have seen them until Wilde[304] (Moffatt's servant) said, "I saw them going into your hole soon after you left."

The Skipper, Wilde and I started to dig. Yes! too true, they had been there a few seconds before, but – in a flash – they were gone for ever.

It was a rotten business getting their bodies out, but we did. Poor Ken – he was heart-broken. They really had been splendid fellows.[305]

Then we got orders to be relieved in the afternoon by the 1/9th King's Liverpool Regiment. The 1/9th King's Liverpool Regiment packed the Communication Trench. The Skipper arranged with me to lead out the Company. I started. The trench was foolishly packed. We had a little exposed stretch to cross, and scarcely had I got up on to this part than I heard two shells coming over. They burst; I could see nothing – it was pitch dark. Bits – lumps of earth, stone, and shell – came down. I was blown off my feet, about 15 yards. When I picked myself up – dazed – I realised that several men must be killed. There were about 15 killed. Sergeant Catterall and Private Wright,[306] who were directly behind me, were never seen again. How on earth I escaped is nothing short of a miracle.[xxxi] We pushed on to try to clear the trench before another came – but it did – something whizzed past my head – it was a man's foot – bootless and sockless. The test of nerves was awful – but I pushed on and collected my men near Battalion HQ. I found about 40 men – but no Skipper. I felt sure that he was killed. However, I decided that I must get my live men away to the old Support Trench in the sunken road near Bernafay Wood and the Briqueterie. I took up my dispositions there, and, leaving Kenders in command, went back to find the Skipper. I met him with the rest of the Company coming down Death Valley looking weary but calm, and as trim as if nothing had happened. That man was a marvel – I was shivering like a leaf – Poor old Skipper, when he met me he burst out crying, "My God, boy, I'm glad to see you – I was certain you were killed with the rest." I was a mess too, my tunic was simply covered at the back with blood. The Skipper insisted that I was hit – but I wasn't; and why is an unanswerable question.

We had now had six days of continuous heavy shelling – practically no sleep – living in filth – polluted ground – the most awful smells of decomposition. We were physically and mentally weary. We had been brought into Reserve, still under shell fire, to get a rest! So it was called, preparatory to attack.

---

[304] Norman also spells the name "Wild".

[305] Private Thomas Richardson, Service no 2959, and Private James Spencer, Service no 2984, are commemorated at the Thiepval Memorial, Pier and Face 3C and 3D. Private J. Spencer's name can be seen in the photograph on the back cover of this book.

[306] Lance Sergeant Richard Catterall, Service no 200756, and Private John Wright, Service no 3158, husband of Ellen Wright of Radcliffe, Manchester (who was aged 41 when he died) are commemorated at the Thiepval Memorial, Pier and Face 3C and 3D. Private J. Wright's name can be seen in the photograph on the back cover of this book.

During the night of August 6th the Boche gave us a very rough time with heavy shells – we had several casualties and men buried by shells blowing in the trench.

We lost one of our stretcher bearers, Private A. Howarth – quite a boy but he had been very good, working hard, fearing nothing – but the strain was too much, and it wasn't surprising.[307] Lieutenant J.B. Packman also got very nervy and had to go to Hospital.

Most of us were feeling nervy, very much so, but we couldn't all go away – someone had to pull themselves together; but it was easy enough to let one's feelings get the upper hand – if you gave way to them in the least.

We moved back to a Strong Point at the Briqueterie, where the Company was occupying an old German redoubt. It was a wonderful place, made of sand bags and concrete. It had originally been made in the Boche Second Line to defend the high ground at Bernafay and Trônes Wood – a wonderful position. It was a maze of trenches, with breastworks 10 feet deep with at least 20 Machine Gun Positions.

The men were simply told to go to sleep.

At about 8.30pm I was sent for to go to HQ. On reporting there, I found Captain Teale of the Lincoln Regiment, our Staff Captain. An officer was required to go along with him to direct Ammunition, Bomb, Water, and Ration Dumps behind the Front Line, ready for the Show. Noton should have gone; he had returned to us about three weeks earlier, after proceeding to Hospital in January 1916 with a nervous breakdown, but he wasn't really fit to come out again. He was a stout fellow, and had done very good work with us, but the last few days had been too much.[308] I suggested that I went with Teale as I had nothing special to do, though I needed a rest very badly.

We started out, and about 40 wagons came up, full of Small Arms Ammunition, bombs and grenades. We had about 800 men working with us. Manse Evans also had a party up the Line, some from "Y", "X", and "Z" Companies.

We had a <u>very</u> unpleasant time unloading the stores – the Boche shelled all the time, and we had no cover.[xxxii] But it had to be done. One huge dump, containing 20,000 rounds of Small Arms Ammunition, 5,000 bombs, 2,000 grenades, rockets, bully beef, and biscuits, was made at the top of Death Valley. It struck me as foolish, but it was in Divisional Operation Orders to do it.

---

[307] Norman makes it clear that Private Howarth – in common with many others during this period – suffered mental, rather than physical, incapacity. See the diary entry for 1st May 1916 for an earlier example of him in action under difficult circumstances.

[308] This is the last time that Lieutenant H.H. Noton (also referred to in the original diary as H.N. Noton) is mentioned in the diary until 20th March 1917 when he travelled on a train with Norman, who was then on his way from Ripon to Bury for a period of leave. He had been with "A" Company of the 2/5th Lancashire Fusiliers when they first landed in France on 3rd May 1915 (the first mention of him in the diary), and has featured frequently up until this point, inter alia as excelling on patrol in No Man's Land, and receiving the honour of the MC, "*the first honour to the Battalion*" (see the diary entries for 12th October to 4th November 1915 on page 105 and 16th to 27th November 1915 on page 125), until, as mentioned here, he unfortunately "*crocked up*" and was admitted to hospital on 5th January 1916, returning to Britain (see the diary entry for 23rd December 1915). He spoke good French (see the diary entry for 4th May 1915), participated in a fishing competition in June 1915 (see the diary entry for 6th to 12th June 1915), enjoyed riding (see the diary entry for 31st August 1915), and sang *The Mountains of Mourne* at a Battalion concert on 9th October 1915 at Aveluy (see the newspaper cutting relating to the diary entry for that date). There is a photograph of him at the end of this chapter which bears the caption "*Wounded Somme 1916*"; The word "*wounded*" is used here to indicate shell shock; the Battalion War Diary records that he was sent to hospital "*sick*" on 7th August 1916, It is not clear whether he ever returned to Active Service. Manse Evans also went to hospital "*sick*" the same day (see next page). According to the Battalion War Diary 2nd Lieutenant H.P. Griffiths, who had joined only on 16th July 1916, was also sent to hospital with "*shock*" on 9th August 1916, while 2nd Lieutenants Frew and Weller, who joined in April and June 1916 respectively, were also wounded – physically – on 5th and 9th August respectively.

The work was completed at about 3.30am. I got back to HQ at 4.00am. Evans was missing; I had spoken to him at 3.15am at the Dump – he said that he wasn't very fit, but I didn't think much about it. I wondered if he had been hit on his way down, so Ashton and I went up the Valley again to look for him, but couldn't find him. We called at several Aid Posts, but no trace. I couldn't do anything else – I was dead beat, scarcely able to stand up.[309] I reported to Major Milnes on my return. He ordered me to go down into his dug out and have a sleep. I was beyond food but I had some – the first real meal for over 24 hours.

The HQ dug out was a marvellous example of German Work and Engineering. It was a huge place, completely hidden below ground. You went down about 20 feet to the first deck, which consisted of a long passage with a dozen rooms opening off it, all furnished. The whole place was wood lined. There was a second deck, just the same, another 30 feet below, which is where I went. I got to bed at about 5.45am, and slept soundly until 9.00am. When I came up for breakfast they were surprised that I had slept – there had been a very heavy bombardment of 12 inch, 8 inch, and 5.9 inch shells for two hours. I never heard a sound. I went over to see how the boys were, and found Kerr. They had had a rotten time with a few casualties. Corporal Hitchon, a fine old soldier, had been killed.[310] He was wounded initially, and, as the bearer party were moving off, a shell struck the party and killed all five.

Captain Teale came along, and said, "Hello, Hall, heard the news? The Boche hit the dump we made last night, and the whole lot has gone up in smoke. Fancy all that work for nothing."

"Well, what's to be done, Sir?"

"Oh, repeat the programme tonight."

[Norman found time to write a letter to his father during this period (pictured right). The original date reads "Sunday 8.8.16". Norman has overwritten the first "8" with "5", but in fact Sunday was 6th August.

The text reads:

My Dear Father,

A very hurried note to let you know I am still pretty fit, but quite tired. I often wonder why I used to sleep for hours at night.

---

[309] This is the last mention of Manse Evans in the diary until 1917. He features later in the diary, initially in January 1917 as a Physical Training Instructor at Ripon, also going to Fountains Abbey with Norman on 18th February 1917, then as sharing a tent with Norman at Scarborough in May 1917; on 9th July 1918, when Norman is with the 1/5th Lancashire Fusiliers in France, there is a reference to "*Evans*" being on leave, which may again be Manse Evans. He had joined the Lancashire Fusiliers in Bury at the same time as Norman (see the diary entry for 4th September 1914), and was with "C" Company of the 2/5th Lancashire Fusiliers when they first landed in France on 3rd May 1915. He has been mentioned quite frequently in the earlier part of the diary, for example as being "*always prominent with very short socks*" on Rouse Parade at Southport (see the diary entry for 8th November to 13th December 1914), also as being involved in a raid on 31st December 1915, and he is one of those specifically commended for doing "*good work*" in the diary entry for 26th to 30th May 1916 on page 184. In the diary entry for 29th to 30th June 1916 he is referred to as being the Lewis Gun Officer.

[310] Corporal Fred Edwin Hitchon, Service no 3322, son of Joseph P. and Ann Hitchon, husband of Margaret of Edenfield, Manchester, was aged 48 when he died, and is buried at Delville Wood Cemetery, Longueval, reference XVI.E.10.

We are having glorious weather over here. So glad the wedding was such a success. I only wish I had been with you all.
Waterhouse is very fit but is looking older.
Please tell George and the others I will write when I have time.
My letters are very short and uninteresting.
However better short and sweet.
Sorry to hear about Alec. Roger seemed very worried when I saw him here.
Where are you going for holidays I wonder. You must all need a change.
Well it is just post time, so good luck,
Your loving son,
Norman]

07.08.16   We received orders that our Brigade would attack Guillemont Village at 6.00am on the morning of August 8th. The first wave was to be the 1/8th Liverpool Irish on the left, and the 1/4th King's Own Royal Lancasters on the right, with the 1/4th Loyal North Lancashires in Close Support, and the 2/5th Lancashire Fusiliers as Brigade Reserve.

The objective was to take Guillemont Village, push through, and occupy a Line on the Eastern side of the Bapaume to Bray road. Several Divisions had made an attempt to do this previously, but had failed. What were our chances with one Brigade, which was already weak after many casualties? But it was typical of the tactics on the Somme – a nibbling, useless waste of good troops; innumerable lives were wasted in this way.

We spent the day making our plans. I knew the ground pretty well up to the village. I had been over most of it during the past few days.

We got up two days' rations per man, extra Small Arms Ammunition – bombs and aeroplane flares – and, in fact, converted the men into human Christmas Trees. The amount of equipment etc. the higher authorities expected a man to carry, and to fight while carrying, was absolutely absurd.

I rested as much as possible during the day.

At about 7.00pm I started out with Staff Captain Teale to make the dumps up again. We had quite as bad a time as the previous night but finished half an hour earlier at 3.00am. I returned to Company HQ after reconnoitring the exact lines of approach for "Z" Company to reinforce up to Fagan Trench, Edwards Trench, Maltz Horn Trench, and Arrow Head Copse. Fagan Trench was blown in three times while I was up there;[xxiii] as Cecil Moffatt used to say – oh, it was a Jolly Little War!

When I returned I found that "Z" Company had moved into our old Support Trench – Chimpanzee Trench.

At about 3.20pm "X", "Y", and "W" Companies moved up to the Close Support area, under Major Barnsdale, Lieutenant Ronald, and Captain G. Gray[311] respectively. We were getting very short of officers. Major Milnes was in command of the Battalion.

---

[311] This is the last time that Captain G. Gray is mentioned in the diary until 23rd January 1918, when he joined the 1/5th Lancashire Fusiliers (with whom Norman then was) at Hinges. He was with "A" Company of the 2/5th Lancashire Fusiliers when they first landed in France on 3rd May 1915 (the first time he is mentioned in the diary), and up to this point has been mentioned frequently, for example, participating in two fishing competitions in June 1915 and winning the latter by catching 14 fish in three hours (see the diary entries for 6th to 12th and 21st to 30th June 1915), attending a rather wild dinner

LT H H NOTON. M.C. W COY Wounded Somme 1916

LT. G. GRAY. Wounded AUG3/16. TRONES WOOD Later joined 1/5". LF ab Hinges in Jan 1918. Wounded and a prisoner Mar 1918.

Top left: 2ⁿᵈ Lieutenant Cecil Henry Moffatt
Left: 2ⁿᵈ Lieutenant Stanley Leslie Moffatt
Above left: Lieutenant H.H. Noton
Above right: Lieutenant G. Gray

party on 8th October 1915 with Norman, Joe Hedley and two Scotsmen, going on leave at the same time as Norman in November 1915, looking for birds' eggs in Martinet Wood (see the diary entry for 18th June 1916), doing *"good work"* in patrolling No Man's Land (see the diary entry for 26th to 30th May 1915 on page 184) etc. He had become OC of "W" Company when Joe Hedley went as an Instructor at the Infantry Base Depot on 27th June 1916. In the diary entry for 4th to 5th August 1916 on page 227 it is reported that *"Gray, though wounded, carried on for some time but eventually had to go down."* It is not clear whether he carried on right through until this entry on 7th August 1916 or had tried to return, but it does seem to be clear that his wound eventually got the better of him and he returned to Britain, as he is not amongst the seven original officers who are reported as still with the 2/5th Lancashire Fusiliers in the diary entry for 21st to 26th August 1916, and the photograph above, and its caption, *"Wounded Aug 3/16 Trônes Wood"*, appears to confirm this. After joining the 1/5th Lancashire Fusiliers in January 1918 he was again wounded at Bucquoy on 25th March 1918, and became a Prisoner of War.

08.08.16   At 4.20am our guns opened the barrage with steady shelling.

The attack was timed to start at 4.20am, but was delayed slightly. "Z" Company were about three quarters of a mile back at this time.

Ken had gone to HQ to be on the spot with Major Milnes, so as to get clear instructions what to do. He left me in command of "Z" Company. At 6.00am he sent for me. I left Armstrong and Kerr in charge while I reported to HQ. While there I had a bit of breakfast – bacon and eggs. Splendid!

At 7.00am we moved up into the sunken road near Trônes Wood.[312] We had the 39th French Division on our right at Maltz Horn Ridge, and the 2nd Division on our left.

At this point, we heard that the Liverpool Irish had been successful on the left. A report from an aeroplane timed at 5.20am had recorded that British Troops were in Guillemont Station . The aeroplanes always observed attacks, and it was the job of those on the ground to site coloured ground flares as pre-arranged signals to show our positions to the aeroplanes.

However, the 1/4th King's Own Royal Lancasters on our right had suffered very severely from Machine Gun fire. They had been held up by some barbed wire which had not been blown away by the barrage, even though it had been terrific, almost awe-inspiring in its intensity, and one might with good reason have thought that nothing could have stood up against it, much less live through it.

Our three Companies, "W", "X", and "Y", had gone up to help them, and by 7.15am the 2/5th Lancashire Fusiliers had been absorbed into the fight. They had already suffered many Casualties. When the 2/5th Lancashire Fusiliers moved up into the fight at 7.15am, our place was taken by a Battalion of the 166th Infantry Brigade (we being the 164th Infantry Brigade). Meanwhile the attack on the right by the 165th Infantry Brigade had successfully overcome the difficulties on that side, and had then captured and consolidated its objectives. The right Company of the 1/6th King's Liverpool Regiment established touch with the French, according to programme.

On the left it was awful – it was extremely difficult to keep communication, and no one seemed to know anything, save that there were hundreds of killed and wounded.

The morning went on with continuous fighting, and by the afternoon the position was as follows:

Right Attack –	1/6th King's Liverpool Regiment	Succeeded, and consolidated.
Centre Attack –	1/4th King's Own Royal Lancasters	Couldn't get forward.
Left Attack (ours) –	1/8th Liverpool Regiment (Irish)	Succeeded to some extent, but the 1/8th Liverpool Regiment (Irish) were lost – cut off; they had gone into Guillemont Village but had not been seen since.

---

[312] For Trônes Wood and Guillemont see the maps/plans on pages 214, 224, 258 and 259.

During the afternoon the position was uncertain – a Bombing Party of three officers and about 50 men was organised to try to fight a way through, but it was hopeless, and half the men were lost doing it.[313] They had a rotten time and couldn't reach the Irish, nor get in touch with the 2nd Division on the left. Up to now only a few of the 1/8th Liverpool Irish who had been wounded early on could be accounted for, while the rest were missing.

The brave fight of the 1/8th Liverpool Irish will always be associated with this battle. It is difficult to make a clear account of the action, but it appears that, in the thick cloud of dust caused by an Easterly wind, and the smoke of the barrage, they lost direction and inclined too far North. Moreover, it is certain that some of the trenches captured by the 1/8th Liverpool Irish and the 1/4th King's Own Royal Lancasters (the advance party of the 164th Infantry Brigade), were not completely mopped up, as they were found to be full of Germans by the two Companies of the 1/4th Loyal North Lancashires who followed up to occupy them. Also, the Bombing Party ran into many Germans in the afternoon. The 1/4th Loyal North Lancashires made a gallant fight, and actually reached their objective in spite of withering Machine Gun fire from their right – i.e. from high mounds, and from Guillemont Village. However, only one or two men got back; the remaining survivors were captured and marched back next day up the slope to Ginchy in full view of our troops across the valley, who were powerless to help them.

At about 5.00pm we got back to our original starting off place, having lost many men and not gained an inch. But our shells must have given the Boche a heavy casualty list.

The Line to be held was re-adjusted so as to run from Arrow Head Copse on the Right to the

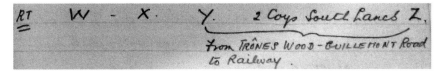

Guillemont to Longueval Railway on the Left. From right to left the Line was held as follows:

The trench we held was awfully packed, just like sardines – it was impossible to get along, except on the top.

The Skipper ordered me to stay with "Z" Company on the left, while he would remain near "Y" Company's HQ, where there was a telephone. We arranged to send reports to each other every half hour, mine to be sent on the hour, and his on the half hour.

"Y" Company only had two officers – Duckworth and Wolfe. We had three – Waterhouse, Armstrong and myself. Kenders had gone to "W" Company.

This night, August 8th, was one of the worst nights I ever spent in my life. Never before or since have I experienced such awful conditions. It had to be experienced to really realise that such conditions could be possible for civilised men to endure.

[313] In the original diary Norman uses the first person plural in describing the Bombing Party, but does not name anyone involved. A report in the Brigade War Diary shows that it was the other three Companies of the 2/5th Lancashire Fusiliers who were ordered to provide this Bombing Party, at about 1.45pm. The same report confirms that "Z" Company never at any time got beyond the Support Trench. Another report in the Brigade War Diary shows that 2nd Lieutenant John Alexander Hamilton Coats (Norman spells the name "Coates") of the 10th Battalion Royal Scots, formerly Chief Petty Officer with the Royal Naval Volunteer Reserve, who had arrived with the 2/5th Lancashire Fusiliers on 24th April 1916 according to the diary entry for that day, and was now attached to 164th Brigade Trench Mortar Battery, was killed early on 8th August 1916. The son of John T. Coats of Leith, he was aged 20 when he died, and is commemorated at the Thiepval Memorial on Pier and Face 6D and 7D.

234

Between 5.00pm and 6.00pm it had been perfectly peaceful – dead still, with a glorious sunset – but, after the excitement of the day, it seemed uncanny.

Suddenly a vivid star expanded over the Boche Line – a rocket. It lit the sky with a milky nimbus, then fell gracefully, like a fairy. It was followed by many flashes behind the Boche Line – a series of detonations. "My God – they're starting again," I thought. The shells came over with their horrible rumble and whizz, and burst one after another around our trench. This prologue was followed by a circle of Red, Green, White, and Orange Rockets fired from the Boche Line – signals to their Gunners to increase or decrease range, and for more Batteries to fire. We knew those Red Rockets all too well! "Now we're for it," I thought.

There was only one thing to do – have a walk around the Company, talk to the men, cheer them up! It seems ironical to go and tell a fellow it's alright, no need to get excited, we're safe enough here – when all the time you're shivering with fright, fear, and cowardice – not at the thought that the next shell might burst right on you, and lay you to rest for ever, but at such times it was strange but occasionally one's thoughts just flashed across the space to Blighty[314] and a feeling of thankfulness came when we realised how fortunate it was that those at home couldn't see this awful place with its horrors, its life, its death, and agony.

"Look another Red one – and what's that Orange Signal, they haven't used that before?" Then the Boche fired some shells which burst above us like shrapnel, but, instead of spreading lead bullets, each shell threw out something which caught fire and fell in blazing worms all round. They were phosphorus shells – liquid burning phosphorus. These were most terrifying, and we had great difficulty in controlling our men in "Z" Company. It was miraculous that no one was burnt. This particular barrage lasted about quarter of an hour. Then they put up some really big stuff. They were dropping all around and in the trench – burying or killing 6 to 10 men at once.[xxxiv] We had now had about two and a half hours of it, and it was about 10.00pm – quite dark.

The congestion in my trench became worse. Men who had been lying out all day in shell holes crawled in under cover of darkness. I had the King's Own Royal Lancasters, the Loyal North Lancashires, 1/8th Liverpool Irish, Engineers, and our own men. How many of these poor fellows ever did manage to crawl in was a marvel – seriously wounded – yet making a last effort to save their lives and get assistance. They told us that there were many men lying out who couldn't get in. We went out and brought about 20 men back. Then the difficulty was to get them away through the shelling to our Aid Post. Many started but never reached the Aid Post, but were killed on the way, while others were wounded a second or third time. It was awful in all this crowd and shelling to have probably 150 wounded men, and only be able to help them ever so little. We hadn't even any water or food to give them. Fortunately the shelling died down and almost ceased for an hour until about 11.30pm, except for the big fellows firing on back areas. The sound of these big shells in their travel is sluggish, it passes perhaps a thousand yards above our heads with a ponderous and increasing vibration like a train, then its heavy whine sounds fainter until it almost dies away, followed a few seconds later by a bright flash in the sky, and a terrific boom. Some of the shells were 16 inches in diameter and weighed about half a ton.

We took advantage of the lull in the storm to get the wounded away, which eased things, and relieved us who were more fortunate; it's awful to have men moaning, crying, shrieking with pain. I went along to the Skipper at our Company HQ – which was merely a hole in the trench wall. He

---

[314] Blighty is slang for "Britain" or "home", and is derived from Hindustani "bilayati", meaning "foreign land".

had heard no news, but Major Milnes had been up and said that we may have to attack again, but, "Don't do anything until you hear from me." I hadn't seen the Adjutant once round our Line. 2nd Lieutenant Walker was sent out to try to get in touch with the 2nd Division. He did a very useful piece of reconnaissance and returned with the information required at about 1.00am. I saw Duckie (Duckworth) once or twice during the night. I tried to keep my fellows busy working on the trench, clearing it where it had been blown in etc. I was jolly glad to have something to do. Luckily Jimmy Bowd, the Quartermaster, arrived with the rations. He had had an awful time over the past ten days getting up to the Line. We were jolly glad to get some cold boiled beef, bread, biscuits, jam, bully, and cold tea – my fellows were just about famished. At 12.30pm the shelling started again – the same old fireworks – the same old tearing feeling in – or, rather, through – your head as each shell burst, heaving up the earth and men, and throwing them down again. The fire got heavier! It began to rain, to lighten – which we scarcely noticed; nor could the thunder peals be heard above the row of battle. 1.00am came, 1.30am, 2.00am – no report from the Skipper – not a bit like him – he was always so prompt – so methodical – could his runner have been killed? – what had happened? Should I send Ashton to find out? No! I'll go myself. I told Armstrong that I was going. I tried to squeeze past the men who were huddled together in the bottom of the trench like rabbits. We had the minimum of sentries on duty – the Boche could never come across <u>that</u> No Man's Land.

I soon got out of the trench and went along the top. It was no use trying to take cover or dodge. Just go and risk it – it would even be a relief to be killed and get out of it, I almost thought. I couldn't find the Skipper at the Company HQ – the trench was blown in – the telephone gone. Was he killed? I felt that he was – but I tried to hope that he wasn't. I learnt that, when the shell had blown the trench in, Duckworth[315] and Company Quartermaster Sergeant Ogden had been wounded.[316] Someone had seen Captain Waterhouse with Mr Duckworth a few minutes before. I couldn't find poor old Ken anywhere. Porter his runner came up and said he thought that "The Captain" must have been blown up. I reported to Battalion HQ that I was taking over command of the Company, and gave my position for messages to be sent to. It was then 3.00am. The South Lancashires in my trench received orders to attack at 4.20am. I had no orders whatever. I didn't know what to do. Eventually I organised my men as well as possible but I could only raise 32 out of the 159 who had come up only about 18 hours before.

---

[315] This is the last time that Captain W. Duckworth ("Duckie") is mentioned in the diary until 20th March 1917 when Norman met him when he (Norman) was on his way to Bury for a period of leave while he was on Home Service at Ripon. At this time he was a temporary captain, his substantive rank being 2nd Lieutenant, but he is not the 2nd Lieutenant Duckworth, Assistant Adjutant, who Norman mentions as being gassed with almost all the other staff officers of the 1/5th Lancashire Fusiliers on 3rd January 1918 in the La Bassée Sector (see page 293 of the *Afterword*), as he was gazetted as a full captain, with effect from 1st June 1916, on 5th August 1917. Duckworth was with "B" Company of the 2/5th Lancashire Fusiliers when they first landed in France on 3rd May 1915, having joined the Lancashire Fusiliers as an officer in Bury in or about September 1914 (see the diary entry for 12th September 1914). There has been frequent mention of him in the diary up to this point, particularly during training in England. He is mentioned as having been involved in a raid on 31st December 1915, and Norman went to dinner with him at "X" Company's HQ on 24th June 1916. There is a photograph of him with Barwood, Hartington and Barnsdale, probably taken in September 1915, on page 65.

[316] Company Quartermaster Sergeant Thomas Ogden, Service no 2645, husband of Mary and son of Peter and Martha Ogden, all of Heywood, died of his wounds three days later on 11th August 1916, and is buried at St Sever Cemetery, Rouen, reference B.35.8.

Supposing I did receive orders to attack, what could I do with 32 men? I sent a report – a strength return – to Battalion HQ, i.e. to Major Milnes. Armstrong and I decided just to await orders – we couldn't do anything except watch and wait.

Poor Armstrong, he nearly went out of his mind. More than once I had to talk to him like a father, although he was 12 years older than me. If I hadn't been there I really believe he would have shot himself.

At times I felt like crying aloud from sheer cowardice – I prayed more than once. Then I pulled myself together, telling myself, "You're a man, not a baby"; and the thought of old Skipper's example helped me. I still did not know what had really become of him.

2nd Lieutenant Walker came to me and said that the South Lancashires were going over the top, and that he was taking "Y" Company over. He asked what I was going to do. I replied that my orders had been to take no further action until ordered. I stood fast with my men. Walker went over the top – we never saw or heard anything of him again. One of the many "Missing believed killed".[317] Life began to have little or no value.

At 4.45am I received an order to the effect.

"You will co-operate in attack with the South Lancs. Barrage will lift at 4.20am. The village of Guillemont must be taken."

It was too late!![xxxv]

Somewhere someone had blundered. I immediately reported to HQ. I had now 27 men with me. I could do nothing but "Stand to".

09.08.16   At 5.00am the Liverpool Scottish went over the top – just as day was breaking. They crossed over our trenches, advancing to the attack across a shell-torn area, every yard of which was swept by Machine Gun fire. They never reached the objective, but their discipline was wonderful; they were held up by barbed wire, and simply stood up firing at the Boche.

At about 9.30am I got orders to move out of the Line, and for the Battalion to rendez-vous at Carnoy.

Just as I moved out with my men I found Kenneth lying dead – it was awful. I just felt heart-broken – this was the final of all things. Dear old Skipper killed – no more.[318] I made absolutely certain that he was dead and just had time to lift him on to the trench side. I

---

[317] 2nd Lieutenant Richard Walker, of the 2/5th Lancashire Fusiliers, formerly of the London Regiment (Artists' Rifles), son of C.W. Walker of Burwash, Sussex, died aged 33 on 9th August 1916, and is commemorated at the Thiepval Memorial, Pier and Face 3C and 3D. He had been attached to the 2/5th Lancashire Fusiliers on 19th June 1916 to run an NCOs' Class of Instruction.

[318] Captain Kenneth Waterhouse, son of the late Joseph and Louisa Waterhouse, husband of Gladys Constance Waterhouse, of Hale, Cheshire, a former pupil of Giggleswick School, was aged 38 when he died, and is believed to be buried at Guillemont Road Cemetery, Guillemont, but his actual burial place has not been identified, and therefore he is commemorated by a Special Memorial, No 2. He had first reported to the Drill Hall in Bury on 12th September 1914 and had applied for a commission, and was with "D" Company of the 2/5th Lancashire Fusiliers when they first landed in France on 3rd May 1915. He had a horse called Sandy Mac, always immaculately turned out by his groom, and spoke French (see the diary entry for 4th May 1915). He and Norman had become friends even before travelling to France, having sat at Mess together with Goldsmith, Barnsdale, and Norman's brother, George (see the diary entry for 8th November to 13th December 1914). Once in France he invited Norman, then a Signalling Officer attached to HQ, to join at "D" Company's Mess, which Norman did from 9th May 1915 until they finished their training at Arques on 8th July 1915; subsequently Waterhouse asked Norman to become his 2nd in Command of what was then "Z" Company, which Norman did with effect from 23rd September 1915. Waterhouse became known as "The Skipper" while they were at Arques (see the diary entry for 21st to 30th June 1915). Despite spending long periods away from the Battalion as an Army School Instructor, he is frequently mentioned throughout the diary up to the date of his death, generally in terms of being cool and collected in the face of adversity, as well as caring deeply about his men. There are examples of this in this current chapter, and also, by way of further example, the following two diary entries:

Captain Kenneth Waterhouse, "The Skipper"

couldn't even get his personal belongings. I had approximately 25 men with me, Armstrong being left behind on an Advanced Post with some of "Z" Company. I reported at HQ to Major Milnes about Captain Waterhouse, and I am afraid that I rather gave way to my feelings. I tried to go back and bring Ken's body down so that we could bury him, but it was impossible to go back with living men to get even old Skipper.

"Z" Company were a sad party and a sorry sight as we tramped back some 5 miles to Carnoy – scarcely able to put one foot before the other. I wouldn't let my fellows rest until they were clear of the danger zone.[319]

At Carnoy we at last had a rest – it was great in the sun, and all was quiet and peaceful – we had left that horror behind. We arrived in Camp to find that Jimmy Bowd had prepared a really good meal for the men, and hot water to wash and shave, the first real wash and meal for 10 days.

After this I felt heaps better and wanted to go back again to get Kenneth's body, but Major Milnes wouldn't let me – he said that it was a useless risk.

However, Captain Newman, the Padre, went, but he couldn't find the body; however he learnt that the South Lancashires had buried him.

Then it was that we realised what had happened to our Battalion. It was a mere skeleton of its former self. Many of our pals had gone. This was the realisation of the awfulness of war, to come back and miss the familiar faces, the greetings; and in the quiet – the privacy – of my tent that night I saw war as never before, and then and then only did I appreciate how mercifully I had been spared through it all.

---

1.   15th April 1916, on his returning for a visit from the Army School: *"As usual we were all delighted to see him, and get a few useful suggestions. He went round to see the Company before leaving. The Skipper really loved his men in "Z" Company, and undoubtedly had their interests at heart. He was very upset about Schofield [who had been killed the day before]."*

2.   30th July 1916, in Happy Valley in the Somme area: *"The Skipper, as usual, was just as cool as if he had been walking down Lord Street to Thom's Café in Southport."*

There is a photograph of him with Norman, Hedley, Latter, Simon, Kemp, and the Mayor and Mayoress of Arques, taken between 20th May 1915 and 8th July 1915 on page 52. See also *Obituaries*.

[319] *The History of the Lancashire Fusiliers 1914-1918* by Major General J.C. Latter summarises the Battalion's actions from 31st July 1916 to 9th August 1916 thus: *"A much less comfortable Minden Day was spent by the 2nd/5th Battalion [than the 17th, 18th and 20th Battalions, who managed to hold a parade in Happy Valley] which from 31st July to 5th August endured many outbursts of heavy shelling in the line near Arrow Head Copse, close to Guillemont. This tour of duty is, however, remarkable for several acts of gallantry by non-commissioned officers and men. A signaller, Private J. Atherton [almost certainly one of Norman's original Signallers – see page 36], earned the DCM by repeatedly and on his own initiative going across the open under heavy fire to repair the only telephone line which was working in the brigade and to arrange lamp signalling with a neighbouring battalion. Corporal J. Newsham and Private T. Cooper were awarded the DCM for gallantry as stretcher bearers. The former twice left his trench in full view of the enemy to attend to wounded men lying in the wire in front of it. The latter secured volunteers to carry wounded back to the aid post through a shelled area; and at another time he remained for a long period in the open giving first aid to the wounded and putting them in as much shelter as he could find. Private J. Eatough and Private W. Booth were awarded the Military Medal for digging out under heavy shell fire four men who had been buried by the explosion of a shell; Eatough also carried a number of other wounded men to the dressing station under fire. The battalion was partially involved in an attack at Guillemont on 9th August, suffering serious losses but being given no definite role. Company Sergeant-Major Burns showed great gallantry in reorganising his men after the attack and was awarded the DCM."* Company Sergeant Major Burns was mentioned by Norman in the diary entry for 26th to 30th May 1916 on page 184 as doing especially *"good work"* with "Y" Company. The Battalion and Brigade War Diaries show that poor communication and congestion in the trenches were identified as issues needing to be addressed after the action on 8th/9th August. Specifically with regard to the 2/5th Lancashire Fusiliers, in the early hours of 9th August there was confusion as to whether the Battalion was to be relieved or take part in the attack. As late as 3.15am the Adjutant of the 2/5th (Best-Dunkley) was ordered by Brigade HQ to carry out the attack, but at 4.00am the CO (Milnes) decided to call it off. It is therefore especially fortunate that Norman did not receive the order to advance in time.

Above:
Photographs of the
Somme battle area,
August 1916
Left:
Carnoy, just behind
the battle area

CHAPTER 22
Carnoy, Bronfray Farm, Méricourt, Franleu and Cayeux-sur-Mer
10th August 1916 to 30th August 1916

10.08.16   We got properly cleaned up, but we didn't have our valises, so had to keep the same clothes. Everyone seemed heaps better, but looked worn out – battle worn – a vacant haggard drawn expression – but very thoughtful.

We had a Brigade Parade in Mass Formation. Major General Jeudwine addressed us. The gist of his remarks was:

Officers, NCOs and men of the 164th Infantry Brigade, I am proud of you – you have had a most trying ordeal during the past 10 days. Your work, your discipline, your morale has been wonderful. Guillemont was a hard task – an impossible task – but everyone did magnificently. The casualties in your Brigade, General Edwards, are very severe. We all miss those of our comrades who have given their lives ... [at this point it was too much – it was impossible to conceal any longer that choking feeling – those tears].
You have every reason to be proud of yourselves, and I hope that before many days are over you will have the true reward of a soldier ..." [we all thought he meant a rest] *"... and be able to carry out the next attack with great success, and avenge the lives of your comrades. Good Morning.*

Three cheers for the General were called – but they weren't too hearty. His last remarks rather damped our hopes.

In the afternoon a new draft of 204 other ranks arrived, and <u>one</u> officer – Lieutenant Packman. We received orders to reconnoitre the trenches held by General Duncan's 165th Infantry Brigade. Back to that shelling!

I went up for "Z" Company with Major Milnes, Kenderdine ("Y" Company), Cooper ("W" Company), S.L. Moffatt ("X" Company), Lieutenant Colonel Hindle, Major Crump, Captain Duckworth,[320] and Lieutenant Strong of the Loyal North Lancashires.

We rode up as far as we could, and walked the last 2 miles. We got heavily shelled, but suffered no casualties.

Coming back I was with Leslie Moffatt. We were chatting about Cecil, and he said, "It will be my turn soon – Cecil and I have never been away from each other for many days at once, and I'm sure that we shall be together again." A strange idea, but it proved too true within the next days.

That night I slept like a log.

11.08.16   It was a quiet day. I slept during the afternoon. I was very tired, not physically so much as mentally.

12.08.16   I got up at 6.00am. It was a glorious morning and I went up with the same officers to reconnoitre more trenches on the 165th Brigade Front – Duncan Alley etc. We also met

---

[320] This must be a Captain Duckworth of the Loyal North Lancashire Regiment, not Captain W. Duckworth of the 2/5th Lancashire Fusiliers, who had been wounded on 8th August 1916.

some of the 1/6th King's Liverpool Regiment, notably Captain Owen and Captain Thompson, who were both were very sorry to hear of the Skipper's death; he was a great favourite with everyone.

On our return Captain Jackson met us and said that the Attack was off so far as the 164th Brigade were concerned. A sigh of relief went round – "Thank God!"

I arrived back in Camp at 11.00am, had breakfast – and went to bed.

I got up at 2 o'clock, when orders were received to "Stand By", ready to move at an hour's notice. I managed to scribble a hurried note home to tell them about Ken, and that I was alright.

At 3.00pm we received orders that the Battalion would move at 6.00pm to Dublin Trench and Casement Trench.

We moved off on the exact stroke of 6.00pm. I was not over keen on going back to the "jolly old war".

We moved along the Carnoy to Maricourt road, where I happened to fall in with 2nd Lieutenant H. Allen of the 1/10th Liverpool Scottish; we walked along together for some distance, and chatted about England and mutual friends.

The Carnoy to Maricourt road

As we came towards Maricourt we came under heavy shell fire, but the only thing to do was to go through it. We got through Maricourt and turned North on to the Guillemont Road, which was also being heavily shelled.

We had several casualties here, and there were large numbers of wounded coming down – men from our Division. "Z" Company were leading, but I only had two casualties.[xxxvi]

13.08.16 I took up my position in Casement Trench at about midnight. There was a Dressing Station here. We were rushed up in Reserve and ordered to get the men as much sleep as possible. I found a stretcher which the MO at this Dressing Station lent to me. I had a narrow escape – a shell burst in the entrance of the Dressing Station, and rather spoilt the entrance to the place.[xxxvii] I slept for about three hours.

We were engaged on working parties and carrying parties all day. The Battalion had been brought up to dig a new trench, about 70 yards from the German Line. We were near the Battery positions, which was not very pleasant.

The parties were working shifts, and I had plenty to do, as I was responsible for seeing that the parties were detailed, and kept to time of programme. The parties were from "W", "X", "Y", and "Z" Companies – practically the whole Battalion, comprising 450 other ranks – except for four small parties of mine, the Tunnelling Company, who worked under the 1/1st West Lancashire REs on the Maricourt to Briqueterie road.

14.08.16   The working parties were out again. We were shelled intermittently during the day.

At night the large working party went out again. While moving up Death Valley this party was caught in a heavy barrage and suffered severely. Many men were killed or wounded. 2nd Lieutenant S.L. Moffatt was wounded, but tried to rally the men, then was again wounded. He died at Dublin Trench Dressing Station – a strange coincidence after his remarks to me only a few days before.[321]

Kenderdine and Cooper re-organised the party and went forward, but couldn't do much work, as they were shelled out. "Z" Company were more fortunate, and dug for about six hours. Both Royal Engineers' Officers were killed. We were very busy all night, and very tired.

15.08.16   It was a glorious morning. I had a shave. We got orders to move to the Transport Lines, moving by platoons at 200 yards intervals. The march was uneventful, with no casualties. I was very tired, and slept for an hour waiting for the other Companies to arrive.

Just when all the men had reported, the Brigade instructed us to find a party of one officer and 60 other ranks to return from where we had come in order to do a job of work – the message had been delayed. Fancy those fellows having to march back about 4 miles, dead tired. Packman took them, as he had seen very little of the fighting. I was sorry for my men, several of whom were lost. Lance Corporal Hampson[322] was killed, while Private Bent was wounded.

We got to the Transport Lines at 12.30pm, and moved off again at 3.00pm, with Major Milnes in command. We got another draft of 140 men for the East Lancashires and the Lancashire Fusiliers.

We moved via the Citadel, Méaulte, and Méricourt. It rained all the way, and I was very tired. I saw several fellows whom I knew en route. The King was at this place the day before.

I rode "Sandy Mac". Poor old "Sandy Mac" – he knew me, but somehow he seemed to understand that his master had gone, and Newhouse, the groom, was a very sad fellow.

---

[321] See the diary entry for 10th August 1916. There is very little information on the Commonwealth War Graves Commission's website for 2nd Lieutenant Stanley Leslie Moffatt, in contrast to the information about his brother Cecil (who died just under two weeks earlier on 1st August 1916), and his headstone has no inscription, simply bearing his rank, surname, initials, date of death, and stating (it would seem incorrectly) that he was with the 2nd Battalion of the Lancashire Fusiliers. The information about his brother includes age at death and his parents' names and address, while there is an inscription on his brother's headstone which reads: "For as in Adam all die even so in Christ shall all be made alive 1 Cor. 15.22". See the footnote to the diary entry for 1st August 1916 for more information about the brothers' family and their background. In Leslie's service record at the National Archives, his age is stated as 20 years 2 months on 31st August 1914, although his registered birth date was 12th June 1895; he presumably falsified his age to facilitate his brother falsifying his. Leslie Moffatt is buried at Péronne Road Cemetery, reference II.G.8. He was in "X" Company, and is mentioned in the diary entry for 26th to 30th May 1916 on page 184 as having done "good work" with them, becoming OC of "X" Company at the end of June 1916. The diary entry for 4th to 5th August 1916, just days after the death of his brother on 1st August 1916, is to the following effect: "2nd Lieutenant S.L. Moffatt had also had an exciting experience with a fighting patrol at Arrow Head Copse, and had the satisfaction of killing several Boche. About 30 Boche had come out to meet him, but with a Lewis Gun and rapid rifle fire his small patrol accounted for most of the Boche party – the remainder rushing off for their lives." There is a photograph of him on page 232.

[322] It has not been possible to find any Commonwealth War Graves Commission record for a man named Hampson (or similar) who died on or about 15th August 1916. A Lance Corporal Hampson is mentioned in the diary entries for 14th to 19th August 1915, 27th August 1915, 18th March 1916, 1st May 1916, and 28th June 1916; on the last date he was said by Norman to have been wounded, which is confirmed in the Battalion War Diary casualty list, where his Service no is given as 2841; the Medal Index Card and Pension Ledger for this man in the National Archives show that he was subsequently re-assigned to the King's Liverpool Regiment, and was awarded a 30% disability pension from 21st September 1918 as a result of a gunshot wound to his right arm.

We arrived at Méricourt at 7.00pm. The Company was in moderate billets, but, after the past fortnight, it was luxury. "Z" Company were in the Public Hall. My Company HQ was on Corbie Road. I was very tired, and slept like a log. It was glorious to be miles away from the shelling – even out of the sound of it.

16.08.16 Lieutenant Colonel Fox, of the Royal Warwickshire Regiment, took over Command of the Battalion, with Captain B. Best-Dunkley as Adjutant.

The Officers in "Z" Company were now Kerr, Armstrong, Packman, and myself.

We allotted the new draft from the previous day, and got the men cleaning up, with fresh clothes, baths etc.

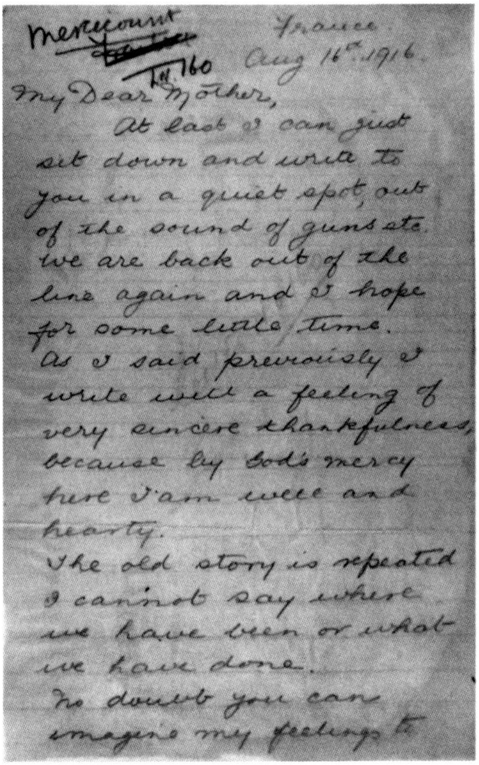

I wrote a letter to my mother. [Part of the letter is pictured above, and reads:

My Dear Mother,

At last I can just sit down and write to you in a quiet spot, out of the sound of guns etc. We are back out of the line again and I hope for some little time.

As I said previously I write with a feeling of very sincere thankfulness because by God's mercy here I am well and hearty.

The old story is repeated. I cannot say where we have been or what we have done.

No doubt you can imagine my feelings to be back here, but one looks for old friends in vain.

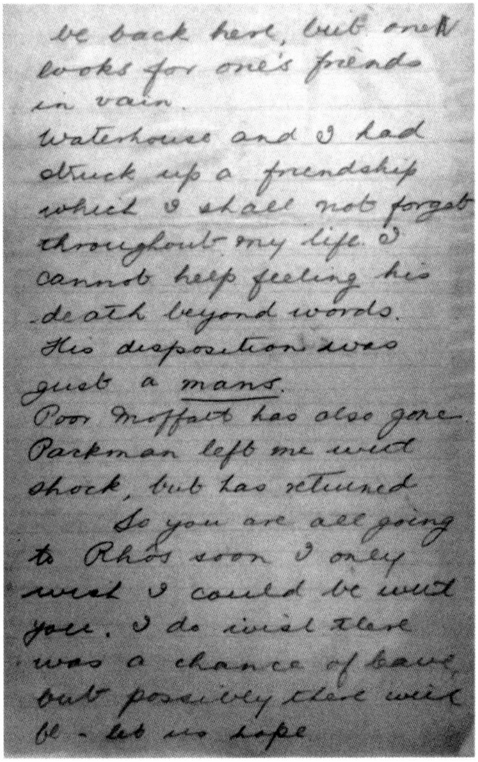

Waterhouse and I had struck up a friendship which I shall not forget throughout my life. I cannot help feeling his death beyond words. His disposition was just a <u>man's</u>.

Poor Moffatt has also gone. Packman left me with shock, but has returned.

So you are all going to Rhos soon. I only wish I could be with you. I do wish there was a chance of leave, but possibly there will be – let us hope.]

17.08.16 and 18.08.16	There was Company Training on some ground near the River Ancre, trying to get the morale back a bit, and also instil our methods into the new draft. It felt glorious to be able to walk about a village without worrying about shells. On August 17th we heard that Guillemont had been captured, but it took a full Division to do it. On August 18th I took part in an FGCM with Major Merriman as the President. It was a glorious evening, with a tremendous number of Observation Balloons in the air – I counted 49.[323]
19.08.16	We got up at 4.30am, and marched to Méricourt Station, where we entrained at 7.00am. We went via Heilly, Corbie, Amiens, and Longpré to Abbeville, where we detrained at about 11.00am. We marched out of Abbeville through Rouvroy, along the Route Nationale N° 25 to Frières, where we left the main road, and proceeded North West to Franleu, our destination and billeting area.

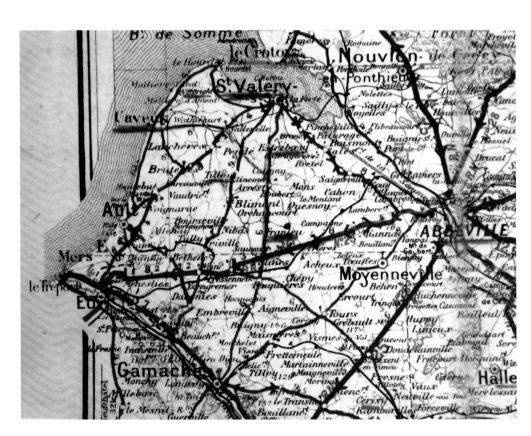

Franleu was a glorious little village, situated in a very fertile district where "the valleys seemed to stand so rich in corn that even they were singing". It was almost impossible to imagine that only a few hours before we had been in shell-swept, devastated Picardy. At

---

[323] These were also called "Sausages", or Kite Balloons. Norman mentions having seen them first six days after landing in France on 9th May 1915, and mentions seeing them again in diary entries for 29th July 1915, 8th to 13th August 1915, 14th August 1915, 2nd July 1916, 26th July 1916, 6th and 12th July 1917 in the vicinity of Gommecourt (on both of which occasions he saw the observers escape by parachute when the balloons were under attack), and 6th and 8th September 1917 in the Ypres Sector. See the photograph on page 47.

any rate our "Contemptible Little Army"[324] had saved some parts of France from German "Kultur".

Things went on normally in this village; the farmers were busy collecting in their wheat, and the countryside for miles seemed a rich golden colour. It was a peaceful spot this, miles away from the War, where – for a few days at any rate – we hoped to be left alone to recover our humanity. Then, in the quietness of these simple hard-working peasants, chiefly old and young – the men of military age being away in the Army – we realised what we had been through, the friends we had lost, our own escapes; and one appreciated what it was to be alive and well.

"Z" Company had excellent billets, for both the men and officers.

20.08.16 We had Church Parade at 10.45am. It was a very nice service – a memorial service and thanksgiving service all in one. It just struck the right note.

I received an invitation to George's Wedding, but never entertained hopes of getting to England, even though I hadn't had leave for seven[325] months. We had even bigger things to do. I was very tired. I had a short ride on "Sandy Mac" in the afternoon.

We got a second message from the GOC Division:

The casualties in the actions in which the Division have recently been engaged have been very severe, but the bravery and courage of the troops in the attack were magnificent, and the Lancashire characteristic, dogged determination, was never better shown. Any ground gained was seldom lost. Our Line was advanced 500 yards on the right, and 300 yards on the left. 13,000 yards of trenches were dug by the Division in the 17 days, and over 3,000 yards were deepened and widened.

21.08.16 We did Company Training.
to
26.08.16 It was glorious weather. Our men were benefiting from their rest. They had baths, clean clothes, and haircuts. Buttons were polished, and guards mounted with – almost – the same precision and ceremony as in Peace time. There is nothing like regular hours, regular meals, and discipline for making a man take an interest in himself and cheer him up. Some called it eye-wash. But this eye-wash kept up the morale and Esprit de Corps of our troops, and made them better men.

Captain J.W. Hedley rejoined from the Base. We were all delighted to see "Uncle Joe's" cheery face again. Naturally he was very sad to hear of our losses. He was looking very fit.

The Battalion organisation was now re-arranged as follows:

In Command	Lieutenant Colonel Fox
2nd in Command	Major H. N. Milnes
"W" Company	Captain J.W. Hedley
"X" Company	Major Barnsdale
"Y" Company	Lieutenant T.H.G. Kenderine
"Z" Company	Captain N. Hall

---

[324] On 19th August 1914 Kaiser William II issued an order that General French's "Contemptible Little Army" be defeated forthwith.
[325] In fact it had only been just over six months since Norman's last leave in February 1916.

Kemp returned on August 22nd, and was posted to "Y" Company.[326]

There were only seven of the original officers now left with the Battalion. [327]

On August 24th we dug a Strong Point as a demonstration to the new drafts – it seemed an awful shame to do this in a field where the corn had just been cut and not then gathered in. Fancy even showing these happy country folk what a trench was like!

On August 25th the Battalion marched to St Valery-sur-Somme, where all the men bathed, and had their dinners on the shore. We officers had a cheery lunch of very good soles in a real Hotel – a very enjoyable day.

On August 26th I got hauled up before the CO by the Adjutant, Best-Dunkley, for not being actually with my Company on Rouse Parade, when I was busy inspecting billets, cookers, and the Company Orderly Room etc. However, Colonel Fox was quite on my side. So enough said!

27.08.16   The Division decided to send three officers and 50 men from each unit to Cayeux-sur-Somme by the sea for three days for a change, with no duties, just a complete rest, which was a fine idea for all the men, NCOs, and officers alike after fighting.

I was ordered to take the first party, and to remain until all parties had had their three days, and to return with the last party. My job was to arrange the billeting and rations, expected to take about half an hour a day.

I left Franleu at 8.00am. It was a glorious sunny morning, and it felt like going for a holiday. Lieutenant Cooper and 2nd Lieutenant Wolfe went with me, along with 50 men.

We marched via Campagne, Orchancourt, Blimont, Tilloy and Lanchères to Cayeux, a distance of 15 miles, arriving at about 1.00pm. We fixed up the men in billets, arranged the cooking, and read out orders, which were:

Breakfast	8.00am
Roll Call	9.00am
Dinners	1.00pm
Tea	5.00pm
Supper and Roll Call	10.00pm

Cayeux was a nice little spot on the Channel. After lunch I had a stroll along the Promenade, and went to sleep on the shore.

In the evening after dinner everyone was walking about on the Promenade, which was just a lot of boards laid down on the levelled shingle. At the North and about a mile away was Nieu Brighton, and a lighthouse. I got an awful shock when it flashed a red light – I immediately got the wind up – it reminded me of the Boche Signal to open a barrage. I'm afraid my nerves were very shaken, and I was feeling pretty cheap and lifeless, and still tired. So, as we walked along we came to some Summer House bathing huts, quite cosy and nicely furnished. It was just getting dark, and I decided to go into one of these. Cooper and Wolfe both disliked the idea. They said, "Oh, you can't – they're private." "Never mind," I said, "I can always apologise and clear out if anyone comes." So in I went, alone! A few minutes later, my quiet think was disturbed by the arrival of the owners; several

---

[326] Norman Kemp had left at the beginning of June 1916 for treatment in England for a hand injury. See page 185.

[327] Major Milnes, Major Barnsdale, Captain Hedley, Lieutenant Bowd, Lieutenant Packman, 2nd Lieutenant Kemp, and Captain Hall; see the diary entry for 3rd May 1915 o page 321 for a full list of the officers who departed for France with the Battalion.

girls about 18 to 22, one or two boys about 16 to 18, and Pa and Ma – at least, I guessed so. I felt awfully guilty, and I tried to apologise in my best French. Then one of the girls spoke in English – this relieved matters, as I felt I could express my apologies quite nicely. They pressed me to stay – said that I was most welcome – were quite interested when I said that I had just come down from the Somme Front …

Well, I soon decided that I didn't need much persuading to stay. Cooper and Wolfe passed several times, looking jealousy – but I never called them along.

These people proved to be a family of friends from Paris, just over at their Summer House. We all talked together till about 11 o'clock. Then they gave me a pressing invitation to meet them the next morning and join their bathing party. I accepted! And bid them Good Night.

Cooper and Wolfe were furious when I told them about my good luck. Of course, it was their own fault. We returned to our Hotel for the night.

28.08.16   I had a look at the men at 9.00am. They had all enjoyed their day and were in good spirits – especially as I paid them some money.

Then we set off for a morning stroll by the sea. It was great – just civilised kiddies playing on the sands and paddling, dogs barking and swimming for sticks, people sitting in deckchairs getting sun burnt – just the typical seaside scenes. There were some tennis courts, and croquet lawns. There were the same little groups of fisher folk lolling about as if all was peace and quiet in the world. And there was the Sea – just the same incessant roll of the waves, with the curl and the splash and the foam as they broke on the shore. And across it – only some 25 miles away – England! So near and yet so far! If only thoughts could have gone over that space like wireless waves!

Why was there a war? Why so much hardship, bloodshed, and devastation – not very far away? As Captain Jeffreys used to say, "It makes you think". Even in war – in the quiet times – one did think; yes, *really* think!

Then as Cooper, Wolfe and I lay on the sands, the Souffrice family, the people I had met the previous evening, arrived – at least, Jean, Simone, and a friend. I introduced Cooper and Wolfe, then we all went off to their house to change for the bathe. We had great fun, about 20 of us, paddling canoes, swimming, and diving – oh, it was great. Afterwards we had cocoa and buns. The girls had been to school in England, and had cultivated many English customs in their home.

They invited us up to their house (Villa Nell) for tennis, afternoon tea, and dinner. There was quite a large party of us, and we had a very cheery time.

One of the boys was in the Army and away in Vosges.

Madame was exceedingly kind, and just made me quite at home. She told us to use their house as our own while we were there. After dinner we walked about – a perfect moonlit evening – and left for our Hotel at 11.00pm.

We had got to bed, when at 12.20am I was disturbed by a motor cycle dispatch rider with bad news. The message read as follows:

You will return with your party to Franleu at 6.00am 29th inst.
URGENT
B. Best-Dunkley, Captain and Adjutant
Acknowledge.

All good things come to an end. I went off to tell Cooper and Wolfe. I told them to warn the men that it would be Reveille at 4.45am, kits stacked at 5.30am, and ready to move at 6.00am.

I went to Jean Souffrice. They were still up. We trotted off to hire a farm cart to carry the kits. Jean said he would come with us.

My Goodness! Back to the Somme – we knew it! Back to all that shelling. Well, orders are orders. Anyway, the best thing was to get some sleep. So we turned in again at 1.00am.

29.08.16   Jean Souffrice came over and had breakfast with us at the Hotel. The family turned out at 6.00am to see us off, and bid us "Au Revoir" and "Bonne Chance!" All our good time cut short – just like the Army.

The cart arrived. We loaded the kits, and away we marched at 6.00am. It started to rain, and came down in torrents. Jean eventually got in the cart.

We arrived at Franleu at 11.30am. All was hustle and bustle. Sudden orders had been received – the Division was to move back to the Somme.

We had no feelings of keenness to get back; we knew what it was like – we had experienced it. The actual starting time for the move wasn't known, so we decided to give the men a jolly substantial meal, and also have one ourselves.

Jean Souffrice came to "Z" Company Mess for lunch. We had a cheery party, Joe Hedley, Kenders, Kemp, Packman, myself, and Godfrey and Jackson, two new officers.

It rained all afternoon.

We left Franleu in pouring rain at 9.00pm to march to Abbeville. I had already done 16 miles and it was another 16 miles to the Railhead. We marched off in full fighting order as we didn't know what was to happen or whether we should see our kits before we went into action again.

It was an awful night. As I marched along, little did I think that at Stubbington they were having a merry evening prior to my brother George's Wedding. But it was no use worrying – I couldn't go.

30.08.16   We arrived at Abbeville at about 1.30am. We formed up in the Military Siding, and waited for our train, all soaked to the skin. I managed to get some tea for my men in "Z" Company.

At about 2.00am the train started for the Somme Front. We traversed our familiar Somme Valley Route to Amiens, Corbie and to Méricourt (which we had left only 11 days before). In the meantime we had re-organised our Battalion and done some useful training.

We arrived at Méricourt at 11.30am, where it was still pouring, and the roads were flooded.

There was no one to meet us to tell us where to go. So Colonel Fox decided to move away from the station to clear the yards. Captain Macready met us and told us where our billeting area was. This was on the sloping ground between the River Ancre and the Albert to Amiens Route Nationale N° 29. Our area was about 2 miles from Méaulte and in the Xth Corps Area.

It was just a field, and a muddy one into the bargain. The wheat sheafs were still cocked, but ruined. We had no cover of any description and a bitter cold North East wind was blowing. It was no use looking at it – the men were wet through, tired, and hungry, having had practically no breakfast. Unofficially I showed my men how to make a bivouac out of the corn cocks and a ground sheet or two for the roof. We also found some wood and corrugated iron sheets and made further bivouacs. Then I got the cooks busy and the men soon had a good meal. Later I met Captain Teale[328] with whom I had worked at Trônes Wood on the dumps (who by the way got the MC for his work on that Show), and he promised to get us some pukker[329] bivvy sheets and a few tents. They arrived at 5 o'clock, so my "Z" Company men settled down fairly comfortably, considering.

I had been busy all day, and had scarcely thought of George's Wedding. I did think of it just for a few minutes, but it only made me discontented and envious, so I got to a job of work quickly.

At 6.30pm I began to feel somewhat hungry, so I decided to go down with Joe Hedley and Kenders to Méaulte for some food – the first since about 7.00am. We got an omelette, eggs, bread and butter. It made quite a good meal.

A day or two later I received a postcard from Simone Souffrice.

18 CAYEUX. — La Plage Sud. — LL.

[The postcard is pictured on the left and reads:

Dear Mr Hall,

We all were very sorry not to go to Franleu. We said we would, but the bad weather obliged us to stay in all the afternoon. John told us you are alright in your camp. We miss you very much and really feel sorry that you could not stay any longer.

I shall send you the photos as soon as they are ready. I hope they will be good, as that will be a souvenir of your too short stay at Cayeux!

*Will you please remember me to your friends M*rs. *Wolfe and Cooper.*

Kind regards to you from Simone.

N.B. The right hand side of the writing is obscured by being pasted to the diary, but it is possible to reconstruct the complete text.]

---

[328] See the diary entries for 6th and 7th August 1916.

[329] Pukker (more normally spelt pukka or pucca) is slang for "proper", derived from the Hindustani for "cooked" or "ripe".

CHAPTER 23
The Albert to Méricourt Road near Millencourt, and Fricourt
31st August 1916 to 6th September 1916

31.08.16
to
04.09.16

On Thursday August 31st we moved into a new camp area nearer to the Albert to Amiens road, near Millencourt, where Captain Simon was buried in August 1915.[330] This camp, although very dirty, possessed enough tents for all – greatly appreciated after the previous two days' soaking. Fourteen new officers joined us, who soon decided that Active Service was rougher than they expected. They were:

Lieutenant McVicker, MO[331]

2nd Lieutenant Godfrey, "Z" Company[332]

2nd Lieutenant Lawrie, "Z" Company

2nd Lieutenant Jackson, "Z" Company[332]

2nd Lieutenant Maw, "Z" Company

2nd Lieutenant Steibel[334]

2nd Lieutenant Essex P.

2nd Lieutenant Laslett

2nd Lieutenant Dickinson[333]

2nd Lieutenant Chiswell

2nd Lieutenant Beesley

2nd Lieutenant Jones, J.B.

2nd Lieutenant Worrall

2nd Lieutenant Mordecai[334]

On Friday September 1st Packman was taken from me and made acting Quartermaster, Jimmy Bowd having at last crocked up – he had been a brick to stick it for so long.[335]

---

[330] See the diary entry for 14th to 19th August 1915.

[331] Lieutenant McVicker (spelt McVickers by Norman) has already been mentioned as having been "with us as MO for a short time" in the diary entry for 12th to 16th July 1916. In fact he had been with the 2/1st Wessex Ambulance, a Field Ambulance unit with the 55th Division, since at least January 1916. According to the War Diary of the 2/1st Wessex Field Ambulance, Lieutenant McVicker was detailed for temporary duty with the 2/5th Lancashire Fusiliers on 2nd September 1916, replacing Captain Bennett (mentioned later on page 266), also of the 2/1st Field Ambulance, who had been detailed for temporary duty with the 2/5th Lancashire Fusiliers on 28th August 1916. It is not clear what had happened to Captain Levine who took over as MO when Lieutenant R.N. Thompson left on 8th March 1916.

[332] Both Godfrey and Jackson have already been mentioned as recently joined new officers in the diary entry for 29th August 1916.

[333] Lieutenant Talbot Dickinson MC, described as a "flamboyant patriot" in Thomas Floyd's At Ypres with Best-Dunkley, died on 31st July 1917 in the 3rd Battle of Ypres. Aged 29 when he died, he was the son of Robert Woolstoncroft and Annie Elizabeth Dickinson of Chorlton-cum-Hardy, Manchester, and is commemorated at the Ypres (Menin Gate) Memorial, West-Vlaanderen, Belgium, Panel 33.

[334] Norman also spells "Steibel" as "Stiebel", and he spells "Mordecai" as "Maudacai"

[335] This is the last mention in the diary of Lieutenant James Bowd, better known as Jimmy Bowd. He was first mentioned as Quartermaster of the 5th Reserve Battalion at Southport in the diary entry for 8th November to 13th December 1914, was Quartermaster of the 2/5th Lancashire Fusiliers when they landed in France on 3rd May 1915, and remained Quartermaster throughout from then until his departure. There have been many references to him in the diary up to this point. He was clearly a man who enjoyed a drink, being described as "tight" and in an argument with the Adjutant Captain Cummins in the diary entry for 31st December 1914, and he and Captain Cummins are again mentioned as being together on the train journey to France on 3rd May 1915 having "imbibed freely rather than wisely", at which point Bowd was regaling the assembled company with a tale of having met an old friend in Bedford who had given him a periscope; again, the diary entry for 5th November 1915 describes how Norman, Joe Hedley and Gray, who were to spend the night with him on their way to going on leave in England, found that he was not in his billet at Bouzincourt at 10.00pm, but he "arrived back at about 2.30am, having dined well but none too wisely with some old pal of his in Albert." The diary entry for 5th January 1916 reads as follows: Jimmy Bowd was in a terrible state at Rainneville; in loading up at Thiepval Wood he had lost 150 waterproof capes – personally I think he was overloaded and somebody dumped them. Anyway a 'Court of Enquiry' settled the business", and the following day it is said that he "had taken on rather a full cargo and he was ragged by everyone." Nevertheless, he seems to have been popular, and good at his job: "Trust an old Quartermaster for having a few blankets to spare", says Norman when he, Joe Hedley and Gray had to fend for themselves on arriving at his empty billet on 5th November 1915. In the days leading up to his "crocking up" Norman says of him when he had arrived at the trenches on 8th August 1916 with much needed supplies, "He had had an awful time over the past 10 days getting up to the Line", and the following day, when the men at last came out of the Line, they "arrived in Camp to find that Jimmy Bowd had prepared a really good meal for the men". It is not clear what happened to him, or whether he ever returned to Active Service. There is a photograph of him with Captain L.H. Bloy on page 97.

We spent the next few days training our new drafts in Trench Duties. We felt that this period of training might have been increased, as our new men were only roughly trained; also, they didn't know their officers, nor did the officers know the men, for they were new to Active Service and the Battalion.

On the night of September 1st we went into the Corps Line for instruction for new men, relieving the 1/4th Loyal North Lancashires at midnight, and spent the night doing patrols, making two Strong Points etc. We had no sleep all night.

On Saturday September 2nd we were relieved in the Corps Line at 10.00am, and returned to Camp for breakfast. Later in the day we had firing on the Range. It was a very wet night, and the camp was absolutely flooded out.

On Sunday September 3rd, we had Brigade Church Parade in the morning, and at 2.00pm took over the trenches again for instruction, until we were relieved at about 1.15am. It was sickening – as if we hadn't seen enough of trenches without further instruction. But it was for the benefit of the new fellows. Some of us who knew we would soon be in the thick of the fighting wanted to rest. But no luck!

On Monday September 4th we had Revolver and Lewis Gun Firing before lunch. This meant two and a half days with about four hours' sleep. It was absurd, having last minute training before a Show; instead of cheering the men up by giving them a good time, we were making them fed up, and taking any keenness out of them. My fellows were bricks – they supported me in every way. None of us wanted to do anything but well in the next Show, but our men weren't going to be fit to fight.[336]

In the afternoon I rode over to Albert and Aveluy to have a look at them.[337]

I turned in early – tired out!

ALBERT. RUINS 1916.

ALBERT. (Somme) 1916

Aveluy. Somme 1916.

Aveluy. Somme 1916.

---

[336] The Brigade War Diary contains a record for 4th and 5th September 1916 as follows: *"The Brigade was training in 'occupation of trenches' in area D.12. Lack of training displayed by the newly-joined officers and men was very noticeable"*.

[337] Norman was last in Albert on 2nd January 1916. See also the diary entry for 29th July 1915 and footnote 88 on page 68. For Aveluy see Chapters 7 and 8, particularly the entry for 29th August 1915 on page 89.

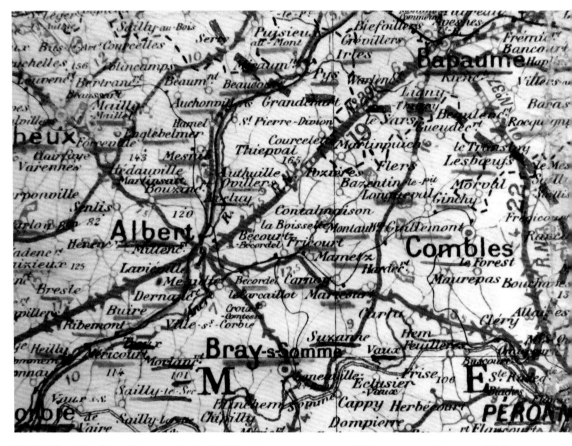

05.09.16　The Battalion marched via Méaulte to a camp near Fricourt, a good camp with huts, tents and bivvies.

06.09.16　Lieutenant Colonel Fox, Major Milnes, Captain Hedley, Kenderdine, Cooper and I set off at 2.30am to reconnoitre the trenches near Delville Wood. We took our horses as far as Longueval and walked the rest. The situation at this time was a peculiar one. The Boche were still holding on with determination to about 20 yards of the North East corner of Delville Wood. Ginchy was still in his hands having been re-captured from the 7th Division (General Shoubridge), after they had held it for only a week. To the South and South East, the Line was held by us, towards Guillemont the Line was held by our 16th and 36th Divisions. The British Front Line was just a series of shell holes organised for defence, in some cases linked up by embryo trenches – but it was like being in the blue. During our Reconnaissance we were sniped at by the Boche several times. He seemed to be all over the place. We didn't waste any time in getting information that we required, and all returned safe by noon.

I made plans for relief of the trenches with Lieutenant Alan Maw,[338] my 2nd in Command of "Z" Company. We held a Conference with my officers, 2nd Lieutenant Lawrie, 2nd Lieutenant Jackson, 2nd Lieutenant Godfrey, and the NCOs and Section Commanders, some of whom were privates.

I had a jolly good night's rest.

---

[338] Norman also spells Maw's first name "Allan".

07.09.16   I was warned that on September 10th I was to proceed to the IVth Army School for a course. Lieutenant Colonel Fox ordered me to hand over "Z" Company to Maw. I was fed up at this, as it seemed as if I was dodging my responsibilities, and going to miss the next Battle – a big one too! The Battalion now had very few officers with even as much experience as I had, and, even though I had comparatively little experience, I felt that I should be of more use than some. However the Colonel said that I needed a rest very badly. I was certainly feeling very done. The August attacks, the worry of our losses, the responsibility of re-organisation, the anxiety of the whole responsibility of taking new men into a big Show, had had an effect on all of us. However, no amount of persuasion could alter the CO's decision. When the CO, Major Milnes and the COs of the Companies again reconnoitred the Line in the afternoon, Maw went instead of me as CO of "Z" Company. However, while they were away, a message came cancelling the decision to send me on a course.[339]

Meanwhile, I had seen Walter Cornall, who had come down from Delville Wood, where they had had a sticky time.[340]

At 7.00pm we received orders to move at once. We moved off in fighting kit, without packs, but just a haversack slung on our shoulders.

The following officers were in charge of the Companies:

"W" Company   Lieutenant Cooper
"X" Company   Lieutenant Kenderdine
"Y" Company   Captain J.W. Hedley
"Z" Company   Captain N. Hall

The order of march was "W" Company, "X" Company, "Y" Company, then "Z" Company.

We started out with platoons at 200 yards distance, and the COs of Companies riding on horses.

We moved up via Fricourt to Montauban. I rode with Uncle Joe most of the way. We chatted about various things, but chiefly about our Companies.

We went along the Mametz to Montauban road. It was a wide road, full of shell holes, and the surrounding country bore every sign of recent heavy fighting. Joe Hedley seemed very upset about the men whom we were taking up. Owing to our <u>heavy</u> casualties in officers and men in August, at least 70% of our strength was composed of officers and men who had never been in action before, some having never even heard a bullet fired – to say nothing of a shell – except at home. Hedley seemed to wonder whether they would stand the test. Even he hadn't seen the Somme fighting, as he had only just returned from

---

[339] When recapping this event in the diary entry for 15th March 1918, Norman says that he had actually started out for the course, but was recalled by a dispatch rider within half an hour. This was the second of four courses that Norman had narrowly missed – see the footnote on page 304 of the *Afterword*.

[340] On 20th October 1917 Norman learned that Corporal Samuel Walter Cornall (Service no 20282, 22nd Battalion Manchester Regiment) had been killed. He had been a fellow pupil at Bury Grammar School, two years younger than Norman. His parents, Samuel Walter and Martha Cornall, lived at Red Bank House, Walmersley Road, Bury. He died aged 23 on 4th October 1917 in the 3rd Battle of Ypres, and is commemorated at the Tyne Cot Memorial at West-Vlaanderen, Belgium, Panel 120 to 124.

Base duty when we were at Franleu. We sat and smoked at one of the halts, and I persuaded Joe not to worry, saying, "It's too late now, we can't alter things. You'll see – they'll do their job when they are put to it."

I was riding "Sandy Mac" – but I little thought that it was the last time I should ride him – or that it was the last ride I should have with Joe.

At Longueval we suffered heavy shelling, by 8 inch, 12 inch, and 15 inch shells – quite as I expected. But luckily my Company had no casualties.

We had previously received very definite orders with regard to the relief, i.e. as to routes, guides, etc. Here are the original orders as I copied them into my message book [followed by a transcription]:

Route to Firing Line

SEPT 7th 1916

Infantry in small parties Platoons

Past Pommier Redoubt.

Through Montauban to Sunken Road running N and S on E side of Montauban.

Up Sunken Road to York and Lancaster Alley.

Leaving York and Lancaster Alley at S. 16 c. 9.5.

Following new trench to Carlton Trench.

Up LIVERPOOL ST or West York Alley.

HALTING PLACES

Before Reaching Pommier Redoubt;

Sunken Road running N and S through E side of Montauban –

Also at MAMETZ.

Unsafe Places to Halt

Pommier Redoubt; Road from S 27 c. 0.4.

Church in MONTAUBAN.

IV ENEMY BARRAGES

(i) MONTAUBAN – heavy shells near church – whizz bangs on W side of village.

(ii) R.E. ALLEY – barrage in S 16 d.

(iii) At S 10 c, through S 10 d, S 11 c, S 11 d and LONGUEVAL.

(iv) Edge of DELVILLE WOOD, Angle trench, WATERLOT FARM, LONGUEVAL ALLEY, TRÔNES WOOD.

OBSERVATION POSTS

CARLTON TRENCH and SAVOY TRENCH to NNE

Small Parties should join MONTAUBAN ALLEY at POMMIER REDOUBT, leaving it at Sunken Road and then to YORK and LANCASTER ALLEY.

GUIDES

The Corps Chief Guide Capt FitzHerbert lives in dug out at S 27 d 7.7 will supply guides to any officers wishing to go up the line.

SAA to be made up.

Certificate by 9AM.

SALVAGE

Coy Dumps

Batt[n] Dumps

Rt BDE[341] Dump S 22 D 9.5.

100 yds N Bernafay Wood

Left BDE Dump S 16 C 9.4.

GREEN Dump

Two large dumps at

F 6 C 2.8 Mametz – Montauban Rd

S 27 C 2.2 Church Montauban

Grenades SAA etc.

MONTAUBAN. Somme 1916.

---

[341] Right Brigade.

RE Material
Same place as BDE Grenade
Dump
Baths
Hot Bath E 16 a 7.4
Sail cloth F 7 a 3.6[342]

MONTAUBAN.
WAYSIDE CROSS
AT ENTRANCE
TO VILLAGE.

We moved up by Pommier Redoubt through Montauban, where we again got shelled according to programme, then took the sunken road running North and South on the East side of the village. We passed the ruined church where the guides were to

MONTAUBAN.
WHERE THE
CHURCH STOOD.

meet us. "Y" Company's guides did not turn up. I found mine, so passed through "Y" Company with Captain Hedley, leaving them in the sunken road. Our guide did not seem certain of his Route. However, passing through several Batteries (where the smell of gas, stale ground, and putrefaction was atrocious) we reached York and Lancaster Alley, which we followed, taking the path on the left, finally arriving at West York Alley, where the Boche put down a short sharp barrage of 77mm and 4.5 inch shells, lasting about 15 minutes.

DELVILLE WOOD
NORTH OF
LONGUEVAL
(*p*. 60).

YoRK and
LANCASTER
ALLEY.

It was a very dark night. However Lieutenant Alan Maw met us, and led us up to our Line on the South side of Delville Wood, i.e. to Diagonal Trench.

It was a fairly good trench immediately in front of Waterlot Farm, which

was no longer a farm but merely a huge scrap heap of cast iron boilers, farm implements etc., which the Boche had collected in the district and dumped, ready – presumably – for removal to Germany as scrap metal. The relief took the greater part of the night. It was with some feeling of thankfulness that we heard that relief of the 20th Brigade was complete, as it would have been quite easy to have walked into enemy Lines, either crossing over our Front Line, or even without coming into contact with our Front Line or troops at all; also the South East corner of Delville Wood was held by a few determined and brave German Snipers.

---

[342] Presumably this refers to washing with cold water in canvas containers, in contrast to the hot baths referred to above.

"W" Company (Cooper) held York Alley, and "X" Company (Kenderdine) held ZZ Trench; "Y" Company (Captain Hedley) were supposed to occupy the Front Line, Stout Trench.

When "Z" Company had been in position for about half an hour, "Y" Company arrived. We directed them to Stout Trench, informing them that, as there were no troops in front of us, I had pushed forward several Advanced Posts from "Z" Company for protection. Uncle Joe had lost one platoon. However, he pushed on with his strolled walk, with a "Cheery oh, Jimmy, Good Luck".

A few minutes later, at about 2.15am, the Boche shelled our area fairly heavily for a short time. At about 2.45am Sergeant Newsome DCM, a stretcher bearer, came to me for two relief stretcher bearers, saying, "Captain Hedley is wounded, Sir! He is hit in the chest and abdomen." Almost at once the stretcher arrived. Joe was badly hit, but seemed quite cheery, and enquired as to the whereabouts of Private Houghton, one of "Z" Company's original stretcher bearers, a boy of 18, who Joe had always promised should carry him down when wounded.

When Newsome returned from the Aid Post the news was that the Doctor was hopeful that Joe would be alright.

Yet another of my <u>very</u> best friends gone. Hedley and Waterhouse had always been like two brothers to me. I saw McVicker later, and he confirmed Newsome's report.

We organised our Line, and my new officers were really splendid. It was all new to them – they were plunged right into the very worst spot on the Somme at the time, Delville Wood – Ginchy – for this village was only some 500 yards East of our position. We had come up to try to do what many hundreds had failed to achieve before us, namely to capture Ginchy, and the commanding ridge East of it. It was imperative for the whole Line that this attack should succeed before anything great could succeed on the Somme. But we didn't know at this time when the attack would be.

Shelling was intermittent during the night, which we spent – what was left of it – improving our trench, and reconnoitring the ground between Diagonal Trench, Elgin Avenue and Stout Trench. There was no Communication Trench to the Front Line – one had been started but it was only about 10 inches deep, just marked out. Consequently the approach from my trench to Stout Trench was across the open. We managed to bury a considerable number of Scotchmen who were lying out, and evidently had been for about 10 days; we couldn't stick the smell – it was awful!

08.09.16 Dawn broke – and a glorious hot, sunny day it was – perfect. It was almost too hot, especially as we had very little water with us.

Nothing happened of much moment – some shelling Hates at 8.00am, 12.00pm to 2.00pm, and 6.00pm, the latter a heavy strafe.

We spent the day clearing up equipment; rifles, Lewis Gun magazines, steel helmets – oh, everything, many of these cast off by those wounded in previous attacks, of which there had been many over this ground. Then we collected new Mills Bombs,[343] Small Arms Ammunition, ground flares etc., ready for issue when orders came to assemble for the anxiously expected "Attack Orders".

The afternoon was quiet, so I had an hour's sleep.

---

[343] See footnote 135 on page 105.

At about 8.00pm heavy shelling began, and continued well through the night.

The original intention of the GOC of the Division, Major General Sir H.S. Jeudwine KCB, was that the 164th Infantry Brigade (ours) was to bomb out the Boche from the enemy Strong Points in Delville Wood, but the scheme was developed, and it was decided at a Conference to carry out the scheme ordered by GOC of the XVth Corps, which stated that the attack on Ginchy would be renewed at 4.45pm on September 9th.

The General Scheme was:

The 16th Division (Irish), XIVth Corps, were to attack on the Right and capture Ginchy;

The 1st Division of the IIIrd Corps were to attack on the Left.

The 164th Infantry Brigade would co-operate in the Centre.

1. The first task of the 164th Infantry Brigade was to take a line of trenches running roughly from the outskirts of Ginchy to the East corner of Delville Wood;

2. The second task was to capture Hop and Ale Alley, which ran at right angles to our Front Line, as far as the junction of Ale Alley and Pint Trench, then at right angles South along Pint Trench to Lager Lane.

This was a very difficult task, as it meant that we would be exposed to Frontal and Enfilade Machine Gun and rifle fire, and would also be between two barrages. We expected these difficulties. When the time came our expectations were more than realised!

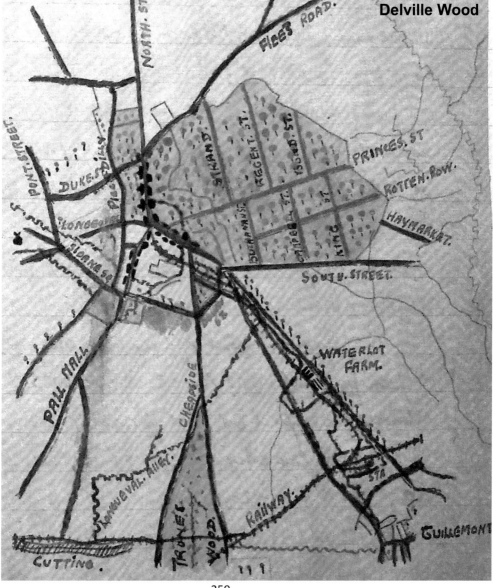

Ginchy, bombarded by the British on July 11, 1916.

Ginchy, ten days later (July 21, 1916).

Ginchy, two days before capture by the British (Sept. 7, 1916). See p. 86.

ILLUSTRATING THE PROGRESSIVE DESTRUCTION AND LEVELLING OF A VILLAGE
BY ARTILLERY.

09.09.16
Some
Day![344]

At midnight on September 8th we received preliminary Attack Orders to be ready to move into Assembly Positions before dawn – this was into Stout Trench. The order of battle would be, from the North, "Y" Company, "X" Company, "Z" Company, "W" Company.

At 3.00am I was ready to move "Z" Company up. I had scribbled a note home – but said nothing of where we were, or that in a few hours I should be in another Big Show. At the same time I had an uncanny feeling about this battle – I really felt that something was going to happen; not that I felt that I should be killed, but there was a feeling …

It was a raw cold foggy morning, fairly quiet, with the usual Machine Gun fire sweeping the ground (just enough to boil the water in the Machine Gun water coolers for morning Gun Fire tea[345]). We moved over the open in single file across about 350 yards of open shell-holed country into Stout Trench. It was a poor Front Line, not deep, and blown in in many places, about 350 yards from the presumed Boche Front Line, and 450 to 500 yards from Ginchy Village, or from what had been the village, as – as will be seen from the photos – not much was left of it.

The enemy started shelling slightly at about 6.00am.

From 7.00am our Heavy and Field Guns commenced deliberate fire-bombardment and continued incessantly until 5.40pm – that was 10½ hours of heavy shelling. The noise was terrific, and, of course, the Boche fired back almost as much, but he seemed to be saving something up for us when we went "over the bags" – as the saying is when an attack is made from a trench.

We had no rations with us, no water, no work to do – we couldn't compose ourselves or walk about, at least the men couldn't; all we could do was Wait! Oh, that waiting to get final instructions as to time, and composition of attacking waves – one could imagine what waiting for the last few hours prior to being hanged is like.

Lieutenant Maw had gone to "W" Company to take over from Cooper, who had gone to command "Y" Company in place of Captain Hedley. My Company officers were now 2nd Lieutenant Lawrie, 2nd Lieutenant Jackson, and 2nd Lieutenant Godfrey. Also, 2nd Lieutenant N. Kemp was attached to "Z" Company for a special Bombing Stunt on Lager Lane.

Hours seemed like days! We were getting very wearied and hungry – that empty sinking feeling. The fog still clung about, and there was very little rifle fire. I was moving along on the top of the parapet seeing that my Lewis Gunners, bombers etc. were in position. Whilst I was walking on the top of the trench the sun broke through, and the fog seemed to lift before I realised it, but the Boche spotted me and opened fire on me with rifles – luckily no bullet found a billet.[xxxviii]

At 12.30 noon I received my Final Attack Orders.

<u>The Order of Battle was:</u>

Our attack was to be made in Four Waves, each of two companies.

1st Wave: two companies of the 1/4th Loyal North Lancashires;

2nd Wave: "Y" and "X" Companies of the 2/5th Lancashire Fusiliers;

3rd Wave: "W" and "Z" Company of the 2/5th Lancashire Fusiliers;

---

[344] *The History of the Lancashire Fusiliers 1914-1918* by Major General J.C. Latter contains a description of the Battle of Ginchy which extends to a page and a half of text, but not unsurprisingly is nowhere near as vivid as the account given by Norman. Norman is mentioned just once in Major General Latter's text, as being in command of "Z" Company.

[345] *"Gun Fire tea"* was sometimes used in army slang to mean tea laced with rum, but here it may just mean ordinary tea produced by using the heat produced by the Machine Guns to boil the water.

4th Wave: two companies of the 1/4th Loyal North Lancashires.

In Support: 1/8th Liverpool (Irish) Reserve, and 1/4th King's Own Royal Lancasters.

The great difficulty from the point of view of "W" and "Z" Company was that we had to file up Stout Trench (running North and South) into Pilsen Lane, which ran East and West, then get out of the trench, attack Ale Alley to support "Y" and "X" Company, then, having taken that objective, to make a right wheel in No Man's Land under heavy fire – which there would be – and attack due East to take Pint Trench from the junction of Ale Alley and Pint Trench, there to link up with the 7th Royal Irish (16th Division), who would by that time have worked through the North end of Ginchy. Also "Z" Company had to make a Strong Point at the junction of Lager Lane and Pint Trench, to bomb up Lager Lane and clear it for 200 yards, and to establish a Bombing Block in Lager Lane. Even if all went well with seasoned troops it was a <u>most difficult</u> operation. However, these were my orders. I at once sat down with my officers, explained the scheme to them, detailed to them their orders, and ordered them to explain to each man his particular job. Kemp I made responsible for the Lager Lane Strong Point and Block with 24 Battalion bombers.

The men got very excited as our own 12 inch shells started to drop in and around my trench – I had 26 casualties from our own shells during the day, but had no means of communication to the Artillery. Ashton had been lost all day. Several men went off their heads. At 3.00pm I received the following message:

OCs of Companies report to HQ at once – URGENT.

Kenderdine, Cooper, Maw, and I met at my Company HQ a few minutes later. A heavy barrage was on the Support Line at the time. We decided that we probably shouldn't get through alive, so handed over our orders to our next seniors, and started off across the 400 yards of open ground. The Boche spotted us and literally sniped at the four of us with 77mm shells and Machine Guns. We ran like hares in a zig-zag course through the bursting shells on the Support Line, and all got to HQ safely, but done to the world – I almost fainted.[xxxix] Major Milnes insisted on us having some food – which, after 36 hours without, under shell fire, was very welcome. Colonel Fox and Best-Dunkley then read out some revised orders, which we took down. It was then 4 o'clock. The attack "kick off" was 5.00pm for the 16th Division.

Our zero time was 4.45pm.

Our attack time was zero + 60 mins i.e. 5.45pm.

So we had to rush back to our Companies through the same barrage. But we got through – all four of us – without casualties.

Very near Stout Trench we met four of my men going towards the Aid Post.

"What's the matter, are you wounded?"

"No, Sir, we've been buried and we're going to the Aid Post."

"Are you wounded – ?"

Poor fellows, they <u>were</u> badly shaken, and no wonder – four fellows were killed by the same shell including Sergeant Russ DCM.[346]

"Well, you can't go down, we want every single man. <u>Go back</u>."

---

[346] Sergeant Stanley Russ DCM, Service no 3374, husband of Alice Russ of Merefield, Rochdale, aged 35, died, according to the Commonwealth War Graves Commission's records, on 26th September 1916; he is buried at Abbeville Communal Cemetery Extension, reference I.C.25; he had been awarded the DCM for his actions in the Blairville raid on 28th June 1916 – see page 200.

I was getting annoyed – very annoyed.

I had drawn my revolver by now. "<u>Go</u> <u>back</u> <u>at once</u> or <u>I'll shoot</u>," pointing my revolver.

They didn't move – I cocked my revolver, and fired one round into the air. They went back!

I met all four of them later at the Aid Post – but wounded. They got what they wanted – Blighties.

I last saw Kenderdine at about 4.40pm when he left me to rejoin his Company, "X" Company.[347]

I never saw him again – he was killed![348]

It was now 4.45pm. A <u>very</u> <u>intense</u> bombardment started – just one whizz of shells – Terrific! Magnificent!

One hour more to wait. Unless killed before.

At 5.15pm the 16th Division left their trenches to attack Ginchy.

Each wave was distinct. Each man moved with his rifle and bayonet at the Post. It was wonderful! The Boche opened Machine Gun fire and rifle fire, like rain pattering on a glass roof. Men fell, wounded or killed – but the more fortunate went on – wave after wave – undaunted, until, about 40 yards from the Boche Line, our fellows waited for the creeping barrage of shrapnel shells, which had rested on the Boche Front Line, to lift – then with a rush! a cheer! they took the trenches – the Boche retired at the double through Ginchy and towards Lager Lane and Pint Trench – there were hundreds of them. My fellows wanted to go over there and then, for fear that there wouldn't be any Boche left. Our time would come, we had only 20 minutes to wait. But I knew that we should have a rough time – the Boche were crowding into our objectives. It was one of the finest, and yet one of the most terrible and inhuman sights that I had ever seen.

At 5.30pm Ashton came to me. "Where have you been, Ashton, all day? I thought that you'd been killed – I'm glad to see you back." "I've been to the Transport Lines, Sir, there's

---

[347] In the original diary Norman has put "Y", not "X", but he must mean "X", as Kenderdine is twice mentioned as being OC of "X" Company in the diary entry for 7th September 1916, and Cooper is said to have taken over command of "Y" Company in place of Joe Hedley earlier in this entry.

[348] Lieutenant T.H.G. Kenderdine is buried at Delville Wood Cemetery, Longueval, reference XIII.C.5. He joined the 2/5th Lancashire Fusiliers on 23rd August 1915. He is frequently called "Kenders" and had the nickname of "Charlie Chaplin", no doubt in part because of his appearance (there is a photograph on page 141), and in part because he was a humourist (he is described as *"very funny"* at football in the diary entry for 25th November to 5th December 1915). Born in Japan, he had come to Britain on the outbreak of war to get a commission. There is virtually no information about him in the Commonwealth War Graves Commission's records, as only his rank, initials, surname, date of death and Battalion appear on his headstone. On arrival in France he was assigned to "Z" Company, and therefore worked closely with Norman from the time of his arrival until he was given his own Company at the end of August 1916. He is frequently mentioned as being out in No Man's Land on patrol or mounting bombing raids (see the diary entries for 14th to 19th August 1915 on page 81-2, 12th October to 4th November 1915 on page 105, 24th December 1915 on page 129, and 26th to 30th May 1916 on page 184); and once he is mentioned as helping Norman to tap German wires (see the diary entry for 16th to 27th November 1915 on page 125). For a few days from 26th January 1916 he was in charge of 20 men forming a working party unloading trains at the Railhead at Pont-Remy, a job that Norman reports that he did *"exceedingly well and was especially thanked for his good work by the GOC of the 46th Division, a feather in Kenders' cap, also in the cap of the 2/5th Lancashire Fusiliers, and, lastly, that of "Z" Company."* Norman tells the following story of when they shared a dug out on the Thiepval Sector on 23rd December 1915: *"It was a filthy wet night, simply coming down in sheets. Kenders was wet through when he turned in. I had slung some ground sheets up in the roof of the dug out to catch the water which was coming through. Poor old Kenders, very tired, had just settled down on the bed, when I was passing the dug out and heard loud – and not altogether Parliamentary – language issuing therefrom, so went to investigate. The weight of water had got too heavy for the ground sheets and had broken the supports, with the result that the whole flood came down on Charlie Chaplin (Kenderdine), and he was again soaked through, including his blankets."* He celebrated a birthday on 30th November 1915, for which occasion his fellow officers made a special effort at dinner. See also *Obituaries*.

steak and chips ready for you at Company HQ, Sir – I thought you'd be better with some food before you went over the top, Sir." 14 miles he had walked, for a steak and chips for me. Just like Ashton! He would have done anything for me.

5.35pm, 5.36pm – minutes seemed like hours. I was really in a funk! Then a runner came, saying "Lieutenant Maw's hit in the head, Sir." "Killed?" "Don't know, Sir." "Tell Mr Petrie I want to see him at once." Petrie came – "Petrie, you command "W" Company when we go over." "Couldn't, Hall – I'm nearly off my head." It was too late to argue. "You command "W" Company, Petrie. I shall be with you, and will try to control our wave."

"Come on, it's 5.40. Time we moved up to Pilsen Trench. Have "Y" Company moved yet, Lawrie?" "Yes, Sir!"

"Right Ho. Come on "Z" Company." Up Stout Trench we moved, and got up there – it was not far – by 5.43pm. All the men were lined up ready – Waiting! Like waiting in a Race for the pistol to start.

Norman and I got on the top – but I didn't like it really!

"Anyway, Kemp, it's no use now. We're in for the Boche this time."

I watched the second finger of my watch – each second seemed an eternal age. 5.44pm …

"Get Ready, you fellows." Shouting was useless – the row was awful – bullets were whizzing about like hailstones – shells bursting like thunderclaps.

The expression on the men's faces was one of thought, fear, farewell – they were silent. 5.44'20".

"They are not the kind of hero one thinks of, but their sacrifices have greater worth than they who have not seen them will ever be able to understand."[349]

Bullets were skimming the top of the parapet – where the heads of men, just concealed, were waiting to give the first leap into that awful No Man's Land.

The end of the day was spreading a sublime but melancholy light on that strong unbroken line of men, comprising "Z" Company and "W" Company, of whom only some would live to see the night.

"Ready." Then with a final spring, 5.45pm. I gave the Advance Signal – I went forward a few yards – my men followed. Some were hit – killed in the first yard or so.

The start has been made very quickly, unexpectedly almost, as in a dream. The rifle and Machine Gun fire was more intense than ever – we moved with difficulty over the already littered ground. Huge shell holes – the whole earth churned up – our first two waves had caught it very severely – even now we were walking over bodies of our own fellows – who only a few minutes before had been hearty strong living men; wounded were crawling back – some walking. It was a hideous sight. But on we went – stumbling. One forgot the shells – the bullets – I looked at Petrie, he was alright – then, instantly, he was shot in the head and killed.[350]

---

[349] Norman does not say where this quotation comes from.
[350] 2nd Lieutenant Donald John Petrie of the 1/10th Battalion Royal Scots, attached to the 2/5th Fusiliers, son of William and May Petrie of Newliston, Kirkleston, West Lothian, was aged 22 when he died, and is commemorated at the Thiepval Memorial, Pier and Face 6D and 7D. Norman says that he joined the 2/5th Lancashire Fusiliers in France on 24th April 1916, the Battalion War Diary says 9th May 1916.

Jackson was hit similarly a few seconds later.[351]

My Companies were losing heavily. We reached a trench – not marked on our maps – not spotted or reported by our aeroplanes. "Y" Company and "X" Company were fighting hand to hand – we joined them – it was every man for himself – but we cleared Haymarket Trench; the few Boche who were there we passed over, and on to Ale Alley. Fire seemed to come from Front, Rear and Flanks all at once – the stridor of the bursting shells hurt your ears, beat you on the neck, went through your temples, I almost cried aloud. We left, scarcely knowing where. The view in front of us was blocked by dust and bursting shells. We were passing through the counter enemy barrage. Here and there I saw forms that spun round, were lifted up – blown into the air – never to be seen again. Bodies literally burnt to charred masses. Now we were nearly running. Some of my poor men fell solidly flat, others foundered meekly, I stepped aside to avoid the dead, quiet and rigid – or else the wounded who lay moaning, crying, asking for help – but we couldn't stop. I was anxiously trying to make out Ale Alley, and, seeing Boche about 50 yards ahead, I turned to look over my shoulder to see how many men I had, and where they were – something struck me – I went on a few yards – a choking feeling – my mouth full of blood – I couldn't breathe for a second.

I'm hit – the whole scene spun round – I fell – then almost at once I got up slowly – not quite certain where I was – tried to go on – managed about 10 yards – fell again. Still a third attempt – when Ashton, my servant, came up behind me – picked me up, and, in a polite way, said,

"Now then, Sir – you're hit – Come on back, I'll carry you – none of your b ——— nonsense."[xl]

It was no use, I had to give in, I couldn't go on, I was hit in my back – I was losing blood quickly from inside. Ashton picked me up, put me on his back and carried me over all that awful ground again. We rested in a shell hole – I helped to dress two fellows' wounds which were very bad. I didn't like leaving them, but Ashton seemed to be in command, and insisted on me going. He carried me two miles to the Aid Post – Major Milnes met us, and rushed me into McVicker.

I remember holding on to Ashton and telling McVicker to plug it with wool and let me go back. I dimly remember him saying, "Oh yes, you'll be alright to go back," and everything went black. I came round – I was on a stretcher. My arm felt stiff; "Doc, am I hit in the arm?" – and then I remembered that, as Ashton had carried me down, I had felt something hit my arm – but didn't worry at that moment. But I had been hit a second time – a bullet had gone clean through my left arm just above the elbow.[xli]

I was lifted out of the dug out – the Boche were shelling heavily. Four bearers came along. One said, "Come on Bill, here's a light weight." McVicker ran out. "Got your helmet?" "Yes, do you want it?" "No fear – put that officer's helmet on, the Boche are gas shelling down the road." So on my Gas helmet went. It was awful breathing and bleeding at the same time. On a stretcher helpless under shell fire is a most trying ordeal. I was feeling very hot and very cold – Shock I suppose. At Bernafay Wood Aid Post I was dressed again, and a

---

[351] 2nd Lieutenant John Henry Jackson, son of Thomas and Hannah May Jackson of Horsforth, Leeds, was aged 25 when he died, and is commemorated at the Thiepval Memorial, Panel and Face 3C and 3D. He had joined the 2/5th Lancashire Fusiliers in France on 31st August 1916, or very shortly before – see footnote 332 on page 250.

Padre very kindly promised to write home for me. I also saw Padre Newman – busy as a bee.[352] From there I was carried about 2 miles over awfully rough roads to Montauban Corner, and dumped to wait for the ambulance. It was then about 8.00pm. The ambulance soon came – but we were shelled all the time and couldn't move – just wait and hope we should be alright. Many were killed or wounded while waiting. I got so fed up that I began to think I didn't mind what happened. Ashton was still with me, and promised to go to the Transport and to send my kit off, and I gave him some money.

Alan Maw[353] was put into my ambulance and we went very slowly, but it was most uncomfortable – every little jar seemed to hurt most. Eventually we reached Bécordel Dressing Station. My dressing felt comfortable and I didn't want disturbing, so the MO decided to send me to the next place. I met an MO at Bécordel whom I knew, Captain Bennett; he saved my life by giving me a drink and a cigarette. About half an hour later we were put into another ambulance and sent via Méaulte to Méricourt to a Dressing Station on the Albert to Amiens road. Here we got ATN[354] injections and were pushed off in another ambulance. It seemed to take hours; we went very slowly, and I began to feel very rotten – I fell asleep or unconscious, I don't know which. We arrived at Heilly Casualty Clearing Station N° 36, and I was soon rushed into an operating theatre. I wouldn't have anaesthetic, persuading them to work without – wished in a few minutes that I hadn't – had a very hot and cold half hour while they removed bits of shrapnel and played about with my back and arm. Eventually I got to a ward, had a wash, was given hot milk and brandy – and clean sheets. It felt like heaven! perfectly peaceful – no shells – not a sound. Just a dim light. I was in great pain now – couldn't sleep. Sister came and rubbed my head. These Hospitals – the Sisters – all the medical arrangements – were wonderful. It was fine to be there after that Delville Wood and Ginchy. I felt awfully bad – had lost a lot of blood, and really thought that I should never get well – then in the middle of the night I pulled myself together and said that I mustn't give way.

---

[352] This is the last mention in the diary of Captain R.E.G. Newman, the Padre. He was first mentioned by name on 2nd July 1916, and in the entry for 30th July 1916 was described as *"one of the very best of fellows … he cheered everyone up and had a word of encouragement for all of us."* *The History of the Lancashire Fusiliers 1914-1918* by Major General J.C. Latter mentions him three times, at the 3rd Battle of Ypres in July/August 1917, when he was awarded the MC in recognition of the fact that he *"exposed himself fearlessly in his efforts to cheer the troops and minister to the wounded"*; in an incident on 17th September 1917 near Wieltje, when a dug out caught fire and he helped get its occupants out to safety and put out the fire; and on 9th April 1918 when the Germans broke through the Line at Givenchy and attempted to take Captain Newman and another Padre prisoner at the Windy Corner Aid Post, whereupon Captain Newman escaped and was able to report the fact that the Germans had penetrated the Line to Battalion HQ, for which action he received a bar to his MC.

[353] Norman also spells Maw's first name "Allan". 2nd Lieutenant Maw had joined the 2/5th Lancashire Fusiliers in France on 31st August 1916, but he may already have had some experience previously, as he was immediately made 2nd in Command of "Z" Company on 6th September 1916, and Norman was originally going to hand over the command of "Z" Company to him for the attack when he was to be sent away on a course at the critical moment on 7th September 1916; then, earlier on 9th September 1916, Maw had taken over command of "W" Company when Cooper went to "Y" Company to take over as OC of that Company in place of Joe Hedley.

[354] This is anti-tetanus serum, which was routinely used in the First World War, and administered as soon as practicable, usually at a field treatment station, though the abbreviation would more normally be "ATS", or simply "AT".

10.09.16   I had a little milk for breakfast. I asked Sister if a Captain Hedley had been through – luckily he had been in that very tent. But – he had died the previous night. Poor old Hedley, gone at last.[355] It upset me very much.

The Doctor came round, and examined me. I heard him say that I couldn't be moved for some days. Cooper was also brought to my ward wounded.[356] I slept a little, then was wakened by Sister saying, "You'll have to leave us after all – all cases are to be evacuated at once."

At 11.00am I was taken by ambulance to the Hospital siding at Heilly, and placed on the Ambulance Train.

Previously I had had several tickets pinned on my pyjamas.

I was very tired and in pain on the train, and was not allowed to eat or drink – which was rotten, as I had ordered a Bass, when Sister arrived at the critical moment and stopped it, so I had to watch another fellow drink it.

The train got very hot and stuffy. I couldn't get comfortable, and was really beginning to feel quite rotten. We arrived at Rouen at 11.20pm. I was very tired. I was taken up to Nº 2 British Red Cross Hospital, near the Bishop's Palace, Rue des Petits Oiseaux. I arrived at about 11.45pm, and had a rotten night – I kept wakening with the thought of shells etc., and I could only lie in one position.

L.T. C. Cooper
wounded
QUINCHY
1.9.16.

---

[355] Captain Joseph Walton Hedley, son of the Reverend Matthew and Jane Alice Hedley, formerly of Langho Vicarage, Whalley, Lancs, BA Brasenose College, Oxford, Assistant Master at Copthorne School, Crawley, Sussex, died on 12th September 1915 according to the Commonwealth War Graves Commission's records, aged 35, and is buried at Heilly Station Cemetery, Méricourt-l'Abbé, reference IV.F.6. He is first mentioned in the diary as being with "D" Company of the 2/5th Lancashire Fusiliers when they first landed in France on 3rd May 1915, and has featured frequently thereafter up to his death. He was a big man, playing in goal at football in the diary entry for 29th November to 5th December 1915, and, describing the billiard table on which he slept on 5th May 1915, Norman adds *"a strong one luckily!"* He was friendly from the first with Captain Kenneth Waterhouse, also of "D" Company, and Norman was invited to join them both in "D" Company Mess on 9th May 1915, which he did until they finished their training at Arques on 8th July 1915. Norman describes both of them as being like brothers to him. Joe Hedley's nickname is said to have been "Hell Fire Joe" (see the diary entry for 21st to 30th June 1915), or, more commonly, simply "Uncle Joe". Inter alia Norman describes how they both attended a rather wild dinner party on 8th October 1915 with Gray and two Scotsmen, and went on leave at the same time in November 1915, on which occasion Joe managed to take with him as a souvenir a German Trench Mortar bomb 2 feet 6 inches long and 1 foot in diameter. During this leave, as they travelled together before dawn in a train carriage without gas or electric lighting, Norman says: *"'forewarned is forearmed', and Joe Hedley, with his usual attention to detail, produced a couple of candles"*. On 27th June 1916 Joe left to take over duties as an Instructor at the Infantry Base Depot at Étaples, therefore being absent when Kenneth Waterhouse was killed on the Somme Front on 8th August 1916, but returning towards the end of August 1916 when the Battalion was at rest at Franleu, in time to go back up to the Somme Front with the Battalion on 7th September 1916. There is a photograph of him with Norman, Kenneth Waterhouse, Latter, Simon, Kemp, and the Mayor and Mayoress of Arques, taken between 20th May 1915 and 8th July 1915 on page 52. See also *Obituaries*.

[356] According to the Battalion War Diary Lieutenant S. Cooper joined the 2/5th Lancashire Fusiliers in France on 23rd August 1915. In both the Battalion War Diary and *The History of the Lancashire Fusiliers 1914-1918* by Major General J.C. Latter his initial is "S", but Norman has put "C" in the caption to the photograph. He is first mentioned in the diary entry for 10th July 1916, and must have been an experienced officer, as he was already commanding "W" Company by 10th August 1916.

11.09.16   I found that I was in Nº 1 Ward. I had a fairly comfortable day, and slept at intervals, but had an awful time having my dressings done. I couldn't move my left arm – my hand was partially paralysed.

Lawrie, one of my subalterns, arrived in the same ward.[357] Thus I knew that all the officers in "Z" Company had been killed or wounded. The Doctor, Major Hudson, seemed very anxious about me, and said that I couldn't be moved for some time.

Nº 2 Red Cross Hospital was a very cheery Hospital, and everybody there was just great. I was feeling pretty bad, but everyone was so kind.

12.09.16   There was a change in orders – the Hospital was to be cleared of as many patients as possible. Major Hudson decided that he would send me over to England.

At 2.00pm that day they started to dress me – umpteen clothes – operation stockings etc. etc. etc. At about 6.00pm I was lifted on to a stretcher and was carried down to the ambulance – one of the carriers slipped and dropped the stretcher, and me included. It hurt very badly, and I'm afraid that I was <u>very</u> rude to him, to say the least of it. I was taken down to the Quay at Rouen and put on board the Hospital Ship, *St Andrew*.[358] It was a fine ship, with everything finely arranged, and with very comfortable swinging cots. I was only allowed a little tea and a piece of bread and butter, although I was very hungry. My back was very painful during night, but I had a morphia injection and got some sleep, and felt much better next morning.

HMHS *St Andrew*

13.09.16   On the morning of Wednesday September 13th I found that we hadn't left Rouen. We sailed at about 11.00am, down the Seine to Havre.

I wanted a cigarette, and sent for my bundle of clothes, but I couldn't find my case with my notes in; then I found my case, but there were no notes – they must have been stolen out of my wallet, because I had had them at Longueval to give Ashton some money. The RAMC had kept up their reputation!

However, I remembered that I had a sovereign given to me by Aunt Jane for an emergency ration; I decided that this was an emergency, so I spent some of it.

I couldn't move in my cot, but a fellow lent me his periscope to look at the view through a porthole. However, I am afraid that I wasn't very interested in views. We arrived at Havre in the afternoon, and crossed over to Southampton.

---

[357] Lawrie had joined the 2/5th Lancashire Fusiliers in France on 31st August 1916. Norman met him again when he (Norman) was based at Ripon in 1917, waiting to be sent back to France; sadly, he says of Lawrie, in his diary entry for 8th June 1917, that he *"was wounded on 9th September 1916 at Ginchy on the Somme – he only had a few days in the Line and was never much use for anything again."*

[358] HMHS *St Andrew* was a screw steamer built in 1908 for Great Western Railways, fitted out by the Ministry of Defence as a Hospital Ship in 1914. Before and after the War she was a cross channel ferry between Wales and Ireland.

On the boat I saw Major Milnes[359] who had been slightly wounded by a shell which had hit the Aid Post in York Alley – it had killed McVicker, the MO,[360] and wounded the Major.[xlii] We travelled up from Southampton on a Hospital Train, a new Lancashire and Yorkshire Railway train, especially made – beautifully equipped, and very comfortable. Alan Maw[361] was on the same train.

14.09.16   On arrival in London I was sent to Miss Birkett's at 7 Mandeville Place, West London, where I arrived at about 2.00am, absolutely wearied and tired out. I was put to bed, and I actually slept. I had been on the way from the Line for four and a half days, moving from one place to another. It was a glorious feeling to be in that cosy bed that night – at last – once again in dear old England – miles away from the fighting.

But the Zeppelin Raiders were busy. One had been brought down at Cuffley on 3rd September. We had several exciting Raid Warnings – not exactly pleasant in Hospital. I had two very nice fellows in my room, Captain E. Greville, Royal Irish Fusiliers, a great fellow who cheered me up no end, and Lieutenant Dixie MC of the Manchester Pals, who was rather a pessimist.

So my Active Service finished at any rate for six months.

I anxiously awaited a report of the Ginchy scrap, having left in the middle of it, and eventually learned the following:

The Battalion was not relieved on the night of September 9th, although the casualties were heavy, 19 officers, and 369 NCOs and men.

The officers <u>killed</u> were Captain Joe Hedley,[362] Lieutenant T.H.G. Kenderdine,[363] 2nd Lieutenant Petrie,[364]

---

[359] Major H.N. Milnes (whose full name was Henry Nicholas Milnes) had been with the 2/5th Lancashire Fusiliers as 2nd in Command when they first landed in France on 3rd May 1915, having trained with the Lancashire Fusiliers at Southport. He has been mentioned frequently in the diary up to this point, having assumed temporary command from time to time, including on 8th August 1916 for the engagement when Kenneth Waterhouse was killed, and Norman's orders to advance in support of other troops luckily came too late. He next appears in the diary at the Infantry Depot at Étaples in June 1917 when Norman returned to France after recovering from being wounded, and, in the diary entry for 26th October 1917, Norman records that he had learned that Major Milnes had returned to the 2/5th Lancashire Fusiliers as their CO. Norman liked Major Milnes from the start; when he went on leave on 19th September 1915 he comments, in the entry for that day: *"We did miss him"*, and in the diary entry for 1st to 15th June 1916, when they found that the Major was not to return to the 2/5th Lancashire Fusiliers on coming back from leave, at least not immediately, he says: *"Officers, NCOs, and men alike were all sorry to lose the Major. He was one of those people who do such a lot in a quiet unassuming way, yet are always busy. The 2/5th Lancashire Fusiliers owed a very great deal to Major Milnes. His very presence, whether on parade or in the Mess, seemed to alter the whole atmosphere. However we hoped that our loss would be his gain, and that we should soon have him back."* Amongst other things, he must have been a good horseman, as he won musical chairs on horseback at Bouzincourt on 6th September 1915, was one of the only two officers who was any good at going over some jumps on 19th January 1916, and came first in a Divisional Competition for "Officer's Charger" at Simencourt on 19th June 1916. There is a photograph of him with Lieutenant Colonel H.J. Shirley, Lieutenant R.N. Thompson and Captain G.C. Hutchinson on page 112.

[360] Lieutenant Edgar Harold McVicker of the RAMC, attached to the 2/5th Lancashire Fusiliers, only son of Mr and Mrs Samuel McVicker of Toronto, Canada, was aged 23 when he died, and is buried at Dantzig Alley British Cemetery, Mametz, reference I.C.8.; the inscription on his grave reads: *"Our son died as he lived careless of self thoughtful for others"*. This is particularly poignant, bearing in mind that he had just treated Norman, and his concern that Norman should have his Gas helmet on (see the diary entry for 9th September 1916).

[361] Norman also spells Maw's first name "Allan".

[362] See footnote 355 on page 267.

[363] See footnote 348 on page263.

[364] See footnote 350 on page 264.

The Thiepval Memorial photographed in 2018; of those mentioned here, Petrie, Elson, Taylor, Essex, Kemp, Jackson and Saxby are commemorated on this monument, having no known graves.

Elson,[365] Taylor,[366] Essex,[367] Norman Kemp,[368] Jackson,[369] Godfrey,[370] and Lieutenant McVicker RAMC.

The officers <u>wounded</u> were Major H.N. Milnes, Captain N. Hall, Lieutenant Cooper, Lieutenant Maw, 2nd Lieutenant Worrall, Steibel, Lawrie and Jones.[371]

<u>Missing,</u> believed killed, was 2nd Lieutenant E.Y. Saxby.[372]

---

[365] 2nd Lieutenant Edwin Arthur Elson of the 9th Battalion Middlesex Regiment, attached to the 2/5th Lancashire Fusiliers, is commemorated at the Thiepval Memorial, Pier and Face 12D and 13B. He had joined the 2/5th Lancashire Fusiliers in France on 15th June 1916 according to Norman (17th June 1916 according to the Battalion War Diary), and is described as a "*rather useful fellow*" on page 185.

[366] 2nd Lieutenant David George Taylor, of the 10th Battalion, Manchester Regiment, attached to the 2/5th Lancashire Fusiliers, is commemorated at the Thiepval Memorial, Pier and Face 13A and 14C. This is Norman's only reference to him. The date on which he was attached to the 2/5th Lancashire Fusiliers in France is not clear, but, excluding McVicker, only 13 new officers are named on page 250, yet the Battalion War Diary confirms that 14 joined on 31st August 1916.

[367] 2nd Lieutenant Percy Clifford Essex, son of Jean Cameron Essex and the late Captain Bertram E. Essex of Lewisham Road, Highgate, London was aged 21 when he died, and is commemorated at Thiepval Memorial, Pier and Face 3C and 3D. He joined the 2/5th Lancashire Fusiliers in France on 31st August 1916.

[368] 2nd Lieutenant Norman Kemp, son of the Reverend Canon R. Lavers Kemp and Mrs Lavers Kemp of West Didsbury, Manchester, was aged 21 when he died and is commemorated at the Thiepval Memorial Pier and Face 3C and 3D. He is mentioned in the diary entry for 4th September 1914 as having joined the Lancashire Fusiliers in Bury at the same time as Norman, and was with "D" Company of the 2/5th Lancashire Fusiliers when they first landed in France on 3rd May 1915. He features frequently in the diary up to his death, having shared a billet with Norman in Bedford in April 1915 (see the diary entry for 18th April 1915), and they got to know each other even better when Norman joined "D" Company's Mess from 9th May 1915 until they finished their training at Arques on 8th July 1915. While they were at Arques he "*pinched a horse from the Transport Lines to ride into Merville*" (see the diary entry for 10th to 11th May 1915), and enjoyed a swim in the canal on 26th May 1915, and he had some "*good sport ratting*" with Norman, Latter and Harker in the trenches at Aveluy (see the diary entry for 14th to 19th August 1915 on page 78). According to the Battalion War Diary he was appointed Bombing Officer on 24th June 1915, and he features prominently as a bomber and on patrol in No Man's Land (see the diary entries for 14th to 19th August 1915 on page 81, 27th August 1915 on page 86 and 12th October to 4th November 1915 on page 105), apart from periods of absence when he was being treated for a bombing injury to his hand (see the diary entries for 20th April 1916, 1st June 1916 and 22nd August 1916). There is a photograph of him with Norman, Kenneth Waterhouse, Hedley, Latter, Simon, and the Mayor and Mayoress of Arques, taken between 20th May 1915 and 8th July 1915 on page 52. See also *Obituaries*.

[369] See footnote 351 on page 265.

[370] 2nd Lieutenant Henry Godfrey had joined the 2/5th Lancashire Fusiliers in France on 31st August 1916, or very shortly before – see footnote 332 on page 250. Norman does not mention the circumstances of his death, while the Commonwealth War Graves Commission's records give the date as being "*between 8th and 9th September 1916*". The son of Joseph Godfrey, and husband of Florence E. Godfrey, he was aged 35 when he died, and is buried at Delville Wood Cemetery, Longueval, reference XIII.C.7.

[371] For Lieutenant McVicker, Major Milnes, Lieutenant Cooper and Lieutenant Maw see footnotes 360, 359, 356 and 353 on pages 266-9 respectively. Worrall, Steibel (which Norman also spells "Stiebel"), Lawrie and Jones had all joined the 2/5th Lancashire Fusiliers in France on 31st August 1916, or very shortly before. See also footnote 357 on page 268 with regard to Lawrie. The Brigade War Diary records that Jones was "Wounded (Shellshock)".

[372] According to the Commonwealth War Graves Commission's records, 2nd Lieutenant Eric Yardley Saxby, of the 9th Battalion Middlesex Regiment, attached to the 2/5th Lancashire Fusiliers, son of Jess and Elizabeth Saxby of Kilburn, London, died aged 23, and is commemorated at the Thiepval Memorial, Pier and Face 12D and 13B. He joined the 2/5th Lancashire Fusiliers in France on 14th June 1916.

General View of Ambulance Train

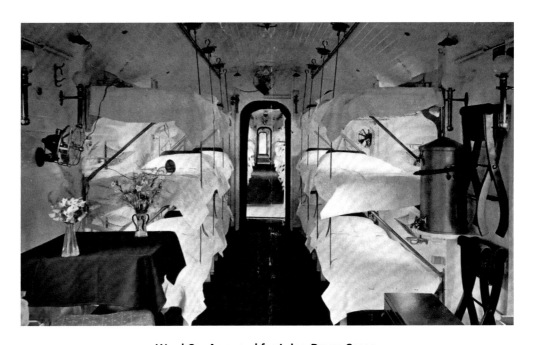

Ward Car Arranged for Lying-Down Cases

During my stay with the 2/5th Lancashire Fusiliers, from May 1915 to September 1916 we had had 74 officers. Major Barnsdale[373] and Lieutenant Packman[374] were the only two officers of the originals who were left with the Battalion. The Battalion had had nearly 1000 casualties in NCOs and men.

The night of September 9th was apparently an awful night. The 164th Infantry Brigade found the objectives impossible to hold, owing to the heavy casualties having reduced numbers too much. The 2/5th Lancashire Fusiliers had to withdraw to their starting off point, Pilsen Trench.

The situation in York Alley was chaotic. There were three Battalion HQs all together, the two Dressing Stations had been blown in, and the trenches were choked with wounded and ration parties, while the Boche had the range to a nicety, and shelled unmercifully. Those men who still remained were worn out, famished, and thirsty. The Battle had been a very trying experience. Luckily our guns retaliated on the German Batteries and silenced them within two minutes (according to the *Lancashire Fusiliers' Annual*). With the exception of the two previously mentioned, this day had cost the Battalion the remaining officers of the 2/5th Lancashire Fusiliers who had trained, come out to France, and fought with them during the anxious times of 1915 and 1916.

---

[373] Captain J.D. Barnsdale joined the Lancashire Fusiliers as an officer in Bury in or about September 1914 (see the diary entry for 12th September 1914), and had already been promoted to Major by the time the Battalion embarked for France on 3rd May 1915, at which point he was in "B" Company. While training in Southport Norman says that he, Kenneth Waterhouse, Norman, and Norman's brother, George, would sit together at Mess (see the diary entry for 8th November to 13th December 1914), and he features frequently in the diary during training in England. After arrival in France he is mentioned as inviting Norman to have dinner with him and some French officers when they are taking over the trenches from the French at Aveluy (see the diary entry for 31st July 1915), but then, on 19th June 1916, Norman writes: *"I believe that Major J. Barnsdale was Town Major of Simencourt at this time for some reason or other."* He returned to the Battalion on 20th July 1916, and seems to have resumed his position as OC of "X" Company, being listed as OC of "X" Company on 8th August 1916, and in the diary entry for 21st to 26th August 1916. But in the diary entry for 7th September 1916 Lieutenant Kenderdine was listed as commanding "X" Company, and Major Barnsdale is not mentioned, so that it would appear that he missed the engagement at Ginchy for some reason. There is a photograph of him with Barwood, Duckworth and Hartington, probably taken in September 1915, on page 65.

[374] Lieutenant J.B. Packman was with "C" Company of the 2/5th Lancashire Fusiliers when they first landed in France on 3rd May 1915, having joined the Lancashire Fusiliers at the same time as Norman (see the diary entry for 14th September 1914). Norman says he went home on 8th May 1915 after only five days in France, giving no reason for this. The Battalion War Diary says he left on 10th May 1915, and records the reason as being that he was *"sick"*. He returned to France at about the beginning of June 1916 (see the diary entry for 1st to 15th June 1916). He was an officer with "Z" Company when the Battalion arrived at the Somme on 25th July 1916, but by 5th August 1916 he *"really wasn't fit. In fact it was certain he ought to go to Hospital"*, and the following day he *"got very nervy"*, and did go to hospital. He returned to "Z" Company on 10th August 1916, but left the Company once again on 1st September 1916 when he was made Acting Quartermaster, thus avoiding the engagement on 9th September 1916, and being one of the only two original officers still to be with the 2/5th Lancashire Fusiliers at this point. In the diary entry for 4th August 1917, discussing the appointments of various comrades to the rank of substantive Captain, or alternatively reversion to their (lower) substantive ranks, Norman has written: *"Packman was also a Captain"*, and has added an exclamation mark. Like Norman, Packman had been educated at Bury Grammar School.

On arrival at the hospital at 7 Mandeville Place Norman Hall spent the first month in bed, then, when he could go out, he and his fellow convalescents enjoyed theatre shows (matinees, as they weren't allowed out in the evenings) and *"used to parade daily at noon at the Long Bar at the Grand in the Strand – quite an amusing place – where Admirals, Generals, and all kinds of folk collected"*. He also called on people whom he knew in London, including Lieutenant Colonel Shirley (CO of the 2/5th Lancashire Fusiliers from June 1915 to June 1916)[376] and Miss Hedley, presumably the sister of Joe Hedley.[376]

Though his wounds were not yet healed, Norman left 7 Mandeville Place on about 1st November 1916, and went home to Bury.

On 9th January 1917 he was passed fit for Light Duty, and was sent to join the 5th Reserve Battalion in Ripon, where he was appointed OC of "V" Company, the "demics" Company,[377] and trained alongside new recruits and other men who were recovering from wounds. In this period he met up again with many former 2/5th Lancashire Fusiliers men, for example, Lance Corporal Burgon, Private Bennett (both of whom were presented with Military Medals during this period), Company Sergeant Major Howard (who had been wounded in Dainville in June 1916), Long Waterhouse, Evans, Latter, Noton, Rothband, Barwood and Duckworth.[378] On 15th February 1917 he was passed fit for Home Service, and two days later did his first Route March, *"most of it on Major Longley's horse"*. On 17th March 1917 he was passed fit for General Service, and at the end of April moved with the Battalion to Scarborough for more training, where he says: *"Life became rather monotonous and one began to get tired of this type of soldiering."*

On 9th June 1917 he left Scarborough to return to France. His diary entry reads:

I was leaving behind many of my old NCOs and men. I wished they were going back with me. They wished they were coming with me – especially my old Company Sergeant Major Joe Howard, my old Company Sergeant Major "Z" Company 2/5th Lancashire Fusiliers, a man for whom I always had, and shall have always, a great regard.
These partings are inevitable, and I had been in England since September 14th 1916 – surely long enough. Fit again, I felt keen (in a way) to be off back to the Front. I say "in a way" because no man can be really keen on war – trenches and the horror of war – especially when you've had experience of it. My companions were different, they were going out for the first time – to them doubtless it was a great adventure – full of excitement, and new experiences. They little realised, I know, what they were really going to – they soon found out.

---

[375] The *Afterword* summarises the key contents of the diary from 15th September 1916 onwards. The passages that appear in italics are quotations from the diary unless otherwise appears. They may have been slightly edited from the original diary, but only in accordance with the principles set out in the Preface.

[376] For Lieutenant Colonel Shirley see footnote 251 on page 192, and for Joe Hedley footnote 355 on page 267.

[377] i.e. the Company for incapacitated men.

[378] For details of when the commissioned officers listed here were last mentioned see page 321. For Lance Corporal Burgon see the diary entry for 14th to 19th August 1915 on page 80; for Private Bennett see the diary entry for 24th to 28th June 1916 on page 200 and footnote 265 on that page; for Company Sergeant Major Howard see the diary entry for 24th June 1916 on page 196 and footnote 254 on that page.

Following his arrival in France on 14th June 1917, Norman reported to the Infantry Base Depot at Étaples, and attended the training centre known as the Bull Ring, where he renewed his acquaintance with Major Milnes, formerly of the 2/5th Lancashire Fusiliers, who had been slightly wounded in the same engagement as Norman on 9th September 1916. He learnt that he was to be posted to the 1/5th Lancashire Fusiliers, then in the 42nd Division. He joined them on 22nd June 1917, and was assigned to "C" Company as 2nd in Command to Captain William M. Tickler, of the 2nd (Garrison) Battalion Cheshire Regiment, attached to the 1/5th Lancashire Fusiliers.

He had previously written to Bertram Best-Dunkley (formerly the Adjutant of the 2/5th Lancashire Fusiliers, now temporary Lieutenant Colonel commanding them in the Ypres Sector) to ask to join the 2/5th. Best-Dunkley's reply is pictured here, and reads: "*Thanks for your wire, very pleased if you can come and join us, I have a Company ready for you to take over. You will however have to pull strings at your end & see what can be done, make friends with the Adj. & O.C. Depot & get into communication with Milnes. If you meet Francis at the base tell him the same thing. Yours B. Best-Dunkley.*"

At first Norman was disappointed to be posted to the 1/5th Lancashire Fusiliers, but he recollected that he and Best-Dunkley "*never were very great pals*",[379] and that in any case most of the officers whom he had known in the 2/5th Lancashire Fusiliers were gone, while he already knew several of the officers serving with the 1/5th Lancashire Fusiliers, for example Captain George Bertram Horridge.[380] Nevertheless, it must have been hard to adjust to life with the 1/5th Lancashire Fusiliers, having lost the camaraderie of those with whom he had shared so many experiences and grown up militarily, as it were, and there were other factors which made it even more difficult; for one thing, it meant that he had to revert from temporary Captain to his substantive rank of 2nd Lieutenant, which naturally he struggled with; for another it meant that he was training with troops who, while they had had experience of the very tough conditions in Gallipoli, did not know as much as he did about fighting on the Western Front. His diary entries for June and July 1917 include:

---

[379] See, for example, the incident on 26th August 1916 on page 246.

[380] Norman often mentions socialising with George Horridge in the 1/5th Lancashire Fusiliers. George had been wounded while serving with the 1/5th Lancashire Fusiliers at Gallipoli. He tied with Norman in a revolver competition on 3rd July 1917 and ran a 3 mile cross country course on 5th July 1917. He was OC of "B" Company until Norman took over this role at Nieuport on 22nd October 1917, following which he became OC of "A" Company. He is mentioned by Norman as having a "*marvellous escape*" when a shell exploded on a crowd gathered at a Ration Dump in the Ypres Salient. Captain Austin Patrick Hudson (Pat), aged 26, a Bury Grammar School pupil, son of Reverend Richard and Mrs Violet Ellen Hudson of St John's Vicarage, Bury, and Lieutenant Thomas Alexander Greenwood Mashiter, Assistant Adjutant, aged 24, son of Mr and Mrs Thomas Edward Mashiter of West Dulwich, London, died in the explosion, and are commemorated at the Tyne Cot Memorial, West-Vlaanderen, Belgium, Panel 54 to 60 and 163A, and Panel 125 to 128 respectively. The Commonwealth War Graves Commission has the date of death as 31st August, the Battalion War Diary 1st September, and Norman 2nd September 1917. Like Norman, George Horridge was, as "*Battle Surplus*" (see page 280), sent to attend a course at Hardelot Chateau when the Battalion went into action in the German Spring Offensive on 23rd March 1918. He was interviewed for the Imperial War Museum's audio-records in 1984, shortly before he died in December 1987.

It seemed very strange to be back at the Front again, and my comrades were very different from the old crowd. My first impressions of the 1/5ᵗʰ were anything but good. They struck me as a poor Battalion, with bad discipline, dirty and badly organised, and obviously not yet used to French methods. They seemed to have little or no idea of living as comfortably as possible under conditions necessitated by war, whereas in the 2/5ᵗʰ we had always lived fairly comfortably and certainly ran our Company Messes better. I could see that the Battalion had a lot to learn … On 25ᵗʰ June 1917 I took over "C" Company Mess, with the idea of getting it something like in order … In my opinion the 42ⁿᵈ Division had fallen to a very low ebb prior to this time from the point of view of a fighting force, and morale, and the health of the troops was far from the standard required from troops likely to be called upon at short notice to go into battle … I wasn't as keen or even interested in "C" Company in the 1/5ᵗʰ Lancashire Fusiliers [of whom Norman was, at the time of writing this, temporarily OC while Captain Tickler was on leave] as my old "Z" Company in the 2/5ᵗʰ, every man of whom I knew so well, in fact I positively loved that Company. In "C" Company I didn't know the men so well and didn't take to them in the same way. Ho! This Battalion – the 1/5ᵗʰ Lancashire Fusiliers was not at this time to be compared with my old crowd, the 2/5ᵗʰ Lancashire Fusiliers …

In the context of reverting to the substantive rank of 2ⁿᵈ Lieutenant, Norman writes:

On 28ᵗʰ July I paraded with my three pips up [i.e. the insignia of a captain]*, and was called out by Colonel Holberton for being improperly dressed, vice three pips in lieu of one. He ordered me to take them down. I refused on the grounds that the Battalion order was insufficient without quoting higher authority, which he did not do. After much arguing I turned up a Territorial Forces regulation for Jenkins, the Adjutant, pointing out that a 2ⁿᵈ Line Territorial Forces officer joining a 1ˢᵗ Line unit would revert to his permanent rank, but could be re-instated in same if the establishment permitted. In my case, the establishment didn't permit, as they wished to promote officers who had joined in Egypt – even after Gallipoli – officers who were actually junior to me. Jenkins at this time was only a Lieutenant, but on my reversion was immediately promoted – of course he was a pal of Holberton. The annoying part of it was that fellows who remained with the 5ᵗʰ Reserve Battalion* [i.e. on Home Service in Britain] *still retained their rank. So I reverted to 2ⁿᵈ Lieutenant.*

Norman respected Captain Tickler, and he also particularly mentions a Lieutenant Foster St Barbe of "C" Company, with whom he got on well right from the outset.[381] However, there were clearly some tensions between him and some of the other officers in the 1/5ᵗʰ Lancashire Fusiliers, especially in "C" Company, and he remained unsettled for a while. In August 1917 he wanted to apply for transfer to the Special Brigade RE (Chemical Corps), but "*the Colonel refused to forward my application … , his excuse being that I was too useful to the Battalion*"; the following month he investigated the possibility

---

[381] St Barbe had been to school in Bedford as mentioned in the diary entry for 18th April 1915, and had become a tea planter in Malaya by the time war broke out. Norman says of him: "*He was a nice fellow, such a gentleman and it was he who stuck by me when I had trouble over my rank question when I first joined the 1/5th in June 1917*"; on 13th March 1918 he began a period of six months' leave in England, under a scheme for "War Worn Officers", to qualify for which an officer generally had to have completed two years' continuous service in France, and Norman was "*delighted*" when St Barbe travelled from Cheltenham to Bristol to visit him in hospital on 21st August 1918. He must still have been on leave at that time, but he had rejoined the 1/5th Lancashire Fusiliers at the front by the date of the Armistice on 11th November 1918. On 7th December 1918 he was dispatched to England in command of a Colour Party of five men charged with bringing the Battalion Colours from Bury to France so that they could accompany the Battalion on its forthcoming advance as part of the occupying force of Germany. The collecting of the Colours involved a ceremonial parade around Bury, and, after the party had rejoined the unit at Charleroi in France on 20th December 1918, another Ceremonial Parade in France on 22nd December 1918.

of becoming employed in the manufacture of explosives at the Gretna Works in Scotland, but *"as I was in France, the War Office would not consider my release for Munition Work"*.

Luckily, one of Norman's problems was resolved fairly swiftly, as on 5th August 1917 he was appointed substantive Captain. His diary entry for 5th August 1917 reads:

I was feeling very fed up with everything these days. In fact I wasn't a bit happy with the 1/5th crowd and wished I had risked Best-Dunkley and gone to the 2/5th Lancashire Fusiliers.[382] However, this day I was gazetted Substantive Captain, which seniority was to date from October 8th 1916, so that I only lost my Temporary Captaincy officially from June 22nd to August 5th. This quite upset everybody's calculations. They had worked hard to get my "reversion" through, and now all their trouble was for nothing, and – no matter whether they liked it or not – I was a pukker[383] Captain; but it wasn't popular. However, I didn't care a —— , I felt I deserved it.

It still took a little time for Lieutenant Colonel Holberton to give effect to Norman's elevation, but on 19th August 1917 he *"had a real 'strafe' with the CO about (his) rank and at last was reinstated in Battalion orders."*

The 1/5th Lancashire Fusiliers were in the 125th Brigade of the 42nd Division. When Norman joined the Battalion it was commanded by Lieutenant Colonel Philip V. Holberton of the Manchester Regiment, while Brigadier General H. Fargus CMG, DSO, of the Duke of Cornwall's Light Infantry[384] was appointed to command the Brigade with effect from 26th June 1917. On 22nd June 1917, the day when Norman reached the Battalion, it had just come into Rest at Ytres, and a few days later moved to be in Reserve in Havrincourt Wood.

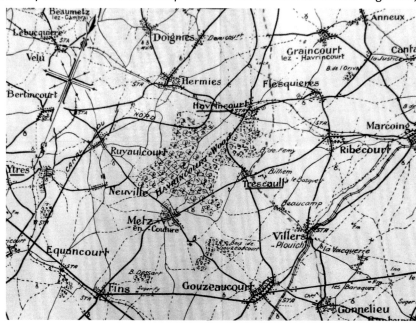

Havrincourt Wood and surrounding area; the British Line is marked in red

---

[382] 5th August 1917 was in fact the very day on which Acting Lieutenant Colonel Bertram Best-Dunkley died, aged 27, from wounds received in an action at Ypres, for which he was awarded the VC. The action is described in Thomas Floyd's *At Ypres with Best-Dunkley*. He was the son of Augusta Martha Edith and the late Alfred Corah Best-Dunkley, and is buried at Mendinghem Military Cemetery, West-Vlaanderen, Belgium, reference III.D.1. See also *Obituaries*.

[383] Pukker (more normally spelt pukka or pucca) is slang for "proper", derived from the Hindustani for "cooked" or "ripe".

[384] In his diary entry for 26th September 1917 Norman writes: *"The Brigadier was a very nice fellow, quite young – and not a bit stiff and starchy."* As appears later in this *Afterword*, page 304, he arranged for his family to visit Norman in hospital at Bristol.

Of Havrincourt Wood Norman writes:

Havrincourt Wood was a huge thick wood, fully a mile square, with long rides running across it laterally. It was really glorious – a beauty spot amidst the chaos of war. As a sector the Hate of the Boche was less demonstrative than in many sectors; still a considerable annoyance was caused by Snipers, Machine Guns, and Trench Mortars. Usually, although there was a lot of Artillery in this area, at sunrise the clamour of the guns ceased and the birds "took over", the cuckoo being particularly active. Nightingales were common here, also the black and yellow golden oriole was often heard. In the centre of the wood the War at times seemed far enough away. The disturbing factor was the peculiar noise and crack which shells and bullets made against the trees, the noise echoing through the whole wood. Crops and fruit were plentiful here … one day we found some fine red currants and gooseberries in the garden of a destroyed farm.

In July 1917 they went for a period of training at Gommecourt, which lasted until 20th August 1917. While they were there Major Gilbert S. Castle joined them as 2nd in Command, and on 26th August 1917 Captain Arthur M. Johnson RAMC also joined as MO.[385] During this period Norman's Company, "C" Company, was sent to the Railhead at Albert to load trains, and Norman took the opportunity to re-visit old haunts while in this area. Part of his diary entry for 21st August 1917 reads as follows:

Gommecourt Chateau which served as the 125th Brigade's HQ in July/August 1917 and also March 1918 (see pages 297-303)

The Company went to bathe in the Ancre near Aveluy. In the afternoon I took the Company to Albert to draw packs. Albert looked much the same as ever.[386]
I got back at about 4.30pm, had tea, then got a bike from the Signallers and rode down to Aveluy village. This village brought back many memories in the good old 2/5th days, when we were with the 51st (Highland) Division. We had some good times here with "The Skipper", Joe Hedley and "Z" Company of the 2/5th Lancashire Fusiliers. I saw the old billets, the Chateau, one time 154th Infantry Brigade HQ, now a Corps "delousing" station – and just to think in the stables of this Chateau had been bred a one time Derby Winner. Well, I rode down to the Cemetery to see one or two graves of fellows I

---

[385] In his diary entry for 30th August 1917, Norman writes: "*Major Castle was a great fellow – quite young – he joined us at Gommecourt from the 5th Gloucesters, and had seen considerable Service. He and Arthur Johnson [the MO] were great pals.*" Norman was good friends with Major Castle, later Lieutenant Colonel (see page 299 of this *Afterword*), and he also found Captain Johnson a congenial companion, visiting him at Louvencourt on 8th July 1918, at which time Norman was on his way to rejoin the 1/5th Lancashire Fusiliers at Couin Chateau and Johnson had moved to a Field Ambulance unit (see also pages 300 and 301 for more about Captain Johnson).
[386] Norman was last at Albert on 4th September 1916, and before that on 2nd January 1916; see the photographs on page 251 and also the diary entry for 29th July 1915 and footnote 88 on page 68; and for the Derby Winner see the diary entry for 31st July 1915.

knew, Major Harry Nickson of the Loyal North Lancashire Regiment,[387] *Privates Park,*[388] *Todd*[389] *and Chadwick*[390] *of the 2/5*[th] *Lancashire Fusiliers, and Werner Albert*[391] *– a German prisoner whom we captured. I then went on to Crucifix Corner, rode along the Authuille road and on across the fields to the edge of Authuille Wood along the familiar track through the wood up to our old Battalion HQ – Post Lesdos.*[392] *It was all blown in, the old log hut, the verandah. Maisoncelle Trench leading up past the Aid Post was still there and a relic of our days still stood up, a Communication Trench sign – "Aintree St". There wasn't a soul there, only myself. Perhaps that isn't quite correct – for I sat down there all alone, on that summer evening – and the whole place came back to me, the old familiar crowd I had seen so often there, Colonel Shirley,*[393] *Major Milnes, Bloy, Hutty, the Skipper, Joe, Thompson, the MO. What changes had taken place since I was last in that place.*

Time was pressing. I would have liked to ramble over the whole area for hours. So I went up to "X" Company's old Line, Earhole Sap, along the old Front Line, past "W" Company HQ, on to Post Donnet,[394] *and over to the Front Line in front of La Boiselle. There, right in the middle of No Man's Land, was a Corps School. It seemed all wrong.*

He was put in sole charge of half of "C" Company at the Albert Railhead, mostly loading wagons side on onto the trains, for which four hours per train was allowed. He proudly reports that their record for loading a train was 35 minutes, which meant that he and his men were able to take the rest of the four hours off.

He again acquitted himself well on 28th August 1917 when he was detailed to command the 125th Infantry Brigade Advanced Party in establishing a camp near Goldfish Chateau, on the way to the Ypres Salient. On finding that there were insufficient tents to accommodate the men he went right to the top, by determination and persistence obtaining an audience with General Harper at

Goldfish Chateau, between Poperinghe and Ypres (it is no longer in existence)

[387] Major Harry Nickson, 4th Battalion, the Loyal North Lancashire Regiment, died aged 32 on 30th October 1915; he was born at Manchester, son of Henry and Elizabeth Nickson of Lytham, married Rita Charlotte Rooke of Liverpool, and is buried at Aveluy Communal Cemetery Extension, reference B.26.

[388] Private F. Park, Service no 2731, "Y" Company 2/5th Lancashire Fusiliers, died aged 20 on 21st August 1915; the son of Thomas Park of Bury, he is buried at Aveluy Communal Cemetery Extension, reference B.8.

[389] Private William Todd, Service no 3087, 2/5th Lancashire Fusiliers, died aged 18 on 31st October 1915; the son of James and Annie Todd of Radcliffe, Manchester, he is buried at Aveluy Communal Cemetery Extension, reference B.27.

[390] Private R. Chadwick, Service no 2961, 2/5th Lancashire Fusiliers, died on 13th September 1915, and is buried at Aveluy Communal Cemetery Extension, reference B.1.

[391] See the diary entry for 27th August 1915 and footnote 113 on page 88.

[392] See the diary entry for 11th September 1915.

[393] The last dates on which Norman had mentioned Lieutenant Colonel H.J. Shirley and Major H.N. Milnes were 21st June 1916 and 13th September 1916 respectively – see footnote 251 on page 192 and footnote 359 on page 269 respectively. For Captain L.H. Bloy, Captain G.C. Hutchinson ("Hutty"), Captain K. Waterhouse ("the Skipper"), Captain J.W. Hedley (Joe), and Lieutenant R.N. Thompson (the MO) see the information on page 321.

[394] See the diary entries for 28th August and 2nd September 1915.

Corps HQ at Proven, 15 miles away. The General personally gave orders for provision of the required tents and their transport to the Goldfish Chateau camp, and also ensured that Norman was provided with a meal, it being then about 8.00pm. When Norman got back to his unit at 10.30pm he found that his servant, Turner, also had a hot meal ready for him, and comments: "*I also ate this – an extra meal on Active Service (when lucky enough to get it) wasn't to be sent away*".

It seems that elevation to the substantive rank of Captain, and also his work at the Albert Railhead and Goldfish Chateau towards the end of August, marked the point at which Norman finally began to find his feet in the 1/5th Lancashire Fusiliers, and his diary entry for 9th September 1917 reads:

Horace Bentley came to have a chat with me in the afternoon, and said a few things which quite altered my feelings towards the 1/5th; apparently I wasn't quite as unpopular as I imagined – in fact rather the reverse, I am glad to say.

Meanwhile, the diary entry for 27th August 1917 is also of interest, inter alia as showing how good communication was at the front, such that it was possible to have up to date information as to where another individual soldier was stationed. The entry reads as follows:

I got permission to have the day off to go and see George, who had returned from leave and was back again at St Omer. I went on one of the Signallers' bicycles – heavy things at the best – but over Belgian cobble-stoned roads not the pleasantest way of getting about. Still I wanted to see George, so how much for a little discomfort.
I went through Steenvorde … to Cassel, a town situated on a hill. The country generally here is flat. But Cassel with its windmill stands out prominently, having a commanding view. Leaving Cassel I followed the Route Nationale N° 42 through Le Nieppe to Arques, past my old billet – the house of Monsieur Saintoyen – and the Mayor's house,[395] where "Z" Company of the 2/5th Lancashire Fusiliers had their Mess in 1915 – but I hadn't time to call and see them, so went on to St Omer. I went to George's billet near the station, he wasn't there so I went round to the Mess at the Barracks. I went into the anti-room and found him asleep. When I wakened him up it was about 2.45pm and I hadn't had lunch, so he got some for me. I felt about done as I had had scarcely any sleep for three days, then this 25 miles ride on a rotten road against a strong wind just about jiggered me. I felt alright after lunch. We had a jolly good chat all about George's leave and home. We had a good look round St Omer. Then George decided I couldn't ride my bike back, so he went to see the Senior Chaplain, whom he knew pretty well. He [the Chaplain] had a little car and insisted on running me back. We started off at 7.30pm, fastening my bike on the side of the car. I wasn't quite sure where I had come from and we got lost. Eventually it went dark and we got more lost. After calling at several estaminets to enquire the way, they eventually dropped me at Abeele near the Corps Transport Park. It was then pouring with rain. Just as I was saying Good Bye, Tod Morgan[396] arrived on the scene – he had had a night out – very much so. I decided it was too wet to go on, so we put into the Corps Workshop Kitchen where there

---

[395] This was in the period from 20th May 1915 to 8th July 1915.
[396] 2nd Lieutenant Morgan was one of the officers of "C" Company who had made life difficult for Norman when he first joined the Battalion.

was a good log fire. George and the Chaplain set off back to St Omer. Eventually we reached Watou St Jean at 5.30am, very tired. But it had been well worth it. I knew we were likely to be in a Show any day, and for that reason I especially wanted to see George.[397]

He describes the scene of men from other units returning from the front in this sector thus:

The troops returning from the Line were literally a pathetic sight – just covered head to foot with mud, weary – and with that awful scared war worn look which troops returning from battle so often have. There was a constant stream of Motor Ambulances and Char-a-bancs with wounded. Gunners were actually riding on their Gun Limbers – sitting up fast asleep. This road had seen hundreds of thousands of such troops along it during the War.

Norman was fortunate in not being required to take part in an attack undertaken by "C" and "D" Companies while in the Ypres Salient. On 30th August 1917 he was kept back from the pending engagement as "*Battle Surplus*", a system which he explains as follows:

A system was now in operation by which a "Battle Surplus" from each Battalion was left out of the Line. Experience had shown that in action Battalions were so reduced by casualties that there weren't sufficient numbers of officers, NCOs and Specialists to form a skeleton of a new Battalion to absorb drafts. Consequently it was ordered as a General Army Order that each unit would leave out of the Line a nucleus of all ranks, e.g. in a Company either the OC Company or 2nd in Command remained behind, and a proportion of Platoon Officers, NCOs and Specialists – Lewis Gunners, Signallers etc. In view of this order I was detailed to remain behind for "C" Company. It was a rotten feeling, because it seemed to flavour somewhat of "dodging the Column".

---

[397] George had joined the Lancashire Fusiliers in Bury as an officer at about the same time as Norman (see the diary entry for 4th September 1914), and Norman mentions that, while they were training at Southport, he, George, Kenneth Waterhouse, Goldsmith and Barnsdale all used to sit together at Mess. Norman heard on 22nd August 1915 that George had been promoted to Lieutenant (see the diary entry for that day), and he was promoted to substantive Captain at the same time as Norman, also with effect from 8th October 1916, as stated in the diary entry for 5th August 1917. He had been much later in coming out to France, however, and it appears that he was still in England on 19th September 1915 when Norman learned that he had become engaged to Effie (see the photograph on page 96). Thereafter Norman visited George and/or Effie when passing through London on his way to or from leave in November 1915 and February 1916. George was married on 30th August 1916, and does not seem to have yet been to France at that point. In January 1917 Norman again visited George and Effie, this time in Colchester, where it seems that George was with the 3/5th Lancashire Fusiliers. It is not clear exactly when he was sent to France. He mentions in the diary entry for 15th July 1917 that Effie went to 105 Walmersley Road on that day, so perhaps that was at about the time George went to France. 105 Walmersley Road was close to Norman's parents' home at 217 Walmersley Road; it may have been the home of Norman's elder brother John Russell, or Jack, as Norman mentions visiting Jack and Effie there on 27th December 1917 while he was on leave in Bury. About a month after meeting with George at St Omer on 27th August 1917, Norman mentions (25th September 1917) that George was in hospital, though he does not say why. On 31st October 1917 Norman heard that George's son Derrick had been born (he saw him for the first time two months later when on leave over Christmas – see page 293, also for a photograph), and then, on 17th November 1917, he says that "*George went to England to Woolwich*". In the diary entry for 16th December 1917 to 2nd January 1918 (i.e. during the period when he called on Jack and Effie at 105 Walmersley Road) he says "*George was now stationed at Heaton Park*" in Bury.

Then on 2nd September 1917 the Quartermaster of the Battalion, Lieutenant Clem Whittaker, was seriously injured by shell fire, eventually losing a leg,[398] and on 4th September 1917 Norman was appointed to act as Quartermaster in his place, which meant he again was excused from going into action. His Company, "C" Company, suffered particularly heavily in the ensuing battle, which had the objectives of taking Iberian, Borry, and Beck House Farms on the Frezenberg Ridge on 6th September 1917. He writes:

The Battalion attacked at 8.00am. "C" Company got the full force of the German fire, and in a very few minutes the Company was practically wiped out; they were reduced from five officers and 157 NCOs and men to two officers and 30 other ranks; this was by 8.30am. Fire came from all directions – even from Boche Snipers who had crept out early in the morning into No Man's Land and concealed themselves amongst the killed who were still lying out from the previous day's attack. These fellows even blacked their faces. They certainly were very brave – but were certain to be shot on the spot if caught – and many of them were.

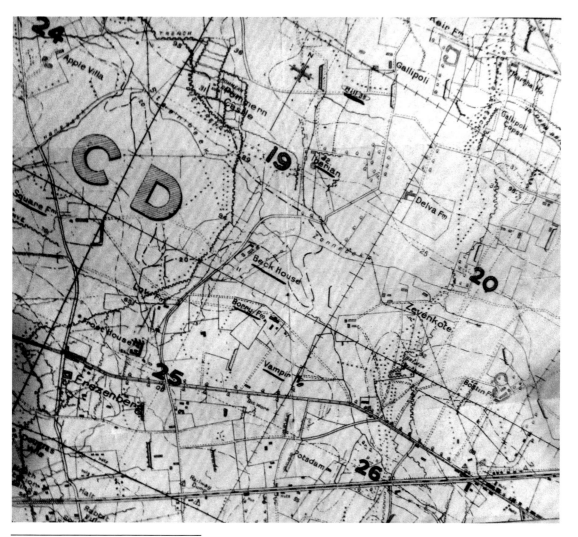

---

[398] According to Norman, this was on the way back from the Ration Dump immediately after Captain A.P. Hudson and Lieutenant T.A.G. Mashiter had been killed – see the footnote earlier in this *Afterword* on page 274.

Unfortunately, despite "C" and "D" Companies having initially partly attained their objectives, they were ultimately forced to retire to their original Line, having suffered considerable losses. Norman comments that *"the 125th Infantry Brigade had had an object lesson in the peculiar strengths of German defensive systems and the futility of 'minor operations'."*

When the Battalion, who had been relieved in the Line on 8th September 1917, arrived at 2.00am the following day at St Lawrence Camp near Poperinghe (where Norman had seen to it that a hot meal was awaiting them), "C" Company were down to two officers (Tickler and St Barbe) and 23 other ranks. Norman says of the Battalion's arrival: *"It was a pathetic sight to see the remains of the Battalion come into Camp. I say 'come' – those men didn't march. They couldn't! They could just about put one foot in front of the other."*

The British officers killed were:

"C" Company	Lieutenant V.H. Morgan[399]
	Lieutenant G. Murphy[400]
	2nd Lieutenant W.L. Briggs[401]
"D" Company	2nd Lieutenant C.H. Harrison[402]
	Lieutenant E.B. Tristram[403]

A number of awards were made to the Battalion as a result of this engagement, including the MC to Captain Tickler.

The Battalion was relieved in the Ypres Salient on 18th September 1917. In looking back at their time in this sector Norman writes:

---

[399] Lieutenant Victor Harold Morgan of the 1st Battalion King's Liverpool Regiment, attached to the 1/5th Lancashire Fusiliers, son of the late Charles James George and Sarah Morgan, died aged 22, and is commemorated at the Tyne Cot Memorial, West-Vlaanderen, Belgium, Panel 31 to 34 and 162 and 162A and 163A. Also known as "Tod", Lieutenant Morgan was an officer in "C" Company of the 1/5th Lancashire Fusiliers when Norman joined it on 22nd June 1917.

[400] Lieutenant George Murphy of the 13th Battalion Royal Warwickshire Regiment, attached to the 1/5th Lancashire Fusiliers, is commemorated at the Tyne Cot Memorial, West-Vlaanderen, Belgium, Panel 23 to 28 and 163A. He was one of the officers in "C" Company of the 1/5th Lancashire Fusiliers when Norman joined it on 22nd June 1917, and Norman speaks of him in affectionate terms, saying: *"Murphy was a nice boy – just a boy, but a nice lad, and full of beans"*.

[401] 2nd Lieutenant William Lonsdale Briggs of the 1st Battalion King's Own Royal Lancaster Regiment, attached to the 1/5th Lancashire Fusiliers, son of the late Mr F.S.H. Briggs and Mrs E.J. Briggs of Workington, died aged 23 on 14th September 1917, a few days after this engagement, and is buried at Étaples Military Cemetery, reference XVII.A.28. 2nd Lieutenant Briggs was an officer in "C" Company of the 1/5th Lancashire Fusiliers when Norman joined it on 22nd June 1917.

[402] 2nd Lieutenant Cyril Henry Harrison of the 10th Battalion South Lancashire Regiment, attached to the 1/5th Lancashire Fusiliers, son of the late William Henry Harrison and Annie Harrison of Worthing, died aged 20, and is commemorated at the Tyne Cot Memorial, West-Vlaanderen, Belgium, Panel 92 to 93 and 162A.

[403] Lieutenant Eric Barrington Tristram, of the Royal Fusiliers, attached to the 1/5th Lancashire Fusiliers, son of Mr C.F. and Mrs M. Tristram of Wimbledon, died aged 21, and is commemorated at the Tyne Cot Memorial, West-Vlaanderen, Belgium, Panel 28 to 30 and 162 to 162A and 163A.

One shrinks from an attempt to describe the conditions that prevailed in the Salient – in fact words cannot describe it. It could only be realised by visiting that area. No part of it was at rest. By day aircraft on both sides tried to spot out every movement that was attempted on either side, and, day and night, guns sprayed the trenches with shrapnel, HE, or gas shells. The approaches to the Line from Ypres were through hundreds of Guns – firing madly. The roads were soon left, and one approached the Line by duckboard paths – it was easier to lose one's way than to keep to the track, and soldiers of both Armies strayed into their opponents' Lines. Along the whole dreary length of duckboards, in places bridging over big shell holes filled with mud and water, the possibility of slipping into these uninviting watery graves was a real menace, a fate which befell many poor fellows in the Salient. At intervals distinctive signs in luminous paint were erected on the tracks. The Front Line wasn't a line at all, but merely a series of shell holes linked together with Battalion HQ and Company HQ in Pill Boxes captured recently from the enemy. The Menin Road and Cambridge Road were well known.

Runners had a most trying time – many were the casualties. Yet their messages were delivered. Losses in personnel were heavy, as were losses in Guns and Transport.

The period in the Salient was most depressing. We had lost a lot and achieved nothing. It was a ghastly place – desolation all around – sickening sights and smells – a ground saturated with gas in many places – that Salient was the worst possible sector of any in all the World.

The Division left it without regrets – feeling that it really hadn't had a fair chance of doing itself justice.

The Cloth Hall at Ypres

Above left: Intact, before suffering war damage
Above: In 1918, in ruins
Left: In 2018, rebuilt

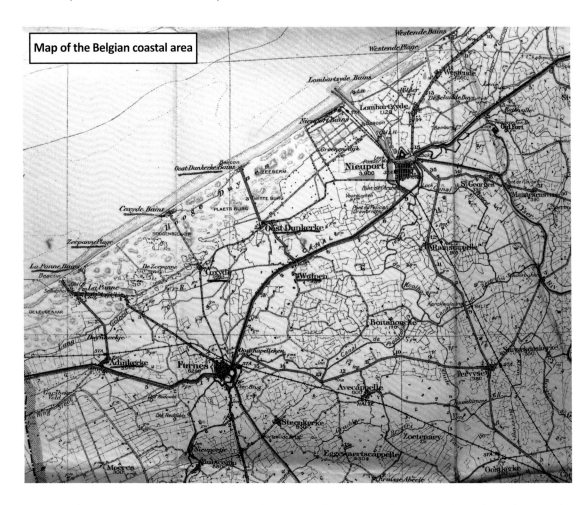

Map of the Belgian coastal area

The Battalion moved into Support in the Belgian coastal area, and then up to the Belgian front in the Nieuport Sector on 5th October 1917. While in Support the Battalion seems to have had a fairly comfortable time, almost a seaside holiday, though they were not entirely clear of the danger zone. Norman writes of bathing in the sea, and says: *"It was rather amusing as the Old Boche had made an extension to the Ostend Pier so that he could observe right down the coast. Occasionally he shelled us while we were bathing – but didn't upset our swim. When we heard "'em" coming we dived under the water so that the shells wouldn't hit us."* On another visit to La Panne he recounts: *"I heard the 41st Division Theatre Party, "the Crumps", who were playing on the shore. It was just like a typical seaside place – kiddies sitting in the front rows, and others digging and paddling on the shore. Unfortunately the Boche shelled La Panne that afternoon and dropped a Crump[404] into the Crumps' show, giving people an awful shock, and unfortunately killing several including children. As a result no more shows were held on the sands."* He also records that they were subjected to almost nightly aircraft bombing, commenting *"and bombs are worse than shells for harassing one's nerves"*.

Of the Nieuport Sector he gives the following description:

---

[404] Army slang for shells, usually German 5.9 inch shells (see the diary entry for 2nd to 6th August 1915), from the sound made by them.

The Nieuport Sector was a curious one – the town itself had practically ceased to exist, for scarce a day had passed when it was free from Artillery fire, and later aeroplane bombing claimed its attention. Nieuport had been thoroughly tunnelled by the French during their original occupation, and though at first the low, slimy, and generally dark tunnels were distinctly unpopular, all ranks appreciated them as we had further experience of Nieuport.

Nieuport – Rue Longue

The tunnels, running parallel to the streets, had been made by connecting up the cellars; they were "at times" lighted by electricity, but even then fully equipped troops found it difficult to pass. The Left, or Lombartzyde Sector, was North and North East of the town, across the wide and deep Yser Canal, held by the 125th and 127th Brigades in turn. The less important St George Sector to the East and South East was allotted to the 126th Brigade, two Battalions being in the Line and two in Reserve.[405] In each Front Line the defences consisted mainly of breastworks, and Island posts; as much of the area was below sea level it was impossible to construct trenches in this flooded marshy ground.

Nieuport – entrance to the cellars

The Front was described as 'one big flood' and when, as frequently happened, a big shell knocked in the bank of one of the many dams, the description adequately fitted the case.

Just across the Yser was the Redan and Indiarubber House. The Redan was a large triangular redoubt with its apex towards the enemy, with an artificial moat.[406] Indiarubber House [see photograph on next page] was a barn like structure formerly used by the Belgian Army as a magazine. It was built of solid concrete, ingeniously disguised. Shells actually rebounded from this building. The building was used as a Battalion HQ for the Left Sub-sector. It was lighted by electricity and really quite cosy.

---

[405] Norman was in the 125th Brigade.
[406] See the map on page 288.

The Redan was linked to the town by three wobbly duckboard bridges, erected by the troops, laid on barrel floats, without sides, and with many gaps between the duckboards.

These bridges, Putney, Crowder, and Vauxhall, rose and fell several feet with the tide, and in addition were carried out of the straight by the inflow and outflow of the tide.

The approaches to the bridges down and up were very steep, over muddy banks, and movement was often very difficult and not without danger. In addition these bridges were well marked by the Boche and were shelled all day and Machine Gunned at night, and the bridges were consequently often damaged, and to and fro traffic held up for repairs. All supplies, food, ammunition, Engineers' stores, etc. had to be manhandled across this river, the only means of approach except by the Five Bridges which was too far away. Troops, ration parties, working parties had to make their way across these swaying planks, and wounded had to be carried on stretchers across the same dangerous way. It was no easy task for a man with full equipment to negotiate these

INDIA-RUBBER HOUSE, USED AS BATTALION HEADQUARTERS.

NIEUPORT, SHOWING REMAINS OF PUTNEY AND CROWDER BRIDGES AND RUBBER HOUSE IN THE DISTANCE.

bridges, carrying only two petrol tins full of water, bags of rations, a trench board, reel of barbed wire, box of ammunition. It was extremely unhealthy to linger on these bridges. Many journeys to and fro were often made in the course of a night.

At the East end of the town several smaller canals joined the Yser, and at this point the Five Bridges so called had been erected. The destruction of dams and locks brought the tide into the canals, causing them to overflow and flood our defensive works. The repairing and rebuilding of dams and bridges was a severe drain upon the resources of the Engineers, and the Infantry working under their direction. The 428 and 429 Field Companies had each more than 30 bridges of various kinds under their charge. Parties were supplied to Tunnelling Companies, who constructed three deep Advanced Dressing Stations in the Nieuport Cellars.

There was really little infantry activity on this Front. Patrolling was very limited – and in some cases was actually done on rafts. But no Front was more active in Artillery and Heavy Trench Mortar bombing. Bridges, dams, roads and back areas were continuously shelled. This was made all the easier for concentration for the Boche because of the very limited lines of approach and the comparatively small change in the Front Line (except on July 1st 1917) in this area. The enemy even shelled Dunkerque with 15 inch guns at a range of 29 miles. The intensity of shelling increased in violence, until, on reaching the Line, its intensity was such as to be unsurpassed on any other sector.

The Boche had the advantage of position in holding higher ground at Lombartzyde village, and his *works and trenches were unaffected by the floods. Consequently, while at times we were wallowing in mud and water often waist deep, the Boche was looking down on us from his hard dry trenches. This advantage in high ground gave him good observation of our movements, and consequently by day movement was very much restricted. The weather had broken, it was very wet and cold, and the whole place soon became a sea of mud.*

Patrolling was difficult and usually necessitated wading and occasionally swimming, with no means of getting dry on one's return. The ration parties had a very hard time getting up to the Line, and to my mind these men deserved great praise for their efforts in – though dog tired – struggling up to the Line under heavy fire, to take their comrades food and letters. Hot food was a difficulty but we managed this by warming the food up in kitchens in the tunnels and then using specially constructed food containers, or straw packs – metal ammunition boxes contained in outer wooden cases and the intervening space packed with straw.

There were no Communication Trenches to most parts of the Line and it was very easy to lose one's way.

Norman enjoyed the work of Quartermaster, his duties including, on the lighter side, taking care of a pet goat which had accompanied the Battalion from Egypt, and buying fresh sole for dinner at La Panne; but, ironically, his new rank of substantive Captain meant that he was now too elevated to remain in the role. He became OC of "B" Company on 22nd October 1917, immediately feeling more comfortable with that Company than he had with "C" Company.

He says of this period "*I often ran across fellows I knew, for example, on 9th October 1917 Harold Downham of the 1/7th Lancashire Fusiliers and Frank Cain of the Highland Light Infantry.*"[407]

His account of part of a tour as OC of this Company in November 1917, just behind the front line, is as follows:

"B" Company moved up to Nasal Walk [see the map on page 288] *in Close Support, taking over from "C" Company of the 7th Lancashire Fusiliers. This was a peculiar spot. It was a narrow neck of land running East from the Five Bridges, bounded on the South by the Yser Canal, and in front by Nieuland Polder. At this time at low tide it was merely mud, and at high tide a small lake. The approach to this isolated spot was over three canals, crossed by rickety bridges made of trench boards floating on barrels. It was very wet, but the chances of attack by the Boche were pretty remote, as our field of fire was good and the old Hun would have had to wade through mud at least knee deep to get to us. On my right I had a Lewis Gun Post holding a small dam. This was blown in the first night, and my Post was flooded out, and isolated from the rest of the Company …*

We could do very little in this trench except general trench repair work. We were shelled intermittently all day. It was wonderful how the Hun seemed to have that bit of land marked, and, unfortunately, we were in the direct line for the Dams, and consequently we got the shorts that were intended for these

---

[407] These were both former Bury Grammar School pupils. For Harold Downham see the footnote to the diary entry for 2nd September 1914. Frank Backwell Cain was the son of Frank James Cain (who owned the Derby Hotel, Bury and died in 1917) and Elvira (who died in 1905). He enlisted as a private in the 20th (Service) Battalion of the Royal Fusiliers (3rd Public Schools) in 1914, but transferred to the 15th (1st Glasgow) Battalion of the Highland Light Infantry as a 2nd Lieutenant in December 1916. He was killed by shell fire at Ayette on 13th April 1918, aged 24. He is buried at Gézaincourt Communal Cemetery extension, reference I.L.10.

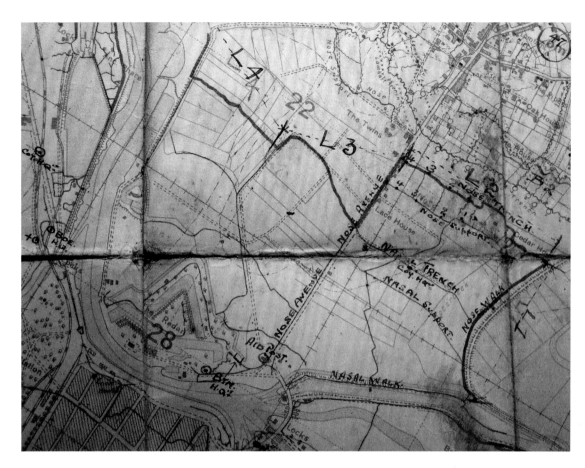

Above is a map showing the area immediately adjacent to Nieuport, to the North and East, including the Redan and the Five Bridges; Norman describes how his Company held a tongue of land bounded to the South by the the Yser Canal, which is just below the word "*Locks*" at the base of the map. The aerial view to the left, which Norman says gives "*an excellent idea of the Lombartzyde Sector*", shows this area, the Canal being just visible diagonally across the bottom left hand corner. North on the map above is about 30° to the right of perpendicular, and on the aerial photograph on the left it is about 40° to the right of perpendicular; after making adjustment for this it is possible to see where the map above and the aerial photograph fit onto the map on page 284, just to the North East of Nieuport.

objectives, but we had no casualties …

On November 18th 1917 we had a pretty rough day. The Boche started shelling early in the morning, and shelled heavily all day; he broke my only means of approach – or rather withdrawal – from my semi-island home – all three bridges being damaged and partly sunk. The real target was the "Cinq Ponts"; he started shelling at 9.00am and continued solidly until 3.00pm.

At about 7.00am Macdonald and Elmes, my runners, left my Company HQ for Battalion HQ (Indiarubber House).[408] They were away all day. I was completely cut off, and my telephone wires were torn to shreds. My Company HQ was a small elephant hut dug into the sand or mud banks – none too safe; still it did offer some cover. When the shelling stopped I decided that the bridges must be mended. So I, along with one or two fellows, got busy – it was a bitterly cold job as it meant being in the water part of the time. We managed to repair one bridge, but even then it was very shaky, and it was doubtful whether it would stand the trench relief crossing, and then ourselves.

At about 5.30pm Ashworth [2nd Lieutenant G. Ashworth] *took the guides to meet the French* [who were to relieve "C" Company], *and he had orders not to let more than three on the bridge at any one time... During the relief the Boche again started shelling, but the Divisional Commander – risking starting an Artillery Battle – applied his Scheme of Punishment Fire, and silenced the enemy in 20 minutes. Much to our relief, Macdonald and Elmes turned up just before the French. I had given them up for lost, killed, wounded, or drowned, however I was glad to see them, and especially so, as the MO had sent six bottles of Bass N° 1 for me, which we enjoyed very much. The relief was very slow, however we got through at about 10.00pm. I remained to cross over to the mainland with Company HQ. One of my Signallers slipped off the bridge with a fullerphone[409] and I had to go into the canal after him to get him out. Then a Lewis Gunner slipped in with his Gun – this, like the telephone, went to the bottom – some expensive relief; still, we didn't lose any men, and that was the main point.*

With my telephone broken down I couldn't report that relief was complete, so had to wait until I got back into Nieuport. When I went to the 125th Brigade to telephone to Jenkins [the Adjutant], *Holberton was somewhat annoyed at first, until I told him my very good reason. I was soaked through with my ducking and had no chance of a change. Captain Needham, the Staff Captain, gave me a hot whisky, which saved the ship. It was now midnight. I had sent the Company on to Brisbane Camp at Oostdunkerque, our Rest Camp, for the night. I walked through Nieuport to Pelican Bridge via Wulpen to Brisbane Camp, arriving at 2.00am, very tired, very wet, and very cold – and it rained all the way. On arriving at Brisbane Camp I went round to see the Company were settled in for the night. They were busy having a really good hot meal, which Acton* [T.E. Acton MM, Company Quartermaster Sergeant] *had so thoughtfully prepared. I then found my billet, an old farm house, scantily furnished, but here again Acton had also thought of the officers, and had a roaring log fire ready, and a hot meal. I just took off every stick of clothing to dry and sat in front of that very welcome fire almost all night.*

---

[408] Describing the personnel in "B" Company, Norman says: "*I had two very keen young fellows – quite boys – Macdonald and Elmes, as my personal Company Runners. They were always together, most reliable, and if it was at all possible to get a message delivered, no matter what the conditions, these two lads would do it.*"

[409] A type of field telephone invented by Captain A.C. Fuller (later promoted to Major General) in October 1915 to overcome eavesdropping by using metallic circuits instead of an earth return, and gradually adopted throughout the Allied Lines.

This was to be Norman's last tour on the Belgian front, and he continues:

So we were to leave the Nieuport Sector, and, not many hours hence, Belgium.
"Remember Belgium!" said one fellow. "Aye – as if we could ever forget it"; or, as Edwards wrote in his Lombartzyde Litany:

> *"From all the trials and tribulations*
> *From all the miseries of mud and water*
> *And from the Lombartzyde Sector*
> *Good Lord deliver us."* [410]

In the latter part of November 1917 the Battalion moved on to the La Bassée Sector, incorporating the La Bassée Canal and Givenchy.

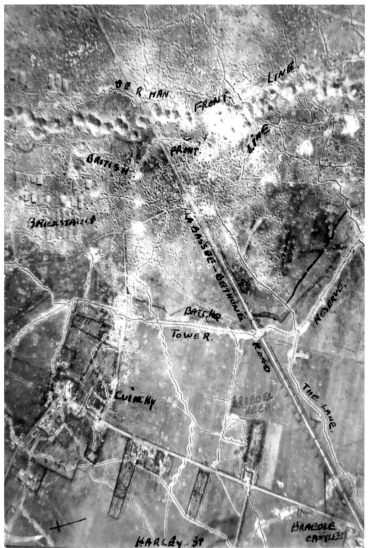

Left: Aerial photograph of the Right or Canal Sub-sector of the La Bassée area, showing the British and German front lines, shell holes, the Brickstacks and Cuinchy.

Below: Aerial photo of the Canal and Railway which divided the Right and Left (Givenchy) Sub-sectors (see the maps on page 291); No Man's Land, the crater-pitted area between the German and British front lines close to the camera, is marked, and the Brickstacks can be seen on the lower right hand portion of the photograph.

---

[410] These lines may perhaps be by one of Norman's comrades, 2nd Lieutenant W.L. Edwards of "D" Company.

Maps of La Bassée Area – Right (Canal) and Left (Givenchy) Sub-sectors

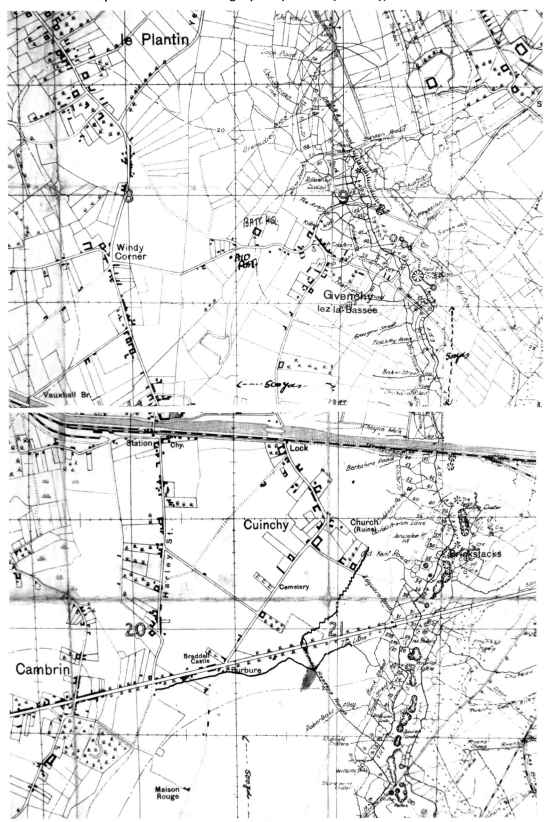

During the period of the move to the La Bassée Sector and for a short time after arrival in the sector Norman was acting as Adjutant, another role that he enjoyed, but it came to an end all too soon on 10th December 1917, on the return from leave of the Battalion's official Adjutant, Captain E.E. Jenkins. On handing back the role of Adjutant Norman writes:

I got another good chit from the CO, although this shouldn't really be put into black and white. In his own words: "Well my lad, Thank you for the excellent work you have done, it has been an eye opener to me that anyone could tackle an Adjutant's job as you have done and not had previous experience. The thoroughness and attention to detail relieved me of much work and worry, and I shall not forget it, and shall take the opportunity to recommend you for Staff work very highly, which I consider you are quite capable of doing well." This was sufficient recompense for those weeks' really hard work – with scarcely a minute off duty except to eat and sleep (and very little of that).

The diary contains the following description of the front line in the La Bassée Sector:

LA BASSÉE SECTOR. THE MILL. –*CRATERS.*

No Man's Land was an almost continuous line of craters, full of stagnant, green, stinking water, with sides of crumbling earth and slimy mud, real death traps for night patrols. We and the Boche each dug sap heads on the lips of these craters and in many cases each were within range of the other's bombs or hand grenades. These saps were cheerless kind of spots for Posts to keep the long watches. The Line itself was a succession of salients and re-entrants.

The Right or Canal Sub-sector was the better sector – this included the Canal and South of it. It included the Brickstacks and a number of tunnels ran up to the Front Line from the Village Line, namely Robertson's Tunnel, Wilson's Way, and Old Kent Tunnel, which tunnels provided excellent dug out accommodation, but to my mind were tactically death traps …

LA BASSÉE SECTOR. THE BRICK STACKS.

On the contrary on the Givenchy Sector (North of the Canal) the land was much lower and the water level only a few feet below the ground level; Princess Island, for example, was like living in mud; furthermore, the trenches were mainly sand bag breastworks, duckboards had vanished, and it was as much as anyone could do to keep his "neck above water" so to speak, to say nothing of developing the offensive spirit and mastery of No Man's Land.

HARLEY STREET AND WINDY CORNER.

Norman was lucky enough to be on leave in England for Christmas 1917, meeting his two month old nephew Derrick, George's son – whom he also calls "Bimbo" or "Bill" – for the first time.

Then, at the time of his return on 3rd January 1918, waiting at Gorre for his unit to come out of the Line later that day he writes: *"I was wired for at 8.00am to proceed to HQ in the Line at once. Orders are orders and there is no asking why! Still we did wonder what was the matter. I had a quick breakfast and started out with my tin hat and revolver, and Box Respirator in the 'Alert' position, i.e. slung on one's chest with the flap loose, so that the mask could be put on and the valve mouth piece placed in position in six seconds."*

On arrival at the front line he found that a gas attack had laid low virtually all the HQ officers of the Battalion, including Major Castle

Norman's mother with baby Derrick

(then acting CO), Captain Jenkins (the Adjutant), Lieutenant H.R. Waugh (the Lewis Gun Officer)[411] and Captain A.M. Johnson RAMC, the MO. Major Castle (who could hardly speak) and Captain Jenkins (who could hardly see), were the only officers left at HQ when Norman arrived. The account in the diary of what happened next is as follows:

Major Castle said I was to take over command of the Battalion temporarily until we got out, then I was to take over the Adjutant's duties, and arrange with Colin Hunt, the Senior Captain, about carrying on. ... Major Castle and Jenkins were evacuated soon after ... so I was completely on my own at HQ. I found I had just time to make a hurried tour of the Line and see where people were, and that all was clear regarding the relief. The 7th Lancashire Fusiliers, commanded by Lieutenant Colonel Brewis, relieved us. Brewis was a very fine soldier, and awfully nice fellow; he realised the position I was suddenly thrown into, and helped me quite a lot in taking over. ... After dinner I sent a note to Colin Hunt ... asking him where I should meet him and the time. He came across to the

Château de Gorre, Beuvry, where Norman was based when out of the Line at La Bassée; on the next page are photographs providing more detail of the accommodation in Beuvry.

Orderly Room in the Chateau to see me. He wanted me to take over command of the Battalion for the time being, as he wasn't very keen and didn't feel equal to it. However I couldn't see my way to do this over him, and I suggested I might be more use to take over the Adjutant's duties (of which I knew a little), and there was no one else to do this so far as we could see. So that was how it was arranged. I then asked him what orders he wished issuing for the following day's programme. However he said, "Oh, you draft the orders – you know more about it – and issue them."

---

[411] In the diary entry for 3rd July 1917 Norman says: *"Waugh was a great fellow – a Scotsman of the King's Own Scottish Borderers"*. In April 1918 Norman and Waugh had some adventures together when returning to the 1/5th Lancashire Fusiliers through the war-torn French countryside – see later in this *Afterword*, page 298

Norman duly did so, after first sorting out the important matter of what the arrangements were to be for the Officers' Mess while they were out of the Line. The following day, in the MO's absence, he even took Sick Parade, as to which he comments wryly, "*As my treatment was mainly Castor Oil or M&D,[412] I wasn't over popular as a 'quack MO'.*"

In the longer term, as instructed by Major Castle, he again took over duties as Adjutant, which – as before – he relished, working hard, and for long hours, as witness a diary entry for 24th January 1918: "*I was still busy at 2.20am – there were no more candles, so I had to stop work.*" Upon his having to relinquish the role once more on 17th February 1918, on the recovery of Captain Jenkins, his comment is: "*I was once again rather fed up at leaving this job … I really felt I was much more use in this type of work than Company Work.*"

On 19th January 1918 Lieutenant Colonel Holberton had put forward a recommendation for him to be appointed to a staff post, but on 5th February 1918 there is the following diary entry: "*Unfortunately I found I couldn't get a staff job, as some new order had come out regarding appointments. I seemed to miss everything I was recommended for, except hard work.*"

On 28th February 1918, his 26th birthday, as a reward for his hard work as Acting Adjutant, he set off for a week's leave in Paris, staying at the Hotel Regina. He met up with the Souffrices of 7 Rue Mulot, the family whose summer bathing hut he had wandered into in Cayeux-sur-Mer,[413] and he spent practically the full week sightseeing and dining with them, particularly mentioning one of the daughters, Simone, and the father, Jean.[414]

---

[412] Medicine and Duty, which was a term for treatment handed out by MOs to those whose ailments were not serious enough to justify the outcome often most hoped for by those attending Sick Parade, namely, being excused from duty.

[413] See the diary entry for 27th August 1916.

[414] 7 Rue Mulot is now a Centre Communal d'Action Sociale (Community Centre); the Hotel Regina, which opened in 1900, and is situated close to the Louvre, is still in business.

Meanwhile, America had joined the War on 6th April 1917, but had had to spend time training troops before sending them across the Atlantic in significant numbers. An American Medical Officer, Wagner, had been among those injured in the gas attack on Battalion HQ on 3rd January 1918, and at about this time Norman mentions American airmen spending time with them for "liaison", and he even had a half hour flight with one of them over the Boche Line and La Bassée.

The German Spring Offensive was now imminent, and Norman reports that on his return from Paris *"the atmosphere seemed to have changed somewhat ... People talked sort of below their breath about the German Offensive, and without doubt in anyone's mind that this was coming, and would have to be faced, but it didn't depress us."*

Soon after his return to the Battalion, which was then in training at Houchin, he was selected to be sent on a three week Army instruction course. It seems that he was quite unusual in not yet having attended any such course. He had been about to go on one in September 1916, just before the engagement in which he was wounded, but was recalled at the last moment.[415] While he was poised to go on the course in 1918, news came through on 22nd March that the German Spring Offensive had begun, and Norman expected that history was about to repeat itself, i.e. that the course would be cancelled at the last moment.

His account of the arrival of the news that the Offensive had begun is as follows:

When dinner was almost over, the Colonel received an urgent Dispatch Rider Letter Service delivery. He excused himself, retired to his room with Jenkins, and a few minutes afterwards sent for the Company Commanders, Horridge,[416] Tickler, Hunt,[417] and myself.
"Gentlemen, I have very grave news to tell you. As we all know the Germans have attacked on a wide Front and have gained much ground, our troops are retiring all along the Line.
The Division (and in particular ourselves) is ordered to be ready to move at half an hour's notice in Battle Order (no packs). Our destination so far as I know is indefinite.
Will you please collect your Company officers <u>at once</u> and explain to them what I have told you."
The Battalion were in bed. The "Alarm" was sounded, and the Battalion turned out at its Company Alarm Posts. Within a few minutes a peaceful camp was turned into a "hive of bees". Parties were rolling blankets, collecting stores, packing valises, and stacking them. Quartermaster stores were being packed. When things in the platoons were well on the way, we officers went out to our billets and packed our kits, leaving out only absolute essentials. This was at about 10.15pm. By midnight most of the stores had been sent off by motor wagon to La Buissière or Vaudricourt, and the Battalion 'Stood by' i.e. the men lay down in their huts with their kits ready at hand.

---

[415] See the diary entry for 7th September 1916.
[416] See the footnote earlier in this *Afterword* on page 274.
[417] Captain C.H.C. Hunt, "D" Company; see also the account of the gas attack on Battalion HQ on 3rd January 1918 earlier in this *Afterword*, page 293.

Rather than the course being cancelled, as Norman expected, it was decided that he would once again be *"Battle Surplus"*, and he therefore proceeded – along with George Horridge and Bernard Hawksey – to the I[st] Army Infantry School at Hardelot Chateau while the rest of the Battalion went into action. His diary entry for 23rd March 1918 reads:

I had to hurriedly hand over to Umpti North,[418] my 2nd in Command of the Company. I felt very upset about this, in fact very much ashamed of myself, although of course it was no fault of my own; still it felt like dodging the Column. I scarcely had pluck to go and say farewell to my Company and wish them "Good Luck" – for I knew that, before many hours had passed, they would be in the thick of the fighting to stop the German onrush …

The Battalion marched out of Camp at Houchin at 8.30am, looking very fit and full of spirits (not wine). Motor Omnibuses were waiting on the Labeuvrière road to convey the Infantry Units of the Division. Many hundreds of buses were used. There was no doubt that the Division was being rushed to the threatened area. The men sang, shouted, passed the usual witty remarks to passers by, and, after leaving the coal mines and the slag heaps near Béthune, went through Bruay, Dieval, Bryas, St Pol – here the country had changed to a well wooded hilly type, with valleys and farmsteads – then proceeding practically due South to Herlin, Nuncq, Frévent, Bouquemaison and Doullens. Doullens, usually a sleepy town – was very much alive. On the way there were little excitements, as, owing to the dense foliage and overhanging branches, it was necessary, if riding on top of the bus, to be constantly on the lookout, otherwise disaster might result to one's head or headgear. Telephone wires proved a source of amusement or annoyance, "Mind the Wire" being continually heard.

They turned due North East along the Route Nationale N° 25 to Arras. On approaching Saulty L'Arbret it was obvious that something was doing, and that the Battle Zone was not very far distant, for the main road was being shelled, and the journey through the hilly narrow streets was very perilous as the streets already had shell holes here and there. Route Nationale N° 25 was followed as far as

Beaumetz-lès-Loges then they turned South East downhill across the Arras to Doullens line, to Rivière and Bretencourt … then proceeding to Ransart and along the Ayette road.

Refugees in straggling groups were met here, some in motor lorries, others in vehicles of all descriptions, some foot slogging it wearily, pushing perambulators, or following farm carts on which were stacked just such possessions as they could hastily collect together before leaving their

"The good lady" referred to in the footnote below

---

[418] Lieutenant S. North MC ("Umpti") survived, and must have remained in contact with Norman after the War, as Norman recounts: *"A rather interesting incident happened to Umpti North. They were in position in the garden at a house in Bucquoy; a small dog came up from the cellar of the house, and, on investigation, Umpti North found an old lady down there. She was in a very bad state of mind, and without rations, which she was soon provided with; however, many attempts to persuade her to leave her house failed. She explained that she had been there all the War, and wasn't leaving it. She had seen the Boche over that same ground twice before, and this was the third time. No amount of persuasion could prevail upon her to move to a safer place further behind the Lines. Later, after the War, Umpti visited this place again, and took [a] photograph of the good lady who was again living there with her daughter."* A print of the photograph is pasted into the diary, and features above in the text.

homes. *Such a sight as this, pathetic in the extreme, is one of the outrages of war, one effect of the War from which our people at home were mercifully spared. These poor homeless villagers from the small hamlets were wending their way to safety out of the reach of this savagery, with no definite destination or shelter at the end of their day's journey. Some had even managed to bring a cow along with them. The sight aroused feelings of pity and anger.*

Progress became more and more difficult, roads being packed with troops moving in the same direction, and an increasing stream of traffic retiring before the enemy's advance. At 5.00pm on March 23rd DHQ was established at Adinfer, 2 miles North East of Ayette, 8 miles South of Arras, and 8 miles North East of Bapaume.

The 1/5th Lancashire Fusiliers found themselves fighting the Germans in the area around Gommecourt, where the ground was already familiar to them from their training in that area during July and August 1917. Although they fought valiantly in and around Sapignies, they were ultimately obliged to withdraw to the Gommecourt Ridge, and then from there to dig in along a new Line between Bucquoy and Ablainzeville, which they were able to do in a relatively orderly fashion owing to their familiarity with the territory.

Ironically, the I st Army School was closed down and dispersed almost as soon as Norman arrived there, so he did not get his course after all,[419] instead rather guiltily spending his time in leisure pursuits,

including playing golf and calling at the Le Pré-Catelan Café at the sixth hole.

At the beginning of April 1918 he was instructed to rejoin his unit, and on 5th April he proceeded up to the front with Lieutenant H.R. Waugh,[420] Lewis Gun Officer, who was also returning to the Battalion after having suffered minor wounds early in the engagemen. On the way they had a close encounter with a party of 50 Germans, who were fortunately rebuffed by the 13th

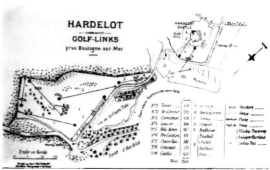

---

[419] This was the third of four courses that Norman narrowly missed – see the footnote later in this *Afterword* on page 304.

[420] Norman has described Waugh earlier as *"a great fellow – a Scotsman of the King's Own Scottish Borderers"*.

Royal Fusiliers, whom Norman and Waugh had been lucky enough to meet shortly before; also *"an enemy aeroplane suddenly came out of the low lying cloud, and he opened fire with a Machine Gun, and many of the bullets came uncomfortably near."*

They also met en route German prisoners coming down from the front. One group Norman describes as follows: *"They were unescorted and looking very miserable and were just about getting along wounded; one big burly fellow had a nasty bayonet wound in his face, and the general appearance was just that of soldiers of whatever Army, who had been in a heavy battle for several days."*

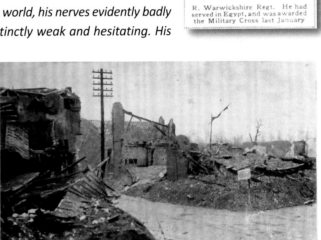

Captain E. E. Jenkins, M.C.
R. Warwickshire Regt. He had served in Egypt, and was awarded the Military Cross last January

Norman and Waugh found Captain William Tickler in the Bucquoy area. Captain E.E. Jenkins, the Adjutant, had been killed on 25th March 1918,[421] and Captain Tickler was now Acting Adjutant. Lieutenant Colonel P.V. Holberton[422] had also died a hero's death on 26th March 1918, and Lieutenant Colonel P.A. Clive, DSO, MP had taken over command of the Battalion. Norman Hall says of this encounter with Tickler at Battalion HQ:

Poor old Bill, he looked absolutely done to the world, his nerves evidently badly in need of a change, for his speech was distinctly weak and hesitating. His first remark was that we had arrived in the middle of a Battle, and that earlier in the afternoon Lieutenant Colonel Clive, while reconnoitring in the village of Bucquoy, about 400 yards South East of this point of Line in the Bucquoy Switch, had been killed.[423] Major Castle had only a short time before taking up the Battalion to counter-attack the Boche.

Norman was expecting to be sent to join Major Castle in the attack, but he continues:

BUCQUOY CROSS ROADS: THE SCENE OF SEVERE HAND-TO-HAND FIGHTING ON APRIL 5, 1918, BY THE 125TH BRIGADE.

---

[421] Norman's first mention of Jenkins, then a Lieutenant, is not particularly complimentary (see page 275), but on the occasion of his death he says *"he was a great favourite of all of us, and a very capable soldier"*. The Commonwealth War Graves Commission's records are to the effect that Captain Edgar Ernest Jenkins MC of the Royal Warwickshire Regiment, attached to the 1/5th Lancashire Fusiliers, the son of Ernest and Louisa Jenkins of Leamington Spa, was aged 31 when he died, and is commemorated on the Arras Memorial, Bay 3.
[422] Lieutenant Colonel Philip Vaughan Holberton, of the 2nd Battalion Manchester Regiment, five times mentioned in dispatches, son of E.R and E.G. Holberton of Teddington, husband of Dorothea Holberton, died aged 38 on 26th March 1916, and is buried at Achiet-le-Grand Communal Cemetery Extension, reference IV.F.8. See also *Obituaries*.
[423] Lieutenant Colonel Percy Archer Clive, of the Grenadier Guards, DSO, MP for South Herefordshire, Legion of Honour, Croix de Guerre, twice mentioned in dispatches, son of Charles Meysey Bolton and Lady Catherine Clive, husband of Alice Muriel Clive, died aged 35 on 4th April 1918, is commemorated on the Arras Memorial, Bay 1.

On our arrival Tickler was almost annoyed to see us for some reason. He was particularly upset that I had come up to the Line, as he had sent a second wire to me, ordering me on no account to come up to the Front Line.

Apparently a special wire had been sent from Division to the effect that Captain N. Hall was on no account to rejoin his unit in the Front Line. Tickler remarked that, if the Division learnt I was up there, there would be a Devil of a row. I had no idea I was considered so precious. I suppose they wanted to keep me as a specimen of an officer who had been in this real fighting. I later learnt that they were keeping me sort of up their sleeves in case the Staff Captain of the 125th Brigade, Captain Needham, got knocked out, at least so Captain Needham himself told me.

So Norman once again resumed the role of Acting Adjutant and prepared for the Battalion coming out of the Line, to billets at Vauchelles. He reports:

The Battalion came out of the Line on the night of April 7th. The weather had been very wet for some days, and, except for two days at Gommecourt, sleep had been impossible to obtain, and they had been fighting pretty well continuously since March 25th. The men were so very weary they could scarcely walk, let alone march. From Bucquoy to Souastre is about 7 miles; it took hours to cover, and the shells which fell near the road could raise no interest, much less fear, in men so utterly exhausted. Motor buses were waiting at Souastre to convey the remains of the Battalion, which only 15 days before had marched out of Houchin looking so spick and span and so full of spirits. Most of the men fell asleep on the buses en route via Hénu, Pas, Thièvres and Marieux to Vauchelles, where they arrived at 6.00am on April 8th.

We in Vauchelles hadn't the least idea what time the Battalion would arrive, but were ready from midnight. I had guides ready to take the Companies to their billets. It was a bitterly cold night, and waiting about in the village was none too cheery a job, but what was it compared with what the fellows had suffered?

The first party to arrive was the Brigade Party, Brigadier General Fargus, Captain Barton (Brigade Major), and Captain A.O. Needham (Staff Captain); they were a weary enough looking party, thoroughly worn out and filthy dirty. The General waited to see the 5th Battalion arrive, although he could just about stand up.

When the Battalion arrived they formed up by Companies and moved off to billets in barns and houses. I never saw such a sight in my life as these fellows. Many could scarcely stand up, to say nothing of walking, and the expression of their faces was one which I shall never forget; many looked more mad than sane, with sunken eyes – yet a vacant stare, blood shot; the mud and general dirty appearance did not improve matters, and it was extremely sad to see the men slowly move off in groups to their billets. Many were too exhausted to eat any food, although they hadn't had a decent meal for days. They simply fell down on the straw in their barns, some even too done to even take off their equipment. After going round Company billets to relieve officers as far as possible of Company Duties in seeing the men settled in, I went to HQ; there it was a sorry sight – scarcely a handful of officers remained from that cheery jolly crowd which gathered together on March 22nd at Houchin.

Major G.S. Castle was promoted to Lieutenant Colonel after this engagement, taking over command of the Battalion; also *"as a result of Tickler's work in this Show he got a Bar to his MC,*[424] *and Arthur Johnson got the MC. Both truly earned it."* In the context of the award to Captain A.M. Johnson, Norman describes how *"on more than one occasion our own MO … showed extreme bravery and absolutely regardless of personal safety in attending to the wounded and getting them away back to the Dressing Stations."*

He also praises the Padre, Captain Lowe, saying: *"Even the Padre – although against the rules of his calling – was a most energetic combatant officer; I say energetic reservedly, because perhaps he wasn't exactly that; anyway he worked tremendously hard taking charge of a carrying party mainly detailed for bringing down wounded from the Front Zone to the Battalion Dressing Station. At his own suggestion he utilised this carrying party on its forward journey to take up rations, ammunition, or any old thing which wanted taking up to the boys in the forward area. Lowe was a great fellow and his practical sympathy and example did a great deal towards keeping up the spirits of the officers and men under most demoralising conditions of body and mind."*

Following on from the engagement the Battalion did another tour of duty in the Line in the vicinity of Gommecourt.[425] Norman describes this area as follows:

Gommecourt was itself now only a name, for the Hun had demolished it so ruthlessly during the Somme Offensive in 1916 … There was a notice board erected by the French Government after 1917 to the effect that the "Historic Landscape of Gommecourt" was being preserved as a war memorial, and that nothing was to be disturbed which would alter its present aspect; no one imagined that the Boche would ever drive us back into this area, but such was the unfortunate state of affairs now … The old Front Line of the enemy, which now formed the Reserve Line, consisted of well revetted deep

trenches with 18 inches of mud on the old duckboards. The old German Front Line facing Hébuterne was now a Communication Trench to our Front Line (for the German Front Line here originally faced South West, and was in 1916 the most Westerly point of the German Line). His original Reserve Lines, which now formed our Front Line, were shallow trenches, lacking in revetment, fire steps, barbed wire defences …

---

424 The MC had been awarded for the action on 6th September 1917, referred to earlier in this *Afterword* on page 281-282.

425 The 125th Brigade had trained in this area in July and August 1917 (see page 277 of this *Afterword*) and had at that stage used the Chateau as Brigade HQ (see the photograph on page 277); Norman says that they used it as HQ again in 1918, but the Chateau shown on this page is in much worse condition, and it is difficult to see how it could have functioned as Brigade HQ, other than as a Camp HQ; either it had deteriorated significantly in the interim, or this is a different Chateau.

The old German light railway from Gommecourt Park to Biez Wood was soon put in working order and used for carrying water, rations, RE material, and ammunition. There were several tunnelled dug outs in the wood, stretching from one side to the other, these being a fine example of German thoroughness. Our Battalion HQ was a fine place, all wood lined, with separate cubicles; evidently it had been a Battalion HQ in 1916. The Mess Room was lined with oak panels, evidently removed from the Chateau by the Boche, and the seats round had at one time been pews in the village Church. It was a bit dirty, but we soon made change and had it looking like home! At any rate a trench home.

The following anecdote is recounted of Captain A.M Johnson and Captain Lowe in this sector:

The Aid Post was some little distance from the Battalion HQ nearer the village, and here lived Arthur Johnson, the MO, and Padre Lowe. Any morning at about 10.00am one might call there and see these two lads sitting up in bed (i.e. on stretchers) eating bacon and eggs. But Lowe was a great fellow – he used to go round the Line nearly every night to see the boys, taking round cigarettes, chocolates etc. We always knew when the Doc and Padre were coming to the Mess for meals, as the Boche invariably spotted them coming down the road and greeted them with a salvo of shells – a regular dinner gong. During this tour, on 20th April 1918, a German soldier named Ferdinand Rohr, aged 24, of Nº 7 Company, wandered into British Lines. Norman, who was present when he was apprehended, reports that *"he really seemed quite glad to be a prisoner, i.e. when he realised his position, and that he was treated decently."* Preserved in the diary are four original pages of handwritten notes taken by 2nd Lieutenant H.R. Ronnebeck recording an interview with him; the notes give, inter alia, an account of various difficulties suffered by German troops, including shortage of food and supplies.

war. Then used to be shot for trivial offences but not now.

The Bavarians were much hated by others because of the atrocities they had committed.

His company had lost 70 men killed alone near Arras.

He did not believe it to be true that a German 240 mm gun was shelling Paris. He believed that our losses by U boats were enormously exaggerated, their U boat losses were never mentioned. All letters from home are severely censored. Every two months they are given the date for the end of the war. Dates given were February 1917, Feb 1918 and now June 21st 1918. He did not believe the war could possibly...

Their canteens sold only tobacco, cigars (very bad ones) and cigarettes also, writing paper sometimes wine could be bought but it is very scarce and dear.

They get no fresh meat, very little meat at all. Bread is bad and the allowance is 750(?) grammes per day. They get peas & beans. Coffee is

sufficient in quantity. Tea is sometimes given.

The Bavarians refused to attack at Arras and his unit (not the 151st but previous one he was with) made the attack. Every man was given a packet of chocolate for this. Chocolate is extremely scarce.

Accommodation is very bad and they have suffered heavily from our night bombing raids. He was quite ignorant of our raids over German towns. They get no newspapers. He had heard nothing of Prince Lichnowsky's revelations.

He believed that after the war Prussia Bavaria and the remainder of Germany would separate.

Every man carries three rounds of anti tank rifle ammunition. Each round is marked with a red ring round the cap and costs about 1.30 Marks = 1/1.

H. R. Rommelbeck
2nd Lieut.

In the diary Norman describes how at this time the tactics of the British Army altered so as to mount a Defence in depth, defending mutually supporting "Localities" rather than simply a long Line. There is a lengthy account in the diary as to how gradually the tide began to turn in favour of the Allies, including commentary extracted from *My War Memories 1914-1918* by Erich Ludendorff,[426] which were first published in 1919. Amongst many other things, difficulties with communication and supply as the Germans advanced are mentioned as factors leading to German defeat, as to which Norman says, "*We had several examples of the failure of this, from prisoners*", an example being the notes of the interview with Ferdinand Rohr referred to above.

In the context of commenting on Ludendorff's memoirs Norman gives the following analysis:

Ludendorff's statements help us to appreciate the enemy, his wonderful organisation, his thoroughness, and yet his weaknesses, leading to failure, and the complete breakdown of that great "War Machine" – the German Army. It is that machine-like quality that appears to be at the root of their failure; somewhere the Boche missed that human touch; instead his Army was developed so much like a Machine that the initiative of the private soldier was not sufficiently developed. When well led, the German was a good soldier and brave, but without leaders he was lost. Not so our men – many of our battles were won by little groups of private soldiers, left without officers or NCOs, who – using their own wits – defended their ground and made ground. The idea of one Britisher equalling 10 Germans, 12 French, 14 Russians etc. is rot. But there isn't any doubt that the British Tommy was a superior fellow to the German private soldier.

---

[426] Erich Friedrich Wilhelm Ludendorff was a powerful German general who promoted the unsuccessful German Spring Offensive.

Possibly the German Staff Officers were better than ours, mainly because they had been trained to think in big things – Armies, Divisions and Corps – before 1914. In contrast our Generals had never been trained in the same way. Our Regular Army was originally 6 Regular Divisions and 14 Territorial Divisions. Further, a large proportion of our Army was always abroad, so that large forces were never collected, even for manoeuvres.

Norman has recorded that while in the Gommecourt sector: *"I was looking a bit worn these days. My shirt was split right across the shoulders and my battle jacket was badly torn and patched, as I had worn it in 1916 when I was wounded on the Somme."* He also says of this period: *"The dug outs were rather dirty and it was rather difficult to keep clean – 'friends!'[427] were prevalent. I suppose the Boche had left them, and – as they hadn't had much to feed on for some time – they made hay while the sun shone."*

At the beginning of May 1918 he contracted PUO[428] or Trench Fever, and was admitted to hospital, initially N° 21 Casualty Clearing Station, then N° 2 British Red Cross Hospital,[429] Rouen, and finally, on 28th May 1918, N° 74 General Hospital, Trouville, the last being a Convalescent

Army Form A. 2042A.

Hospital Redirection Card.

On the admission of a Soldier to Hospital this card should be filled in and forwarded to his next-of-kin.

Number (if any),
Rank and Name } Captain N. Head.

Battery, Company
or Squadron }

Battalion, Regiment,
Service, &c. } 1/5. Lanc: Fusiliers

has been admitted into

No. 2. B. R. C. HOSPITAL,
A.T.O2. British Expeditionary Force.
(Letters should be addressed as above.)

Sick*

Wounded* T. U. O.

Signature of Chaplain,
Medical Officer, Sister,
or Wardmaster } L. L. Dowling.

* Indicate here briefly nature of wound or sickness.
W3597—M2317 350,000 6/17 HWV (P1166) Forms/A20124/3

Hospital, where he was asked to take charge of German prisoners constructing a bath house, and trenches for the Sisters in case of the hospital being attacked; presumably this was to give them cover rather than to enable them to mount a defence, as the Sisters would hardly have been suited for the latter, given Norman's comment after he had commenced the construction of the trenches: *"I had a few Sisters sent over on apro[430] to see whether they were the right fit – as some of the good ladies were almost as broad as long."* He observes of the task: *"It was an easy, but interesting, job and gave me something to do; I was getting a bit tired of doing nothing – particularly as I was feeling <u>really</u> fit again."*

He remained at Trouville until 2nd July 1918, then made his way back via Étaples to the 1/5th Lancashire Fusiliers at Couin Chateau on 9th July 1918. Had Norman not contracted Trench Fever in May when he was Acting Adjutant, it seems likely that he would have been promoted to Adjutant, but, not surprisingly given his eight weeks' absence, Captain Rouse had now been appointed to that role, and Norman found he had *"no definite job … [but was] employed as a sort of 'pal to the CO'"*, i.e. to Lieutenant Colonel Castle. He again covered as Adjutant for a short time while Rouse was on leave, then he covered as Intelligence Officer, then as Signals Officer, which happened to be the role that he had started out in on arrival in France. His diary entry for 27th July 1918 reads: *"A bit of bad luck happened*

---

[427] i.e. lice.
[428] Pyrexia of Unknown Origin.
[429] This was where he had initially been treated after being wounded on 9th September 1916 – see the diary entry for 10th September 1916.
[430] Approval.

– I missed a Staff Course because one of our Brigade Dispatches arrived late.[431] *I had a very bad attack of nerves and seemed to have no confidence – a rotten feeling."*

In the event, by a twist of irony, the role of Signals Officer, his first role in France, also proved to be his last, as, on 29th July 1918, when he was riding to Louvencourt to buy beer for the men for Minden Day[432] on 1 August, *"in attempting to avoid a runaway limber with two mules, also some troops of the 57th Division, and trying to take the fence on the road side, the horse failed and fell back on me. My right foot stuck in the stirrup and the horse rolled back on to me."* He had broken his ankle, and was again (for the third time) admitted to N° 2 British Red Cross Hospital,[433] via N° 3 Canadian Hospital at Doullens, then sent across the Channel on HMHS *Essequibo*, narrowly (by a margin of three men) avoiding being sent on the next ship, the SS *Warilda*, which was torpedoed and sunk.[434]

H.M.H.S. "ESSEQUIBO"

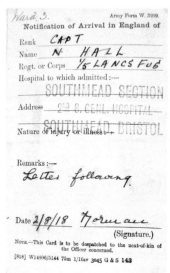

On arrival in Britain on 2nd August 1918 he was sent to the 2nd Southern General Hospital at Southmead, Bristol, where he spent nearly six weeks, being visited by – and, when he was mobile enough to leave the hospital, visiting – friends and family of Brigadier General Fargus and Lieutenant Colonel G.S. Castle,

---

[431] This was the fourth course that Norman had narrowly missed for various reasons, and, in fact, he never attended any significant residential course throughout his War Service, which must have been very unusual for an officer. The first such course was a Musketry course in Southport, which he missed because he was sent to Bedford with the 2/5th Lancashire Fusiliers on 18th April 1915 (see the diary entry for 11th to 18th April 1915); the second was when he was recalled at the last moment for the Ginchy engagement on 7th September 1916; and the third was during the German Spring Offensive, when on 23rd March 1918 he was sent to the Ist Army Infantry School at Hardelot Castle for a course, but the School was closed down (see the account earlier in this *Afterword*, pages 295-297).

[432] See the footnote to the diary entry for 1st and 2nd August 1914.

[433] The first two occasions were after being wounded on 9th September 1916 (see the diary entry for 10th September 1916), and on contracting Trench Fever in May 1918, as mentioned earlier in this *Afterword*, page 303.

[434] At 1.35am on 3rd August 1918 a torpedo fired by German Submarine UC-49 took out the SS *Warilda*'s starboard propeller, so that the port engine could not be shut down as the engine room had been flooded, and she continued to move in a circle at about 15 knots until she ran out of steam. The lifeboats could not be lowered until that happened. Of the 801 people on board 123 lost their lives, including 101 *"walking patients"* from the lowest ward, and all the engine room staff.

as well as receiving visits from his own friends and family, including his fellow officer in the 1/5th Lancashire Fusiliers, St Barbe.[435]

He was discharged from the Bristol Hospital on 10th September 1918, and was sent to a Convalescent Hospital in Blackpool, where he was appointed Adjutant of the Brighton Hydro, a role which does not seem to have been especially onerous. Of this period he says: *"We followed the Rapid Progress of our Armies in France with much interest, but never realised that the War was going to end so quickly. I had many regrets that I wasn't out with the Battalion helping to kick the Boche back, and really having the satisfaction of being in at the finish, particularly as I had many experiences of the reverse kind. But then, 'Fate', or something, had ruled things differently for me. Perhaps for some things I was fortunate, but it seems a very feeble finish up to the War for me."*

On 11th November 1918 his diary entry reads:

Kathleen came over to stay at Blackpool. I met her, and we went up to the Savoy Café at about 11.00am. I rang up Squires Gate, and got the news that the Armistice was signed. I had the honour of making this announcement in the Savoy Café and everyone stood in silence after the first burst of cheering had subsided. Kathleen and I went to a Service at South Shore in the afternoon at 2.00pm. It was a most impressive Service, and we both enjoyed it. Processions were organised and the whole town generally went mad. Kathleen and I went North to Park Street for the evening, and got back at 11.45pm. I got to bed very late. There were many absentees – but no trouble.

It seemed <u>very</u> difficult to realise that Hostilities were actually finished, and one had a fear that they might be renewed.
The terms of the Armistice to the Germans were fairly severe.
The Country as a whole received the news with tremendous excitement. Everyone went mad and paraded the streets.
It felt as if a tremendous load had been taken off one's back, but what the feelings of the men actually at the Front could have been one can only surmise.

On 16th November 1918 Kathleen returned home to Bury, and his account of the remainder of the day reads: *"There were Torchlight and Fancy Dress Processions in the afternoon and evening. I went along in the evening with the Manageress at the Brighton, Doris Barker, and Mademoiselle Toby. I had my wrist watch[436] cut off my wrist in Talbot Square, where there was a bonfire and a burning of an effigy of the Kaiser."*

---

[435] See the footnote earlier in this *Afterword* on page 275.
[436] This was the watch that had been purchased on 26th April 1915 in Bedford.

He was passed fit for Home Service on 23rd December 1918, thus narrowly missing being appointed as Camp Adjutant of what he calls "the whole Blackpool Centre", presumably the King's Lancashire Military Convalescent Hospital, which he says would have carried with it the rank of temporary Lieutenant Colonel, and would have meant that his Army pension would have been based on that rank.

After spending Christmas at home, he proceeded to Thirtle Bridge, Withernsea on the Yorkshire Coast on 9th January 1919, ostensibly to help man the coastal defences. However, after the small excitement of his train jumping the buffers at Withernsea Station, and ending up halfway across the village street, he was assigned "Light Duty", which involved reporting on parade first thing and then going for walks along the cliffs. He was demobilised on 19th January 1919, thus bringing his Army career to an end, apart from a short period from 10th April to 13th July 1921, when he volunteered to serve in a Defence Force formed by Lloyd George's government to support the police during a National Emergency precipitated by widespread strikes.

Norman's own summary of his service during the First World War is as follows:

I had served from September 9th 1914 to January 19th 1919:	*4 years 132 days*
I had actually been in France:	
May 3rd 1915 to September 9th 1916	*1 year 129 days*
June 14th 1917 to August 2nd 1918	*1 year 49 days*
Active Service Total:	*2 years 178 days*

I had started as a Private in the 3rd City Battalion, The King's Liverpool Regiment, on September 9th 1914, and terminated my service as Substantive Captain, with effect from October 8th 1916, during which time I had been Acting 2nd in Command of the 1/5th Lancashire Fusiliers from June 30th 1918 to July 22nd 1918, as Temporary Major (?!!).

The question mark and two exclamation marks in parentheses are rather enigmatic. There is no other mention of his having been appointed temporary Major, but the period seems to coincide with that when he reports that he was employed as a sort of "pal to the CO".

After demobilisation, Norman went back to his pre-War employment as a Chemical Engineer at Port Sunlight, but continued to support the Lancashire Fusiliers as an ex-serviceman. He was selected to be a member of the Colour Party which represented the 5th Battalion in the Victory Parade in London on 19th July 1919, of which he says:

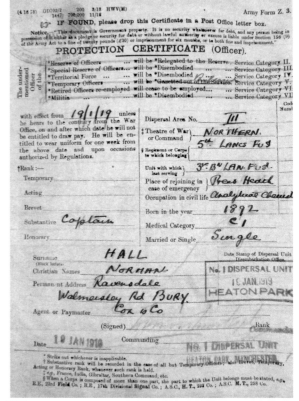

I never knew why I was selected, and the only reason I could possibly imagine was the fact that I was I think the only officer who had served with all units of the 5th Territorial Force during the War.

I was one of the first commissioned officers of the 2/5th Lancashire Fusiliers, I assisted in the formation of the 3/5th Lancashire Fusiliers at Bury in January 1915. I served with the 2/5th Battalion and 1/5th Battalion in France, and I was posted to the 5th Reserve Battalion at Ripon and Scarborough from January 1917 to June 1917. So that perhaps I was in the fortunate position of really being able to represent all units ... From the 42nd East Lancashire Division there were seven officers. I was therefore very lucky and I may say that I felt it a very great honour to have the privilege to represent the very fine officers, NCOs and men of all units of the 5th Lancashire Fusiliers who served in the Great War.

The Memory of that Day – July 19th 1919 – will never be forgotten. It is very difficult to put into words exactly what one's own personal feelings were on that occasion. Perhaps they were even too sincere, too personal to put into words. Certainly they were mixed – those of Rejoicing for Peace, and Sadness for the Memory of one's friends of all Ranks...

As we passed into Sloane Street the crowd was intensely thick on either side and there was one almost continuous unending cheer throughout the whole route. There seemed to be no place along the route where another person could be put; and at some points – particularly from Westminster Bridge to Buckingham Palace – people scarcely seemed to have room to move an eyelash. At first the effect

was most discomforting. It gave us a cold chill down our backs – an empty feeling inside, and to be perfectly honest it was somewhat difficult to suppress that choking feeling in your throat or the tears. Practically everyone agreed on this point when we compared notes after.

In time the strangeness and the sort of feeling you were on show passed off and we were able to take an intelligent interest in the whole affair. The people were wonderfully expressive in their cheering and one almost felt it was worth while having put up with a little

A newspaper cutting showing the procession passing through Trafalgar Square into the Mall from Whitehall *discomfort out in France to feel the appreciation.*

The other members of the Colour Party were Acting Company Sergeant Major J. Hutchinson VC, Lance Sergeant E. Smith VC DCM, and Lieutenant R. Max Barlow MC.[437] A fifth person, Regimental Quartermaster Sergeant A. Mooney, went as reserve.

---

[437] For Acting Company Sergeant Major J. Hutchinson see footnote 261 to the diary entry for 24th to 28th June 1916 on page 200. Edward Benn Smith of the 1/5th Lancashire Fusiliers was a coal miner from Maryport, Cumbria who enlisted in 1917. He earned his DCM and VC within a fortnight of each other on 10th and 22nd August 1917 respectively. At 19 he was the youngest man to be awarded a VC in the First World War. The action which won him the DCM was to lead a small party in attacking about 40 Germans after lying in wait for them in their own trench, while the citation for the VC records *"Sergeant Smith ... personally took a machine-gun post, rushing the garrison with his rifle and bayonet. The enemy, on seeing him advance, scattered to throw hand grenades at him. Regardless of all danger, and almost without halting in his rush on the post, this N.C.O. shot and killed at least six of the enemy"*. He later assisted another platoon to attain its objective, and the following day led his section forward to restore a portion of the Line which the Germans had taken. Both actions are mentioned in Major General J.C. Latter's *The History of the Lancashire Fusiliers 1914-1918*, where his qualities of leadership and tactical acuity are particularly praised. He remained in the Army as a regular soldier, but unfortunately was killed early in the Second World War on 12th January 1940.

Richard Maxwell Barlow (Max) was awarded the MC as a 2nd Lieutenant in an action near St Julien on 20th September 1917 in the 3rd Battle of Ypres, in which, according to *The History of the Lancashire Fusiliers 1914-1918*, *"although severely wounded in the first few minutes* [Second Lieutenant Barlow] *refused to leave his platoon until he had led them to the Schuler Galleries"*, i.e to their objective; this was also the engagement in which Captain J.C. Latter was awarded his MC (as to which see the footnote to the diary entry for 25th September to 3rd October 1915).

Left to right: Acting Company Sergeant Major J. Hutchinson VC, Captain N. Hall, Lance Sergeant E. Smith VC DCM, and the reserve member of the Party, Regimental Quartermaster Sergeant A. Mooney; Lieutenant R. M. Barlow MC, the fourth person who actually carried the Colours, was not photographed.

Norman also represented the 2/5th Lancashire Fusiliers on the unveiling of the Memorial to the 55th Division at Givenchy[438] on 15th May 1921 (when he was serving in the Defence Force during the period of National Emergency, as mentioned above). With regard to this occasion he says:

It was a very strange feeling to arrive at Cuinchy by train; the last time I crossed this railway it was by short rushes under shell fire ... I went off on my own to see some of the old spots, rambling about trenches and No Man's Land and the Boche Line. It seemed so strange – all so unreal. Could one be dreaming! Was the War on or had it finished? Many thoughts flashed across my mind as I sat on the edge of one of the huge craters, still full of barbed wire and the only smelly water in its bottom. For a moment the silence was only disturbed by the singing of a lark. Only anyone who had been through hard times on this ground could realise the feelings that were felt on that day ...
I always felt it was a great privilege to have been chosen to represent the 2/5th Lancashire Fusiliers

---

[438] Where Norman had been based between November 1917 and February 1918.

at the Unveiling of the Givenchy Memorial, and to be present and personally pay my own tribute to the memory of those Gallant Fellows of the 55th Division – and particularly the 2/5ᵗʰ Lancashire Fusiliers – who had laid down their lives for a great cause, "A War to End War" – not only on the Givenchy Front, but all along the Western Front from Ypres to the Somme: "May their sacrifices not have been in vain, for the benefit of the generations yet unborn."

The other men who represented the 2/5ᵗʰ Lancashire Fusiliers at the unveiling were Captain J.C. Latter MC,[439] indicated in the photograph below, Acting Company Sergeant Major J. Hutchinson VC,[440] Sergeant W. Cadden DCM[441] and Sergeant A. Wroe, all of whom had proceeded to France with the unit on 3ʳᵈ May 1915.

While at Givenchy, Norman saw and photographed the graves of 2ⁿᵈ Lieutenant John Schofield VC[442]

The moment when the Memorial to the 55th Division was unveiled on 15th May 1921

No. 8—Givenchy Memorial Ceremony: Officers of the 55th Division.

---

[439] For Captain J.C. Latter see the footnote to the diary entry for 25th September to 3rd October 1915.
[440] For Acting Company Sergeant Major J. Hutchinson see footnote 261 to the diary entry for 24th to 28th June 1916 on page 200.
[441] For Sergeant W. Cadden see the diary entry for 2nd July 1916.
[442] 2nd Lieutenant John Schofield (Norman spells it *"Scholfield"*) was the son of John and Martha Schofield, of Coniston, formerly of Blackburn, and died aged 26 on 9th April 1918. He is buried at Vieille-Chapelle Military Cemetery, La Couture, reference III.C.8. The citation for his posthumous Victoria Cross reads: *"For most conspicuous bravery and devotion to duty in operations. 2nd Lt. Schofield led a party of nine men against a strong point which was reported strongly held by the enemy, and was attacked by about 100 of the enemy with bombs. He disposed his men so skilfully, and made such good use of rifle and Lewis gun fire, that the enemy took cover in dug-outs. This officer himself then held up and captured a party of twenty. With the help of other parties this position was then cleared of the enemy who were all killed or captured. He then collected the remainder*

The 55th Division Memorial at Givenchy photographed in 2019

SOMME 1916
YPRES 1916-17
CAMBRAI 1917
GIVENCHY-FESTUBERT 1918
THE ADVANCE IN FLANDERS 1918

The inscription on the central panel of the Memorial to the 55th Division at Givenchy, photographed in 2019; the other two sides read:
Units of the West Lancashire Territorial Force, which was formed in 1908, fought in France and Belgium from 1914. On 3rd January 1916 it was re-assembled as the 55th (West- Lancashire) Division and served under that title throughout the remainder of the campaign.
Around this site from the 9th to the 16th April 1918 the Division, continuously attacked from the Canal to Festubert by three German Divisions and with its left flank turned, held its ground, and inflicted severe loss upon the enemy.
... "this most gallant Defence, the importance of which it would be hard to overestimate" ...
Sir Douglas Haig's Despatch date 20-7-18

and Sergeant Sleigh[443], both of the 2/5th Lancashire Fusiliers, at the British Cemetery, Windy Corner, marked at that time by wooden crosses.

At the end of the text of the diary, completed on 30th March 1928, Norman quotes with approval the following passage from R.H. Mottram's *Sixty-Four, Ninety-Four:* [444]

The war is only tolerable as a memory when one can feel that we have all learned something from it. Otherwise it becomes a mere nightmare of waste. Let us leave our children such a memorial that, seeing it, they may be able to imagine a way of settling disputes more intelligent than maintaining, during years, a population as large as that of London, on an area as large as Wales, for the sole purpose of slaughter by machinery. If we cannot provide the information which will make it possible to avoid this, and if those children of ours cannot use it, then indeed the nightmare of waste will visit us. More than a nightmare, a reality in which our children and with them the whole civilisation of Western Europe may disappear. Deservedly so, for we shall have betrayed all those dead comrades of ours, rendering their willing sacrifice a ridiculous futility.

---

of his men, made his party up to ten, and proceeded towards the front line, previously informing his Commanding Officer as to the position, and that he was proceeding to retake the front line. He met large numbers of the enemy in a communication trench in front of him and in a drain on his right and left. His party opened rapid rifle fire, and he climbed out on to the parapet under point blank machine gun fire, and, by his fearless demeanour and bravery, forced the enemy to surrender. As a result, 123 of the enemy, including several officers, were captured by 2nd Lt. Schofield and his party. This very gallant officer was killed a few minutes later."

[443] Sergeant Harry Balfour Sleigh (for some reason Norman has his intitial as "F."), Service no 200013, was the son of Mary Ellen and the late Thomas Sleigh of Bury, and died aged 28 on 9th April 1918. He is buried at Vieille-Chapelle Military Cemetery, La Couture, reference III.C.7.

[444] Ralph Hale Mottram was born in Norwich in 1883, the son of a banker. He served in the First World War, and made his name as a war poet and novelist. *Sixty-Four, Ninety-Four* was written in 1925, one of three novels called *The Spanish Farm Trilogy*, filmed in 1927 under the title *The Roses of Picardy*, drawing on his experiences in the First World War.

Name	Regiment	Date of Death[445]	Place of burial or commemoration
Bampton, Lance Sergeant Tom	2/5th Lancashire Fusiliers	23.07.15	Rue-du-Bacquerot (13th London) Graveyard, Laventie, France
Baxter, Lieutenant Edward Felix VC	1/8th The King's Liverpool Regiment	18.04.16	Fillièvres British Cemetery, France
Bentley, Captain Frank Mercer MC	1/5th Lancashire Fusiliers	13.10.18	St Souplet British Cemetery, France
Best-Dunkley, Lieutenant Colonel Bertram VC	2/5th Lancashire Fusiliers	05.08.17	Mendinghem Military Cemetery, Belgium
Bloy, Captain Laurence Henry	2/5th Lancashire Fusiliers	29.06.16	Fillièvres British Cemetery, France
Brooks, Lance Corporal Harry	2/5th Lancashire Fusiliers	29.04.16	Le Fermont Military Cemetery, Rivière, France
Briggs, 2nd Lieutenant William Lonsdale	1st Bn. King's Own Royal Lancaster Regiment, attached 1/5th Lancashire Fusiliers	14.09.17	Étaples Military Cemetery, France
Cain, 2nd Lieutenant Frank Backwell	15th Bn. Highland Light Infantry	13.04.18	Gézaincourt Communal Cemetery Extension, France
Cameron, 2nd Lieutenant W.G.[446]	1/2nd Duke of Wellington's West Riding Regiment, attached 1/5th Lancashire Fusiliers	04.09.18	Adanac Military Cemetery, Miraumont, France
Catterall, Lance Sergeant Richard	2/5th Lancashire Fusiliers	06.08.16	Thiepval Memorial, France
Chadwick, Private R.	2/5th Lancashire Fusiliers	13.09.15	Aveluy Communal Cemetery Extension, France
Christie, Major William Charles	1st Bn. Royal Warwickshire Regiment	13.10.14	Méteren Military Cemetery, France
Clive, Lieutenant Colonel Percy Archer DSO, MP	1st Bn. Grenadier Guards, attached 1/5th Lancashire Fusiliers	04.04.18	Arras Memorial, France
Coats, 2nd Lieutenant John Alexander Hamilton	2/5th Lancashire Fusiliers, attached 164th Trench Mortar Battery, formerly RNVR	08.08/16	Thiepval Memorial, France
Cornall, Corporal Samuel Walter	22nd Bn. Manchester Regiment	04.10.17	Tyne Cot Memorial, Belgium
Davies, Lieutenant Colonel Oswyn St Leger[447]	6th Bn. Manchester Regiment	05.04.18	Bienvillers Military Cemetery, France
Dickinson, Lieutenant Talbot	2/5th Lancashire Fusiliers	31.07.17	Ypres (Menin Gate) Memorial, Belgium
Downham, 2nd Lieutenant Harold	1/7th Lancashire Fusiliers	29.09.18	Grévillers British Cemetery, France
Elson, 2nd Lieutenant Edwin Arthur	3/9th Middlesex Regiment, attached 2/5th Lancashire Fusiliers	09.09.16	Thiepval Memorial, France
Essex, 2nd Lieutenant Percy Clifford	2/5th Lancashire Fusiliers	09.09.16	Thiepval Memorial, France
Fryer, Lieutenant Eric Hamilton	2/5th Lancashire Fusiliers	03.08.16	Thiepval Memorial, France
Godfrey, 2nd Lieutenant Henry	2/5th Lancashire Fusiliers	08/09.09.16	Delville Wood Cemetery, Longueval, France
Hampson, Lance Corporal[448]	2/5th Lancashire Fusiliers	15.08.16	Not known
Harrison, 2nd Lieutenant Cyril Henry	10th Bn. South Lancashire Regiment, attached 1/5th Lancashire Fusiliers	06.09.17	Tyne Cot Memorial, Belgium

---

[445] According to the Commonwealth War Graves Commission's records.

[446] The death of 2nd Lieutenant W.G. Cameron is mentioned in the original diary as occurring while Norman was absent from the Battalion during the final advance across France, in an action to take the village of Metz-en-Couture. He was the son of Mr W.F. Cameron of Leeds, and was 28 when he died. The cemetery reference is VIII.J.34.

[447] Lieutenant Colonel O. St L. Davies died at Bucquoy while commanding the 8th Battalion of the Lancashire Fusiliers during the German Spring Offensive. He was the son of Mr J.M. and Mrs J.E. Davies of Llanwrda, Carmarthenshire and was aged 44 when he died. The cemetery reference is XVII.A.4.

[448] See the footnote to the diary entry for 15th August 1916 regarding the absence of any mention in the Commonwealth War Graves Commission's records of the death of Lance Corporal Hampson on 15th August 1916.

Name	Regiment	Date	Cemetery
Hartington, Lieutenant John Ernest MC	2/5th Lancashire Fusiliers, attached 164th Company Machine Gun Corps	13.07.17	Lijssenthoek Military Cemetery, Belgium
Hawksey, Lieutenant Bernard Richard[449]	1/5th Lancashire Fusiliers	28.09.18	Caudry British Cemetery, France
Hedley, Captain Joseph Walton	2/5th Lancashire Fusiliers	12.09.16	Heilly Station Cemetery, Méricourt-l'Abbé, France
Hitchon, Corporal Fred Edwin	2/5th Lancashire Fusiliers	06.08.16	Delville Wood Cemetery, Longueval, France
Holberton, Lieutenant Colonel Philip Vaughan	2nd Bn. Manchester Regiment	26.03.18	Achiet-Le-Grand Communal Cemetery Extension, France
Hope, Lieutenant Colonel George Everard MC[450]	1st Bn. Grenadier Guards, attached 1/8th Bn. Lancashire Fusiliers	10.10.17	Ramskapelle Road Military Cemetery, Belgium
Howarth, Company Sergeant Major N. DCM	2/5th Lancashire Fusiliers	17.06.17	Longuenesse (St Omer) Souvenir Cemetery, France
Hudson, Captain Austin Patrick	1/5th Lancashire Fusiliers	31.08.17	Tyne Cot Memorial, Belgium
Jackson, 2nd Lieutenant John Henry	2/5th Lancashire Fusiliers	09.09.16	Thiepval Memorial, France
Jeffreys, Captain Darrell Richard	1st Bn. Devonshire Regiment	11.07.15	Chester Farm Cemetery, Belgium
Jenkins, Captain Edgar Ernest MC	Royal Warwickshire Regiment, attached 1/5th Lancashire Fusiliers	25.03.18	Arras Memorial, France
Kemp, 2nd Lieutenant Norman	2/5th Lancashire Fusiliers	09.09.16	Thiepval Memorial, France
Kenderdine, Lieutenant T.H.G.	2/5th Lancashire Fusiliers	09.09.16	Delville Wood Cemetery, Longueval, France
Kerr, 2nd Lieutenant Arthur Douglas Garnett Odell	3/10th Middlesex Regiment, attached 2/5th Lancashire Fusiliers	03.08.16	Thiepval Memorial, France
Loring, Lieutenant Colonel Walter Latham	2nd Bn. Royal Warwickshire Regiment	23.10.14	Ypres (Menin Gate) Memorial, Belgium
Lucas, Company Sergeant Major Thomas Turner DCM	2/2nd London Regiment (Royal Fusiliers)	01.05.18	Crouy British Cemetery, Crouy-sur-Somme, France
Manock, Lance Corporal Joe[451]	2/5th Lancashire Fusiliers	28.06.16	Arras Memorial, France
Martin, Sergeant T.[452]	1/5th Lancashire Fusiliers	13.01.18	Gorre British and Indian Cemetery, France
Mashiter, Lieutenant Thomas Alexander Greenwood	10th Bn. York and Lancaster Regiment, attached 1/5th Lancashire Fusiliers	31.08.17	Tyne Cot Memorial, Belgium

---

[449] Lieutenant B.R. Hawksey is frequently mentioned in the original diary from 1917 onwards. He was with the 1/5th Lancashire Fusiliers in June 1917 when Norman joined them in France, and often socialized with Norman. He lost a horse – or had it stolen – in Béthune in February 1918 while they were in the La Bassée Sector, bringing back only the saddle, which led to "*some row*", and a Court of Enquiry. Like Norman, he was, as "*Battle Surplus*", sent to attend a course at Hardelot Chateau when the Battalion went into action in the German Spring Offensive on 23rd March 1918. Norman mentions that during the final advance across France (at which time Norman was not with the Battalion), following attacks on Highland and Welsh Ridge, 2nd Lieutenant Hawksey, "*who had done splendid work throughout*" was found to be missing. He was aged 28 when he died, the son of William David and Elizabeth Hawksey of Manchester, and his memorial reference is Sp. Mem. 1, meaning that he is known to be buried in the cemetery, but it is not known exactly where.

[450] Writing about the Nieuport area on 10th October 1917, Norman says: "*The Commanding Officer of the 8th Lancashire Fusiliers, Lieutenant Colonel Hope MC, late of the Grenadier Guards, was missing. While making a tour of his Line after relief he walked into a Boche post, a fight followed, and poor Hope was never heard of again – a complete mystery.*" His body must have been found later, as he is buried in Ramskapelle Road Military Cemetery, reference VI.A.1. He was the only son of Henry W. and Lady Mary Hope of Luffness and Rankeillour.

[451] Norman spells this "Maynock".

[452] In the original diary Norman mentions that while they were in the La Bassée Sector the Boche blew in a post at "F" Sap, manned by Norman's own Company, "B" Company, under the command of Umpti North. He says that this happened on 10th January 1918, not 13th January 1918. He records that Sergeant Martin and four others were killed, and four were wounded. He does not name the others who died, but the graves of three other privates of the 1/5th Lancashire Fusiliers who died on 13th January 1918 are near that of Sergeant Martin; Sergeant Martin's cemetery reference is V.B.22, while at V.B.19, 17 and 18 are respectively the graves of Private R. Butterworth, Service no 201446, Private T. Jones, Service no 201550, and Private W.H. McMahon, Service no 201417. The Commonwealth War Graves Commission's records do not list any fourth man from the 1/5th Lancashire Fusiliers who died on 13th January 1918 or shortly afterwards in the La Bassée Sector.

Name	Regiment	Date	Cemetery / Memorial
McVicker, Lieutenant Edgar Harold [453]	Royal Army Medical Corps, attached 2/5th Lancashire Fusiliers	09.09.16	Dantzig Alley British Cemetery, Mametz, France
Moffatt, 2nd Lieutenant Cecil Henry	2/5th Lancashire Fusiliers	01.08.16	La Neuville British Cemetery, Corbie, France
Moffatt, 2nd Lieutenant Stanley Leslie	2/5th Lancashire Fusiliers	13.08.16	Péronne Road Cemetery, Maricourt, France
Morgan, Lieutenant Victor Harold	1st Bn. King's Liverpool Regiment, attached 1/5th Lancashire Fusiliers	06.09.17	Tyne Cot Memorial, Belgium
Murphy, Lieutenant George	13th Bn. Royal Warwickshire Regiment, attached 1/5th Lancashire Fusiliers	06.09.17	Tyne Cot Memorial, Belgium
Nickson, Major Harry	4th Bn. The Loyal North Lancashire Regiment	30.10.15	Aveluy Communal Cemetery Extension, France
Ogden, Private Francis [454]	2/5th Lancashire Fusiliers	28.06.16	Arras Memorial, France
Ogden, Company Quatermaster Sergeant Thomas	2/5th Lancashire Fusiliers	11.08.16	St Sever Cemetery, Rouen, France
Oldfield, Captain Edmund George William	8th Bn. Manchester Regiment	05.06.15	Helles Memorial, Gallipoli, Turkey
Page, Captain John Kenneth Samuel MC [455]	9th Bn. Royal Warwickshire Regiment, attached 1/5th Lancashire Fusiliers	22.08.18	Sucrerie Military Cemetery, Colincamps, France
Park, Private F.	2/5th Lancashire Fusiliers	21.08.15	Aveluy Communal Cemetery Extension, France
Petrie, 2nd Lieutenant Donald John	1/10th Royal Scots, attached 2/5th Lancashire Fusiliers	09.09.16	Thiepval Memorial, France
Quinlan, Private Richards	2/5th Lancashire Fusiliers	19.07.15	Le Touret Memorial, France
Richardson, Private Thomas	2/5th Lancashire Fusiliers	05.08.16	Thiepval Memorial, France
Russ, Sergeant Stanley DCM	2/5th Lancashire Fusiliers	26.09.16	Abbeville Communal Cemetery Extension, France
Saxby, 2nd Lieutenant Eric Yardley	3/9th Middlesex Regiment, attached 2/5th Lancashire Fusiliers	09.09.16	Thiepval Memorial, France
Schofield, 2nd Lieutenant John VC [456]	2/5th Lancashire Fusiliers	09.04.18	Vieille-Chapelle New Military Cemetery, La Couture, France
Schofield, Private John [457]	2/5th Lancashire Fusiliers	15.04.16	Le Fermont Military Cemetery, Rivière, France
Simon, Captain Eric Conrad	2/5th Lancashire Fusiliers	17.08.15	Millencourt Communal Cemetery Extension, France
Sleigh, Sergeant H.B. [458]	2/5th Lancashire Fusiliers	09.04.18	Vieille-Chapelle New Military Cemetery, La Couture, France
Smith, 2nd Lieutenant Alec	10th Bn. Lancashire Fusiliers, formerly 11th Prince Albert's Own Hussars	08.07.16	Thiepval Memorial, France
Smith, Sergeant Roger MM	16th Bn. Manchester Regiment	15.10.16	Warlencourt British Cemetery, France

[453] Norman spells this name "McVickers".
[454] See the footnote to the diary entry for 28th June 1916; in this table Private Francis Ogden is listed in place of J. Turner.
[455] The death of Captain Page (nicknamed "Peggy") occurred after Norman had left the 1/5th Lancashire Fusiliers and returned to Britain. It happened at Miraumont while he was commanding "D" Company during the final successful advance against the Germans. Captain Page was the son of Mr S.W. and Mrs M.A. Page of Wolverhampton, and was aged 22 when he died. The cemetery reference is I.J.3.
[456] Norman spells this name "Scholfield".
[457] Norman spells this name "Scholfield".
[458] Norman refers to Sergeant Sleigh as Sergeant F. Sleigh.

Name	Regiment	Date	Memorial / Cemetery
Spencer, Private James	2/5th Lancashire Fusiliers	05.08.16	Thiepval Memorial, France
Stott, Lieutenant William Ernest[459]	1/5th Lancashire Fusiliers	08.08.18	Euston Road Cemetery, Colincamps, France
Taylor, 2nd Lieutenant David George	10th Bn. Manchester Regiment, attached 2/5th Lancashire Fusiliers	09.09.16	Thiepval Memorial, France
Thewlis, Lieutenant Harold Darling	1/7th Manchester Regiment	04.06.15	Helles Memorial, Gallipoli, Turkey
Todd, Private William	2/5th Lancashire Fusiliers	31.10.15	Aveluy Communal Cemetery Extension, France
Turner, Private John[460]	2/5th Lancashire Fusiliers	12.09.16	Delville Wood Cemetery, Longueval, France
Tristram, Lieutenant Eric Barrington	Royal Fusiliers, attached 1/5th Lancashire Fusiliers	06.09.17	Tyne Cot Memorial, Belgium
Walker, 2nd Lieutenant Richard	2/5th Lancashire Fusiliers, formerly London Regiment Artists' Rifles	09.08.16	Thiepval Memorial, France
Waterhouse, Captain Kenneth	2/5th Lancashire Fusiliers	09.08.16	Guillemont Road Cemetery, Guillemont, France
Watson, Private A.	15th Bn. Highland Light Infantry	21.12.15	Authuille Military Cemetery, Authuille, France
Wright, Private John	2/5th Lancashire Fusiliers	06.08.16	Thiepval Memorial, France
Young, Lieutenant Edmund Taylor	6th Bn. Manchester Regiment	10.06.15	Helles Memorial, Gallipoli, Turkey
Young, Lieutenant Malcolm Henry	2/5th Lancashire Fusiliers	29.06.16	Fillièvres British Cemetery, France

Far left: Heilly Station Cemetery, Méricourt-l'Abbé, where Captain Joe Hedley is buried.

Left: Guillemont Road Cemetery; Captain Kenneth Waterhouse's Special Memorial is second from the left.

[459] Norman refers to W.E. Stott as a 2nd Lieutenant, but the Commonwealth War Graves Commission's records refer to him as a Lieutenant. He died after Norman had left the 1/5th Lancashire Fusiliers just before the final successful advance against the Germans. Norman describes the death as having occurred in the area of Serre-lès-Puisieux while Lieutenant Stott's unit was on patrol, gaining control of No Man's Land. He was aged 24 when he died. The cemetery reference is V.G.6. His brother, Lieutenant Robert Sebastian Stott MC, attached to a Trench Mortar unit, also died, aged 21, on 12th October 1918. They were the sons of Mr J.R. Stott (who predeceased them) and Mrs C. Stott of Heywood.

[460] See footnote 269 on page 201.

Obituaries

Norman included a number of obituaries in his diary. Some take the form of newspaper cuttings pasted into the diaries, some are included in the narrative itself, and some appear at the end of Volume 3 of the diary as obituaries separate to the narrative written in his own words; here, after describing his Battalion's involvement in the Somme Offensive, he wrote: *"In closing this stage of my experiences – it would hardly be fitting to do so without a few words of appreciation of my dearest friends who fought and died for their Country"*, and there follow tributes to Kenneth Waterhouse, Joe Hedley, T.H.G. Kenderdine and Norman Kemp.

Lieutenant Colonel Bertram Best-Dunkley

Bertram Best-Dunkley joined the 4th Battalion in 1907 as 2nd Lieutenant, and was promoted Lieutenant in 1908. By profession a schoolmaster, he was when war was declared in Tientsin, but at once returned to England and joined the 4th Battalion.

In May 1915, he went to the 2nd Battalion, thence to the King's Own Lancasters, and subsequently to the 2/5th Battalion, all serving on the Western front. He was also employed as Claims Officer. He acted as Adjutant of the 2/5th for some months. In October, 1916, he was promoted temporary Lieut.-Colonel to the 2/5th Battalion. He was in command of the Battalion on the 31st July, and from the wounds received died on August 5th, 1917.

On the 31st July when his Battalion was in a tight place, his gallantry was conspicuous and is best described in [the] following notice, which appeared in the *London Gazette*, when the posthumous award of the Victoria Cross was conferred.[460]

Lieut.-Colonel B. Best-Dunkley, V.C.

[Reproduced from a newspaper cutting pasted into the diary]

Captain Laurence Henry Bloy

Captain Laurence Henry Bloy entered the University *[Victoria University, Manchester]* in Sept., 1911, after a course of education at Hindley and Abram Grammar School. He was a science student, and at the time of joining the Army had obtained his Inter-B.Sc. He took a keen interest in sport, and had played in several of the footer teams.

He received a commission in Sept., 1914, having been an O.T.C. member from 1911-1914, and was promoted lieutenant at the beginning of 1915. In March of the same year he gained his captaincy, and left for

---

[460] The notice does not actually appear in the diary, but the citation was *"For most conspicuous bravery and devotion to duty when in command of his battalion, the leading waves of which, during an attack, became disorganised by reason of rifle and Machine Gun fire at close range from positions which were believed to be in our hands. Lt.-Col. Best-Dunkley dashed forward, rallied his leading waves, and personally led them to the assault of these positions, which, despite heavy losses, were carried. He continued to lead his battalion until all their objectives had been gained. Had it not been for this officer's gallant and determined action it is doubtful if the left of the brigade would have reached its objectives. Later in the day, when our position was threatened, he collected his battalion headquarters, led them to the attack, and beat off the advancing enemy. This gallant officer has since died of wounds."* This action was at Wieltje near Ypres.

France early in May. There he was appointed Adjutant of the *nth [sic]* Lancs. Fusiliers. During a raid on the German trenches on June 28, 1916, he was seen fighting against great odds, and after the engagement was amongst the missing. In February, 1917, he was reported to have died of wounds as a German prisoner, at the age of 23. Both officers and men of his company felt his loss keenly, and remember him as one who was unfailing in energy and had an utter contempt of danger.
[Reproduced from a newspaper cutting pasted into the diary]

Lance Corporal Harry Brooks

Lance Corporal Brooks was a very good fellow, and a very promising NCO; he was only 21, and lived with his widowed mother at Booth Street, Tottington.
[Taken from the diary entry for 1ˢᵗ May 1916]

Captain Joseph Walton Hedley

He joined the Battalion in January 1915 at Southport, and proceeded to France in May 1915. He was initially 2ⁿᵈ in Command of "Z" Company, then took over as CO of "W" Company when Goldsmith left us.
He was always known as "Uncle Joe" by the officers in "Z" Company. To me he was like a brother.
He was a typical, truly British, character, with a kind, happy, and cheerful disposition, a man of the highest principles. He loved his men, and was loved by all of us. He died of wounds received in Action at Delville Wood, on September 8ᵗʰ 1916 at 2.30am. He was one of the best fellows I ever met, and I spent the happiest days of my Active Service with him and the Skipper – they were always together.
[Included in the obituaries at the end of Volume 3 of the diaries]

Lieutenant Colonel Philip Vaughan Holberton

He was the third son of the late E.R Holberton of The Lawn, Teddington, and was born in 1879. He was educated at Shrewsbury School, and Sandhurst, where he won the sword of honour, the last presented by Queen Victoria. He was gazetted to the 2ⁿᵈ Battalion of the Manchester Regiment in January 1901, and joined it in South Africa. There he was slightly wounded and received the King's medal with two clasps. After holding the Adjutancy of his Battalion, to which he was appointed at the early age of 23, he was appointed to the same position to the West African Regiment, and was in Sierra Leone for three years. Following that he was again Adjutant to a Territorial Battalion of the 6ᵗʰ Manchester Regiment and proceeded with them to Egypt in 1914, and to Gallipoli in 1915. He was through that Campaign and appointed a General Staff Officer at Suez. Six months later in October 1916 he became Brigade Major of the 126ᵗʰ Infantry Brigade, and was appointed to command the 1/5ᵗʰ Lancashire Fusiliers. Colonel Holberton was four times mentioned in Dispatches – receiving his Brevet Majority in 1915, a Serbian Decoration, and his Brevet Lieutenant Colonel in 1917. He was killed at Gommecourt on March 26ᵗʰ 1918. His loss affected us all very much; he was a charming personality, a brave soldier, a true gentleman, and a friend.
[Taken from the original diary entry for 8ᵗʰ April 1918]

2nd Lieutenant Norman Kemp

Norman Kemp was the elder son of the Rev. Canon and Mrs. Lavers-Kemp, The Rectory, Radcliffe, Lancashire. He was 21 years of age and was educated at Rossall. He had gained an open Mathematical

Exhibition at Magdalen College, Cambridge, but on the declaration of war he was granted his commission in the 2/5th Lancashire Fusiliers. He was with the Battalion from the time of its being raised in Bury in September 1914. He went to France in May, 1915, and was wounded in December and returned to England for some months. He returned to France in March, 1916, but the wound had caused further trouble and May found him again in Hospital in England. He finally left for France on July 18th, 1916. His Battalion took part in the great push on the Somme in September, 1916, and he was killed at the capture of Ginchy on September 9th, 1916. Earlier in this battle he had been badly wqounded in one of his arms by machine gun fire. His men begged him to return to the dressing station to have his wounds attended to, but he refused to do so, as all the officers were at the time either killed or wounded. He had been in charge of the bombers, but when he saw the other officers "down" he took command of "Z" Coy – his old original company, and led the attack to the German Position. Just when the objective was gained, he was hit by a machine gun bullet as he was leading his men on. We all feel the loss of Norman Kemp. He was a good officer, full of promise & ability, brave. He forgot his own danger for the safety of his men. He was a most popular officer and his loss was one which was very difficult to replace.

[Reproduced from a newspaper cutting pasted into the diary, completed by Norman in his handwriting]

Lieutenant T.H.G. Kenderdine

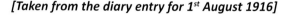

He was born in Japan, and came to England to get a commission in 1915. He joined the 2/5th Lancashire Fusiliers in September 1915 at Aveluy.
He was a cheery fellow, brave, a hard worker, and a humourist – often known as Charlie Chaplin. He was killed in the attack at Ginchy on September 9th 1916.

[Included in the obituaries at the end of Volume 3 of the diaries]

2nd Lieutenant Cecil Henry Moffatt

Cecil Moffatt was one of the bravest, most cheerful, unselfish fellows I ever knew. We had been great pals. His men loved him – we all did. He was a very capable officer … He will never be forgotten by those of us who have been more fortunate.

[Taken from the diary entry for 1st August 1916]

Private John Schofield

Schofield was an exceedingly nice fellow; quiet, unassuming, but always doing his job whether on sentry, patrol, or work, a "Brave Soldier", efficient and thoroughly reliable.

[Taken from the diary entry for 14th April 1916]

Captain Kenneth Waterhouse

He joined the 2/5th Lancashire Fusiliers at Bury in October 1914. He had never done any soldiering before, and he was about 38 when he joined us. We all loved him from the first day he came.

By January 1915, at Southport on the formation of the double Companies, he became Captain and CO of "Z" Company. He was a strict disciplinarian, a man of sound common sense, an organiser, a man with a keen sense of justice, and full of thought for the welfare of his men, who loved him when they got to understand him. I first joined him at Caionne in May 1915, when, although I was HQ Staff, I lived with "Z" Company. Then he claimed me as his 2nd in Command of "Z" Company in September 1915. We were like brothers. I literally worshipped him. He was <u>the</u> greatest friend I have ever had, and my ideal of what a man should be – firm, determined, working with an object; yet kind, sympathetic, temperate. He was a <u>man</u> – a <u>soldier</u>. Without doubt – had he lived – he would have made a big name for himself in the Army. He never got any decorations – but he earned them time and time again. His death meant a great deal to me – more than anyone can ever understand. Poor old Skipper; his body is dead, but his character – his example – will live with me for ever.
[Included in the obituaries at the end of Volume 3 of the diaries]

Lieutenant Malcolm Henry Young

Malcolm Henry Young was the youngest of three sons of the late Colonel Pilkington and Mrs. Young, of Stand Hall, Whitefield. He was educated at Marlborough, where he showed a partiality for field sports. In games and boxing he won some distinction. On the 2/5th Battalion being raised, Malcolm Young joined it, which was very fitting, as his father commanded, and was long and honourably connected with the 1st Volunteer Battalion. Lieutenant Young accompanied his Battalion to France, and served with it uninterruptedly until the end of June.

He commanded the strongest party, composed of some of the best men. They were to get into the German fire trenches, and bomb them for twenty-five minutes. This was successfully carried out, but there were more Germans in the trenches than was expected.

The party left the trench and Lieutenant Young was the last to ascend the ladder, the place of every honourable officer; when doing so the man in front of him was shot through the shoulder. Lieutenant Young pushed him up and told him to get home. He was at this moment wounded on the parapet of the trench, close to Captain Bloy, and died within a few hours, on June 29th, 1916, in his twenty fourth year. A gallant youth of great amiability, he was beloved by his men, and many are the tributes that have been paid to his memory by brother officers. His elder brother, Edmund, fell in Gallipoli when serving with the 6th Manchesters.[461]
[Reproduced from a newspaper cutting pasted into the diary]

---

[461] Lieutenant Edmund Taylor Young died on 10th June 1915, and is commemorated at the Helles Memorial, Panel 159 to 171.

Time Line of Norman Hall's War Service

03.09.1914	Joined up as a Private with the 3rd City Battalion King's Liverpool Regiment
12.09.1914	Corporal, N° 7 Section, "B" Platoon, 3rd City Battalion King's Liverpool Regiment
14.10.1914 from 07.10.14	Gazetted 2nd Lieutenant, 5th Reserve Battalion, Lancashire Fusiliers
08.11.1914	Appointed OC "B" Company of the 5th Reserve Battalion, Lancashire Fusiliers
07.01.1915 from 23.12.14	Gazetted Lieutenant, 5th Reserve Battalion, Lancashire Fusiliers
19.04.1915	Appointed Signalling Officer to the 2/5th Lancashire Fusiliers
03.05.1915	Landed in France for the first time
23.09.1915	Appointed 2nd in Command of "Z" Company of the 2/5th Lancashire Fusiliers
07.07.1916 from 08.05.16	Gazettted Temporary Captain, 2/5th Lancashire Fusiliers
09.09.1916	Wounded at Ginchy
11.01.1917	Appointed OC "V" Company, 5th Reserve Battalion, Lancashire Fusiliers, Ripon
14.06.1917	Returned to France
22.06.1917	Joined the 1/5th Lancashire Fusiliers, 2nd in Command of "C" Company
27.06.1917	Reverted to substantive rank of 2nd Lieutenant in Battalion Orders
29.06.1917	Appointed Acting Rail Transport Officer
05.08.1917 from 08.10.16	Gazetted Captain, Lancashire Fusiliers, Territorial Force
04.09.1917	Appointed Acting Quartermaster of the 1/5th Lancashire Fusiliers
22.10.1917	Appointed OC of "B" Company of the 1/5th Lancashire Fusiliers
23.11.1917	Appointed Acting Adjutant of the 1/5th Lancashire Fusiliers
10.12.1918	Reverted to OC of "B" Company of the 1/5th Lancashire Fusiliers
03.01.1918	Appointed Acting Adjutant again (also briefly CO Battalion and Acting MO)
21.02.1918	Reverted to OC of "B" Company of the 1/5th Lancashire Fusiliers
08.04.1918	Appointed Acting Adjutant of the 1/5th Lancashire Fusiliers
10.05.1918	Admitted to hospital with Trench Fever

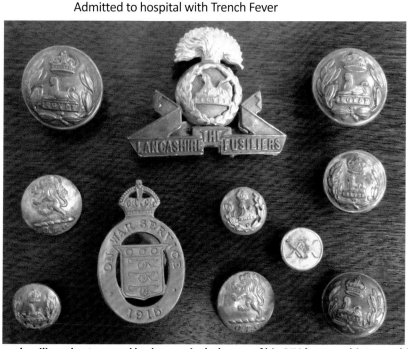

Some of Norman's military buttons and badges, to include two of his OTC buttons, his Lancashire Fusiliers cap badge, a War Service 1915 badge, and a button with the insignia "XX", denoting the Twentieth Foot, the precursors of the Lancashire Fusiliers; the sphinx emblem and the word "Egypt" which feature on the Lancashire Fusiliers items originated from the Regiment's distinguished service in Egypt in 1801.

09.07.1918	Returned to 1/5th Lancashire Fusiliers, again as Acting Adjutant[462]
14.07.1918	Acting Intelligence Officer of the 1/5th Lancashire Fusiliers
22.07.1918	Acting Signalling Officer of the 1/5th Lancashire Fusiliers
29.07.1918	Injured in a riding accident
13.09.1918	Duty Officer at Brighton Hydro, Blackpool, subsequently Adjutant
09.01.1919	Posted to 5th Battalion, Lancashire Fusiliers, Withernsea
19.01.1919	Demobilised

On landing in France on 3rd May 1915 the 2/5th Lancashire Fusiliers were (along with the 1/4th King's Own Royal Lancasters, the 1/8th King's Liverpool Regiment (Irish) and the 1/4th Loyal North Lancashires) in the 3rd Infantry Brigade – later the 154th Infantry Brigade – and the 1st Highland Division – later the 51st Highland Division – in the Indian Army Corps. In January 1916 the 154th Brigade moved to become the 164th Brigade in the newly formed, or re-formed, 55th Division, the West Lancashire Division, in the VIIth Corps and the IIIrd Army, but subsequently Norman refers to them as being in the VIth Corps area, and mentions senior personnel of the VIth Corps.[462] On 25th July 1916 on moving to the Somme they transferred to the XIth Corps in the Vth Army, though on 30th August 1916 they are mentioned as being in the area of the Xth Corps.

When Norman joined the 1/5th Lancashire Fusiliers following his return to France in June 1917 they were in the 125th Brigade in the 42nd Division. The first specific information given by Norman as to the position of the 42nd Division is on 28th August 1917, when he says that they were in the Vth Corps and the Vth Army. On 15th October 1917 he says they were now in the XVth Corps, and the IVth Army, where they remained until they were transferred to the 1st Corps in January 1918. By 23rd March 1918 they were taking orders from Lieutenant General J.A.L. Haldane of the VIth Corps, but two days later they moved from the VIth Corps to the IVth Corps under Lieutenant General Sir G.M. Harper. On 15th March 1918 Norman was warned he was to be sent to the 1st Army School at Hardelot, so presumably they were in the 1st Army by that stage, but from at least 1st April 1918 the 1/5th Lancashire Fusiliers were fighting on the IIIrd Army front, which remained the case until the end of the War.

5th Battalion, The Lancashire Fusiliers; the undermentioned to be Majors. Dated 15th October, 1914:—

George Alfred Kay (late Captain and Honorary Major, 1st Volunteer Battalion, The Lancashire Fusiliers).

Henry Nicholas Milnes (late Captain and Honorary Major, 5th Battalion, The Lancashire Fusiliers).

John Davison Barnsdale (late Captain, 1st Volunteer Battalion, Nottinghamshire and Derbyshire Regiment) to be Captain. Dated 7th October, 1914.

John Joseph Pemberton Cummins to be Quartermaster, with the honorary rank of Lieutenant. Dated 7th October, 1914.

The undermentioned to be Second Lieutenants. Dated 7th October, 1914:—

Robert Spencer Ashworth.
Richard Henry Barnes .
Lawrence Henry Bloy.
William Duckworth.
Mansfield Priestly Evans.
George Hartley Goldsmith.
George Hall.
Norman Hall.
Geoffrey Clegg Hutchinson.
Norman Kemp.
Reginald William Kirkman.
John Booth Packman.
Newton Dukinfield Thompson.
Kenneth Waterhouse.
Malcolm Henry Young.

5th Battalion, The Lancashire Fusiliers; the undermentioned Second Lieutenants to be Lieutenants (temporary). Dated 23rd December, 1914:—

Charles W. Laughlin.
Lawrence K. Bloy.
George H. Goldsmith.
Norman Hall.
Geoffrey C. Hutchinson.
Reginald W. Kirkman.
Kenneth Waterhouse.

Lancs. Fus.
2nd Lt. (temp. Lt.) N. Hall to be temp. Capt. 8th May 1916.

Extracts from the London Gazette for 14th October 1914, 7th January 1915, and 7th July 1916

---

[462] At the end of the main text of the diary, under the entry for 19th January 1919, there is a tantalising entry to the effect that Norman had been *"Acting 2nd in Command of the 1/5th Lancashire Fusiliers as Temporary Major from June 30th 1918 to July 22nd 1919"*, but this is followed by a question mark and two exclamation marks in brackets, and is not otherwise referred to in the text (see page 306).

[463] Norman mentions RE Officer Parkinson on 7th April 1916, who was *"attached to VIth Corps HQ"* (page 169), and on 22nd June 1916 he says that they were *"still in the VIth Corps area"* (page 193), while he says that Captain Merriman was *"a member of a VIth Corps FGCM"* on 24th June 1916 (page 195), and on 17th July 1916 that they were rumoured to be about *"to move from the VIth Corps area South"* (page 208). The Battalion War Diary entry for 6th May 1916 confirms the position, stating *"The Division has now apparently taken its place in VI Corps."*

List of Officers who Went to France with the 2/5th Lancashire Fusiliers on 3rd May 1915, and other Officers with the 2/5th Lancashire Fusiliers who are Frequently Mentioned by Norman, Including the Dates of the Diary Entries when they are Last Mentioned as being in France with the 2/5th; also Page Numbers where Information about them is Summarised in a Footnote

			Page
Those who went to France on 3rd May 1915:			
Headquarters:	Lieutenant Colonel J. Hall, CO	13.06.15-20.06.15	54
	Major H.N. Milnes	13.09.16	269
	Captain J.J.P. Cummins, Adjutant	13.06.15-20.06.15	54
	Lieutenant J. Bowd, Quartermaster	01.09.16	250
	Lieutenant W. Abbotts, Transport Officer	05.11.15	113
	Lieutenant C.W.B. Hill, Machine Gun Officer	13.07.15	60
	Lieutenant N. Hall, Signals Officer	14.09.16	–
	Lieutenant R.N. Thompson, MO	08.03.16	159
	Captain Gillenders, Chaplain	25.07.15	65
"A" Company	Captain G.H. Goldsmith	10.09.15	95
	Captain E.R. Ramsden	08.07.15	57
	2nd Lieutenant G. Gray	07.08.16	231-2
	2nd Lieutenant H. Waterhouse	30.07.16	215
	2nd Lieutenant H.H. Noton	06.08.16	229
"B" Company	Major J.D. Barnsdale	14.09.16	272
	Captain L.H. Bloy	24.06.16-28.06.16	201
	2nd Lieutenant W. Duckworth	08.08.16	236
	Lieutenant A.V. Barwood	06.09.15	94
	2nd Lieutenant J.E. Hartington	25.01.16	140
"C" Company	Captain G.C. Hutchinson	24.06.16-28.06.16	200
	Lieutenant R.W. Kirkman	18.07.15	64
	2nd Lieutenant B.H. Rothband	04.08.16-05.08.16	227
	2nd Lieutenant M.H. Young	24.06.16-28.06.16	201
	2nd Lieutenant M.P. Evans	06.08.16	230
	2nd Lieutenant J.B. Packman	14.09.16	272
"D" Company	Captain K. Waterhouse	09.08.16	237-8
	Captain J.W. Hedley	10.09.16	267
	Captain E.C. Simon	14.08.15-19.08.15	78-9
	2nd Lieutenant J.C. Latter	25.09.15-03.10.15	99-100
	2nd Lieutenant N. Kemp	14.09.16	270
	2nd Lieutenant J.F. Harker	29.07.16	213-4
Other officers with the 2/5th Lancashire Fusiliers who are frequently mentioned by Norman:			
	2nd Lieutenant H.M. Ainscow	24.06.16-28.06.16	199
	Lieutenant S. Cooper	10.09.16	267
	Lieutenant E.H. Fryer	04.08.16-05.08.16	227
	Lieutenant G.H.A. Humble	24.06.16	196
	Captain J.W. Jeffreys	14.08.15-19.08.15	62
	Lieutenant T.H.G. Kenderdine	09.09.16	263
	2nd Lieutenant C.H. Moffatt	01.08.16	218
	2nd Lieutenant S.L. Moffatt	14.08.16	242
	Captain R.E.G. Newman	09.09.16	266
	Lieutenant Colonel H.J. Shirley	21.06.16	192

Endnotes Referring to Narrow Escapes In Chapters 1-25, and Narrow Escapes after 14th September 1916

(N.B. not every incidence of being under shell or gun fire etc. is included here)

Endnotes Referring to Narrow Escapes in Chapters 1-25

End-note	Date	Event
i	17.06.1915	Brush with danger in a lightning storm, away from the Front.
ii	14.07.1915	Bullet just missed Norman in Laventie trenches.
iii	14.07.1915	Man killed near gap in the hedge soon after Norman and Captain Shirley had moved on.
iv	16.07.1915	Bullet meant for Norman at Laventie trenches just missed him.
v	08.1915	Bullets raining on Aveluy trenches.
vi	08.1915	Whizz bang shells on Aveluy Wood.
vii	22.08.1915	Shell on the verandah at Aveluy, where Norman and other officers had been sitting shortly before.
viii	23.08.1915	A bullet hit the heel of Norman's boot in the trenches at Aveluy.
ix	31.08.1915	Shell at cross roads at Aveluy.
x	10.09.1915	Shell accidentally exploded in bank at Machine Gun demonstration.
xi	16 to 27.11.1915	Nearly "got" by the Boche when tapping wires in an old Communication Trench.
xii	21.12.1915	Shell exploded at a place at Thiepval Wood where Norman had been 10 minutes earlier.
xiii	25.12.1915	Shell exploded just outside dug out at Thiepval Wood.
xiv	12.1915	Trench Mortar exploded close to Norman at Thiepval Wood.
xv	31.12.1915	Machine Gun at Thiepval Wood trained on open ground that Norman had to cross.
xvi	03.01.1916	Trenches in Thiepval Sector attacked the night after the 2/5th Lancashire Fusiliers had moved out.
xvii	26.02.1916	Shell at Beaumetz within a few yards of Norman's platoon.
xviii	01.05.1916	Rifle fire from the Boche when trying to recover Lance Corporal Brooks' body from No Man's Land.
xix	24.06.1916	Anti-aircraft shell fell on Norman's billet in Dainville when he was at dinner elsewhere.
xx	27.06.1916	Shell exploded in his sleeping quarters after he had vacated them, lodging shrapnel in his belt.
xxi	19.07 1916	Shell landed in garden of house in Beaumetz where Norman was a member of an FGCM.
xxii	28.07.1916	Shell within 40 yards in the Somme area.
xxiii	31.07.1916	Going along the top of the trench to make sure men had taken cover, shells falling all around.
xxiv	03.08.1916	Buried without his gas helmet on, while going along the trench to warn of gas shells.
xxv	03.08.1916	Norman had to cross open ground through a hail of rifle and Machine Gun bullets.
xxvi	04.08.1916	Nearly ran into a German Post.
xxvii	04.08.1916	Encountered a German while out reconnoitring.
xxviii	04.08.1916	In a shallow advanced trench with both the Boche and the British firing across it – several wounded.
xxix	04.08.1916	Still in the advanced trench – British guns fired short at the Boche.
xxx	06.08.1916	Norman cleared their trench as Boche shelling got nearer, just before a shell hit the trench.
xxxi	06.08.1916	Shell exploded at Trônes Wood, killing several in Norman's immediate vicinity.
xxxii	06.08.1916	Making a Dump of ammunition etc. near Bernafay Wood, under shell fire and with no cover.
xxxiii	07.08.1916	Re-making the ammunition dump under shell fire, and being near Fagan Trench when it was blown in.
xxxiv	08.08.1916	Burning phosphorus fell on the trench where Norman's Company was.
xxxv	08.08.1916	Orders to advance on Guillemont (doomed to failure) delivered too late.
xxxvi	12.08.1916	Shelling at Maricourt and on the Maricourt to Guillemont Road.
xxxvii	13.08.1916	Shell burst in the entrance to the Dressing Station where Norman was sleeping.
xxxviii	09.09.1916	Boche rifles fired when Norman was caught standing out of his trench when fog lifted.
xxxix	09.09.1916	A dash over open ground through shell and sniper fire to get revised orders.
xl	09.09.1916	Wounded, rather than killed, after going "over the top".
xli	09.09.1916	Bullet through the elbow after having already fallen from first wound.
xlii	09.09.1916	Aid Post where Norman had just been treated shelled, killing the MO.

Narrow Escapes after 14th September 1916

29.07.1917	At Gommecourt: *"There was a very heavy thunderstorm. [Captain William] Tickler got his tin hat struck, and I got an electric shock crossing the wet boards to the Orderly Room."*
30.08.1917	Selected to stay behind as *"Battle Surplus"* when "C" Company went into the Line on the Ypres Salient (see the *Afterword*, page 280).
04.09.1917	Stood in as acting Quartermaster, thus not going up to the Front Line with "C" Company for an attack two days later (see the *Afterword*, page 281).
05.09.1917	In camp at Goldfish Chateau: *"Things quietened off and I went to bed in my tent. I had not been in long when the shelling started again. One shell burst so uncomfortably near my tent that I got bits of shrapnel whizzing through the tent. It was a bit too hot for me, so I decided to roll up my valise*

and retire to some dug out about 200 yards away for the night. The next morning I came back to find half my tent torn to shreds and a huge hole taking half the floor space. Why I moved I don't know – only blue funk. Anyway I was jolly glad I had moved."

11.10.1917   While riding from Oostdunkerque to Nieuport: "*Near the Signal Station between Nieuport and Oostdunkerque the Boche started to shell the road, dropping them first behind, and then gradually increasing the range about 50 yards at a time. I put my horse to full gallop – practically lying along his back. Wallace, following closely behind, thought I had been hit and my horse was simply running away. One shell burst very near; I didn't get hit – but my horse got a bit of shrapnel. At Oostdunkerque we stopped for a breather. A narrow escape indeed!*"

17.10.1917   Shelled in Coxyde village: "*In the evening we had a very unpleasant experience of shelling. Our billet was practically in the centre of the village of Coxyde, where several roads converged. Also the tower on our billet was an excellent ranging mark. When they started I was sitting near the window. A shell burst in the middle of the road and smashed our windows - and I narrowly escaped getting hit in the head.*"

10.11.1917   Shell exploded in a tunnel at Nieuport: "*We [Captain Edwards of the Coldstream Guards and I] got back to the Redan at 5.00pm, but had rather an unpleasant experience. We walked from Canada Camp via the Zouave Track, and as we approached Nieuport the Boche were shelling the town heavily. We entered the tunnel at Arch Bridge as usual, and had only proceeded up it a few yards when there was a terrific crash, the electric lights went out, pieces of stone and brick flew about, and we were choked with dust and covered with dirt. A shell had burst in the tunnel and completely blown it in. I produced an electric torch and we examined the damage, which was only about 10 yards in front of us – it was a very narrow escape and somewhat shaking.*"

10.12.1917   Relieved at La Bassée Right Sub-sector: "*Our relief was only just in time, for the 10th Manchesters who relieved us had a bad time that night. The first Gas Projector Attack ever made by the Boche was made only a few hours after we got clear. These Gas Projectors were drums of liquid Chlorine or Phosgene (or both), which were fired over, and were detonated on contact with the ground, emitting a very heavy concentration of gas. The only warning one had of such a Gas attack was a tremendous report – a big flash, and then hundreds of star like trails in the sky. From hearing the report to the bursting of the drums in our trenches was about 10 seconds as a maximum, not much time to get one's helmet on – even from the "Alert" position – and take cover in gas-proof dug outs protected by double blanketed entrances. "C" Company of the 10th Manchesters were practically wiped out by this preliminary Gas attack, but they manned the parapet and beat the Boche before he got a footing in our trench. Private Mills won the VC. We, away back in cosy billets in Beuvry, were unaware of this until late that night. But we were lucky to be out of it by such a narrow squeak.*"

12.12.1917   In the town of Béthune: "*Here Cooper and I had a meal. We had a very unpleasant experience while having a 'short one' before our meal. The peace was disturbed by the nightly visit of Boche Aeroplanes which had become very common of late. The familiar whirr of an aeroplane bomb descending was followed immediately by a terrific explosion on the opposite side of the street, accompanied by the row of the whole house front falling across the street and completely blocking the way with bricks and masonry. Our windows were shattered, and pots and glasses rattled. It gave us all a pretty good shaking, but we were none the worse for our experience. I began to wonder whether I should go on leave* [due to commence five days later] *even yet!*"

25.02.1918   At the cross roads near Vermelles Church: "*We got shelled on the road. While we were having a pow-wow near Vermelles Church, at the corner shown in this picture* [see the photograph on the opposite page]*, a shell burst on the cross roads, luckily none of us got hit.*"

05.04.1918   German aeroplane opened fire near Bucquoy (see the *Afterword*, page 298).

05.04.1918   Instruction to return from the Front Line at Bucquoy village (see the *Afterword*, page 299).

02.08.1918   Norman narrowly avoided being put on board SS *Warilda*, which was torpedoed in the Channel (see the *Afterword*, page 304).

09.01.1919   Train jumped the buffers at Withernsea Station (see the *Afterword*, page 306).

Oostdunkerque – see the narrow escape on 11.10.17

Coxyde – see the narrow escape on 17.10.17

Note: in the postcard above Norman's billet at Coxyde-sur-Mer is marked with a cross and dots, and the billet of the Transport Officer and Quartermaster next door is marked with a plain cross.

Béthune – see the narrow escape on 12.12.17

Above Norman has written *"To Railway Station – and leave?"*

Vermelles – see the narrow escape on 25.02.18

Index of People

1. Names beginning with "de" are listed under the second part of the name.
2. The rank attributed in this index is the highest rank that the person held when last mentioned by Norman; if it is known from facts mentioned in this book that the person attained a higher rank later, reference to that is added in brackets.
3. Norman Hall is not included in this Index as he appears virtually throughout the book.
4. Page numbers underlined in bold indicate the page on which key details appertaining to the person are summarised in a footnote.

Index of Place Names

including the names of bridges, canals, islands, rivers, roads, stations, towns, villages, woods (some roads feature in the Military Posts Index)
N.B. Streets/Buildings etc. are listed under the town in which they are found, sometimes without the number(s) of the page(s) on which they appear being specified separately.

Index of Military Posts, Trenches etc.

Including buildings in France/Belgium commandeered for military purposes, camps, farms, roads and other landmarks in the battle area (Aid Posts, Casualty Clearing Stations, Dressing Stations and Hospitals are in the General Index); for La, Le, Les or St see note to Index of Place Names.

Index of Fighting Units etc.

Note: the 2/5th Lancashire Fusiliers are not listed here, as they appear virtually throughout the main text of the book.

Index of Armaments